P9-DFW-083

The Professor's Guide to
Teaching

The Professor's Guide to
Teaching

Psychological Principles and Practices

Donelson R. Forsyth

American Psychological Association
Washington, DC

Published by
American Psychological Association
750 First Street, NE
Washington, DC 20002
www.apa.org

To order
APA Order Department
P.O. Box 92984
Washington, DC 20090-2984

Tel: (800) 374-2721; Direct: (202) 336-5510
Fax: (202) 336-5502; TDD/TTY: (202) 336-6123
Online: www.apa.org/books/
Email: order@apa.org

In the U.K., Europe, Africa, and the Middle East, copies may be ordered from
American Psychological Association
3 Henrietta Street
Covent Garden, London
WC2E 8LU England

Typeset in Goudy by EPS Group Inc., Easton, MD

Printer: United Book Press, Baltimore, MD
Cover Designer: Naylor Design, Washington, DC
Technical/Production Editor: Kristen R. Sullivan

The opinions and statements published are the responsibility of the authors, and such opinions and statements do not necessarily represent the policies of the American Psychological Association.

Library of Congress Cataloging-in-Publication Data
Forsyth, Donelson R., 1953–
   The professor's guide to teaching : psychological principles and practices / Donelson R. Forsyth.
      p. cm.
   Includes bibliographical references and index.
   ISBN 1-55798-960-5 (alk. paper)
      1. College teaching.   2. Educational psychology.   I. Title.

   LB 2331 .F632 2002
   378.1'2—dc21

                                                                                    2002071717

British Library Cataloguing-in-Publication Data
A CIP record is available from the British Library.

Printed in the United States of America
First Edition

To Claire, David, and Rachel, with love

CONTENTS

PREFACE

I am not a born teacher as some of my colleagues seem to be. Indeed, in graduate school I was all about the research, and so when I took my first academic post, I was ready to measure, manipulate, and publish, but I was unprepared to teach. I, like many other new college professors, was relatively untrained in the pedagogical arts, for I had adopted the world-view that teaching was a duty, whereas scholarly research was a joy.

To say I struggled a bit those first few years would be putting it mildly. The misery of leaving a class, knowing I'd failed. The visits to the chair's office. The intrusive thought, "I wish I was going someplace else," that popped into my mind during the too-short walk to each class. And the evaluations. I came to dread the time of year when those feedback reports arrived in faculty mailboxes. I would bury the large manila envelope at the bottom of my stack of mail, steal back to my office, pick out the bad ones, and lose confidence in myself. Some comments, such as the following, were simply negative.

- Forsyth is a jerk; he should be fired.
- He is the worst teacher I have ever had.

Other comments were critical, if insightful.

- Although there is no doubt that Forsyth is well versed in his field, his attitude in the classroom left something to be desired.
- Contrary to what Don may believe, he is not God's gift to psychology.
- I force myself to come to this class and tolerate the elementary way you approach this class most of the time.
- Your jokes are seldom funny or effective as teaching methods,

and it shows how egotistical and self-centered you probably
are.

Some comments were poignant.

- At first he had the attitude he didn't really care about us—
  then we all started flunking and dropping his course. He became somewhat concerned, but it was too late for us.

And, in response to the question "What was the single most important
learning experience for you in this course?" one student wrote, "I cannot
think of one, other than not to take this instructor again."

I wanted to blame my students: to question their abilities, preparation,
and raw intellect. But I could not overlook the irony of the situation. In
my research I studied how people react to failure: how they tend to deny
responsibility for negative outcomes by blaming others. I could not ignore
my own findings, so I listened to my students. They became my teachers,
I became their student, and I learned the lessons about instruction and
pedagogy that I had too long ignored.

What were these lessons? The first, most fundamental one was that I
had to redefine my role as a member of the faculty at a university. I had
always considered myself to be a psychologist and recognized that my first
duty was to my field. I was content to spend long hours in my laboratory
carrying out research, analyzing results, and writing scholarly reports of the
findings. I pursued external funding, trained graduate students in research,
published regularly, and attended national and international meetings. But
in time I learned that scholars who only expand their own knowledge fall
short of the ideal. It is not enough to generate the knowledge; one must
also convey this knowledge of the field to others. The researcher who does
not teach is the flip side of the teacher who does not do research: Both
are only parts and not wholes.

The second lesson was that I had to find meaning in the day-to-day
actions that go into teaching. As a novice instructor I gave lectures, administered exams, held office hours, and assigned grades, but I was only
going through the motions. I did not know how these various activities fit
together, and so I literally did not know what I was doing. So, like any
good teacher, I began to actually think about why and how I was teaching.
What are my goals, I wondered, as I planned a lecture or learning activity?
How difficult is this material? How much help will my students need to
grasp the key concepts? What are the key concepts, anyway? Should I stress
application, conceptual understanding, or interpersonal skills? And what
learning activities will work best to achieve these goals? I ruminated over
these questions, and the results of that rumination were a thoughtful, coherent approach to my classes.

The third lesson was that I needed to respect my students and their abilities. I realized that my students were capable learners who could grasp the most complex topics in my field so long as I taught these topics properly. But I also realized that students are sometimes reluctant learners. With their busy lives, their earlier learning experiences, and their quite natural focus on grades over learning, they were often reluctant to take responsibility for their work. So, just as I had once blamed students for my poor work, I recognized that students sometimes shrug off responsibility for their failures to learn. So I reminded them of their skills and abilities but at the same time refused to be the center of their learning. If they are to become true scholars—to be capable of finding the answers to questions as yet unposed—then they must take responsibility for their learning. I was not the expert dispensing knowledge but rather a guide helping them learn how to learn.

I learned many other lessons—so many that I decided to write them down in the form of a book. These lessons eventually helped me improve as a teaching psychologist, for in time the 2s and 3s I had been earning on a 5-point teacher evaluation scale became 4s and 5s. And students' comments changed from hostile and negative to complimentary and appreciative. This n-of-one case study suggests that good teaching can be learned, just like any other scholarly skill.

Although I deserve the blame for the portions of this book that readers may find objectionable (e.g., conjectures about learning that are not supported by research, simplistic bits of advice about teaching, distracting personal opinions), many other people deserve credit for the good parts. I must credit the many professors who, by teaching me so well, served as role models for how it should be done, and also my many colleagues in psychology and other disciplines who shared their views of teaching with me. Dr. Thomas McGovern of Arizona State University–West tops that list; his unswerving devotion to teaching clarified my own understanding at a time when I was most malleable to others' influences. He also read the entire manuscript of this book, as did Dr. Lisa Sherwin of Georgia Southern, and their careful commentary contributed enormously to the project. I also appreciate the support of the dean of the College of Humanities and Sciences at Virginia Commonwealth University, Stephen Gottfredson, who (as ironic as it may sound) reduced my teaching load for a semester so that I would have time to complete this project. Susan Reynolds, Anne Woodworth, Kristen Sullivan, Jennie Reinhardt, and the many other expert staff members at the American Psychological Association also earn my thanks for deftly guiding the book along its journey from an ill-formed idea into published work. The real credit for this book, however, belongs to the thousands of students who have sat in my classrooms over the years and were so happy to give me feedback. Some comments were negative, some were positive, but all of them were helpful.

The Professor's Guide to
Teaching

INTRODUCTION

Have you ever really had a teacher? One who saw you as a raw but precious thing, a jewel that, with wisdom, could be polished to a proud shine? If you are lucky enough to find your way to such teachers, you will always find your way back.

—Mitch Albom
Tuesdays With Morrie (1997, p. 192)

Psychologists are not only researchers, statisticians, therapists, and consultants but also teachers who promote the dissemination of the field's stock of knowledge, skills, and outlook to others. Like their colleagues in other departments and programs, psychology professors must deal with issues related to learning and instruction, such as lecturing, testing, grading, and evaluating instruction, but unlike professors in other disciplines, they approach these issues informed by their broad understanding of psychological theory and research. Because the processes that are involved in teaching and learning are the very processes studied by psychologists, when psychologists teach, they can take advantage of the same knowledge, skills, and abilities that they use in their other professional roles as theoretical scientists, researchers, and practitioners.

*   *   *

Many psychologists are scientists who test hypotheses about the causes and consequences of cognitive, emotional, and behavioral processes. Others are therapists and consultants who use their skills to improve clients' adjustment and promote well-being. But some psychologists are teachers: professors who promote the dissemination of the field's stock of knowledge, skills, and outlook to other professionals, students, and the lay community. They teach in small liberal arts colleges and huge universities; they teach inveterate doctoral students, disdainful upper-level majors, enthusiastic first-year students, and distracted high school students. These professors are full-time members of the faculty who balance their teaching against their

3

research and service duties, adjunct faculty who help their department meet its need for teachers, and part-timers who return to campus when their work schedules permit. Some remember teaching in a world without computers, e-mail, and "Student Evaluations of Teaching" forms, but others are graduate students standing at the lectern of their first classroom unsullied by all but the most vicarious of preparation for their professorial obligations.

These teaching psychologists are similar in many ways to professors in other disciplines within the academy. Like colleagues in such departments as English, chemistry, foreign languages, management, sculpture, or music, they must achieve an extraordinary degree of mastery over their chosen field. College professors are not just teachers who summarize the work of others for students but are scholars who share their unique and penetrating understanding of their field through teaching. All professors, too, are the experimenters delivering the manipulation in one of the most elaborate social programs ever devised: higher education. They share the goals described so eloquently by Cardinal Newman in 1852, including "raising the intellectual tone of society," "cultivating the public mind," "purifying the national taste," "giving enlargement and sobriety to the ideas of the age," "facilitating the exercise of political power," and "refining the intercourse of private life" (Newman, 1852/1973). All, too, are members of the community of scholars who teach, study, and sustain their disciplines and their universities through their service.

But teaching psychologists, *qua* psychologists, differ from professors in other disciplines within the academy in a fundamental way: They command a profound understanding of psychological, behavioral, and interpersonal processes that influence their teaching and their students' learning. Whereas chemistry professors may wonder why their students are not motivated to learn the material they present in lecture, psychologists can call to mind a dozen explanations of students' indifference—and use those theories and the research that they have generated to identify ways to ignite students' interest in their studies. Although engineering professors may be convinced that experiential activities enhance learning, psychologists can draw on emerging studies of memory, cognition, and learning to test and refine this assumption. Whereas professors of music may not understand the difference between a test's reliability and a test's validity, psychologists do—they invented these concepts. When psychologists teach, their efforts are informed not only by their personal experiences but also by the stock of knowledge of their entire discipline.

The role of teacher is also consistent, in many respects, with the other roles that comprise the psychologist's professional persona, including scientist, researcher, and practitioner. As scientists, psychologists are skilled builders of theories, synthesizers of empirical findings, and perspicacious critics who can find conceptual weaknesses in even the tightest conceptual argument. These skills not only help them generate new understandings of psychological processes but also provide them with the means of organizing and communicating that understanding to others. As researchers with data collection and analysis skills honed through years of practice, psychologists approach questions of measurement, assessment, and classification with confidence rather than confusion. Psychologists' applied skills—their knowledge of the symptoms of dysfunction, their familiarity with conflict and its resolution, their commitment to prosocial values, and their helping skills—are as useful in the classroom as they are in the clinic, counseling center, and community.

Because teaching psychologists command a profound understanding of the causes of human thought, emotion, and action, their instructional methods, their examinations, their one-on-one tutorials, and even the support they give their students should be the envy of professors in other academic disciplines. Yet, in too many cases, psychologists do not exploit their discipline's resources when they teach. Some, when teaching 300 students in an auditorium, use the same procedures as the chemistry professor down the hall. Others give their students tests that include mostly multiple-choice items that ask about facts and information. Some never require that their students write any papers, ask questions in class, or take part in discussion. And some, when they get the feedback from the previous term's teacher evaluations, remark that "the quality of teaching cannot be measured." Some professors spend all their time looking at their students through the eyes of a teacher rather than through the eyes of a psychologist.

But what insights does psychology offer to the professor in the classroom? This book offers a partial answer to this question by breaking college-level teaching down into its behavioral components. It begins at the beginning, with the steps that the professor takes when planning a course, and ends, as it should, at the ending: documenting one's contributions in teaching by developing a teaching portfolio. Each chapter frames the major issues surrounding one aspect of instruction and then offers an overall conceptualization of these issues that draws on current psychological theory and research. The chapter dealing with lecturing, for example, conceptualizes the lecturing method as a form of communication and then uses research dealing with persuasion processes to identify how this teaching method can be best used. Similarly, the chapter dealing with classroom testing approaches the issue from the standpoint of psychological assessment and so considers how testing requires the same care that psychologists use when developing questionnaires and inventories.

The book is ultimately practical, however. It reviews theory and research, but its primary focus is on application in the educational setting. The analysis of lecturing as a form of communication, for example, offers a series of recommendations for best practices in teaching that stresses the importance of considering the source of the message, the nature of the message, and the characteristics of the receiver of the message. The chapter dealing with the development of classroom assessment methods reviews the fundamentals of test development and item analysis and offers rec- ommendations for alternative means of assessment. The chapters are se- quenced by a just-in-time heuristic, with topics reviewed in the order in which they demand the professor's attention during a typical term's teach- ing schedule. Although teaching is more than the sum of these parts, I consider in turn planning, lecturing, using student-centered teaching meth- ods, leading discussions, using collaborative or experiential activities, test- ing, grading, helping students through feedback and guidance, managing classroom dynamics, using innovative technology, evaluating teaching ef- fectiveness, and documenting one's contributions as a teacher.

This book assumes that you, the reader, are a psychologist—or, at least, someone who is familiar with the fundamental assumptions, contro- versies, data, and other key elements of the discipline's paradigm. This assumption lets the analysis step beyond general questions about curricu- lum, instruction, and learning to focus on specific questions pertaining to the psychological processes involved in teaching and learning. The book is not, however, aimed at any particular kind of psychologist—only those who teach. It therefore strives to satisfy the needs of readers who are only beginning their careers as well as those who have been teaching for many years. These two groups' interests are in some ways incompatible, for novice teachers are often searching for techniques that will miraculously change their ho-hum courses into scintillating intellectual masterpieces, whereas veterans seek insights into perennial problems that still nag them each time they teach a course. This book tries to satisfy both these demands by organizing specific suggestions for teaching within an overall conceptual framework that is consistent with existing psychological theories and con- cepts.

I hope psychologists will find these suggestions useful, but I recognize that this book's basic goal is a presumptuous one. The suggestions offered may not add much to what readers already know about teaching. Like so many self-help or how-to books, it may fail to deliver on its promise of fresh insight and wise counsel. True, people who read self-help books often express satisfaction with them, and some evidence has suggested that this satisfaction is related to actual improvement (Halliday, 1991). But self-help books can also mislead readers rather than help them by proffering sim- plistic solutions to complex problems; their recommendations are often at variance with current research findings; they raise expectations but not awareness; and they delude people into thinking that they will improve by following the simple formulas the author presents (Rosen, 1987). As Starker (1987) concluded, "Self-help titles, by and large, are repositories of unproven, sometimes unprovable, advice on matters of considerable importance and complexity" (p. 453).

I tried to avoid these pitfalls by not oversimplifying the complexities of teaching or drawing conclusions that overstepped the limitations of the available data. For the most part, however, the implications of psychology for teaching were too plentiful rather than too few. Teaching and learning are extraordinarily complex behaviors, but psychologists' models, theories, and findings offer insight after insight into these processes. To some professors in the academy teaching and learning may seem mysterious and unpredictable, but to psychologists they are intriguing phenomena that fall squarely within our domain of expertise. Because the processes that sustain teaching and learning are the very processes studied by psychologists, the classroom is a veritable laboratory and clinic for the teaching psychologist.

1

PREPPING: PLANNING TO TEACH A COLLEGE CLASS

Consider how an ordinary day is put together. . . . whether it is crowded or empty, novel or routine, uniform or varied, your day has a structure of its own—it fits into the texture of your life. And as you think what your day will hold, you construct a plan to meet it. What you expect to happen foreshadows what you expect to do.

—George A. Miller, Eugene Galanter, and Karl H. Pribram
Plans and the Structure of Behavior (1960, p. 5)

Preparation to teach psychology begins many months before that first day of class. This planning must take into account not only the nature of the class to be taught and the kinds of students who take it but also the purposes of the class itself. All who teach must, before they walk to the classroom's dais on the first day of the term, identify and prioritize the goals they will attempt to reach, including their broad objectives and their more narrow specific aims. They must also decide how they will teach by selecting the techniques they will use to help their students reach their learning goals. They must plan discussions, write lectures, select readings and texts, design assessments, and sequence the topics they hope to cover. This planning comes to an end on the first day of class when these plans, and the syllabus that details them, are shared with students.

* * *

The nightmare always begins the same way. I stand at the lectern in a teaching auditorium I have never seen before. Countless students pack the vast room, sitting in hundred-seat rows that stretch back into the room's dark, distant recesses. I lean forward, clear my voice in the microphone, and the students fall silent as I begin to welcome them to this, the first day of class. But before I am halfway through my first sentence, I realize that I have inexplicably forgotten to prepare any remarks. With no notes on the podium that provide an eloquent overview of the course's purposes and procedures, I decide to skip the oration and just review the syllabus.

9

My confusion becomes panic when the empty desk by my side tells me that, despite an unbroken record of 25 years of dutifully meeting each first class with a carefully prepared syllabus, I forgot to make one up for this class. So I take a deep breath and steel myself to the task of bluffing my way through 30 minutes reviewing course goals and procedures until the awful truth becomes apparent to me: I have no idea what course I am supposed to be teaching.

The nightmare's lesson: Prepare. Indeed, psychologists' teaching-related thoughts often revolve around "prepping": I haven't finished prepping that class yet. Is that course a new prep for you? I cannot go to that colloquium—I have to prep for a class. How many preps do you have this semester? I need to have a few minutes of quiet so I can prep. Apparently professors are so busy preparing that they do not even have time to say the whole word.

Teaching psychologists' near obsession with preparation reflects the thoughtful nature of teaching. As Woodworth (1958) explained some time ago, most complex actions are organized in two stages: the preparatory stage and the consummatory, or behavioral, stage. During the preparation stage, people create the organization for their actions: They identify their objectives, set their goals, develop strategies, make plans, and select their tactics. All this planning, as Miller, Galanter, and Pribram (1960) explained, provides the blueprint for specifying "the order in which a sequence of operations is to be performed" (p. 16) and in doing so, structures actions effectively. Armed with a plan, individuals no longer react to situations; rather, they proactively control situations so that their expectations are affirmed.

Miller and his colleagues (1960) pointed out that "any Plan complicated enough to be interesting will include steps that are executed for no other reason than to pave the way for what we really want to do" (p. 159). For teaching, these steps include setting the goals for a class—the broad, general outcomes as well as the more specific outcomes that are more easily documented when the term comes to an end. Planning also involves identifying the paths to follow in reaching those goals. Will you lecture or lead discussions? Will you give tests and of what type? Will you use a textbook or a collection of readings? What topics will you cover and in what order? Will you assign papers and projects? These sorts of questions must be considered before class even meets, making preparation the first step on any journey into teaching.

GOALS TO SEEK

A professor's course planning includes the formulation of general goals for the class—for example, to instill knowledge, create critical thinkers, hone research skills, transform students into scholars—as well as the specification of specific, content-based goals such as to "teach students that correlations do not imply causality," "help students learn to respond in positive ways to people who are different from them," "encourage an attitude of healthy skepticism," and "write all research papers in APA style with ragged right-hand margins." This planning helps professors cultivate and maintain a thoughtful, coherent approach to their teaching. Like a corporation's mission statement, a set of strategies gives purpose to the small day-to-day actions that, although insignificant in isolation, sum to create an overall approach to teaching. Such an inclusive perspective provides an antidote for the relentless drift toward meaninglessness that can overtake action. The original purpose of an act can change over time until its original purpose is replaced by some new, and less coherent, understanding (Vallacher & Wegner, 1987). The professor, reading over material that must be covered in tomorrow's lecture, may forget she is "prepping a class" and instead think she is "just reading." The professor who stops on the street to answer a student's question may think he is wasting time when, in fact, he is teaching. If people enter a situation without a conceptualization of action in mind, their actions are easy targets for reinterpretation. Before they know it, they become test givers, attendance takers, experts, disciplinarians, or speakers, but not what they intended to be: teaching psychologists.

Goals also sit atop a pile of factors that psychologists have identified in their studies of motivation and performance. People working at jobs ranging from hauling logs to generating creative ideas to proofreading were found to be unproductive if their goals were vague or absent but productive if they were laboring to attain clearly established goals (Austin & Vancouver, 1996). Students tend to be more interested in course materials and their performance improves when they can identify the goals they are seeking (Elliot, 1999; Husman & Lens, 1999). Individuals experiencing interpersonal and psychological difficulties cope more effectively when they can identify the goals they hope to achieve and the paths they can take to reach these goals (Snyder, Cheavens, & Sympson, 1997). These findings suggest that students and their professors will perform better if they know what goals they are seeking and whether those goals are important to them (Kleinbeck, Quast, & Schwarz, 1989). This chapter therefore reviews several models of goals in higher education and includes ones that vary in terms of specificity; some focus on the specific content to be examined in the course, whereas others include a wider range of outcomes when specifying the purposes of college teaching.

Bloom's Taxonomy: Global Cognitive Outcomes

In the late 1940s Bloom and other educational psychologists began formulating a classification of "the goals of the educational process"

(Bloom, Englehart, Furst, Hill, & Krathwohl, 1956). Bloom and his colleagues developed taxonomies in three domains: affective (emotions, attitudes, appreciations, values, feelings); psychomotor (physical skills such as coordination, athleticism, dance, body awareness); and cognitive (thinking, reasoning, evaluating). However, his hierarchical model of the cognitive domain is what so frequently guides educators' attempts to identify the critical goals they seek in the classroom. The cognitive taxonomy's six levels range from low to high in terms of cognitive complexity, from simple recall or recognition of facts to evaluation (see Table 1.1). Bloom's model, despite advances in our understanding of the actual relationships among cognitive skills and domains (e.g., Anderson & Sosniak, 1994), offers a useful way of categorizing learning goals.

Knowledge

Many college classes focus on transmitting basic information about the discipline's facts, concepts, theories, researchers, and theorists to the student. Knowledge, as the lowest level of learning, involves only the ability to recall the information and not the use of the information to solve problems or the integration of information with other knowledge. When

TABLE 1.1
Bloom's Taxonomy of Educational Objectives (Bloom et al., 1956)

Level of learning goal	Sample learning objective
Knowledge: remembering factual information, such as names, dates, studies, concepts, theories, and researchers	List the six levels described by Bloom's taxonomy, in order from least to most complex
Comprehension: understanding the meaning of an idea, concept, theory, or procedure	Generate five verbs that describe the learning outcomes associated with each of the six stages of Bloom's taxonomy
Application: describing the specific, concrete implications of a concept or idea in a new context or situation	Give an example of a test question that measures learning at the application level of Bloom's taxonomy
Analysis: identifying the elements of a complex concept and identifying the interrelationships among these elements	Compare and contrast Bloom's taxonomy and Anderson's revised model of learning goals (Anderson & Sosniak, 1994)
Synthesis: integrating concepts and information to yield new insights or structures	Use recent findings in the field of cognitive science to update and refine Bloom's original taxonomy of educational objectives
Evaluation: gauging the value, quality, usefulness, and worth a concept, theory, set of works, and so on	Critique Bloom's taxonomy in terms of the key characteristics of a good theory (parsimony, disconfirmability, coherence, consistency with empirical findings)

professors explain that the first laboratory in psychology was founded in 1879, that many theorists believe five dimensions form the bedrock for individual differences in personality, and that R^2 indexes the percentage of variance accounted for in a multiple regression, they are stressing knowledge. When professors hand out study sheets before the first exam that list key terms, dates, studies, theories, and theorists, they are stressing the goal of increased knowledge.

Comprehension

Whereas knowledge goals can be attained through memorization, comprehension requires more than just recall of data from memory. When students comprehend a concept or idea, they grasp its basic meaning and interpretation. Instead of just naming the three parts of personality described by Freud, students who understand the tripartite theory of personality can describe the basic nature of each component, the dynamic interconnections among the components, and the implications of strengths and weaknesses of each component for overall psychological adjustment. When students can interpret charts and graphs, translate text material into symbolic forms such as equations or predictions, defend the methods used in a particular study, or poke holes in the logic of a theory, then they demonstrate comprehension rather than knowledge.

Application

When professors require their students to *use* the course's theories and concepts—to solve practical problems, to identify avenues for future research, to explain unexpected findings, and so on—they are stressing applications over simple knowledge or comprehension. Application questions are particularly important in psychology, for psychology's applied fields are often grounded in the theoretical substrates of more basic areas of knowledge. Application questions also require more creativity from students, for they must move from the conceptual and general to the concrete and specific. Knowing the names of the eight stages of Erikson's theory of psychosocial development may be sufficient for them to demonstrate knowledge, but to demonstrate application they need to use this information in some way—say, by specifying how therapeutic interventions should be structured for individuals at each of the eight stages.

Analysis

When students analyze concepts, ideas, issues, or phenomena, they must break them down into their component parts while recognizing the interconnections among those parts. Such analysis, according to Bloom, requires an understanding of the structure of knowledge, in addition to an understanding of the content of the knowledge. The classic essay question that begins "compare and contrast" is an analysis question, for it asks the learner to take at least two concepts, break the concepts down into their basic elements, and then compare these elements with one another to determine areas of similarity and difference.

Synthesis

Professors who hope that students grasp the larger significance of the material presented—the field's outlook—are pushing for synthesis: the ability to put parts together to form a new whole. One of the most traditional ways to facilitate the attainment of this goal is to require students develop a paper or project that integrates material from various segments of the course. Theses and dissertations in psychology represent the epitome of synthesis, for students must integrate vast amounts of theory and prior evidence in a coherent, organized framework.

Evaluation

Bloom, anticipating work dealing with personal commitment to interpretations of complex ideas (e.g., Perry, 1970), argued that one of the most advanced forms of learning involves the capacity to judge the value of course material. Bloom was careful to note, however, that he was concerned with evaluations that are based on established criteria, rather than personal likes and dislikes. The student who answers the question, "What is your evaluation of Skinner's theory of behaviorism?" with "I don't like it much," is not demonstrating a sophisticated level of educational attainment. Rather, the theory must be evaluated by arguments that support the position taken, as well as by arguments that refute alternative interpretations. Bloom placed such learning outcomes at the top of the cognitive hierarchy because they require elements from each of the other categories and they demonstrate personal commitment to a viewpoint.

Angelo and Cross's Model of Teaching Goals

Angelo and Cross (1993) surveyed a range of diverse resources as they developed their model of basic teaching goals in higher education, including Bayer's (1975) national survey of instructional goals, Bowen's (1977) classification of the basic individual and social values associated with higher education, Bloom et al.'s (1956) taxonomy of educational outcomes, and a number of earlier studies of college outcomes (e.g., Astin, 1977, 1993; Chickering, 1969; Feldman & Newcomb, 1969). They noted that these sources, despite their varying emphases, repeatedly stressed a common core of outcomes that included higher order thinking skills, basic academic success skills, discipline-specific knowledge and skills, liberal arts and academic values, work and career preparation, and personal development.

Angelo and Cross (1993) developed a series of items to assess a professor's emphasis on these types of educational outcomes, and they administered their inventory to faculty at 2-year and 4-year colleges. They then used cluster and item analysis to fine-tune the inventory and to confirm the clusters of outcomes that they had identified in their review of the literature. They then developed the Teaching Goals Inventory (TGI) to measure the six clusters of outcomes summarized in Table 1.2. Respondents complete the TGI by rating the importance of each goal on a scale from "essential" to "unimportant."

Angelo and Cross (1993) surveyed more than 2,000 professors at community colleges and 4-year colleges to determine which goals were considered "essential." The professors in their study emphasized higher order thinking skills, with discipline-specific knowledge coming in a close second. These professors also rated personal development and work–career preparation as collateral goals, with liberal arts and basic academic skills receiving relatively fewer endorsements as essential. A few more of the professors in 4-year schools rated goals pertaining to increased appreciation of the liberal arts as more essential than did professors at community colleges, who tended to stress personal development, work and career preparation, and the development of basic skills. They also found that the majority of these professors generally agreed in their ratings of the specific goals that

TABLE 1.2
Angelo and Cross's (1993) Six-Factor Model of Teaching Goals

Goal	Description
Higher order thinking skills	Analyzing and synthesizing information; rationality; identifying solutions to new problems; creativity; critical thinking
Basic academic success skills	Improving concentration, memory; listening, speaking, reading, writing, and math skills; development of study skills
Discipline-specific knowledge and skills	Knowledge of terms, facts, concepts, perspective, values, methods, and theories specific to the subject; preparation for advanced study; ability to use tools and technologies
Liberal arts and academic values	Appreciation of the arts, humanities, and sciences; development of a historical perspective; recognition of role of science and arts in society; multiculturalism; ethics
Work and career preparation	Ability to work with others; development of management and leadership skills; commitment to personal achievement and skilled performance
Personal development	Development of a sense of self-worth and personal responsibility; respect for others; commitment to honesty; capacity to make wise decisions

are the least and most essential to teach. The three top goals, all rated by more than 50% of both community college professors and 4-year college professors as "essential," were "develop ability to apply principles and generalizations already learned to new problems and situations," "learn terms and facts of this subject," and "develop capacity to think for oneself." The least important goals, rated as essential by fewer than 10% of the faculty, were "develop a commitment to exercise the rights and responsibilities of citizenship" and "cultivate physical health and well-being" (Angelo & Cross, 1993, pp. 399–406).

What were psychologists' top three goals? Angelo and Cross did not single out psychologists in their analyses, but they did differentiate between social scientists and professors in other disciplines such as the natural sciences, business, arts, and so on. This analysis indicated that social scientists' ratings matched the overall ratings reported by the professorate. Angelo and Cross (1993, pp. 20–21) discovered that 57% of professors in the social sciences they surveyed rated "develop ability to apply principles and generalizations already learned to new problems and situations" as an essential goal. The second and third highest rated goals were "learn to understand perspectives and values of this subject" (52%) and "develop capacity to think for oneself" (50%). Social scientists, as a group, tended to be more varied in their rankings of the various outcomes in comparison to professors in the arts, humanities, and sciences. More than 75% of the professors in the arts, for example, felt that the development of an appreciation of art was an essential goal. More than 80% of the math professors felt that the development of problem-solving skills was an essential goal. But only 50–57% of the social science professors agreed in their ratings of the goals just mentioned, suggesting that social science professors' courses do not converge on a single set of shared outcomes.

Angelo and Cross's (1993) survey also indicated that professors remain more concerned with their own discipline's specific forms of knowledge than general academic and scholarly skills such as writing and mathematics. For example, even though the "Writing Across the Curriculum" movement stresses the importance of teaching students to express their knowledge of their major field through writing, most professors "still regard the improvement of writing as the responsibility of English departments" (p. 368).

Psychology's Goals

Angelo and Cross's conclusions about professors' goals are generally consistent with analyses that have focused on psychologists' goals in their classes. Although psychology's lack of any widely shared paradigm and its practitioners' penchant for specialization ensures a high level of disagreement about the field's ultimate purposes, the three sets of educational outcomes noted in Table 1.3 are those most widely accepted across the field (Kimble, 1984; Levy, Burton, Mickler, & Vigorito, 1999; McGovern, Furumoto, Halpern, Kimble, & McKeachie, 1991). Many psychologists would take exception to this list—suggesting critical goals that should be added or targeting some that should be deleted—but it is generally consistent with the spirit of prior reviews of the psychology undergraduate curriculum, such as the APA Committee on Undergraduate Education's 1991 report (McGovern et al., 1991), the Quality Principles generated by conferees at the 1991 National Conference on Enhancing the Quality of Undergraduate Education in Psychology (McGovern, 1993; McGovern & Reich, 1996),

TABLE 1.3
Three Sets of Goals in Psychology Classes

Goal	Subgoals
Knowledge base	Content: a conceptual framework for learning significant facts, findings, theories, and issues in psychology
	History: knowledge of evolution of psychology's theories and systems
	Methods: understanding of research procedures, measurement, and statistics
	Interdisciplinary context: recognition of connections between psychology and other disciplines
Intellectual skills	Thinking skills: proficiency in critical thinking, evaluating research methods, thinking scientifically about behavior and mental processes, basing judgments on psychological theory and research
	Language skills: comprehension of psychological texts and scientific reports, skill in speaking and writing
	Research and technological skills: ability to conduct (and critically evaluate) research and statistical analyses
	Information-gathering skills: ability to locate and synthesize information needed
Practical skills and personal development	Applied skills: proficiencies that are useful in psychology-related jobs and careers (e.g., testing, management, counseling)
	Self-improvement: improved well-being, happiness, motivation, self-control, stress management, creativity, and so on
	Interpersonal skills: enhanced capacity to relate well with, appreciate, and respect other people
	Interpersonal sensitivity: increased sensitivity to diversity and individual differences
	Ethics: understanding of the role of ethical values in scientific and personal context

and Halpern and colleagues' (1993) analyses of outcomes for psychology majors.

Knowledge Base

Most psychologists would agree with McGovern et al. (1991) that "there are significant facts, theories, and issues in psychology that a student needs to know" (p. 601). Although the core content changes over time as the discipline changes, the emphasis on teaching that core to students does not. This agreement, however, does not extend to other questions of content such as: What topics constitute the core of psychology: biopsychology, learning, cognition, social psychology, developmental psychology, personality, abnormal psychology, measurement? Should professors devote significant portions of the course to the history of the field? Should the connections between psychology and (a) other sciences and (b) the humanities be covered? The changing nature of the discipline's knowledge base and the lack of consensus on these issues support a focus on creating a foundation for lifelong learning rather than a focus on the accumulation of isolated facts and findings.

Intellectual Skills

Students need to know things like "Theory Y predicts this will happen" or "Such and such experiment supported this hypothesis," but they also need to be capable of *doing* psychology. Students need the intellectual skills required to generate theories, do research, communicate ideas and information to others, evaluate conclusions statistically, and locate the information they need for all these intellectual pursuits. As Sternberg (1999c) suggested, psychology's basic content "will change greatly over the years, but the tools for thinking critically and creatively about psychology will not" (p. 38). Of the 10 specific outcomes specified in the Quality Principles, half focus on intellectual skills, including the ability to think scientifically, critique research findings, communicate effectively, and use psychological theory and research when making decisions (McGovern & Reich, 1996).

Practical Skills and Personal Development

Psychology is both a basic science and an applied science. Although its courses often stress fundamentals of the field and basic intellectual skills, much of psychology's content can be applied to oneself, one's relationships, and one's career (Grasha, 1998; Quereshi, 1988). At the *personal level*, studying psychology often helps people better understand themselves—and their problems. Courses like personal adjustment and stress management address the goal of self-improvement explicitly, but even the most basic of psychology courses will yield ideas that have personal implications. At the *value level*, the field of psychology openly examines important contemporary issues, including racism, sexism, ethics, social policy, and political values. A course in psychology teaches not only psychological facts but also interpersonal sensitivity, respect for diversity, appreciation of individual differences, and ethical decision making. And at the *practical level*, psychology courses often seek to apply the field's theories, methods, and findings to industrial, organizational, educational, judiciary, and therapeutic contexts. Courses that deal with interviewing, testing, counseling, and substance abuse are devoted primarily to practical applications of psychology, as are community-based courses such as fieldwork placements and service learning (Levy et al., 1999; McGovern & Reich, 1996).

Prioritizing Goals

Different professors emphasize different goals in their teaching. Professor A may do all she can to impart content to her students; when the term ends she hopes they will be familiar with the basic assumptions of the field's theories, theorists, and major findings. Professor B may be more interested in teaching his students the analytical and methodological skills of the field. He hopes that successful students can "do" things when they finish the course. Professor C may insist that her students learn to think critically, and she may let students sharpen these skills by debating controversies. Professor D may want students to apply material in their own lives. Rather than just read about the topics and methods, D wants his students to recognize the extent to which their own lives are shaped by factors discussed in class. Professor E may share the goals of A, B, C, and D but also want students to apply an academic field in a practical pursuit, such as a business enterprise. These professors' approaches, although very different in their emphases, are nonetheless consistent with a subset of the goals specified in Table 1.3. Indeed, the guarantee of academic freedom ensures that each scholar can pursue his or her own interests and teach those interests in his or her own way—at least, within the constraints of the department's curriculum policies (Levy et al., 1999).

Overall, however, applied goals tend to get less attention in the curriculum, particularly at the undergraduate level. Whereas applied graduate training programs focus on the development of skills needed in mental health treatment facilities, community agencies, corporate settings, and so on, undergraduate courses focus more on psychology's knowledge base and helping students develop their intellectual skills (Belar & Perry, 1992; Miller & Gentile, 1998). These priorities are not, however, always shared by students. Students, more so than faculty, expect that their course work will give them useful, practical skills that can be applied in a profession—with a particular emphasis on a mental health setting (Brown, 1980; Malin & Timmreck, 1979; McGovern & Hawks, 1986). McGovern and Hawks

(1986) documented this disparity by asking students and faculty to rate the importance of goals like those summarized in Table 1.3 on a scale from 1 (not at all important) to 7 (extremely important). They found that psychology faculty gave high ratings to such outcomes as learning the scientific principles of behavior, developing skills needed to evaluate psychological research, and using statistical methods. Students, on the other hand, stressed more immediately useful goals. They gave the highest ratings to these two goals: "get practical experience" and "help other people." They also gave higher ratings to such personal goals as improved relationship skills and skill at modifying their own behavior. When the faculty and students rated the importance of 40 courses, they agreed that core courses like experimental methods, statistics, history, and testing are needed for learning the scientific side of psychology. The faculty's list also included physiological psychology and learning, whereas the students' list included abnormal psychology. Similarly, when the American Psychological Association (n.d.) asked graduates from undergraduate programs to identify those courses that were the most useful to them in their current careers, these respondents named courses with practical content, such as courses in clinical and abnormal psychology. McGovern and Hawks (1986) suggested that this gap between professors' visions of their goals and students' expectations about their courses can be narrowed through academic advising and curriculum revision.

PLANNING THE CLASS

If the first step in prepping a class is the identification of goals—the knowledge base to build, the intellectual skills to foster, the personal development to actuate—then the second step requires identifying the means to achieve those ends. Indeed, when Stark, Lowther, Ryan, and Genthon (1988) asked faculty how they prepare for their classes, few of them said "I think deep thoughts about my general approach to teaching and learning" or "I ask myself 'What qualities should I build into my classroom to promote learning?'" Rather, they reported that they spent time reviewing the topics they would be covering and the materials that they would need for the teaching activities they planned. They also claimed that they considered the characteristics of the students who would be taking the class, as if to coordinate their planned teaching approaches with the students' abilities, goals, and needs. Pondering arcane questions about goals, long-term outcomes, and strategies is all well and good, but apparently professors cannot do it for too long, for they must get ready to teach the class.

Professors, like people in general, differ in their approach to making their plans (Karoly & Ruehlman, 1995). Some like to sketch out their plans in extraordinary detail, laying out each step along the way to the final goal. Others, in contrast, prefer the flexibility of a sketchy plan or just a set of heuristic orienting principles. People also vary in how willingly they disclose their plans to others; some are "very cagey about announcing what their Plans are, whereas others feel quite free to describe them to anybody who inquires" (Miller et al., 1960, p. 121). Some, too, prefer to craft their own plans and will refuse to listen to the advice of others. Others seek out information about others' plans and adopt them as their own if they deem them to be effective. But the complexity of the task facing the college professor, and the need for a syllabus that accurately describes the course's elements, increases the need for an explicit plan of action for each course taught. This plan need not be extensive, but it must at least take into account the type of course being taught, the characteristics of the students who are likely to enroll in the class, and the teaching activities that will be enacted as well as the grading procedures to be implemented.

Consider the Class

When Perlman and McCann (1999b) reviewed the course catalogs from more than 400 psychology departments in colleges and universities, they generated a long list of common courses. The introductory course was universally offered, but abnormal, social, personality, learning, history and systems, tests and measures, cognitive, statistics, child, physiological, experimental, industrial/organizational, developmental, methods, adolescence, life span, human sexuality, counseling, biological psychology, adjustment, sensation and perception, comparative, special topics, field experience, independent study, and research participation courses appeared in many college catalogs. They also identified a number of laboratory co-requisites and newer courses, such as the psychology of women, the psychology of the African American, prevention of social and psychological problems, the psychology of substance abuse, and so on. These courses may all be part of the field of psychology, but the unique content, assumptions, emphases, and complexities of each make unique demands on the psychologists who teach them.

What Does the Course Cover?

Professors who teach a course regularly may not have to review the topics that they need to cover in their assigned courses for the coming term, but professors who are doing a new prep or who are teaching the course again after several years away from it need to refresh their memories of the course's content. One obvious source to consult for information is the university catalog. These descriptions, in most cases, have been officially sanctioned by curriculum review committees, but they can also be out-of-date and inaccurate. Colleagues who have taught the course regularly are another good source of information about content, and they can also clarify what the local mores are about veering away from the catalog's description. Textbooks are another key source of information about content, if the course is one of the more traditional psychology courses previously noted. A review of a few good textbooks can tell you far more about what the course usually covers than a colleague's old syllabus or a dusty description in your college's catalog.

Do You Have a Commanding Grasp of the Course's Contents?

Many professors remember their first term teaching with mixed emotions. They were thrilled to have completed their graduate training and to, at last, be professors. But in many cases they did not feel as though they were ready to teach it. First, many felt uncertain about teaching because they were not trained in teaching, per se (e.g., Benassi & Fernald, 1993; Meyers & Prieto, 2000). Second, even though they were well trained in their particular field, their expertise was often narrower in scope than the courses they would be teaching. Sure, they knew the topic of their dissertation better than anyone else, but did they know an entire terms' worth of material in a course that surveys a larger topic in psychology? Preparation, then, requires a personal review of critical concepts, theory, and research in the area examined in the course; otherwise, one risks falling into the "staying one chapter ahead of them" trap.

Fortunately, professors are scholars, and so they are experts when it comes to building their own understanding of material. Some rules-of-thumb for this process include:

- Begin with very general (and lower level) treatments of each topic before moving to more specific and higher level treatments (Marques, 1999)
- Review several textbooks' analyses of each significant topic that you will cover to sharpen your understanding of theoretical concepts and empirical results
- Supplement this general understanding with more advanced sources, such as *Psychological Bulletin* and the *Annual Review of Psychology*
- Use original sources, scholarly monographs, and resources located on the Web to round out the review and resolve any questions not answered by more general sources.

Chapter 2's analysis of lecture development offers other suggestions to professors who must quickly transform themselves from novitiate into expert.

What Is the Level of This Course?

Psychology courses range from the introductory overview course that samples topics from the entire field to graduate seminars for students who are working on their dissertations, and skilled professors strive to match their instructional and assessment strategies to the level of the course. Course level is often confounded with other influential variables such as course size, general goals, and student maturity, interest, and skill. A 100-level course is often a large-enrollment course, in contrast to a senior capstone course or a graduate seminar in some highly refined topic. Lower level courses are also more content focused than process focused, for in many cases they are prerequisites for advanced classes that assume students are familiar with basic content. When seniors sitting in an advanced psychology class raise their hand and ask, "What's a correlation?" or "What is the difference between classical and operant conditioning?" or "What's an independent variable?" their professor will likely wonder about the quality of the instruction these students received in the prerequisite courses. Course level also determines, in large part, the types of students who will enroll in the course. At many universities, introductory psychology is considered to be a first-year (i.e., "freshman") course, and so it includes a relatively high proportion of students who may not yet have developed the learning skills they need for academic success. Care must therefore be exercised when setting the course's level of difficulty.

What Is the Size of the Course?

Applying Simmel's (1902) taxonomy of groups to classes, a small class numbers from 4 to 20 members, a moderate class from 20 to 40 members, and a large class contains more than 40 members. And perhaps we should add another category, huge, to describe those college classes with 100 or more students taught in vast lecture halls.

Size, per se, changes many of the structural, pedagogical, and practical features of a class. Professors who design their courses for small classes of 10 to 20 students will need to make substantial changes when they discover that 200 have enrolled, just as professors who typically teach mega-sections will need to adopt new techniques when they teach small classes. For example:

- *Style:* As groups increase in size, the need for a task-organizing leader increases. In consequence, an informal style that works so well in a small class may fail when applied to a large class, just as a highly structured, organized approach may be overly constraining in small classes.
- *Interdependence:* Very small classes possess many unique characteristics simply because they include so few members. In such classes, each student becomes more important, and each student therefore has a more profound impact on the quality of the class. In a small class, all the members can develop

individualized relationships with one another, and each student has more of an impact on each class session.

- *Instructional choices:* As classes get larger, the reliance on student-centered teaching methods becomes smaller. One can lecture to a group of five students, but such classes can also be taught through discussion, student presentations, small group activities, and other methods that increase student-to-student interaction. Many such activities can be used in large classes, as chapter 2 notes, but such classes generally force professors into the role of lecturer.

- *Testing methods:* Even though professors may wish to use open-ended, essay type tests in their classes, such testing methods become unwieldy in large classes. When courses reach beyond 20 members, most professors find themselves reaching for tests that can be scored by computers.

- *Engagement:* The intimacy of smaller classes and the anonymity of larger classes create unique demands for students. Because smaller classes are more personal social experiences, confident students often enjoy the opportunity to work closely with others. Less confident students, in contrast, may find the evaluative pressures of the small group to be too great. In contrast, students in larger classes often describe these classes as impersonal and uninvolving, yet some find the anonymity of such classes comforting. If they wish to skip class, their absence will go unmissed. If they get behind in their reading, they will not be embarrassed publicly when they cannot understand the class discussion. If they read the text material casually and cursorily, their blunder goes undetected, for even their test scores are rarely linked to them personally.

- *Management:* Very large classes are more dramatic social experiences, and the sheer number of individuals gathered together puts unique demands upon both the professor and the students. Some of the most time-extensive aspects of teaching—office hours, record keeping, make-up examinations, help sessions, advising, responding to specific students' questions—multiply in direct proportion to the number of students in a class. Technical problems, too, arise as classes swell in size and professors become media specialists, photocopy wizards, and crowd control experts. Students, too, must take more responsibility for their own learning in larger classes, and fewer exceptions can be made for them in terms of testing procedures, missed classes, and other exceptions to procedures.

In general, larger classes require more time to plan and organize. When a professor must give a 10-page test to 10 students, she can print the copies she needs in 10 minutes. But when the class numbers 400, she must develop the exam far in advance of the day that it is needed. When a teacher in a small class gives the wrong date for the test on Monday and corrects the error on Wednesday, he can make a mental note to tell Juanita since she was not in class on Wednesday. In a large class, however, such slips cannot be so easily corrected, for what can be done for the 50 of the 400 students who skipped class on Wednesday and did not hear the correction? One can give a few students a make-up test when they are sick on test day, but what about 20 sick students? These problems cannot be entirely avoided, but planning decreases their frequency.

Consider the Students

Each year Beloit College releases a list of facts about the incoming first-year class. The list recognizes that these students, if they are entering college immediately after they complete high school, were born only 18 years before—and so their experiences are confined to the past 2 decades. These incoming students bring not just cell phones, Palm Pilots, credit cards, and laptop computers, but also a different set of life experiences. The Beloit College (2001) Mindset List noted that for these students:

- There have always been ATM machines.
- They have never referred to Russia and China as "the Reds."
- There has always been a national holiday honoring Martin Luther King, Jr.
- Around-the-clock coverage of Congress, public affairs, weather reports, and rock videos has always been available on cable.
- Women sailors have always been stationed on U.S. Navy ships.
- They have never heard a phone "ring."
- They never dressed up for a plane flight.
- They have never used a bottle of "White-Out."
- "Spam" and "cookies" are not necessarily foods.
- They feel more danger from having sex and being in school than from possible nuclear war.

The Beloit list reminds professors to consider their students' background —their life experiences, their attitudes and interests, the level of preparation, their ethnicities, their cultural backgrounds, and their goals—when ruminating about the best ways to teach them.

Novice Learners or Savvy Seniors?

The matching of students with their classes is an assortive social process that reflects students' stages of their academic careers, their personal interests, and in many cases the requirements of their programs. As noted earlier, students often take introductory psychology in their first year of school, along with English, biology, history, and other general education classes. Not only are these students relatively unskilled learners, but they may also be coping with a number of personal issues related to such things as dormitory living, establishing friendships, and even homesickness, and so their performance can be surprisingly variable as their concentration on the course material ebbs and flows. Such students are also the youngest students on the campus, so the cautions of the Beloit list apply: Students will not know what you are talking about when you mention "old" rock groups (they are not even called "rock groups" anymore), ancient history (e.g., the Bill Clinton–Monica Lewinsky scandal), or long-gone television programs (e.g., *Beavis and Butthead*) in your examples. In many cases, too, local examples do not work with such students because many are new to campus and do not know the local lore of the school or the town or city where it is located.

Psychology Majors or Nonmajors?

The introductory course (and advanced courses that are particularly relevant to other disciplines, such as abnormal psychology, industrial/organizational, and developmental) are often *service courses* for which a substantial proportion of the students who enroll are in another degree program that requires them to take this course. In service courses one is teaching not only the devoted majors in the discipline, but also students whose interests lie elsewhere than psychology: humorless biology majors, pragmatic business students, disdainful future physicists, tattooed and pierced art students, expressive theater majors, and so on. But many advanced courses in psychology, and the methods and statistics offerings in particular, are populated primarily with students who have chosen to major in psychology. Indeed, teaching psychologists have the luxury of teaching to the choir, for the four-fold increase in psychology majors that surprised many departments in the 1970s shows little sign of abating.

Socially Diverse or Homogenous?

In the 1950s most college students were men in their early 20s, they lived on campus, attended classes full time, and their parents were college graduates. But over the past 3 decades, women, African Americans, Hispanics/Latinos, Asians, Pacific Islanders, people with disabilities, international students, openly gay and lesbian students, and those students from families whose members have never gone beyond high school have entered college in record numbers. As college classrooms become more diverse, professors must sometimes revisit their methods, policies, and course contents to be certain they are appropriate for, and fair to, the students in their classes (Border & Chism, 1992; Chism, 1999). When classes are filled with students who range widely in ethnic, cultural, personal, and social background, then the professor must be ready to respond positively to variations in communication styles and skills, interactional and learning styles, achievement orientation, and experience with Western culture's norms and expectations. Moreover, and as considered in more detail in chapter 6, diverse classes provide professors and students with the resources they need to develop their sensitivity to diversity and individual differences.

Traditional or Nontraditional?

The traditional, full-time, 18–22 year-old college student is being gradually outnumbered by older students who are returning to school after a long hiatus. Allen (2000) explained that teaching nontraditional students creates challenges when planning the course for the complexity of students' lives often means that they miss more classes, have less time for non-classroom activities, and can't take advantage of on-campus resources. She recommended exercising care when selecting readings (providing more background for students who took prerequisite courses long ago) and when making decisions about assignments that require students to invest considerable amounts of time outside of class.

Consider the Teaching

No one assumes that lawyers can only bill their clients for time spent in the courtroom or that an orchestra's conductor should be paid only for performances. Yet when people outside the hallowed halls of academia condemn professors for spending so little time teaching, they usually calculate time spent teaching with a single index: How much time do you spend in the classroom lecturing to students? This narrow view of teaching overlooks the wide range of actions that fall under the category *teaching*.

What Will You Do?

When Stark et al. (1988) interviewed faculty who were planning their courses very few of these professors spoke of making deliberate choices among various teaching strategies. Most assumed that they would rely on the tried-and-true lecture method in their teaching, without giving much thought to alternative methods such as discussion and collaborative learning procedures. These faculty make the same error that outsiders do who complain about the "professors' cushy jobs," for they assume that teaching = lecturing. But, in actuality, teaching requires many actions besides lecturing, such as reviewing with students passages from the textbook or previous lectures, guiding classroom discussions, answering students' questions in and out of class, e-mailing course material to them, posting instructional information on the Web, and so on. Even preparing to *not teach*, say by arranging for guest lecturers or by developing a colloquium series that students attend in lieu of class, counts as teaching.

What Will Students Do?

When developing the course, professors plan not only their own actions but also their students' actions. Will they do specific readings? Carry out writing assignments such as term papers? Discuss material in class and make oral presentations? Will they undertake collaborative learning assignments, group and individual projects, take part in service learning experiences, or go out into the field to conduct research? Given the limited amount of time available during the term and students' commitments of time and energy to any one class, the number of learning activities must be assigned carefully. Classes with too few assignments and activities, like work environments where workers have too little to do and too much time to do it in (Wicker & August, 1995), are often boring, unchallenging, and inefficient because learning outcomes that would be accomplished through the activities are neglected. Too many assignments, though, will leave the students, and the professor who must grade the activities, feeling harried. A course where activities follow one after another gives the impression that students' are completing busy work rather than meaningful educational experiences.

What Activities Will the Students Undertake?

One of the advantages of teaching a course in psychology, rather than, say, astrophysics, is that the subject matter can be created and studied within the confines of the classroom. Many classroom activities work by asking students to consider their own behavior from a psychological perspective and may require the development of personal insight. Some activities also make use of simulation and role-playing methods. These learning methods, when they work effectively, help students apply psychological concepts to their own lives, get them involved in the learning process, and challenge them to think about themselves (Mathie et al., 1993). Publishers often provide useful activities in the materials that they have prepared to support their book, and the journal *Teaching of Psychology* publishes and evaluates learning activities in each issue. Indeed, Benjamin, Nodine, Ernst, and Broeker (1999) and Ware and Johnson's (2000a, 2000b, 2000c) compendia of hundreds of activities cut across all areas of psychology, including statistics, research methods, history, physiological–comparative, perception, learning, cognitive, developmental, personality, abnormal, and social. I consider the use of such activities in more detail in chapter 3.

What Technology and Media Will Be Used?

Years ago, high-tech teaching psychologists prepped by ordering films from distribution centers, sorting their slides, and changing the bulb in the overhead projector. Today's high-tech professors source out audiovisual materials from films, videos, DVDs, and laser disks; update their PowerPoint presentations; and check to see if the digital projection system in their lecture hall has been upgraded. The well-prepared teachers of yesteryear visited the classroom before the term started to check the microphone, the lectern, the blackboards, and lighting, but now they need to troubleshoot the network connection and verify that all the gizmos they want to use were not stolen over the break. They must also consider what types of technology their students will be using, and if they decide to use a virtual classroom they must check their Web links and their e-mail system, and field test any new technologies that they are considering implementing.

What Will You Do to Support Students' Learning?

Some professors, anticipating that their students may have problems with the material, plan in advance the sorts of educational support they will provide. Some may, for example, decide to provide students with their lecture notes, partial outlines, or skeletal notes prior to the lecture. Students generally appreciate this indulgence, although they may skip class more frequently if they know they can refer to the printed notes when they study. This practice also means that the lecture cannot be revised extensively the night before class, for students must have enough lead time to purchase the notes from the bookstore or download them from the Web. Some professors schedule review and help sessions before each examination, either as part of class-time or as optional outside sessions for those who need more structure. Other forms of educational support include delivering lectures on study skills, encouraging students to form study groups, holding tutorials during office hours, arranging for students to meet online before exams to review material, giving practice quizzes, and so on. Like social support, educational support has its greatest impact when students need it the most.

Consider the Texts

Scholars acquire much of their knowledge through reading rather than listening. Indeed, humans' capacity to read others' words gives literate people access to the knowledge of past generations while reducing their dependence on oral forms of communication and information exchange

(Stanovich, 1993; Stanovich & Cunningham, 1993). McKeachie (1999) went so far as to suggest that students learn more from their textbook than they do from their teacher, making the choice of texts and readings one of the most important components of adequate preparation (Parsons, 1957).

What Text Should You Use?

When identifying a textbook for your class, you can turn to colleagues for input, both informally and more formally by reading reviews of texts published in such journals as *Contemporary Psychology* and *Teaching of Psychology* (Dewey, 1999). You can also ask students to evaluate which texts they prefer. When Britton, Guelgoez, Van Dusen, Glynn, and Sharp (1991) asked college students to read text passages that had been previously tested for clarity and "learnability," they found that the students were 95% accurate in their judgments, suggesting that students can tell the difference between books that they can learn from and books that will baffle them.

But McKeachie (1999) was correct when he stated, "there is no substitute for detailed review of the competing texts for the course you are teaching" (p. 13). That review requires that you obtain copies of all the texts that you are considering by contacting the field representatives of the publishers, writing directly to the publishers, or by using the Web to request review copies. Acquiring these copies takes time, and most college bookstores like to have professors' book orders far in advance of the start of the term, so the selection of a text usually occurs well before all other preparatory activities. Some characteristics to consider include:

- *Scope, accuracy, and currency:* A good text should present a unified but comprehensive review of all major topics and concepts in the field you are teaching. The material itself should be clearly presented, painstakingly accurate, and representative of current thinking in the field, although a mix of classic and contemporary references is usually desirable. A check of the references should reveal that critical monographs and journal articles are cited.
- *Level:* Different textbook authors write for different audiences. Some write lower level books, deliberately focusing on critical points but presenting the material so that students with minimal reading skills will be able to comprehend it. Others write more challenging books, stressing depth of coverage and detail. Others write books that fall between these extremes: not too hard, not too easy, but, like Goldilock's porridge, just right in terms of students' backgrounds and their course goals. A text's level is determined in large part by the scope of the contents. As an author introduces more

concepts, provides more details about research procedures, and includes more statistical information and more chapters, the book grows in complexity. The book's difficulty is also determined by how easy or hard it is to read and understand the author's writing. Reading level can be estimated by considering the length of the average sentence, the complexity of sentence structure, and the use of longer words (three or more syllables), but you can also precisely index reading level with such word-processing programs as Word or WordPerfect. A few clicks in the Tools areas of these programs indicated, for example, that the preceding paragraph was written at the college level, uses the passive voice 33% of the time, and is average in terms of sentence and vocabulary complexity.

- *Students' background:* The level of text should match the backgrounds and capabilities of the students in your classes. As Wolfe et al. (1998) verified, learning is enhanced when the text matches the conceptual background of the student. They found that students who knew very little about the material they were studying learned the most from a basic text, whereas more advanced students learned the most from a higher level book.

- *Conceptual orientation:* Texts can differ profoundly in terms of theoretical orientation, and one should generally try to avoid selecting a text that is just too different from one's own view of the field (e.g., Rheingold, 1994). Although disagreements with the text are inevitable, the fewer the better, both in terms of learning and classroom relations. Adopting a textbook and then not using it makes the top-10 list of students' pet peeves (Ludewig, 1994).

- *Emphasis on research, application, and diversity:* Textbooks differ in how much they integrate research, applications, and diversity issues. A traditional text will focus on the field's concepts' and conclusions, whereas a more research-focused text will stress how this content was generated through research. Texts also differ in the number of pages they spend on applications and multicultural issues related to racial, ethnic, and gender diversity. They also differ in the way they achieve this integration. Some texts integrate this material throughout the book, others present such information in special boxes within chapters, and others collect this material in a single chapter near the end of the book.

- *Writing quality:* A good textbook should not just present information, but also teach it through a clear presentation that *engages* the reader (Sadoski, Goetz, & Avila, 1995; Sadoski,

Goetz, & Rodriguez, 2000). Dewey (1999) recommended checking the quality of the writing in 5 or 10 sections scattered throughout the book. He noted that a book with an excellent table of contents, a good sequencing of chapters, compelling summaries, a great test bank, and up-to-date references may nonetheless fail "at the level of individual sentences and paragraphs" (p. 26). Students will learn more from a textbook in which the authors replace wordiness with crisp sentences that use the active voice; pepper the text with vivid examples that touch on topics with which readers are already familiar; help the reader grasp the overall organization of the chapter by clearly signaling its structure with headings, summaries, and transitions from section to section; vary their sentence and paragraph structures appropriately; and create coherent paragraphs that make one or two points clearly.

- *Organization:* A good textbook should be well-organized, both in its ordering of chapters and in the ordering of material within chapters. True, if the book's materials are not ordered they way you want them to be, you can always ask students to read them in the order your prefer (e.g., Rheingold, 1994). But assigning entire chapters at a time, and also following the order of the chapters exactly, is less confusing for students. Telling students to "read the next chapter" is far simpler than having them check the syllabus or Web to find out where to go next.

- *Pedagogy:* Textbooks contain elements designed to help the reader remember the material. These pedagogical elements may include the use of boldface for key terms, a glossary, learning objectives, chapter preview, chapter summaries, review questions, embedded self-assessments, boxed material, graphs and charts, summary tables, annotated readings list, and suggested activities.

- *Ancillaries:* Most publishers provide the professor who adopts their books with an array of supporting material, including suggestions for additional classroom activities, lecture ideas, information about resources available on the Internet, and extensive test banks.

Should You Use Readings?

When students read the textbook only, they study only one psychologist's description of the field, or what Rheingold (1994) called "restless thought distilled into static outlines" (p. 36). But when they read articles, they are exposed to many styles, approaches, and orientations. Readings, too, require students to organize the material themselves and make decisions about importance, meaning, and implications. One must, however, select papers carefully, for students cannot grasp the meaning of the article if they lack statistical training and a substantial vocabulary. Not all undergraduate students can, for example, read a *Psychological Review* article and glean the essential points. Articles published in the field's research journals can also be narrow in focus, so the yield for the student who labors through the work may be rather meager. Banyard and Grayson (1999) suggested testing each candidate for the reading list with these questions:

- Does it have star quality?
- Does it stimulate students' questions?
- Does it stimulate ideas for practical work?
- Does it raise contemporary issues?
- Do the studies illustrate a range of psychological methods?
- Do the studies illustrate a range of psychological ideas?
- Do the studies illuminate the lives of a wide range of people?

Problems can arise, however, in simply getting the outside readings to students. Copyright laws have made it more difficult for faculty to create packets of readings, and in some cases university libraries will not even place photocopies of articles on reserve for fear of running afoul of U.S. copyright laws. Some academic publishers will create a customized package of readings, provided your classes are sufficiently large to justify the cost of production. Alternatively, if you are willing to use someone else's collection of readings, then you can adopt an edited volume, such as *Forty Studies that Changed Psychology* (Hock, 1999). Last, some journals, such as *Psychological Science*, permit the use of their contents in educational settings provided your university's library subscribes to the journal.

Consider the Assessments

Well-prepared professors usually know what kinds of tests and scored assignments students will be completing during the 12 to 16 weeks of the term. The possibilities are nearly limitless; *tests* may include examinations, quizzes, take-home tests, and pop quizzes; and *scored assignments* may include reaction papers, book reviews, article summaries, term papers, research reports, journals, and group projects. Assessment planning requires a series of difficult choices about number, timing, and type of tests and assignments that generate opportunities but exact costs as well (Walvoord & Anderson, 1998).

Number of Tests and Assignments

The term's procession of educational events—its lectures, discussions, activities, and assignments—is punctuated by tests. As chapter 4 notes, tests serve as explicit milestones that break up the months of continuous study and so provide a clear deadline that forces students who would otherwise procrastinate to review what they have learned. Tests also yield feedback for students about their progress toward their learning goals, with grades functioning as powerful motivators for all kinds of useful behaviors, such as studying, attending class, taking notes, and reading the text. Because of these motivational benefits, frequent tests on smaller amounts of material are generally more desirable than infrequent tests on massive amounts of material (Dempster & Perkins, 1993). Although a mid-term and final may be sufficient for high-level courses where students are self-motivated and sufficiently skilled learners, the structure of tests may be needed to keep students who are less adept on task. Indeed, some systems of instruction, such as Keller's (1968) programmed learning with integrated feedback, require constant self-testing.

The general warning against "too much of a good thing" applies to tests, however. Frequent testing keeps students on task, but too frequent testing distracts them from the ultimate goal of learning. Instructors who stress tests, evaluations, and grades over all else produce students who are striving to earn a particular grade rather than to learn the course material (cf. Harackiewicz, Barron, & Elliot, 1998). Professors should also describe the nature and purposes of assessments carefully, because even evaluations described as achievement tests serve as extrinsic motivators, whereas tests described as feedback mechanisms stress intrinsic motivation (Ryan, Mims, & Koestner, 1983). Students who are told that a grade of A means they are doing well in a subject respond to the testing better than students who are told that the A is a reward for working hard (Miller, Brickman, & Bolen, 1975). Frequent tests may also create high levels of competition among students. Although introducing competition among students is a popular way to prompt them to expend greater effort, competition may focus students' attention on winning, to the extent that they eventually conclude that "learning something new" is not nearly as important as "performing better than others" (Ames, 1987, p. 134). Tests also take class time away from other activities, with the result that the more one tests, the less one lectures, leads discussions, presents demonstrations, and so on.

Timing of Tests

Most professors schedule their tests to maximize motivational impact, but they do so within the constraints imposed by the term's calendar of class meetings and holidays. Every term has unique events—religious holidays, big football games, basketball tournaments, rush week, homecoming revelries, vacation breaks, and so on—and the ideal testing schedule works around these events. When tests are scheduled on the day after such events, the results are often disappointing, for if students must choose between taking part in campus events and studying, their extracurricular interests generally trump their curricular requirements. Few students will, for example, use their spring break to study for their psychology exam that is scheduled for the day they return to campus, so scores will be better if the assessment is taken before rather than after the break. As Duffy and Jones (1995) noted, professors find that their classes go more smoothly—and students learn more easily—when their tests and teaching activities are consonant with the naturally occurring rhythms of the semester.

Type of Tests

Students' achievement can be measured in many ways, but in most cases the choice boils down to two basic options: *choice-type (CT) tests* and *supply-type (ST) tests*. Tests that use multiple-choice items, true–false questions, and matching are choice-type tests, for students must select the correct answer from a list of alternatives. Short- and long-answer essay questions and fill-in-the-blank items ask students to supply the answer to the question posed. Chapter 4 considers some the strengths and weaknesses of these two basic approaches to measurement, but this choice is often driven by practical considerations rather than pedagogical ones. Because supply-type tests must be hand-graded by either the professor or a well-trained assistant, the time demands they impose become too great in large-enrollment classes.

Cumulative Tests

Dempster and Perkins (1993) suggested that learning is more durable when cumulative testing methods are used. A cumulative mid-term examination and cumulative final examination, for example, could be offered in addition to smaller, unit-specific individual tests. The more cumulative the testing program, however, the greater the retention rates students show. Rohm, Sparzo, and Bennett (1986), for example, found that students who were tested weekly outscored students who were tested biweekly, but that students achieved the very best scores when all the tests were cumulative —when each test contained items dealing with the current material but also items testing the understanding of material from previous units.

Cumulative testing methods require, however, that more time be spent reviewing the results of tests with students. When students will be confronting the material again in the near future, they expect and deserve clear feedback about the items that they answered incorrectly. Because this review can be both time-consuming and contentious when conducted in an open-class discussion, many instructors prepare standardized feedback information that can be distributed to all students. This feedback identifies common problems as identified by the test results and alerts students to which learning objectives will likely be tested on future examinations. Such feedback procedures also reduce the need to return the actual examination items to students. Control of items is less of an issue for professors who use short-answer and essay tests, but instructors who reuse choice-type items each year may find that their items begin to lose validity if they return the tests to students to use in preparation for cumulative finals. These old tests often become part of the test files maintained by campus groups (e.g., fraternities), giving members of such groups an unfair advantage over students who do not have access to the old tests.

Some type of heavily weighted examination at the end of the course is usually needed, even if it is not cumulative. This final examination, in addition to being required at many universities, also prevents the motivational crash that can occur when students' work during the final weeks of class has little influence on their grades. If, for example, students' grades are based on a series of five equally weighted examinations, and the test given during finals week is just the fifth test, students whose prior four tests have virtually locked them into a particular grade will disappear during one-fifth of the class.

Dropping and Making Up Tests

Because of circumstances both within and beyond their control, students sometimes miss tests. Although some professors tell students that no make-up tests will be given, these same professors must then bend their policies for students who have excuses from their physicians, who are required to take part in institution-sponsored activities (i.e., sports), or who are experiencing life events that psychologists recognize as extremely distressing (e.g., death of a loved one). Rather than simply installing a rigid policy that punishes students who miss examinations, many professors establish student-centered make-up test policies that include (a) advance notification of the absence, (b) a time-limit for taking a make-up test, (c) the location and time of the testing, and (d) the type of test to be given (e.g., multiple-choice, essay, true–false). They also share their rationale for their policy with their students so that the system is viewed as a fair, nonarbitrary one (Whitley, Perkins, Balogh, Keith-Spiegel, & Wittig, 2000).

Some professors avoid the problems associated with make-up tests by letting students drop their lowest test grade when computing their final score in the class or by counting another test (or the final) twice. Such procedures, however, likely reduce the overall level of student learning. Grabe (1994), for example, compared the performance of students who could drop tests to students who could not. He found that scores on individual tests were lower, overall, when students' grades were based on a subset of their tests, although the impact on final examination scores was not significant. These findings nonetheless suggest that students may not prepare as diligently when they know that they can drop a test score. The findings also underscore the importance of having a cumulative final examination when using such methods. A "nondroppable" cumulative final prevents students who are satisfied with their grade based on the earlier tests from skipping class entirely during the final segment of the term because they will drop that test anyway.

Pop Quizzes

Few instructors would be shocked to learn that students sometimes come to class unprepared: They have not reviewed their previous session's notes, read the text material assigned for the day, or spent much time ruminating about the issues and concepts under consideration. One way to increase preparation is to put students on a variable-interval reinforcement schedule by giving them unannounced quizzes (Burchfield & Sappington, 2000). Thorne (2000) administered quizzes regularly, and found that they were useful for (a) giving students feedback about their studying (or lack of); (b) desensitizing them to the testing process; (c) sharing samples of the types of questions on the major course exams; (d) gathering feedback about areas where students are having problems; and (e) increasing their level of preparation for class. Ruscio (2001) reported increased preparation in classes when he quizzed students with questions that would be easily answered if they had read the assigned materials.

Nitko (2001), however, argued that random quizzing may increase the level of anxiety of the class and is in some respects inconsistent with one of the most revered principles of education: Diligent, deliberate studying is essential to learning. Nitko (2001) wrote:

> Some teachers advocate "surprise" or "pop" quizzes. Their reasoning is often some vague notion that a good student should always be prepared to perform on command. This seems to be an unrealistic expectation of students. Teachers, for example, make lesson plans and prepare to teach these lessons in advance. They are often resentful (and rightfully so) if asked to teach a class for which they have not had sufficient time to prepare. (p. 311)

Nitko (2001) also noted that such quizzes could harm the grades of students with special learning needs and concludes they should never be used to punish a class that is not obedient or falls behind in its reading.

Consider the Policies

A classroom, like any group, develops norms: consensual standards that describe what behaviors members should and should not perform. A classroom's norms, however, are often deliberately manipulated by professors who hope that they can create normative structures that are consistent with, or even supportive of, scholarship and learning. They do so by developing policies and letting students know the consequences of violating their policies.

Is Attendance Required?

College students are adult learners, so many instructors feel that students should be given the right to miss classes without being penalized. But students learn more when they attend class. Lindgren (1969), for example, reported that students who performed poorly were frequently absent from class, whereas most of the successful students rarely missed classes. These findings offer compelling support for an attendance policy that will prompt students to attend even when they would prefer not to. Students should also be urged to arrive on time and remain in class until its end unless the class is a very informally structured one (e.g., a recitation section, independent study).

A strict no-skip policy can, however, creates both organizational (roll must be taken, excuses for missed classes processed) and instructional (classes filled with unprepared, uninterested students) complexities. Sleigh and Ritzer (2001) therefore recommended reducing absenteeism by increasing student motivation rather penalizing students for non-attendance. Their recommendations, which included reducing the overlap between in-class lectures and the text, are considered in more detail in chapter 2.

What Is Your Academic Integrity Policy

Virtually all colleges and universities have an academic integrity policy that describes the kinds of activities that are considered inappropriate, immoral, or punishable (e.g., plagiarism, cheating, destruction of materials). In preparing for class, you should familiarize yourself with your university's code and let students know that you will enforce the code. Students must also, in some cases, be reminded about common courtesy and classroom civility. Although discourteous actions may not qualify as actionable under the code, some behaviors are considered to be so rude, distracting, or disturbing to others that they create tension in the classroom—and you may wish to ban them.

What Special Considerations Apply to This Class?

Students should be warned about any unique, unexpected, and potentially irritating aspects of the class. If, for example, you expect students to use e-mail to do some of their coursework, then they should be told of this requirement. Some psychology courses deal with very sensitive topics, including personal adjustment, sexuality, and abnormality, and students should be warned about subject matter that they might find personally upsetting.

Should Students With Special Needs Contact the Professor?

Section 504 of the Rehabilitation Act of 1973 and the Americans with Disabilities Act of 1990 require colleges and universities to provide academic adjustments or accommodations for students with documented disabilities. Students seeking academic adjustments or accommodations should be invited to identify themselves as soon as possible so that adjustments or accommodations can be arranged.

SHARING THE PLAN

Professors' plans for their classes are what Miller, Gallanter, and Pribram (1960) called *shared public plans*. Unlike private plans executed by single individuals, public plans usually call for the integration of multiple, interlocking plans. This integration requires communication among all those individuals who play roles in the execution of the shared plan. Most public plans are also more elaborate than private ones. A private plan can remain vague and protean, but public plans must be "prescribed in great detail because an attempt has been made to obtain optimal, not just satisfactory, performance" from each person who is part of the plan (Miller et al., 1960, p. 100). Professors can achieve this communication and specification of their shared plan in two ways: by writing a syllabus and by carefully presenting that syllabus, and the overall plan, to the class at its first meeting.

The Syllabus

A syllabus was originally a very concise list of the topics that would be covered by a lecturer during a protracted course of studies. In time, though, the syllabus has evolved to include all sorts of basic information about the course. Different schools and departments have varying standards about the course syllabus and its contents, but a syllabus is usually considered a contract that defines professors' and students' responsibilities. A syllabus forces professors to share their private plan: It "compels you to publicly reveal your previously well-concealed assumptions. In other words, it makes explicit that which was implicit" (Appleby, 1999, p. 20). Table 1.4 describes some of the categories of information included on a syllabus and summarizes the preceding analysis of course planning.

Professors may not include all of these categories on their syllabus, and students may not pay much attention to all of them, either. As Becker and Calhoon (1999) discovered when they surveyed students about syllabi, students pay the most attention to information about assessment, especially the dates of the exams and when assignments are due. They take less notice

TABLE 1.4
Types of Information Supplied to Students in a Typical Course Syllabus

Subject	Questions answered
Instructor	What is your name and what should students call you?
	Where is your office, and do you hold office hours?
	What is your educational, research, and teaching background?
Course description and goals	What are the overall goals for this course?
	How does this course contribute to general educational goals?
	What are the specific goals?
	What should students know when the course is over?
	How will this course change them?
Course topics	What topics will be covered in this course?
	Why these topics?
	Why this order?
	What are the prerequisites?
Teaching and learning methods	What methods (lecture, discussion, seminar, tutorial) will be used to teach this material?
	Will the course make any unusual demands on students (e.g., heavy writing requirements, use of technology, special projects)?
	Why are these methods being used?
Textbook and readings	What textbook will be used?
	Will other reading assignments be made?
	Why were these texts chosen?
	Are these primary or secondary sources?
Activities and assignments	What types of learning activities and assignments will be made?
	Will papers be required?
	What is their purpose and how will they influence grades?
Grades	How will student progress be measured?
	Is the grading criterion-reference or norm based?
	How much is each activity and test worth?
	Can tests be dropped?
	Is the final examination cumulative?
Policies	What is the attendance and test make-up policy?
	Do you have any other special policies or expectations about the class?
	Any extra credit?
Sources of support	Will you hold review sessions prior to examinations?
	Are the lecture notes or the outline available?
	Will students be given the opportunity to form study groups?
	Does this institution have academic support programs that students can use if they encounter academic problems?
Calendar	When are the assignments due and when should readings be completed?
	When are the tests?
	When will vacations occur?
	What is the timetable for covering the various topics?
Academic integrity policy	What type of academic integrity policy is in force at the university?
	How is this policy applied in this class?
Special issues	What special considerations apply to this class?
	Should students be warned about material and activities that they might find objectionable?
	Should students with special needs contact the professor?

of general course information, withdrawal dates, and the titles and authors of readings. First-year students were more interested in prerequisites than were continuing students, and they were also more concerned about sources of academic support and location of course materials. Nontraditional students attended to the syllabus' description of course goals and the readings, but they were not as concerned about holidays and penalties for late work and honors infractions. All students do expect, however, that professors will honor the syllabus as they would a contract. Hence it is important to include, somewhere on the syllabus, a statement that explains that aspects of the course may be changed if unforeseen circumstances arise, and that these changes will be announced before they are initiated.

The First Day of Class

Asch's (1946) classic studies revealed a primacy effect when perceivers form impressions of others: Initial judgments influence subsequent judgments even when subsequent information contradicts these initial inferences. Asch's findings remind the teaching psychologist to take full advantage of the ambiguity, excitement, and potential of the first meeting with a class (Babad, Kaplowitz, & Darley, 1999; Widmeyer & Loy, 1988). That day comes but once, and it is an opportunity to be seized, a chance to do far more than simply take roll and disseminate information about the text and test. Hilton (1999, p. 118), who has taught classes with as many as 1,200 students, wrote: "I firmly believe that I win my class or lose them in the first 15 minutes, and 50 years of person perception research supports that belief." The first day of a class is the ideal time to (a) give a clear introduction to your course that includes information about yourself, your goals, and the nature of evaluation; (b) set the norms and tone for the classroom; (c) motivate students by arousing their interest, involving them in the learning process, and displaying your enthusiasm for the course material; and (d) correct any misperceptions or inaccurate social norms that pertain to the class.

Identifying Course Goals

Students do not always know why they are taking your course. Perhaps it is required, the only one open, or a course they have always dreamed of taking. The first day of class is the time to let them know what is in store for them, so their expectations are in line with reality. Reviewing the goals as listed on the syllabus provides clear information about *your* goals, but it may not help them identify *their* goals. One way to stimulate this goal analysis is to carry out a simple ice-breaking exercise like the one described by Angelo and Cross (1993). Working alone or in groups, ask students to identify five critical goals they hope to accomplish in the class.

Pool their goals in through a class-wide discussion, and contrast their goals with the ones on the syllabus. Students, by the way, generally do not like to perform such icebreakers on the very first day of class. Instead, they prefer to get out of class early after the professors have reviewed the goals of the course and details about the exams, assignments, and grading methods (Perlman & McCann, 1999a). The first day of class, though, is a unique teaching opportunity that should not be squandered by concentrating exclusively on logistics and requirements.

Setting the Tone

Instructors vary in their approaches and methods, and courses vary in difficulty and demandingness. On the first day, students are busy searching for information that helps them understand where you stand with respect to their in-class behavior (taking notes, arriving on time, showing deference, participating in discussions) and out-of-class behavior (homework, amount of time to spend studying). They also want to know what you are like as a person. You can help them get a clearer understanding of you and the class by adopting the behavioral style that you will take for the entire term. If you hope to start class on time, start the first day on time. If you will keep the class to the very end of the hour, do the same on the first day. You should also begin to build a relationship with your students by disclosing personal information about yourself, gathering some information about them, and responding to their questions.

Motivating the Students

Students are not always excited about plunging into a new area of study, so a little motivational packaging on the first day never hurts. Although many professors simply review the syllabus, explain how grades will be determined, or install their policies about absences and make-up tests, others take the opportunity to highlight the stimulating intellectual tasks to be accomplished, pique students' curiosity, challenge traditional views, and hint at inconsistencies to be resolved. Instead of spending the entire session dealing with procedures and logistics, they instead consider such basic questions as "Why take this course?" "What will people learn by the end of the course?" and "How does this course relate to fundamentally important personal and scientific goals?"

Correcting Misunderstandings

Students often enter psychology courses with a set of expectations about the course and its content, and in many cases these expectations are inconsistent with reality (Friedrich, 1996, 1998). They may assume that the introductory course will concentrate, almost entirely, on psychological dysfunction. They may think that psychology courses will demand little of their time, for psychology is not as difficult as such "real" sciences as physics or chemistry. They may assume that their instructor, as a psychologist, is a compassionate individual who is willing to listen to their personal problems and give them therapeutic advice. The first day of class is an excellent time to prepare them for the realities of the class: the topics to be covered, the procedures to be used, and the amount of time they can expect to spend each week in and outside of class.

One myth that is common on many campuses—psychology courses are easy—should be debunked but not so sharply that students' rosy expectations are transformed into dire prophecies. Positive expectations, even if somewhat unrealistic, facilitate performance. Students who "think they can," in comparison to students who "think they can't," work harder on class assignments, take a more active role in their learning by asking questions, learn more material, and come to think of themselves as high achievers (Harris & Rosenthal, 1986). However, students also need information about the types of behaviors they will need to engage in to achieve desired outcomes and the amount of time they must spend on the class. The old standard, "Look to your left, look to your right: By the end of the term these people will have dropped out of this class with failing grades," is likely too strong—it will create negative expectations that might interfere with performance. But some type of base-rate information such as a chart of the distribution of grades from prior sections of the course should be sufficient to help students calibrate the class's demands (Forsyth & McMillan, 1991).

A FINAL SUGGESTION: USE BEST STRATEGIES

Where do plans come from? Miller et al. (1960) pondered this question before concluding, "probably the major source of new Plans is old Plans. We change them around a little bit each time we use them, but they are basically the same old Plans with minor variations. Sometimes we may borrow a new Plan from someone else. But we do not often create a completely new plan" (p. 177). So this year's syllabus looks very similar to last year's syllabus. New professors base their teaching on the way they were taught. Professors use familiar assessment methods, give lectures from ancient yellowed notes, and forget to try anything new. The old plan becomes the template for all future plans.

Miller et al.'s (1960) warning about the power of old plans to shape new plans suggests that professors, before they rush to write the syllabus, sequence the topics, and craft compelling lectures, should take a little time to consider the general strategies that will guide their teaching. Rather than rely on the values provided by the default program, they should review those strategies and consider replacing them with alternative, innovative, and possibly more effective ones.

What alternative strategies should they consider? Although no one has succeeded in forging the definitive guide to teaching, Chickering and Gamson's (1987) *Seven Principles for Good Practice in Undergraduate Education* is a reasonable place to begin the search for alternatives. Chickering and Gamson, working with a select group of experts in higher education, developed a set of principles that they believe defines "effective practice" in college teaching. They considered developing an exhaustive, comprehensive listing of factors identified in prior research, but in the end they heeded the wisdom of Miller's (1956) magical number 7 ± 2 and opted for a shorter, more memorable list. Their final product, the *Seven Principles*, does not focus on content, for it assumes that good professors know which theories to teach, which skills to nurture, and which findings to push into students' memories. Instead, the *Seven Principles* focuses on the *way* in which the content, skills, and knowledge of the course are taught to students. As shown in Table 1.5, students will be able to reach their learning goals more efficiently and completely if professors create learning environments that are "active, cooperative, and demanding" (Gamson, 1991, p. 5).

Student–Faculty Contact

The *Seven Principles* argues that "frequent student–faculty contact in and out of classes is the most important factor in student motivation and involvement" (p. 4). When in the classroom, professors who use good practices build rapport with their students by learning their names, answering their questions, coming to class early to chat with them, and remaining after class to listen to their ideas and comments. When outside of the classroom, effective professors are willing to talk to students whenever they encounter them, on the sidewalk, by the faculty mailboxes, walking to the commuter parking lot, or even in the checkout line at the local grocery. This student–faculty contact may center on psychology, but it should also include discussion of students' career interests, values, aspirations, and personal interests. Indeed, Pascarella (1980) found that discussion of art, music, politics, literature, and film has a more profound impact on students than discussion of topics within the professors' realm of psychological expertise.

Cooperation Among Students

The *Seven Principles* suggests that professors, when planning their courses' learning activities and grading procedures, should include elements that require students to work in collaborative, positive ways. Professors

TABLE 1.5

A Summary of the Seven Principles of Good Practice Developed by Chickering and Gamson, 1987

Principle	Behavioral indices
Good practice encourages student–faculty contact: Frequent contact in and out of classes	Remembering students' names Involving students in lab and field research projects Taking students to conventions, regional conferences Disclosing personal values, when appropriate Attending student-sponsored events Mentoring and informal advising
Good practice encourages cooperation among students: Collaborative, noncompetitive learning in small groups and student-to-student networks	Encouraging self-disclosure to one another Facilitating the formation of study groups Assigning group projects Using peer evaluation techniques when grading Teaching through group discussion Promoting student-to-student tutoring/teaching Grading by criteria and not by interstudent comparison
Good practice encourages active learning: Teaching methods that require more than passive listening and note taking from students	Requiring class presentations Assigning papers and projects that promote critical thinking Asking students to integrate contemporary events with course material, discussing real-life cases, etc. Assigning term projects and independent studies Involving students in research
Good practice gives prompt feedback: Assessment of baseline knowledge, frequent testing of progress in learning, and global assessment of educational outcomes	Giving quizzes and homework assignments Returning examinations and papers within a week Providing feedback to students early in the term Writing comments on exams and papers Pretesting students Calling or e-mailing students who miss classes
Good practice emphasizes time on task: Setting appropriate time demands and helping students learn to manage their time	Establishing deadlines for completing assignments Discussing course demands with students Helping students set challenging goals Encouraging practice runs before oral reports Stressing self-regulation, studying, and attendance Meeting with students who fall behind
Good practice communicates high expectations: Setting reasonable but high standards for achievement	Warning students about time commitment to the course Stressing high standards of achievement Establishing performance expectations orally and in writing Helping students set challenging goals Explaining penalties for missed or late work Assigning writing Calling attention in class to excellence by class members

Table continues

TABLE 1.5 (*Continued*)

Principle	Behavioral indices
Good practice respects diverse talents and ways of learning: Providing a variety of learning experiences and assessment options	Encouraging questions Discouraging off-task, divisive comments Using a variety of teaching methods Discussing the contributions of women and minority psychologists Developing and using alternative teaching methods Exploring students' backgrounds, learning styles, and outlooks

should not abdicate all instruction to the students, but the more they share the work of teaching with their students the better. Psychology students, in particular, are often thirsting for opportunities to expand their interpersonal skills and so welcome cooperative elements such as peer teaching, small-group activities, student mentoring and counseling, and joint projects. The drawbacks associated with collaborative learning methods, which are discussed in more detail in chapter 3, can be avoided by allowing students flexibility in their choice of work partners and establishing standards that regulate each student's contributions.

Active Learning

The *Seven Principles* questions the heavy reliance on lectures as the default method of instruction in many college courses, favoring instead the use of methods that require an observable response from the learner. Even professors who do not agree with Chickering and Gamson's (1987, p. 5) sweeping salvo at lectures ("students do not learn much just sitting in classes listening to teachers, memorizing pre-packaged assignments, and spitting out answers") still build nonlecture learning activities into their courses: activities and assignments that require students to respond cognitively, behaviorally, and even emotionally to the material. Such activities include independent study projects, writing assignments, speeches, involvement in research, preparation of papers and posters for conferences, analysis of data, simulations, demonstrations, case discussions, debates, and so on.

Prompt Feedback

Even though college students have years of experience in learning settings, many of them are still unable to calibrate their own learning; they do not always know when they have learned material and when they have not. Students also are not sufficiently skilled in regulating their time and motivation, so they need external goals to punctuate and validate their work: tests, exams, and other forms of feedback. As Sorcinelli (1991, p. 19) concluded, "immediate, corrective, and supportive feedback is central to learning." The *Seven Principles* pushes this point even further by recommending pretests prior to beginning of a course of study and occasional global reviews of goals and progress toward those goals.

Time on Task

Studies of the relationship between time spent in teaching, learning, and studying generally support the *Seven Principle's* position on the mindful management of time in and out of the classroom (e.g., Cotton & Wikelund, 1989; McKeachie, Pintrich, Lin, & Smith, 1986). As professors' set about planning their course, they must carefully sequence the topics and activities, allocating time to each goal depending on its complexity, the depth of coverage, and the topic's importance. The *Seven Principles* also suggests that professors let students know how much time the typical student will need to allocate to the class and its activities, and even provide help to students who are woefully inadequate when managing their time.

High Expectations

Research on students' perceptions of their instructors, which chapter 8 reviews in some detail, has suggested that professors who set challenging goals in their courses do not necessarily create headaches for themselves and indignation among their students (e.g., Cashin, 1988). Instructors who set high standards for students are rated more positively than easy graders, so long as they grade fairly and provide students with the resources they need to reach their preferred outcomes. High expectations, even if unrealistically positive, can also set in motion social and psychological processes that will increase the quality of professors' teaching and students' learning (Rosenthal & Jacobson, 1968; Wright, 2000).

Respect Diversity

Teaching psychologists, as psychologists, are enjoined by the APA code of ethics to recognize and respect differences in their students. They should be aware of, and adapt their teaching practices as needed to take into account "cultural, individual, and role differences, including those due to age, gender, race, ethnicity, national origin, religion, sexual orientation, disability, language, and socioeconomic status" (APA, 1992, p. 1599). They should, then, consider their audience when they plan their teaching, and when possible include topics, materials, and activities that mesh with their students' backgrounds, interests, and goals (Puente et al., 1993). The *Seven Principles* suggests that skilled professors, when faced with great diversity in the students they teach, cope by using a wide array of teaching methods.

2

LECTURING: DEVELOPING AND DELIVERING EFFECTIVE CLASSROOM PRESENTATIONS

Should one start with his strongest arguments or save them until the end? Which types of content are most effective when stated explicitly and which types are best left implicit? Answering questions of this sort at present is much more of an art than a science.

—Carl I. Hovland, Irving L. Janis, and Harold H. Kelley
Communication and Persuasion (1953, p. 99)

Teaching psychologists often specialize by becoming particularly adept at one form of instruction, but nearly all must lecture. The effectiveness of a lecture, like any type of influential communication, depends ultimately on the professor, the content of the lecture, and the characteristics of the students: or who says what to whom. Lecturers who combine intellectual excitement and interpersonal rapport are more influential than their less charismatic colleagues, but they will fail to teach well if they have little of meaning to convey to their students. Effective lecture classes must involve the students, for when students withdraw emotionally and cognitively from the classroom, the exchange of information slows.

* * *

He paced about the front of the room, shifting his gaze from one student to another as he explained that today's lesson would reveal one of psychology's great truths: that behaviors followed by reinforcers increase in frequency of occurrence. We listened properly and took a few notes as he systematically ticked off B. F. Skinner's basic assumptions about behavior, but before our minds could wander he launched into one of his stories. This one was set in his high school, which was ruled by an autocratic principal who handed out punishments for the slightest indiscretion. One

49

day a package arrived at the school, and the staff paid the exorbitant collect-on-delivery shipping charges before realizing what the box contained: a 50-pound rock. Furious, the principal called an assembly of the entire school, wheeled the rock in on a dolly, and demanded that the student who had managed the prank confess. No one stepped forward to take the blame, but over the next few days the post office delivered boxes containing rock after rock. The principal had reinforced the wrong behavior. Instead of punishing the student who sent the rock, he unintentionally rewarded him or her and provided other potential miscreants with a model to imitate. The lecturer's story made all these contingencies clear to us, and we left class that day capable of explaining the law of effect and applying it in a real-life example.

Professors are often experts at certain techniques of instruction. Some are masters at leading discussions. Others prefer to stimulate with Socratic questioning and answering. Still others excel in a one-on-one mentoring setting. Nearly all, however, must be able to lecture. Before books had been either written or read, lecturing was the primary means by which the teacher's special knowledge of the field could be passed along to students, and despite advances in the technology of teaching, lecturing remains a staple of college instruction. One expects college professors to *profess*: to state aloud their beliefs and understanding of topics on which they are academic authorities. Indeed, in many colleges our positions are lectureships; when we make presentations in colleagues' classes we are guest lecturers; and when our good teaching is recognized, we are given awards with such names as *outstanding lecturer* or *lecturer of the year* rather than *outstanding professor*.

Yet, academics often debate the worth of the lecture as teaching tool. Critics complain that the lecturer, in taking the stage and holding forth on pet theories, actually teaches very little. With statistics like "people remember only 10% of what they hear in a lecture" and "17% of all information transmitted orally is forgotten in an average of 2.5 days," the antilecturites assault the usefulness of this old-fashioned method of teaching. Chickering and Gamson (1987, p. 5), for example, argued that students do not learn much "just sitting in classes listening to teachers, memorizing pre-packaged assignments, and spitting out answers." But prolecturites answer that lectures provide the scholar with the means of not just disseminating information but also transforming that information into a coherent, memorable package. Scholars, when they reveal their unique interpretation of questions they have spent years researching and contemplating, are an unmatched source of information and interpretation. Not to mention that nearly all teachers can develop a rudimentary lecture that they can use in a wide variety of classes—from the smallest to the largest.

Both sides in this debate have merit, for the question "Is lecturing an effective way to teach?" cannot be answered with a simple "yes" or "no." Lecturing is a complex communication process, involving a series of reciprocal exchanges of semantic and nonverbal messages between the lecturer and the listeners, and the outcome of that exchange is shaped by the interaction of a host of personal and situational factors. Lecturers who read their dull talks in a monotone to a bored audience are not communicating or teaching. But, as Penner (1984, p. 79) puts it, why abandon "the lecture method, just because there are many poor lecturers, who, in actuality, are not really lecturers at all but are unskilled blunderers in a perfectly legitimate educational activity?" The well-prepared lecture, delivered to an attentive class by a dynamic speaker, is a superb means of creating a shared understanding of a topic.

Rather than ask, "*Is* lecturing an effective way to teach?", this chapter asks, "*When* is lecturing an effective way to teach?" This question is similar, in many ways, to the one that guided the work of Hovland, Janis, and Kelley (1953) and their colleagues in the Yale Communication Group during the 1940s and 1950s. They were puzzled by the dramatically differing impacts of communications on audiences. In some cases, a message would have profound effects, prompting long-lasting change in the people who heard the message. But in many more instances, the message was quickly forgotten and resulted in no change in attitudes or behaviors. To explain these differences, the Yale researchers assumed—quite reasonably—that the impact of a communication depends on the source of the message, the nature of the message, and the person who listens to the message (Hovland et al., 1953). Applied to teaching, their model suggests that the impact of the lecture on learning depends on the professor, the professor's lecture, and the students: who says what to whom.

THE LECTURER

Hovland, Janis, and Kelley (1953) discovered that all communicators are not created equal: Even when two speakers give identical messages to listeners, one speaker may be far more influential than the others. As they explained, the "effectiveness of a communication is commonly assumed to depend to a considerable extent upon who delivers it" (p. 19).

Lecture Style

The role of lecturer defines the behaviors that professors should and should not perform as they teach their classes. This role, like most such roles, is created both by the expectations of the professor and by the expectations of the students rather than any objectively defined set of standards. Certainly the role has standard features, no matter who is lecturing:

The professor, usually positioned in a cleared space facing a seating area, communicates verbally and nonverbally to students. But how each teaching psychologist enacts that role varies. Like actors who bring unique interpretations to even the most stock characters, all professors create a unique lecturing persona that they carry with them from class to class. Dr. Showman may enter the teaching stage from a rear door at the moment class begins, orate without interruption for the entire session, and then depart through the same door. Dr. Feely arrives at class well before the session begins, talks informally to the class as he slowly makes his way to the front of the room where he starts class a few minutes late each day. Dr. Avee lectures with a full array of PowerPoint slides, video clips, and computer-generated graphics while wearing a cordless microphone and driving home each point on the bulleted list with a laser pointer. Dr. Quanda lectures in 10-minute units, but punctuates each segment by asking her students thought-provoking questions and guiding the class's discussions. Dr. Reeder distributes an extensive outline of the lecture to students before each class and spends most of the class hour reading from notes or the textbook. These professors are all lecturers, but each adopts a unique style that reflects his or her general demeanor, personality, and assumptions about how a professor is supposed to act.

Although the variety of professorial lecturing styles is undoubtedly vast, Brown, Bakhtar, and Youngman (1984) identified five general types when they asked 258 lecturers such questions as "Do you write out your entire lecture when preparing?" "Do you use humorous asides in your lectures?" "Do you use a blackboard or overhead project during lecture to list important points?" and "Do you like to lecture?"

- *Ramblers* (amorphous lecturers) did not structure their lectures in terms of objectives, organization, or summaries. They generally did not have clear objectives when they began their lecture, and so did not have any materials prepared to support the delivery of their ideas. They did not review prior lectures, provide an outline of the day's lecture, or summarize the content that they presented. Brown et al. (1984) used the word *amorphous* to describe this lecture style because it seems shapeless and unformed.
- *Self-doubters* did not reach the organizational and educational benchmarks set by the orators and lecturers, but they did present material adequately and efficiently. Self-doubters, however, confessed to considerable uncertainty about the contents of the lecture. They felt in many cases that they had structured the material inadequately and did not feel that they had achieved their teaching goals when the class was over.

- *Newscasters* (information providers) delivered well-organized lectures and, like the lecturers, used the blackboard or overhead project to present graphics, objectives, and other material. Newscasters, though, tended to write out their lectures in great or even complete detail. In class they tended to read their lectures, and so they rarely asked students questions, used humor, or digressed from the material. They generally delivered too much content.
- *Orators* (oral lecturers) delivered solidly structured lectures. They often began the lecture by reviewing the prior lecture's major points, and then described the objectives of the current lecture. In some cases orators provided students with a list of the major headings in advance of the lecture, but they relied almost exclusively on the spoken word to make their point. In consequence they used the blackboard or projector primarily to display diagrams, charts, or figures. They did not write out their lectures in full before class, but they were nonetheless confident in their lecturing prowess.
- *Lecturers* (exemplary lecturers), like orators, confidently presented well-structured material without reading from or relying on detailed notes. But lecturers augmented their oral presentation by using visual aids, stressing the relationship between ideas, and summarizing the major points at the class's end. They also reported using a wide range of pedagogical devices, such as humorous asides, repetition and restatement, involving the audience, questioning, and quoting from texts. The lecturers reported that they liked lecturing and were strongly interested in their material.

Brown and his colleagues, after reviewing differences in lecturing style by discipline and level of expertise, cautiously concluded that these teaching styles reflect dispositional tendencies rather than an unfolding developmental progression from less-effective styles (e.g., ramblers) to more-effective styles (e.g., orators and lecturers). They did discover that full professors were more likely to be classified in the "lecturer" category than were less senior professors. But when they classified the lecturers according to their level of experience (1–3, 4–7, 8–10, and more than 10 years), they found few differences in terms of teaching style. The novice professor was as likely to be an excellent lecturer, a self-doubter, or a rambler, as was the seasoned veteran.

Lowman's Two-Factor Model

As Hovland, Janis, and Kelley (1953) explored the impact of communicators on listeners, they soon discovered that how a message is stated can be as influential as what a message says. In many cases people respond to messages in an utterly rational way. When they are exposed to new information, they review the new data, consider its strengths and weaknesses, reexamine their own stock of information pertaining to the topic, and then adjust their position if the new information warrants such change. At other times, people's responses are shaped more by their relationship to the speaker than by their analysis of the speaker's message. An effective communicator, "if he is a striking personality and an effective speaker who holds the attention of an audience . . . can increase the likelihood of attentive consideration of a new opinion." But a good communicator can also influence others; if "he is personally admired or a member of a high status group, his words may raise the incentive value of the advocated opinion by suggesting that approval, from himself or from the group, will follow its adoption" (Hovland et al., 1953, p. 20).

Hovland et al.'s recognition of the importance of the style and the substance of the lecture is consistent with Lowman's (1984, 1995) analysis of master teachers. Lowman examined students' perceptions of teachers, observed expert teachers at colleges and universities, and systematically analyzed the content of letters written by students when they nominated their professors for teaching awards before concluding that these diverse sources all underscored two critical themes: intellectual excitement and interpersonal rapport. Masterful lecturers do not plod slowly through dull material, ignore students' questions, then leave the classroom through a back door behind the dais. Rather, they spend the lecture hour fervently articulating their understanding of the subject's key issues and concepts, while demonstrating that they care about their students' satisfactions and successes.

Intellectual Excitement

Lowman (1995), when comparing the professor who creates intellectual excitement to one who does not, pinpoints two key differences: clarity of presentation and degree of emotional stimulation. Exciting lecturers are clear lecturers: They do not just understand their material but also know how to convey that understanding to others by defining, illustrating, clarifying, comparing, and contrasting. Students describe such lecturers with adjectives like *clear, knowledgeable, organized*, and *prepared*. Master lecturers also seem to be excited about what they are doing: Students used the word *enthusiastic* frequently to describe such lecturers, followed by *inspiring, humorous, interesting*, and *exciting*. Less effective lecturers, in contrast, strayed too frequently from the path of clarity, leaving students confused and uncertain about what point was being made. Such professors also seem uninterested in the material themselves, and so their students also show signs of boredom and withdrawal. Lowman (1995, p. 25) summed up these professors' style in two words: *vague* and *dull*.

Interpersonal Rapport

But what is the difference between professors who establish rapport with students and those who do not? Lowman suggested that professors who create a bond between themselves and their students do so by stimulating positive emotions and *not* stimulating negative emotions. They are warm and open in their dealings with students, show a high level of sensitivity to students' concerns and issues, and provide students with encouragement and praise for their accomplishments. Their students describe them with such adjectives as *concerned, caring, available, friendly, helpful,* and *encouraging.* They also avoid doing things that will engender ill will. They rarely say negative things about their students' capabilities and interests, lose their tempers or display other signs of defensiveness, or act in dismissive ways when students ask questions.

Lowman conceded that his findings pertaining to interpersonal rapport clash with the ideal of the formal, impersonal, and "irascible 'Herr Professor' of the nineteenth-century German lecture hall" (1995, p. 28). But his analyses should not take psychologists by surprise. The teacher–student relationship, like the therapist–client relationship or leader–follower relationship, joins people in a complex web of relationships, roles, and networks. And just as these relationships influence the success of therapeutic treatment or a team's cohesion, so they influence the success of professors' teaching and students' learning. Although therapists' primary goal is to help their clients change their cognitions, emotions, and behaviors, most pursue this goal by establishing a therapeutic alliance with their clients: "Clinicians of all persuasions adhere to the common sense belief that the quality of the client–therapist relationship is an essential, if not sufficient, ingredient in effective treatment" (Higgenbotham, West, & Forsyth, 1988, p. 75). Similarly, leaders who prefer to focus on the task at hand and the procedures to be followed by the group members must also be aware of the socioemotional side of the group. Leadership involves not only directing others' actions but also boosting morale, increasing cohesiveness, reducing interpersonal conflict, establishing rapport, and illustrating concern and consideration for group members (Forsyth, 1999). Professors must stake their claim to the leadership role in the lecture hall by blending task expertise with socioemotional expertise.

Style + Substance = Effective Lecturing

Table 2.1 summarizes Lowman's (1995) overall recommendations for combining elements of intellectual excitement and good rapport when teaching. This two-dimensional taxonomy assumes that the finest professors are successful both intellectually and emotionally, but that intellectual excitement is a more important ingredient than rapport. In other words, a

TABLE 2.1
Lowman's (1995) Two-Dimensional Model of Effective College Teaching

Dimension I: Intellectual excitement	Dimension II: Interpersonal rapport		
	Low: cold, distant, highly controlling, unpredictable	**Moderate:** relatively warm, approachable, and democratic; predictable	**High:** warm, open, predictable, and highly student-centered
High: extremely clear and exciting	**Cell 6: Intellectual authorities** Outstanding for some students and classes but not for others	**Cell 8: Exemplary lecturers** Especially skilled in large introductory classes	**Cell 9: Complete exemplars** Excellent for any student and situation
Moderate: reasonably clear and interesting	**Cell 3: Adequates** Minimally adequate for many students in lecture classes	**Cell 5: Competents** Effective for most students and classes	**Cell 7: Exemplary facilitators** Especially skilled in smaller, more advanced classes
Low: vague and dull	**Cell 1: Inadequates** Unable to present material or motivate students well	**Cell 2: Marginals** Unable to present material well but liked by some students	**Cell 4: Socratics** Outstanding for some students and situations but not for most

Note. From *Mastering the Techniques of Teaching* (p. 34), by Joseph Lowman, 1995, San Francisco: Jossey-Bass. Copyright ©1995 by Jossey-Bass Inc. Reprinted with permission of Jossey-Bass, Inc., a subsidiary of John Wiley & Sons, Inc.

professor who has little rapport with students but is very exciting intellectually will likely be successful in the classroom, but a professor who is all
rapport and no content is likely to be effective in only a limited range of
situations. Lowman's model also describes professorial styles that are more
effective in lecturing and ones that are better suited to more student-
centered forms of instruction, such as discussions or seminars. In particular,
he feels that professors who are high in intellectual excitement and at least
moderately capable of establishing rapport will be the most successful in
the large lecture setting, whereas professors who are very good at establishing rapport but only moderately strong on intellectual excitement will
shine in smaller, nonlecture classes. Lowman's model of effective teaching
offers clear advice to lecturers who want to evolve into more effective
lecturers.

Be Clear

Clarity requires an organized, well-constructed message but also an
articulate, communicative messenger. Tongue-tied, note-reading ramblers
and self-doubters are likely to leave a worse impression than silver-tongued
orators and lecturers who weave together their ideas in a texture of terms,
examples, and implications.

Clarity in public speaking takes practice. Just as plumbers become
more skilled with each toilet installed and chess players become more wily
with each game played, each time the professor delivers the lecture it becomes clearer. This clarification occurs, in part, because lecturers use their
own personal standards and cues from the class to ferret out places where
fuzziness still intrudes. Even if they discount their own internal monitor's
warning ("You don't really seem 100% sure of what you are talking about
at the moment"), the puzzled looks of students will motivate lecturers to
rework that portion of the day's lecture. But practice also increases clarity
by reducing the cognitive load demanded by the lecture. Once portions of
the lecture become more automatic, the lecturer can use these freed-up
cognitive resources to monitor and adjust the current performance (Ericsson & Lehmann, 1996).

Practice also lessens the anxiety most people feel when they must
speak before an audience. Standing before others in the lecture hall can
be an unnerving experience, and those prelecture butterflies often interfere
with clarity. Lecturers' nervousness leaks out in their stammers, long pauses,
annoying filler sounds such as "ah," a loss of tempo, and repetitions. In
such situations even skilled lecturers can lose their natural ease of self-
expression as they become preoccupied with distracting thoughts about
their lack of ability or skill. Their natural expressiveness may also become
labored when they monitor their presentation too closely and forget to
regulate their breathing properly. As Leary and Kowalski (1995) noted,

nervous speakers' voices often quiver, and their mouths become so dry they have difficulty speaking clearly. Practice, however, replaces nervousness with calm, as the once-novel experience of lecturing before an attentive audience becomes a mundane one.

Penner (1984) warned against trying to boost clarity by developing extraordinarily detailed notes and then following those notes too closely. Indeed, Penner suspected that lecturers who read their notes may do so because they are worried that their weak grasp of the material will be obvious if they digress, but ironically their reliance on notes betrays the very weakness they hope to conceal. "The lecturer gives the unmistakable impression to his students that he really does not know himself exactly what he is talking about, because he reads his lecture notes slavishly, instead of fluently presenting material from the vast store of knowledge in the subject area, so that the listening students will recognize his competence and respect him for his expertise" (p. 78). The solution is not to write out the lecture but to develop a habitual way of speaking clearly and articulately.

Be Knowledgeable

Hovland, Janis, and Kelley (1953) noted that lecturers, unlike persuaders, do not usually need to worry that their audience does not believe what they are saying, for "typically the classroom audience has initial expectations that the communicator's conclusions will be the 'correct answers'" (p. 290). But when the class feels that the issues being discussed are matters of opinion or, even worse, they doubt their instructors' depth of preparation, then they are less likely to attend to and accept the information the lecturer is dispensing. Hendrix (1998) described the special credibility problems faced by faculty who are members of minority groups or who are teaching about racism, ethnicity, or sexism yet are not themselves members of the group they are examining. An Anglo American teaching about racism, for example, may be regarded as liberal but somewhat uninformed, particularly by African American students. As one wrote, "They can only get so close. . . . I'd want a minority perspective" (p. 46).

What factors influence perceptions of expertise? Social psychological analyses of source credibility have suggested that students likely notice three types of cues when estimating their professor's expertise (Corrigan, Dell, Lewis, & Schmidt, 1980). First, evidential cues include primarily nonverbal stimuli such as physical appearance, style of dress, office location, and age. As most young professors have always suspected, students likely associate age with wisdom and would thus be more likely to conclude that the older professor is more the expert than the newly minted PhD. Female professors, too, may find that their students do not grant them the same level of respect that they give to male professors, for the students unfairly assume a connection between sex and expertness (Martin, 1984). Second, reputational cues pertain to the professor's level of experience and expertise and can include degrees, titles, and other professional credentials. In many cases, professors carefully post their diplomas and certificates so that their students know that they have been properly trained, and graduate student instructors face an uphill battle convincing their classes that, despite their lack of credentials, they are nonetheless qualified to teach the course. Last, behavioral cues include the nonverbal and verbal actions that students associate with effective and ineffective interventions. Large, sweeping gestures, a relaxed but poised posture, an attentive expression, and a direct gaze are all actions that lay a claim to status. People who speak clearly and loudly are also viewed as higher in expertise than are those who speak softly and pepper their comments with nervous giggles.

Be Enthusiastic

Williams and Ware conducted a series of telling studies of classroom influence in the late 1970s. They arranged for an actor named Fox to deliver a pair of lectures using one of two presentational styles. In the high-expressive condition, "Dr. Fox" spoke with much enthusiasm, charisma, warmth, and humor. In the low-expressive condition, Dr. Fox presented the scripted lecture adequately, but he did not put any emotion into its delivery. The lectures themselves were also manipulated to create three levels of content: high, moderate, and low. Williams and Ware's examination of students' ratings of the lectures and their performance on tests of the content covered in the lectures confirmed what is now known as the Dr. Fox effect: Not only did students consider the expressive lecturer to be more interesting, but they also got higher scores. Significantly, students rated the lectures with more content more positively so long as Dr. Fox did not deliver the material with great enthusiasm; when he was enthusiastic, students felt the low-content lectures were just as good as the high-content lectures (Ware & Williams, 1977; Williams & Ware, 1976).

Subsequent studies of the Dr. Fox effect have suggested that students, over a series of lectures, come to distinguish between the professor who is all style and no substance (Williams & Ware, 1977). However, research still indicates that students learn more from professors who can capture their attention by delivering material in an interesting way (Marsh & Ware, 1982). Most professors are truly excited about the topics that they are presenting to their students, yet their manner sometimes reveals little of this passion. This understated presentational style undermines impact, however, for as Lowman (1995) explained, "The ability to stimulate strong positive emotions in students separates the competent from the outstanding college teacher" (p. 23). This impact need not be manufactured through dramatic lecturing methods, such as role playing Freud or telling detailed stories about clients—although such techniques do probably leave students thinking that the professor is "into teaching." Even the introverted can create the impression of enthusiasm by:

- *Stimulating emotions:* Lowman (1995) noted that the outstanding lecturers in his studies "use their voices, gestures, and movements to elicit and maintain attention and to stimulate students' emotions. Like other performers, college teachers must above all else convey a strong sense of presence, of highly focused energy" (p. 23). A good lecture is not just informational, but inspirational. As Axtell (1998) so eloquently explained, "Many students will soon forget the details and even general themes of their college courses, but few will forget the passion with which their professors approached the subject day after day or the inspiration they gave them to think the subject important and worth pursuing, at least for a semester" (p. 60).

- *Improving vocals:* A lecture is a spoken presentation to the class, and so its impact depends in part on the quality of the voice that delivers it. A variety of factors influence the quality of one's speaking voice—pitch, speech rate, loudness, vocal clarity, tone, and so on—but if any of these qualities is held constant, the result is monotony. When Murray and Lawrence (1980) taught faculty how to vary their vocals, pauses, and nonverbal behaviors, these faculty's teaching ratings rose in comparison to faculty in a control group.

- *Improving nonverbals:* Skilled lecturers are usually in motion, and these body movements send implicit messages about emotion, interest, and excitement. By adopting an open posture—knees and feet spaced apart, arms extended out, hands open, and body leaning forward toward the audience—one appears friendly, warm, and outgoing. Closed, symmetrical postures seem unfriendly, cold, and nervous (Mehrabian, 1972). The way the lecturer walks across the stage, too, can reveal information. In one study, people who adopted a youthful gait that included sway in the hips, knee bending, arm swinging, loose-jointedness, a bouncy rhythm, and a rapid pace were judged to be happier and more powerful than sedate or stiff walkers. A masculine gait characterized by a long stride and forward body lean was also viewed as a sign of power (Montepare & Zebrowitz-McArthur, 1988). Certain hand gestures also communicate enthusiasm, and their use may also improve verbal performance by enhancing the retrieval and processing of verbal information (Krauss, Morrel-Samuels, & Colasante, 1991).

- *Declaring interest in the material:* Because enthusiasm, like perceived expertise and clarity, depends more on the subjective judgment of the perceiver than on the objective behavioral data the target provides, lecturers are well advised to control their students' perceptual conclusions by monitoring self-disclosures. When one apologizes for having to "cover this boring material," one is letting students know that their attention will soon be wandering.

- *Preparing for class:* Professors who are enthusiastic about their work usually prepare to teach it. Students take inadequate preparation as a sign of disinterest in the course.

These prescriptive recommendations can be summed up in a single proscription: Do not be boring. Boredom, as a psychological process, occurs when individuals have difficulty focusing their attention on the content of the lecture. This difficulty can usually be traced to disinterest in the content itself, as when students drift off during the slide show "Structures of the Eye," and protracted analyses of the causes of the fundamental attribution error. Boredom also occurs when a lecturer's "long-winded, rambling, and tedious exposition of an otherwise interesting subject" weakens even the best-intentioned students' control over their focus of attention (Leary, Rogers, Canfield, & Coe, 1986, p. 969).

Leary and his colleagues (1986) identified the key components of boredom listed in Table 2.2 by asking students to describe the things boring people do. Bores, these researchers discovered, would make bad lecturers, for they are passive, tedious, easily sidetracked, but oddly ingratiating. They show little enthusiasm, seem unnecessarily serious, are caught up in their own trivial concerns and they, themselves, seem to be bored. These investigators discovered that once a person is labeled a bore, his or her social value plummets; as boringness increases, one's apparent intelligence, competence, popularity, security, friendliness, and reliability decrease. Boring individuals "are at a distinct disadvantage in social life and may experience dysfunctional consequences" (Leary et al., 1986, p. 975).

Build Rapport

The lecturer is free to use techniques and tools that vary in terms of interpersonal involvement. Some lecturers rely primarily on more impersonal methods and maintain a teacher–student relationship that is similar to that of author and reader or newscaster and audience. They can, for example, remain apart from the class, lecturing in a detached, information-dissemination style, and keep all their in-class discussions focused on the course material. But such an approach fails to take advantage of the unique

TABLE 2.2
The Components of a Boring Lecture Style as Suggested by Leary
et al.'s (1986) Studies of Boredom

Dimension	Forms and behavioral indicators
Passivity	Adds nothing new to the course; doesn't express opinions; unresponsive to classroom circumstances; format of class and lecture is predictable, routine; reacts minimally to student questions
Tediousness	Low rate of activity; lectures at a sluggish pace; rambles; goes into too much detail; pauses a long time before responding to questions
Distraction	Easily sidetracked into talking about topics that are irrelevant and not interesting; excited by trivial details; uses inappropriate body language; uses a great deal of slang
Low affectivity	Lacks enthusiasm; speaks in a monotone voice; makes little eye contact; shows little emotion; few facial expressions
Boring ingratiation	Awkwardly tries to impress others; tries too hard to be funny, nice, friendly
Seriousness	Doesn't smile or laugh; flat affect; rarely uses humor in lecture; pompous
Negative egocentrism	Complains about class, students, text, classroom, university; acts bored, disinterested; not interested in what others say
Self-preoccupation	Talks about self too much; often reveals personal problems, difficulties; includes questions on test about self
Banality	Interested in only one topic; talks about trivial, superficial things; repeats dull stories and jokes; avoids all controversial topics

interpersonal dynamics of the face-to-face lecture situation. When Samuel Johnson proclaimed "now when we all read, and books are so numerous, lectures are unnecessary," he was overlooking the human connection between lecturer and listener (as cited in Zakrajsek, 1999, p. 81).

Just as there are many ways to engage students in the course material, so there are many ways to strengthen the bonds between the lecturer and the class. Most, though, are consistent with Dale Carnegie's (1937) recommendations on how to "win friends and influence people." Carnegie always maintained that the best way to create positive relationships with others is to become sincerely interested in them. Rather than ignoring the social needs of their students, interpersonally skilled lecturers use a variety of relatively simple methods to establish rapport, including:

- *Learn students' names, even in classes of 100:* Carbone (1998) suggested having students state their name each time they ask a question in class to help professors remember their names, but she also describes more elaborate methods. Some professors videotape their students announcing their names in the first week of class, others download rosters with photographs from university data bases, and some take Polaroid snapshots of each student so that they can learn their names. Carbone also recommended practicing the correct pronunciation of names that are unusual.

- *Decrease social distance:* Gleason (1986) suggested that lecturers think of their large halls as they would small, intimate classrooms, and act accordingly. Come early to class, linger after class answering questions, and move about the room when lecturing if possible. Carbone (1998) described professors who eat regularly at the student cafeteria and those who hold office hours at the student center. Even if students never take advantage of these opportunities to interact with their professor, they will likely feel that the lecturer is more accessible to them.

- *Decrease physical distance:* Rietz and Manning (1994) urged lecturers to get as close as they can to their students, even if it means leaving the rostrum and lecturing from the seating area. They flatly stated "never use a stationary or goosenecked microphone attached to a lectern. An immobile mike traps you in place: you cannot move or even turn and still be heard. Furthermore, the lectern becomes a barrier between you and the audience" (p. 247). They recommended a cordless microphone that will allow lecturers to move freely about the room, allowing them to approach closer to students who ask questions or who need to be reminded—by mere physical presence—to pay attention.

- *Lecture with less formality:* Another way of reducing the psychological gap between lecturer and lecturee is to use a less formal style of presentation. As Zimbardo (1997, pp. 10–11) noted, lecturers who move "vigorously about the teaching stage, hands flying, arms waving, gesturing broadly in best Italian fashion, talking fast, sometimes furiously, sometimes not completing sentences except with a finger flourish marking end points" flatten the status hierarchy of the classroom. They move themselves closer to their students, all the while increasing their students' interest in what is being said.

- *Smile (and make eye contact):* Carnegie (1937) felt that people who smile are not only communicating happiness but also signaling their acceptance of other people. Eye contact, too, is a critical indicator of involvement. People generally assume that downcast eyes signal embarrassment, shame, and disinterest, but when lecturers make eye contact with the class, they imply involvement, intimacy, attraction, and respect (Buskist & Saville, 2001). People also consider eye contact or the gaze as evidence of certain personality traits. People who gazed at others only 15% of the time were judged to be cold, pessimistic, cautious, defensive, immature, evasive, submissive, and indifferent. Those who maintained eye contact 80% of the time were seen as friendly, self-confident, natural, mature, and sincere (Exline & Messick, 1967).

- *Self-disclose, appropriately:* Hilton (1999) and others recommended using personal examples and anecdotes during the lecture when appropriate to the topic under discussion. Such materials, Hilton felt, "avoid the chasm of impersonal indifference" and remind students that their professor is a human being who experiences the field at a personal level. Hilton, of course, urged professors to monitor their level of self-disclosure, for there is "a fine line between personalizing your lectures and wallowing in narcissism" (p. 118).

- *Listen to students:* Only in the most formal of presentations do listeners hold their questions until the end of the presentations. In most cases, lecturers urge students to ask questions during the lecture, and they take the time to answer these questions respectfully. Many lecturers, too, punctuate their lecture with carefully developed questions that require a response from students. Another way to gather feedback from students is to take a quick opinion poll about some issue relevant to the lecture topic.

- *Take an interest in students:* Reciprocity is one of the most powerful determinants of attraction; people tend to like those who like them. Professors who show concern for their students, seem to like their students, and act as though they want their students to succeed are rated more positively by their students, and these more positive ratings are also highly correlated with students' self-reported motivational levels and grade expectations (Wilson & Taylor, 2001). H. W. Marsh (1982) found that students consider professors who seem genuinely interested in their students and seem friendly when dealing with specific students to be better teachers.

Do Not Be Negative

Much of the good work done to build a relationship with students can be undone by an ill-chosen word or regrettable lapse of affect management (Buskist & Saville, 2001). As Ludewig (1994) discovered when he asked students and faculty to point out each other's irritating behaviors, students can provoke a professor's ire in many ways: They carry on personal conversations during lecture, cheat on exams, skip class, fall asleep in class, routinely come to class late, do not keep up with the readings, miss exams and expect to be given a make-up, do not bring materials needed for class, skip too many classes, and miss entire lectures and then ask for the notes or a recap. Professors can irritate students by assigning what students consider to be an unfair amount of work, lecturing too quickly, making students feel inferior when they ask questions, delivering lectures in a boring way, getting behind schedule and then cramming in material just before the exam, and requiring a textbook and then never using it. When these irritations mount, the professor and the students may display any of a host of negative reactions documented by Mann and his colleagues (1970), including scorn, sarcasm, mistrust, belittling, and suspicion. For example:

- One professor began his first class of the semester with a smile and an open, down-to-earth self-description, but when he described his goals for the class all he said was, "I want everyone to learn to spell the word *psychology*" (p. 226).
- During a lecture on learning theory, the professor asked the class questions every few minutes as he moved from point to point, but the students consistently gave incorrect answers. His lecture began to slow, and his enthusiasm dipped and reached a low point when no one responded to his question about a study of problem solving involving chimps. Finally he said, "Come on, people. The monkeys were able to solve it" (p. 55).
- After a student offered an opinion during a pause in the lecture, the professor seemed critical of the comment. The student, responding defensively, reminded the professor that he had said that all opinions were welcome. The professor replied, "What is the purpose of my giving you information if you don't use it? If I wanted your opinions, I would say, OK class, now we're going to do nothing for the next six weeks but sit around and listen to your opinions" (p. 60).
- The professor asked for comments and questions on a guest lecture. A student remarked that the lecture seemed "poorly organized, irrelevant, and lacking continuity." The professor replied that he was looking for more substantive comments and that the student "probably misunderstood the lecture anyway" (p. 81).

As noted in more detail in chapter 6, the professors in these examples could have managed these irritating circumstances more constructively than they did.

THE LECTURE

Even lecturers with all the right stuff—credibility, expertise, warmth, and sensitivity—fail as teachers if they organize and present their lectures ineffectively. Anyone who has ever suffered through a disorganized lecture, listened to a colloquium that made no sense, or read an article that harped on trivial issues that were largely irrelevant to the central topic can understand the importance of developing a powerful message. And what makes a message powerful? According to Hovland et al.'s (1953) analysis of the *what* component of their "who says what to whom?" model of communication, an effective lecture must first capture the student's attention, for despite the claims for subliminal learning, communications that are ignored generate little in the way of learning. Second, the lecture must be understandable; the students must comprehend what the lecturer is saying. Third, the lecturer should strive to make the message so compelling that listeners will accept it. Fourth, the points in the lecture must be memorable so that they will be remembered long after the lecture ends. The sections that follow consider some of the ways that the teaching professor can create lectures that meet the Hovland et al. (1953) call for attention-getting, understandable, convincing, and memorable lectures.

Becoming Familiar With the Topic

College professors are not just educators but also scholars with a well-defined command of a particular subject matter. In consequence, their lectures should offer students their unique interpretation of their field's concepts and discoveries rather than the verbalized restatement of someone else's ideas and insights. The first lecture one gives on a topic may not completely satisfy the scholar's demand for originality, but with repetition and revision the pedestrian lecture should grow into the profound oration.

Writing a lecture requires the exercise of the basic skills one uses to write a thesis, journal article, or book. Most experts on authoring scientific papers recommend reviewing general background material on the topic before submerging oneself in more detailed, original source material (Rosnow & Rosnow, 1995; Scott, Koch, Scott, & Garrison, 1999). One obvious starting point is the textbook; one must read it, anyway, so it can also be used as the initial source of information on each topic that the course covers. Next, compare your text's treatment of each topic to similar treatments offered by other texts in the same field. Textbook writers have spent considerable time studying the material that you must teach, so their insights are invaluable; as Sternberg (1997b, pp. ix–x) noted, "they *have* to have given the course much thought." Assemble three or four good texts that range in difficulty and viewpoint, and use these texts to sharpen your understanding of theoretical concepts, identify points that your adopted text does not cover, and harvest their examples to put to your own use. Because textbooks must omit many details, side issues, and empirical exceptions in their quest to communicate major points unambiguously, advanced scholars must supplement such sources by reviewing original sources. Although one may need to review the original journal article to obtain the data points needed to make a chart or table, in many cases summary articles and chapters that appear in such publications as *Psychological Bulletin*, *Annual Review of Psychology*, and the *American Psychologist* provide enough detail for most lecturers' purposes. These sources not only offer up-to-date and comprehensive overviews of topics, but they also offer this information to the reader in an organized, understandable framework. Topical articles in the *American Psychologist* are particularly useful because they are written by experts but are aimed at psychologists in general. These articles are also, in many cases, based on actual lectures, and so they already have the form needed for an oral presentation. The letters published in the *American Psychologist* are also a rich source of hotly debated issues that can be used to generate discussion in even the most verbally circumspect classes.

Two other sources of information should also be exploited, when possible: materials provided by the textbook's publisher and files accessible through the Internet. Particularly in courses that have a large market, the publishers have devoted considerable resources to the development of teaching supplements: newsletter-like reviews of key concepts, biographical information about prominent psychologists, detailed lecture outlines, glossaries of key terms, and suggestions for issues to use in discussion groups. The Internet, although still evolving as an archival tool, offers rapid access to text and graphic information about a number of key topics in psychology. Full-text versions of many journals are now available online, so the scholar who needs to review the exact findings obtained in a particular study can extract that information from his or her desktop computer rather than go to the library.

Connecting the Lecture to the Text

Penner (1984), a passionate advocate of the lecture method, is almost vitriolic in his condemnation of the lecturer who reads the textbook to the class: "Any unqualified person can stand before a class and merely *flip pages* in the textbook! The combination of reading the text or stale notes, and poorly at that, in a monotonous manner, devoid of a sense of humor —that is really depicting a dullard" (p. 78). If students can take notes in class just by following along and highlighting passages from their textbook, then the lecture adds little of value to the learning process.

Gray (1997) offered a strong argument for carefully integrating the textbook with the contents of the lecture. He noted that many instructors seem to be laboring under two false assumptions. First, they assume that they cannot test students' understanding of material covered in lectures if that material is not also examined in the text. Second, they also assume that if material is covered in the text, but not discussed in a lecture, then students cannot be tested on that material either. Both assumptions, however, are false—or at least they can be defined as false by a clearly written syllabus. Gray (1997) wrote:

> Students can read a textbook with understanding if it is well-written; they can also listen in class and take notes if the lecture is clear; and they do both of these if they know that the test includes ideas and evidence from both sources. My own formula, stated on the course syllabus, is that 70% of the points on each test are based on the textbook and 30% are based on lectures. (p. 55)

Gray assumed that even for the introductory course in psychology, students can read and understand the material presented in the textbook.

Structuring the Lecture

The content of the lecture should be established during those long hours of preparation with source materials. But once one reaches a comfortable level of understanding, then the lecture itself must be built and decisions made about what topics are so important or complicated that they must be covered, the desired level of complexity and depth of the presentation, the amount of information that can be adequately presented given the time available, and—perhaps most important—the overall organization for the lecture.

Organizing the Topic

Most theories of memory and cognition suggest that people, as active processors of information, select and organize information into categories based on natural and perceived similarities, discontinuities, and clusters. Rosch (1973, 1975), for example, maintained that categories are created when a number of objects are considered equivalent on one or more dimensions that exist in multitiered, hierarchical taxonomies. A structured lecture that mimics this naturally occurring cognitive process by presenting information in a hierarchically tiered framework should, in theory, increase encoding and storage efficiency and retrieval success (Day, 1980).

Bligh (1998) described hierarchical and flat organizations for lectures. Hierarchical structures organize the material into a series of nested clusters, with relatively specific concepts, examples, and applications organized into superordinate categories that connect the subordinate elements conceptually. Such lectures can typically be summarized in an outline form or as a graphic. A hierarchical lecture on Freud's basic ideas, for example, could

EXHIBIT 2.1
An Outline of a Hierarchical Lecture on
Freud's Contributions to Psychology

I. Fundamental assumptions
  A. What motivates people?
  B. What is the unconscious?
  C. What causes anxiety?
II. Structure of personality
  A. Id
  B. Ego
  C. Superego
III. Stages of psychosexual development
  A. Oral
  B. Anal
  C. Phallic
  D. Latency
  E. Genital
IV. Defense mechanisms
  A. Repression
  B. Regression
  C. And so on
V. Treatment
  A. Psychoanalysis
  B. Free association
  C. Transference

be divided into interdependent superordinate and subordinate categories as shown by Exhibit 2.1.

Not all lectures are hierarchically organized, however. Bligh (1998) noted that in some cases, material can be presented in a flat, linear pattern rather than a tiered one. Bligh terms this type of organization *chaining* and recommends it when material is ordered in a temporal or cause-effect-cause-effect sequence. The Freud lecture, for example, could be presented by tracing the development of each of the key concepts from his first insights into the nature of anxiety to his eventual conclusions about personality structure and defense mechanisms.

Providing the Organization to Listeners

Given that the lecture has an organization, should this organization be shared with students, either in advance of the lecture or during the lecture? And how detailed should the outline of the lecture's structure be? Should only superordinate categories be listed, or should the outline be highly detailed? Arguments can be made both for and against revealing the lecture's organization to the students. On the one hand, most theories of cognition and memory argue that listeners' memories will be enhanced (i.e., they will show increased rapidity and detail at encoding, greater storage capacity, more complete and accurate retrieval) if they can organize the data into meaningful chunks. Moreover, if the students must actively detect the lecture's organization and then use it to build their own schematic cognitive structures, then their memories of the organization and the material it organizes will likely be more durable and detailed.

On the other hand, studies of students taking notes suggest that their cognitive load is already so heavy when they are listening to a lecture that they cannot divert sufficient cognitive resources to creating a suitable structure for the incoming information. One rule of thumb is to provide more detail to students who are not yet well-practiced note takers. In large, introductory sections, students often do not have the note-taking skills and acumen needed to both listen to the lecturer's points *and* create an organizational structure for the notes. In a graduate course, in contrast, students should be able to follow the lecturers' path through the material without an outline as a guide.

No matter what the level of detail in the lecture outline provided to listeners, lecturers should nonetheless use organizational signals in their presentations to let listeners know where they are in the lecture's sequence of topics. They can do this by using the verbal cues summarized in Table 2.3 to help listeners recognize key points, restatements, definitions, examples, comparisons, lists, asides, summaries, and so on. They can also signal movement through the elements of the lecture nonverbally, by counting on their fingers, referring to their notes when they want to summarize, and by raising their eyes to the classroom when opening the floor to questions (English, 1985).

Capturing Attention

When William James (1892) discussed the nature of attention more than a century ago, he distinguished between passive and active attentional processes. Passive attention (or stimulus-driven, bottom-up attention) is dictated by the stimulus itself—students pay attention because the material itself is so arresting that it captures and holds attention. Active attention (or goal-directed, top-down attention), in contrast, depends on those aspects of the perceivers (e.g., expectations, goals, conceptual structures) that determine what is noticed and what is overlooked (Egeth & Yantis, 1997). The following suggestions, although a varied assortment, exploit James' (1892) two methods for capturing attention: create attention-grabbing stimuli and instigate cognitive mechanisms in the listeners that will increase their attention to what is being said.

Telling Stories and Anecdotes

Some lecturers teach critical concepts by embedding them in stories and anecdotes. Some stories may be personal ones: tales of one's own ex-

TABLE 2.3

Cues Used by Lecturers to Reveal the Organizational Elements of
Their Lectures

Organizational indicator	Example
Introductions, overviews, and orientations to the topic	Today we will be discussing Freud's psychodynamic theory by focusing on four basic elements of that perspective: his assumptions, his beliefs about personality's structure, his notions about how people protect themselves from anxiety, and the implications of this perspective for treatment.
Shifters from lecture to question/answer and discussion	Are there any questions about these three assumptions? . . . Let's discuss this for a moment. Specifically, what do you think of Freud's idea that women, because of their weaker superegos, are less moral than men?
Enumerators	Freud identified five stages of psychosexual development, if one counts the latency stage as a true stage. First. . . . Second. . . .
Definition indicators	What did Freud mean by the word *repression*? Freud defined repression as motivated forgetting; the motivated caching of unpleasant or anxiety-producing information in the unconscious rather than conscious mind.
Example and elaboration identifiers	What are some examples of repression? One of Freud's patients, Little Hans, was very fearful of his father, but he was not aware of these feelings . . .
Repetition designators	This point is so critical that I need to say it again. Freud's belief that conflicts in the unconscious mind could be so anxiety-provoking that . . .
Comparison and contrast identifiers	So what is the difference, then, between Freud's conceptualization of dream imagery and Jung's interpretation of dreams? Freud, in calling dreams the "royal road to the unconscious . . ."
Elaboration markers	Let's look more closely at one of Freud's most controversial ideas: his belief that boys' development depends on their ability to resolve the Oedipal conflict.
Sidetrack or aside identifiers	Even though it's only peripherally related to the point I was trying to make, it's nonetheless interesting to consider the Freudian undercurrents in most modern advertising. Take for example . . . Anyway, to get back to our analysis of Freud's ideas about defense mechanisms . . .
Transitioners	We have seen that Freud believed that anxiety is, in many cases, caused by deep-seated conflicts that the ego cannot keep in check, even through the use of defense mechanisms. Given this assumption, what then would be the best way to treat people who are suffering from such problems?

Table continues

TABLE 2.3 (*Continued*)

Organizational indicator	Example
Highlighters	Sometimes people overlook the importance of this point, but it is a crucial one to grasp fully if one is to understand Freud's perspective. . . . What is the point in studying such an old theory that many people feel is sexist and historically limited? Well, Freud's thoughts pertaining to the unconscious mind are one of the cornerstones of modern psychology.
Summary and topic completion markers	So, Freud's remarkable view of the human being is based on three key assumptions. As we have seen, Freud believed that psychological energy, our motivation, results from basic biological motives. Also, we are, in large part, unaware of these motivations because they are locked in the unconscious mind. Last, anxiety arises from the dynamic interplay of these psychic energies.

periences that illustrate some psychological process, such as toilet training a first-born child, a case of one-trial learning that created a long-lasting conditioned response, dealing with a loved one's psychological troubles, and the like. Stories can also be drawn from the experiences of psychologists: John B. Watson's withdrawal from academia, Olds' (1958) serendipitous discovery of the brain structures responsible for pleasure, Skinner's bowling pigeons, Friedman and Rosenman's (1974) initial insights about Type A behavior patterns, and Allport's (1968) meeting with Freud convey content and increase students' interest in the material.

Stories probably do much more than just increase interest and endear the lecturer to the listener. Interesting stories, instead of presenting information in a pallid, dull format, create an emotional reaction in the listener. Stories are more exciting, in many cases, than bulleted lists and charts. But stories also work to create a deeper level of processing. In many cases, when students think about the class, it's the stories they remember, not the definitions and the findings in critical studies (Kaufman & Bristol, 2001; Kintsch & Bates, 1977). Storytelling is an old and effective means of relaying information from one person to the next, and shared stories often form the basis for collective memory and beliefs (Bar-Tal, 2000). These narratives, even though they were experienced by others, nonetheless have many of the memorial features of detailed episodic memories rather than semantic, paradigmatic memories (Bruner, 1996).

Asking Questions

A question will bring students back to the point at hand faster than any joke, aside, or anecdote. When lecturers question, they take advantage of the association between questions and embarrassment—an association likely created during the early school years by teachers who, when they see Johnny or Susie daydreaming, punish them by asking them a question. Now even a simple question, like "What was Freud's term for the part of the mind that people cannot directly access?" can be enough to make students perk up, or at least avert their eyes momentarily in the universally understood nonverbal message, "I don't know the answer. Don't ask me." But questions are also useful for stimulating a thoughtful analysis of information. Indeed, a lecture's outline can be viewed as a series of answers to unasked, but implicitly assumed, questions. For the Freud lecture, for example: What was Freud thinking when he came up with this theory? What were the basic parts of personality that Freud identified? How do people protect themselves from anxieties? How can we put Freud's ideas to use when helping people deal with psychological problems?

Questioning students, particularly in large classes, requires advance planning and the use of appropriate mechanics. Although a question that pops up on the spur of the moment might be an excellent one to use in class, lecturers should also develop possible questions to ask as they are writing the lecture itself. Some of these questions can be answered by the entire class, by vote: for example, "How many of you feel that Freud's theory is unfairly biased against women?" or "How many of you have ever dreamed that you were locked out of your house and no one would answer the door?" Others may be primarily fact-based, such as "What did Freud think was one of the primary motivators of human behavior?" and "What word did Freud use to describe the psychological defense mechanism that keeps memories out of the conscious mind?" Time allowing, questions that call for more detailed discussion, such as "How would Freud explain Leonardo da Vinci's preoccupation with painting women's portraits?" or "If you were a parent of a young boy, how would you help him negotiate his way through the Oedipal conflict?" should also be considered. Lecturers should also use good mechanics when asking questions.

- Signal the question clearly, perhaps by repeating it or presenting it on the board or overhead.
- Give students time to think about the question; tolerate a period of silence in the room.
- If the room is a large one, repeat each student's answer to make sure all students hear the reply and to indicate the importance of listening to the answer.
- Reward students' answers to questions.
- Use care when asking specific students to answer the question, as students sometimes feel intimidated by faculty who "call on" students (B. G. Davis, 1993).
- Distribute the questions that will be considered during class to students in advance of the session.

- Praise students when they ask and answer questions.
- Correct students when their answers are inaccurate, but use tact to diffuse the students' embarrassment.
- Use rhetorical questions sparingly, if at all. Research suggests that such questions tend to distract students rather than stimulate them (Howard, 1990; Petty, Cacioppo, & Heesacker, 1981).

Quoting Original Sources

An English professor discussing some author's work invariably examines the author's words themselves, reading them aloud or displaying them verbatim on the overhead projector. Although psychology is a science rather than a fine art, studying the words that theorists and researchers themselves used lets another voice be heard in the classroom. When considering behaviorism, provoke students' interest with John B. Watson's (1924) famous claim:

> Give me a dozen healthy infants, well-formed, and my own specified world to bring them up in, and I'll guarantee to take any one at random and train him to become any type of specialist I might select—a doctor, lawyer, artist, merchant-chief, and, yes, even into a beggar-man and thief, regardless of his talents, penchants, tendencies, abilities, vocations and race of his ancestors. (p. 10)

Mix in Freud's views on clinical insight when discussing his conception of psychotherapy:

> He that has eyes to see and ears to hear may convince himself that no mortal can keep a secret. If the lips are silent, he chatters with his finger tips; betrayal oozes out of him at every pore. And thus the task of making conscious the most hidden recesses of the mind is one which is quite possible to accomplish. (1953/1905, pp. 77–78)

When struggling to clarify the uniqueness of William James' theory of emotion, give several examples of the emotion sequence before presenting James' own example of fear at the sight of a bear:

> My theory . . . is that *the bodily changes follow directly the perception of the exciting fact, and that our feeling of the same changes as they occur is the emotion.* Common sense says, we lose our fortune, are sorry and weep; we meet a bear, are frightened and run; we are insulted by a rival, are angry and strike. The hypothesis here to be defended says that this order of sequence is incorrect . . . and that the more rational statement is that we feel sorry because we cry, angry because we strike, afraid because we tremble. (1892, pp. 375–376)

When describing the power of the Stanley Milgram (1963) studies of obedience, include a brief description of how people reacted to the experimenter's demands:

> Many subjects showed signs of nervousness in the experimental situation, and especially upon administering the more powerful shocks. In a large number of cases the degree of tension reached extremes that are rarely seen in sociopsychological laboratory studies. Subjects were observed to sweat, tremble, stutter, bite their lips, groan, and dig their fingernails into their flesh. (p. 375)

These quotations are particularly arresting when they are taped in advance by a colleague with an expressive voice who reads the material with enthusiasm or projected on the overhead or large screen.

Using Humor

Evidence has indicated that exposure to humorous material promotes health—but it promotes attention as well. Most humor falls into one of four overlapping categories: stories about psychologists, descriptions of research studies humorously related, jokes concerning psychological topics, and puns/cartoons. Any of these forms may simply break up the monotony of the lecture, but in many cases they relate content. Perhaps the most frequently reprinted cartoon used in psychology is one picturing two rats in the Skinner box; one remarks to the other, "I really have these guys conditioned—every time I press this bar, they give me food." Here, the behavioral psychologist is portrayed as having been gotten the better of by his or her rats. Other jokes, puns, and cartoons reveal psychologists' biases, assumptions, and values. Light bulb jokes, for example, indirectly describe the paradigmatic nuances of each sub-area of psychology (e.g., "How many clinical psychologists does it take to change a light bulb? Only one, but the bulb has to want to change," and "How many counseling psychologists does it take? Four: one to change the bulb, and three to share the experience").

Work by Babad, Darley, and Kaplowitz (1999) has suggested that students value humor in their lecturers the most during the early stages of their academic career. When Babad et al. correlated students' rating of their instructors at Princeton and the descriptions of these instructors in the student-generated university "Student Course Guide," they discovered that the instructors' humor—not their expertise, expressiveness, or approachability—was the only significant predictor of students' ratings of course and lecture quality in general survey courses. In more advanced courses, however, humor became less important and was replaced by greater emphasis on the quality of course content and the absence of criticism. By the time students reached their senior level courses, their evaluations were correlated with only judged quality of readings, course interest level, and instructor's knowledge and expertise.

Offering Asides and Personal Views

An aside occurs when the lecturer strays from the day's outline and presents information—personal views, a self-disclosure, a forewarning of a future topic—that is only tangentially related to the topic at hand. Asides, like humor, provide the listener with a short recess and so reduce the cognitive burden of an information-rich lecture. Asides, however, should be used sparingly, or the flow of the lecture may be sidetracked, and students may have difficulty concentrating on the main content when the lecturer returns to on-task material. Movement in and out of an aside should also be explicitly acknowledged to help students return to a note-taking mode, although the phrase "This won't be on the test, but it's interesting to consider" should probably be avoided because it invites students to woolgather.

Using Multimedia Material

When the angry adolescent says "Don't lecture to me," or the disgruntled employees mutter to one another "Here comes another lecture" just before the boss sits them down for a performance review, they are equating lectures with the delivery of words. But most lecturers combine their words with tables, charts, graphs, images, art, video, and audio materials. The lecture on Freud often includes a picture of Freud, probably smoking a cigar; a baffling graphic representation of the mind-as-iceberg with portions labeled *id, ego,* and *superego*; charts of the defense mechanisms and stages of psychosexual development; a video clip from a Hollywood movie that features an actor who, as a psychoanalyst, is offering a penetrating Freudian analysis of a patient's problems; photographs of art from various cultures that feature phallic symbols or other totemic images; and a graph showing the levels of anger displayed by individuals who either did or did not have the opportunity to vent hostility through a cathartic emotional experience (e.g., Hokanson & Burgess, 1962). Images, graphs, sounds, and other media capture attention precisely because they are not words, and so are salient stimuli that stand out as figures in the ground of the auditory verbal information. Although these materials may seem like gratuitous distractions, they are actually attention gatherers. As Lutsky (1999) noted, distracted students often regain control over their wandering attention each time a new overhead or slide goes up—and once their attention is recaptured, the lecturer can return to verbal material. Verbal presentations that include visual material also initiate dual processing, and as a result students are more likely to remember and understand explanations that intermingle the verbal with the visual (Mayer, 1997; Mayer & Anderson, 1991; Mayer & Gallini, 1990).

Sequencing

Professors, when writing a lecture, must sometimes choose when to present the most challenging material. Should they begin with conceptually difficult information as soon as possible during the lecture (primacy), or should the initial minutes of lecture be used to set the stage for the intellectually challenging concepts revealed in the lecture's final minutes (recency)? This question has no obvious answer, for even though Hovland et al. (1953) spent considerable time trying to understand when primacy versus recency effects occur in persuasion contexts, they eventually concluded "whether primacy or recency effects (or neither) occur depends upon the conditions of the communication situation" (p. 287). When listeners are unfamiliar with key issues in the communication and they grasp their significance only late in the presentation, then recency becomes more likely. Recency also trumps primacy when the lecture builds to a climax, or when listeners' energy rebounds after a mid-lecture sag as they anticipate the end of the session. The occurrence of primacy or recency effects ultimately depends, however, on attentional variables. If attention is high, then the material will be better remembered no matter where it appears during the lecture.

Demonstrations and Activities

Many skilled lecturers will build a demonstration, activity, or other type of student-centered exercise into their presentation. These activities, which are discussed in more detail in chapter 3, provide a break from the predictable lecture-type class, and they also draw students back into the lecture. Rather than simply describing Freud's states of psychosexual development, the lecturer can ask the class to play Carlson's (2000) board game, Psychosexual Pursuit, in which students move through each stage of development through the use of defense mechanisms and the expenditure of libidinal energy. Miserandino (2000) asked students to estimate the impact of Freud's theory on their own thinking by indicating degree of agreement with such statements as "Little boys should not become too attached to their mothers" and "It is possible to deliberately 'forget' something too painful to remember" (p. 22). These activities take up class time that could otherwise be spent lecturing, but "as a means of holding students' attention, motivating them to read and ask questions, and making teaching more enjoyable, demonstrations are hard to beat" (Bernstein, 1999, p. 108).

Mix Lecture and Discussion

Gray (1997) recommended mixing lecture phases with discussion phases in what he calls his idea-based lectures. Consider, as an example, the typical Sigmund Freud lecture. This lecture is an easy one for both the teacher and the students, and after 50 minutes filled with terms and sexually tantalizing examples, "everyone feels that education has occurred: Information has been transferred" (p. 51). But Gray suggested replacing this approach with an idea-based lecture that focuses on one key element of Freud's approach rather than the specific terms and structures (which are described clearly by the textbook, in any case). The steps include:

- Begin the presentation by writing the key idea on the board (e.g., "The human mind actively defends itself against certain kinds of knowledge as a means of reducing anxiety").
- Lecture, briefly, on the idea, putting it into historical context and illustrating its various psychological and practical implications.
- Invite students to express their opinions on the issue either by calling on particular students or by polling the entire class.
- Record students' comments, if appropriate, on a transparency or the blackboard.
- Through lecture, review evidence and examples that support or disconfirm the idea; this critical portion of the lecture involves identifying the key points to be made in advance and preparing suitable materials.
- End the presentation by asking students to vote again on the issue or complete a brief reaction paper.

Enhancing Memorability

Listening to a lecture on a new topic, and taking notes that summarize key points, is no easy feat. Given what we know about memory and the limited cognitive resources available for processing information online, it is little wonder that students don't remember you mentioning that test next week.

Repetition

Advertisers believe that any good ad is worth repeating—and repeating and repeating. As Cacioppo and Petty (1979) discovered in their studies of attitude change, when information is repeated several times, listeners think more about the message and generate more pro-message thoughts each time they hear the message. But they also discovered that too much repetition generated more anti-message and irrelevant thoughts, so excessive repetition will interfere with learning (Bromage & Mayer, 1986).

Pace

Even though the expression "fast talker" is a pejorative one, calling up the image of a slick salesperson who talks a lot without saying anything of substance, listeners think that rapid-fire delivery is a sign of intelligence and expertise. A rapid delivery, however, interferes with students' ability to process the information at a deep level and causes encoding and retrieval problems because new information interferes with older information. As Bligh (1998, p. 39) concluded, "Interference is probably the chief cause of forgetting in lectures, particularly when the lecture is too fast."

Pauses and Silences

Most lecturers, like radio disk jockeys, scrupulously minimize "dead air," prolonged periods when no sound is issuing from the students or the lecturer. But when professors pause every 10 to 15 minutes when lecturing, students' scores on subsequent examinations improve—sometimes by as much as a letter grade (Ruhl, Hughes, & Schloss, 1987). Such silences are the adult learner's version of recess. They enhance learning by giving students the opportunity to review their notes for completeness, relax and let their minds wander, or identify questions about the material just covered. These periods should not be used by students for conversation or cell phone calls, so the instructor should explain the purpose of the periods of silence and explicitly signal their beginning and end.

Giving Examples

Skilled teachers recognize the value of a good example. Learners, and novice learners in particular, rely heavily on examples to build their understanding of concepts. Experts can often make sense of new information by relating it back to their existing stock of knowledge, but novices need concrete, specific illustrations of the concept. When learning about conditioning, for example, students will be baffled by lecturers who immediately present the definitions of an unconditioned stimulus, conditioned stimulus, unconditioned response, and conditioned response. Instead, students need to work out multiple examples of conditioning by identifying each component, just as they might learn an algebraic operation by working a series of practice problems (Reimann & Schult, 1996).

A good example enhances encoding, elaboration, and depth of information processing, but what makes an example good? First, good examples are clear rather than fuzzy—they fit the concept under review neatly, with no distracting ambiguities. Second, a good example should be memorable; the vivid, intriguing example will be remembered long after the pallid, mundane one. Pavlov's dogs and the rat in an operant chamber are examples of conditioning, but so are more creative, unusual examples: the conditioning of Alex in *A Clockwork Orange*, the cat and the can opener, soft drink advertisements, particular songs and emotions, and so on. Third, a good example creates associations between students' existing knowledge and the new construct by relating the abstract concept to topics that personally interest the students.

These aspects of strong examples signal the ways examples can mislead learners. Examples should be clear-cut, but in many cases the example is so complex or so forced that students must strain to make the connection between the specific instance and the general construct. When lecturing on a particularly complex concept (e.g., Kelley's 1967 cube model of attribution, Sternberg's 1985 triarchic theory of intelligence, mediator vs. moderator relationships, or Kohut's 1984 self-theory), be careful to assemble workable examples well in advance. Ad lib examples suggested by circumstances or students may fit the concept well or only roughly. A vivid example can also be so distracting that students don't tie it back to the concept, and some examples are so involving for students that they lose their objectivity. Personally relevant examples can also estrange students in the class who are not interested in the example's focus. Sports examples, as Galliano (1999) noted, can irritate the nonathletic, just as bawdy examples can offend those with heightened sensibilities. Because of these problems with examples, once you find one that works, save it and use it again and again.

Summaries

One of the most frequently recommended methods of lecturing involves three steps: (1) preview the information ("This is what I am going to say"), (2) present the material ("This is it"), and (3) summarize the material ("This is what I said"). This approach helps listeners follow the course of the lecture and provides them an opportunity to double-check their own interpretation of the material against the lecturer's recapitulation. As Lowman (1995) noted, however, excessive summarizing can dull the lecture's message. Indeed, when students know that the final few minutes of class will be spent in a review and recapitulation of material that they think they understood clearly the first time, they often use that time to zip and unzip their book bags and backpacks, collect their coats and belongings, and bid the students seated around them adieu. Davis (1993) therefore recommended a strong ending that will punctuate, rather than reiterate, the lecture's key themes:

> End with a thought-provoking question or problem; a quotation that sets an essential theme; a summation of the major issue as students now understand it, having had the benefit of the lecture just delivered; or a preview of coming attractions. . . . Don't worry if you finish a few minutes early; explain that you have reached a natural stopping point. But don't make it a habit. (p. 117)

THE LISTENERS

The articulate, expert, and engaging lecturer prepares a well-organized lecture filled with vivid examples, memorable stories, and important points. Yet, some of the students, when tested on their understanding of the concepts covered, show little evidence of having learned the lecture's lessons. Why? Because learning does not depend only on "Who says" and "What is said," but also on "Who is (or is not) listening" (Hovland et al., 1953).

Hovland et al. (1953) offered a general orientation for organizing the many individual differences that influence message processing. They recognized that listeners vary in many ways, but they tied these differences back to the basic information-processing steps they identified in nearly all their empirical efforts. If differences among individuals influence their levels of attention, comprehension of the message, and acceptance of the message, then they will likely respond very differently to the same instructional experience.

> Some individuals might generally fail to be influenced by communications because of lack of ability to direct and sustain attention; others primarily because of a low degree of ability to grasp explicit and implicit verbal meanings, resulting in poor comprehension; and still others because of deficiencies in other types of intellectual skills that are directly related to acceptance, as when they have difficulty in responding to verbal incentives with appropriate anticipation of rewards or punishment.... Even when a person possesses the essential abilities, however, lack of responsiveness might occur as a result of motivational deficiencies. For example, an individual may be inattentive because of general lack of interest in what other people say or because he has developed involuntary defenses against anxiety which inhibit or interfere with sustained attention to communication stimuli. (p. 289)

Lectures and Learning Styles

Studies of individual differences in how people acquire and process information have suggested that the lecture format, with its emphasis on sequential organization, verbal content, and minimal social interaction, is an ideal means of learning for only some students in the classroom. Other students' preferred learning style may require more active processes, such as performing exercises or experiments. Others may learn best through reading and independent study. Others may excel in small groups, whereas others may prefer visually stimulating experiences. Claxton and Murrell (1987) categorized these individual variations in learning styles into four categories: personality, information-processing, social-interactional, and instructional preference. Personality models relate differences in learning style back to basic traits of the individual, such as field dependence–

independence (Witkins, 1977). Information-processing approaches suggest that students vary in the way they encode, store, and retrieve new information. Social-interactional models are based on variations in students' motivational goals, such as their interest in learning for learning's sake versus learning to outperform others. Instructional preference models take into account students' attitudes toward different teaching methods, such as small group discussions, formal lectures, readings, and so on. Table 2.4 presents a small sampling of the dozens of learning style models that theorists and researchers have developed.

Although some educators feel that these individual differences are so powerful that students will not be able to learn in a setting that does not match their personal proclivities or characteristics, others suggest that this conclusion overreaches the empirical evidence (e.g., Davis, 1993; Pintrich, 1988). Similarly, some investigators believe that particular types of learning style might be more prevalent in different cultural, ethnic, and gender groups; others feel that learning styles are likely confounded with stereotypes and may contribute to inappropriate and unfair treatment of group members (e.g., Anderson, 1988; O'Neil, 1990). Moreover, even students who prefer to learn by doing or assimilate knowledge more rapidly by carrying out projects in groups should learn to augment their scholarly skills so they can learn in lecture classes as well as other settings. The ability to listen critically to a presentation and cull the most essential elements from the hour-long message is an important skill; even visual or interpersonal learners need to be able to understand the points made by the anchorperson on the evening news. Hence Davis (1993) judiciously recommended

TABLE 2.4
A Sampling of Models of Individual Differences in Learning Styles

Model	Types or dimensions
Fuhrmann-Jacobs Model (Fuhrmann & Grasha, 1983)	Dependent, collaborative, independent
Grasha-Riechmann Model (Grasha, 1972; Riechmann & Grasha, 1974)	Competitive, collaborative, avoidant, participant, dependent, independent
Gregorc Style Delineator (Gregorc, 1982)	Concrete sequential, abstract random, abstract sequential, concrete random
Kolb (1976) Learning Styles	Accommodators, divergers, convergers, assimilatory
Learning Process Questionnaire (Biggs, 1987)	Deep learning, achieving orientation, surface learning
VARK Learning Styles (Fleming & Bonwell, 1998)	Visual, aural (auditory), read/write, and kinesthetic, multimodal sensory modalities
Witkin's (1977) Field Sensitivity Model	Dependent learners (field sensitive) and independent learners (field independent)

incorporating a range of methods when teaching, so that students become familiar with a number of modes for learning.

Readiness to Learn

College students are motivated to learn things that interest and challenge them, and these interests are determined, in part, by their level of cognitive and emotional development (Widick, Parker, & Knefelkamp, 1978. Chickering's (1969, 1981) work, for example, assumes that traditional college students have particular developmental tasks or concerns pertaining to developing competence, managing emotions, developing autonomy, establishing identity, freeing interpersonal relationships, developing purpose, and developing integrity. Students' concern for autonomy, for example, expresses itself in their striving for independence from their parents, comparing themselves with peers to learn how to act in various situations, and relying more on their own thoughts and values. Some of these motivations sustain their efforts to excel in the classroom, but others draw their attention away from scholastic concerns (Widick et al., 1978).

Perry's (1970) work with college students suggested that students are most likely to be engaged when they are challenged by thinking that is different from their current viewpoints. He contrasted students who are dualistic thinkers—those who feel that all questions can be answered clearly and definitively as either right or wrong—with more relativistic thinkers, who realize that different perspectives can be taken on most issues. Perry found that lecturers who introduce conflicting ideas, admit their uncertainty about questions, and encourage students to debate issues among themselves challenge dualists and help them move to a more relativistic stage of development (Schommer, 1998). But when professors also take a stance on an issue and base that commitment on their interpretation of relevant research findings, they stimulate relativists to move from ambivalence toward personal commitment (King, 1978).

Lectures and Studentship

To gain perspective on what it was like to be a student in a lecture class, McGovern (1987) attended four different classes one day and wrote up his experiences in this sobering report:

> I was stunned and saddened by the level of passivity in three of the four classes. In the Psychology 101 class students chatted too long after a provocative point had been made. A student to my left took excellent notes, even raising his own higher order questions in his margins as he recorded the main points of a well-structured lecture. To my right, three women chatted incessantly. In front of me, an individual spent the entire class reading and re-reading a wonderfully sensuous letter

from her weekend partner. In the two 300 level classes, the quality of note taking by the students around me was uniformly poor. In one class, the structure of the content needed significant improvement and I could understand the paucity and scatter of the notes. However, in the other class taught by an adjunct, the organization was quite good, the blackboard recorded major points, and still students took poor notes. Even in the Science class, many students recorded the teachers' words like line items in a budget, with neither integration nor analysis. (McGovern, 1987, p. 12)

The range of students' scholarly skills can be striking. Some students attend class regularly, do the assigned readings before the day's lecture, take good notes, and study at least 3 hours for each hour spent in the class. Others, in contrast, lack what Pressley, Van Etten, Yokoi, Freebern, and Van Meter (1998) call *studentship*: the skills, knowledge, and attitudes needed to master their many academic demands. In lecture classes, the general lack of studentship can escape detection. Students can skip classes and their absence will go unnoticed. If they get behind in their reading, their failure will likely escape detection. If they are sick, hung over, or sleepy, they can "gut out" the lecture hour note free. But if students do not attend, if they do not connect to the professor, and if they do not take good notes, then they will likely learn little from even the best instructor.

Attending Class

No lecture will be effective if it is never heard (Knight & McKelvie, 1986), but lecture classes, because they tend to be large and professor-centered, provide students with the anonymity they need to skip class without fear of detection. In a small class, students who miss class regularly will be noticed, and their actions can be questioned and corrected, but when classes are large and if attendance is not taken, students may soon find that other demands on their time will prevent them from getting to class. Unfortunately, as Lindgren (1969) reported, attendance and performance are highly correlated. When he reviewed the attendance records of high-scoring and low-scoring students, he discovered that 84% of the high scorers attended nearly every class session, whereas only 47% of the low scorers attended faithfully. His findings argue in favor of required attendance in class, but such policies can result in classes filled with students who are so inattentive that they might as well be elsewhere rather than distracting the students who want to pay attention to the lecture. Sleigh and Ritzer (2001), recognizing this problem, suggest structuring the class "so that those who attend experience obvious benefits, such as better grades, personal growth, and 'informative entertainment.'" Specifically, a professor should

- include items on tests and exams that cover information and activities from the class sessions rather than the text,

- spend class time covering aspects of the material that are not considered in readings or on-line,
- provide only the outlines of classroom materials (e.g., lecture notes) at remote locations rather than verbatim transcripts,
- involve the students in the presentation by presenting ideas in interesting ways, making use of examples they can relate to, and involving them in the discussion,
- give students grades for classroom participation and make use of in-class quizzes and activities, and
- create an atmosphere of mutual respect and individual accountability in the classroom.

Listening and Note-Taking Skills

Every professor has had a student who did not take notes but performed marvelously in class. I once had a student who never took a single note, but got 100s on 3 exams and a 98% on the final. She stared at me throughout the class, never jotting down a single comment. It was eerie. But most learners benefit in a number of ways from taking notes (Bligh, 1998). Memories are so fallible and fragile that most people must strengthen them by jotting down summaries of what they learn in each class. Note taking is even more important in large classes, for these complex environments interfere with the sometimes automatic production of lasting memory traces. Notes make salient the lecture's outline, organize information presented in the lecture, force students to identify key points, provide a written record for later review and study, and increase attention to the lecture's content (McKeachie, 1980). Chapter 5 offers some ideas for instructors who want to give their students pointers on how to take useful notes while listening to their lectures.

Lecture Hall Ecology

Even if students show up for class in a physical sense, they sometimes remain disconnected psychologically from the lecturer and the lecture's content. Indeed, many students deliberately select their seats in the lecture hall to avoid having to pay attention to the lecturer. According to Haber (1980), students who sit close to the front identify more with the lecturer and are likely trying to increase their focus on the course material. Those who sit in the rear areas of the class identify more with their peers than the professor, whereas those on the far sides of the class are connected to neither their peers nor the professor. In general, however, students in the center and front areas earn higher grades and participate more than students who sit at the rear of the room (Knowles, 1982; Sommer, 1969). Some evidence indicates that these differences are found because the more intelligent, talkative, or more interested students choose central territories

(Levine, McDonald, O'Neal, & Garwood, 1982). Other studies underscore the impact of spatial factors, such as proximity to the instructor (Stires, 1982). When Griffith (1921) assigned students to their seats alphabetically, students in the front rows scored 3–8% lower than students in the central areas, and students in the rear rows scored 10% lower than the central students.

Who Says What to Whom

Teaching psychologists, perhaps more than any other academics, realize that the students in their classes differ in a host of ways that influence the teaching and learning process. Some may be well prepared for the experience, but others may be ill equipped for the rigors of a psychology course. Some students may be enthusiastic learners who are considering majoring in psychology, but others may be uninterested in the field or actively dislike it. Some learners may enjoy turning concepts over in their minds and contemplating the puzzles of behaviors, but others may engage in deep thought only reluctantly. Some students are confident in their abilities, but others are so uncertain of their skills that they create mental roadblocks to their own success. Listeners come in many shapes and sizes; a lecturer must use flexible and varied methods so that students, no matter what their background, approach, and preparation, can learn something from the day's presentations. But even the finest lecture, delivered by an excellent teacher, will fail if the students—the third element in the who-says-what-to-whom model—are unready, unskilled, or simply unwilling to learn.

3

GUIDING: STUDENT-CENTERED APPROACHES TO TEACHING

I have come to feel that the only learning which significantly influences behavior is self-discovered, self-appropriated learning. Such self-discovered learning, truth that has been personally appropriated and assimilated in experience, cannot be directly communicated to another. As soon as an individual tries to communicate such experience directly, often with a quite natural enthusiasm, it becomes teaching, and its results are inconsequential.

—Carl Rogers
On Becoming a Person (1961, p. 276)

Rather than acting as "sages on stage," professors sometimes act as "guides on the side" by mentoring, facilitating, collaborating, and coordinating. Student-centered forms of teaching, such as full-class discussion, small-group discussions, experiential activities, writing assignments, independent studies, and internships, shift the focus of the class away from the instructor to the student. These methods may not be the most efficient means of transmitting information to students, but they are useful in other ways: They teach students to think clearly and critically about psychology's theories, concepts, ideas, and findings; they encourage students to express their knowledge of psychology in their own way and in their own words; they create opportunities for collaborative learning experiences; and they remind students and professors that students must take responsibility for their learning.

* * *

Many of the world's greatest educators did not reveal their insights to students through their lectures, texts, or papers. Socrates, for example, led his students to draw their own conclusions by asking them series of questions. He also used examples, metaphors, and stories to make each point. Siddartha Gautama, better known as Buddha, taught for 45 years from the period of his enlightenment to his death, but his teachings are recorded as give-and-take dialogs between him and his students. Confucius taught primarily by answering students' questions, often in very general, metaphorical ways. He believed that his greatest strength, as a teacher, was his ability to "listen silently, to learn untiringly, and to teach others without being wearied—that is just natural with me" (Confucius, 500 BC/1994, book 7, chapter 2). And Maria Montessori, the originator of the teaching method that bears her name, believed that students absorb knowledge through their own actions: "Education is not something which the teacher does, but . . . a natural process which develops spontaneously in the human being. It is not acquired by listening to words, but in virtue of experiences in which the child acts on his environment. The teacher's task is not to talk, but to prepare and arrange a series of motives for cultural activity in a special environment made for the child" (Montessori, 1949/1995, p. 8).

These educators, by centering the learning environments that they created around their students rather than themselves, used teaching methods that were similar in some respects to the therapeutic strategies favored by the humanistic psychotherapist Carl Rogers (1961, 1969). Rogers, reacting to the therapist-centered approaches to treatment advocated by psychoanalytic and behavioral psychologists, advocated relinquishing some of the psychologist's control over the therapeutic process to clients. His client-centered therapy emphasized the importance of establishing a personal relationship with clients, but it also emphasized clients' responsibility for their improved adjustment. Rogers eschewed the use of interpretation, directives, and instruction, preferring instead to help clients help themselves. "No approach which relies upon knowledge, upon training, upon the acceptance of something that is *taught*, is of any use" he wrote. Rather, the client must "discover within himself the capacity . . . for growth, and change, and personal development" (Rogers, 1961, pp. 32–33).

Many teaching psychologists, like Rogerian therapists, prefer nondirective, student-centered teaching methods. Rather than lecturing, they stay out of the classroom's limelight by guiding, mentoring, facilitating, collaborating, and coordinating. They may want students to learn concepts, facts, and information, but they also want them to become independent learners who can think critically, express their ideas cogently, and locate the information they need to solve the problems they face. These professors give much of the responsibility for learning back to the students by using one or more of the teaching methods listed in Table 3.1. Each of these methods has unique features. When the professor uses full-class discussion, for example, students must express their ideas and opinions orally and listen to what their classmates are saying. Writing assignments also require self-expression, but through writing rather than speaking. Whereas independent studies require that students organize (with some supervision) their projects and expend considerable time and effort on individual tasks, many group activities require collaboration with others. Regardless of their specific features, these methods are alike in that they actively engage the students in the learning process (Mathie et al., 1993; Miserandino, 1999).

TABLE 3.1
Types of Student-Centered Teaching Methods

Teaching method	Characteristics
Discussion	A two-way dialog between the instructor and the intact class; students' interact through the professor, but they also sometimes interact with one another directly; the professor sometimes controls the discussion through Socratic questioning
Small group discussion	The class "breaks out" into smaller groups and discusses topics and questions without the professor, although one member of the group may be appointed the leader or report giver
Activities	Structured and semistructured learning exercises such as case studies, problems, or simulations of psychological processes that students can complete either individually or in groups
Composition	Assignments such as term papers, free writing, "journaling," and response papers that require students express themselves through their writing
Presentations, panels, and seminars	Students make formal and informal presentations, including didactic overviews of specific topics, summaries of research studies, discussions of research, and reviews of the text material; in many cases specific topics are assigned to individuals or groups, who are responsible for teaching the material to the rest of the class
Projects, independent study, research	Various types of projects, such as library and psychological research, guided readings, and empirical research, that are carried out under the direction and supervision of the professor
Field placements, internships, practica, service learning	Students use their knowledge of and skills in psychology as they perform services in community, educational, therapeutic, medical, business, military, or industrial settings

LEADING DISCUSSIONS

Sykes (1988), in his indictment of college teaching, includes discussions on his list, "Five Ways to Teach Badly." When unprepared, he suggests, professors should "turn their classes into rap sessions, a tactic that has the advantage of being both entertaining and educationally progressive" (p. 61). But a good discussion is not a rap session; it is, instead, an organized, if unstructured, class session during which the professor and the students "consider a topic, issue or problem and exchange information, experiences, ideas, opinions, reactions, and conclusions with one another" (Ewens, 1985, p. 8).

Discussions come in two types. In the full-class discussion (FCD), the professor leads the discussion, asking questions to move the group from one point to the next, summarizing key points, and interceding to redirect the flow of ideas and information. In a small group discussion (SGD), the class breaks up into groups and each group discusses the issue. These groups may report back at the end of the session and the professor may selectively facilitate their discussion, but the group's processes are not coordinated by the instructor. I consider the nature of professor-led discussions in this section and that of small group discussions in the next.

Preparing for Discussions

Preparing for a discussion taps many of the same skills that researchers use when planning their next study, for discussions are student-centered in the same sense that psychologists' research studies are participant-centered. In an experiment, survey, or observational study, participants are the center of attention—their responses are the data that determine the results of the project. But their responses are given meaning only because they occur in a research context that has been carefully created by the researchers. Few researchers would hope that their studies would yield interpretable findings if the studies were unplanned, spontaneous experiences. Yet teaching psychologists sometimes expect that class discussions will be fruitful even if they do not put in much planning time. Although discussions are student-centered teaching methods, they nonetheless require more preparation and investment than professor-centered methods.

Identifying the Function

Sykes (1988) may think that all discussions are rap sessions where students can express their likes and dislikes, express their feelings, or impress one another with their understanding of the subject matter, but a good class discussion can be used to accomplish a variety of instructional objectives, including:

- *Sharing information:* Exchanging information about psychology's theories, concepts, findings, issues, and orientations
- *Application and critical thinking:* Applying psychology to better understand specific issues, identify possible solutions to problems, and gain insight into specific examples
- *Expression:* Enhancing students' ability to express their own viewpoints concerning issues and their understanding of concepts in the field
- *Collaboration:* Stimulating interdependence among students and faculty

- *Value clarification:* Exploring and clarifying attitudes and values.

Significantly, discussions that serve one function, such as value clarification or self-expression, require different types of materials and preparation than ones that involve pooling of shared information or critical thinking. If students are to discuss their experiences with people who suffer from psychological problems, or the origins of their social attitudes, or their beliefs about human nature, they must have adequate lead time before class so that they can read the text, carry out research, or simply collect their thoughts. In some cases, however, a few minutes at the beginning of class spent writing an informal paragraph on the topic is sufficient to prepare students.

Selecting the Topic

Virtually any topic in psychology can be tackled using discussion, although some are easier than others. Students are quite willing to wade in with personal opinions and insights pertaining to Freud's theories of sex differences, experiences with stress, intuitions about the causes of drug abuse, opinions pertaining the ethics of animal and human experimentation, questions about altered states of consciousness, and reactions to studies of obedience to authority. Other topics—such as intercellular transmission, schedules of reinforcement, causes of memory loss, sleep, and psychotherapeutic approaches—given their emphasis on information, do not readily lend themselves to a discussion, but even these topics raise such provocative questions as: Is the need for sleep an instinct? If you could take a "happy pill" that would elevate your mood and have no physiological side effects, would you use it? What are the different ways that people are "paid" for their work? Does the mind defend itself from unwanted memories, emotions, and motivations? Given what we know about memory, how should college classes be taught? Is the Scholastic Aptitude Test (SAT) a good psychological test? All of these questions, coupled with a series of subordinate questions and issues, can provide the structure for a content-focused discussion so long as students have prepared by studying the text before hand.

Developing Openers and Closers

Groups need help starting and stopping their discussions. Because group discussions build gradually over time through a process of social contagion, the first few minutes are often slow going as ideas and energy rise. Many discussion leaders, to help the group get started, use an opener that serves as a springboard for the discussion: an icebreaker activity, intriguing case, video clip, puzzling question, or involving anecdote (B. G. Davis, 1993). The professor can, for example, ask students to vote through a show of hands on a controversial question, such as the validity of the SAT, the accuracy of retrieved memories, or the impact of day care on development. Another quick-starting activity is to ask the class to generate a list of some kind: the causes of stress in their lives, the good and bad features of discussions, the characteristics of a psychologically healthy person, everyday forms of intelligence, and so on.

The teaching professor should also consider ways to end the discussion. All discussions have a natural ending point, although in many cases the group can continue to generate ideas, opinions, points, and insights after the first slowdown. But once the group's analysis has reached its conclusion, the professor should help students reach a degree of closure on the issues being considered. If the discussion was structured by a series of questions, each one can be displayed on the projection system and the class's comments recapped. The instructor may also ask students to spend 5 minutes at the end of class writing a brief analysis of the discussion, and this paper can be used as a record of participation that day. Some instructors generate their own summaries of discussion, which they circulate to students, or ask different sets of students to write summaries for the class.

Discussion Techniques

The heart of the discussion is the exchange between the members of the class—the give-and-take of ideas and opinions. But this exchange can be facilitated by using any one of a variety of procedures that, to a degree, regulate the process. These procedures are particularly useful when classes are large or students are inexperienced with discussion formats, for they bring order and predictability to the process. They also satisfy professors' needs to exercise a modicum of control over their class's procedures.

Debating Controversies

Psychology is filled with controversial topics that can be used to structure in-depth, multilayered analyses of psychological concepts, theories, and findings. Students are more readily drawn into a discussion of a pro—con issue, for only the most uninvolved will refuse to choose and defend a particular side or viewpoint. Consider, for example, a class session on the question "Is discussion a good way to teach college classes?" Each side of the issue could be presented, and points that support it could then be gathered from the class, yielding a list of pro-discussion and con-discussion arguments (see Exhibit 3.1). After building this list of points and counterpoints, the class can review each one carefully to determine its merit and relevance for the issue under review. At the end of the session, a final ballot can be taken in which students decide about the issue.

Professors who regularly use debates may wish to consider using the

EXHIBIT 3.1
An Example of the Ideas and Arguments Generated in a Debate About Discussions

Pro discussion	Con discussion
• An active form of learning compared to reading or listening	• Not enough content
• Connects students to each other, collaborative, builds cohesion	• A few students tend to dominate class
• Teaches expressive skills	• Many students do not get involved (unequal participation)
• Yields information about students' progress (informal assessment)	• Depends too much on student input
• Encourages dissemination of multiple viewpoints, diversity	• Only works for some topics
• Promotes modeling, skill acquisition	• Promotes anxiety, nervousness
• Shifts focus, and responsibility, to students	• Grading is difficult
• Increases interest, involvement, motivation levels	• Difficult to do well
• Prompts students to think about their own position and attitudes	• Difficult to keep track of material covered, generates few notes
• Takes less preparation (in some cases)	• Too inefficient and time-consuming
	• Requires too much preparation
	• Risky procedure compared to lecturing
	• Requires careful preparation
	• Students react negatively to this method

text *Taking Sides: Clashing Views on Controversial Psychological Issues* (Slife, 2001) in their classes. *Taking Sides* organizes psychology's content areas around highly debatable issues, such as: Is there evidence that homosexuality is biologically determined? Do evolutionary and genetic factors determine our sexual behaviors? Are children of divorced parents at greater risk for psychological problems? Do physically punished children become violent adults? Are memories of sex abuse always real? Can intelligence be increased? Is schizophrenia a disease? Do diagnostic labels hinder treatment? Does religious commitment improve mental health? *Taking Sides* provides background readings for each of these issues and decomposes each side in the debate into a series of points and counterpoints. These points and counterpoints can be assigned to specific students, who are responsible for communicating them to the class during the debate.

Brainstorming

When groups are seeking creative, convergent, or unique ideas, opinions, and solutions to problems, they often turn to a discussion method called *brainstorming*. Alex E. Osborn (1957), an advertising executive, developed brainstorming to stimulate ideas via group discussion. He complained of constantly having to struggle for new ideas for his advertising campaigns, so he developed four basic rules to follow to ensure group creativity (Forsyth, 1999, p. 295):

- *Expressiveness:* Express any idea that comes to mind, no matter how strange, wild, or fanciful. Don't be constrained or timid; freewheel whenever possible.
- *Nonevaluation:* Don't evaluate any of the ideas in any way during the generation phase. All ideas are valuable.
- *Quantity:* The more ideas, the better. Quantity is desired, for it increases the possibility of finding an excellent solution.
- *Building:* Because all ideas belong to the group, members should try to modify and extend others' ideas whenever possible. Brainstorming is conducted in a group so that participants can draw from one another.

Brainstorming sessions, when used in teaching, can be used to generate extensive lists of the consequences of mental health policies, ideas for research, examples of psychological processes, and novel applications of theories to practical problems.

People who take part in brainstorming sessions generally think that their sessions generate many ideas (Polzer, Kramer, & Neale, 1997). The bulk of the empirical evidence, however, weighs against Osborn's method —at least as a tool for generating creative ideas. Brainstormers generally do not expend maximum effort on the task, and the group-centered discussion blocks the flow of ideas. The originators of the brainstorming concept thought that hearing others' ideas would be cognitively stimulating, but people must wait their turn to get the floor, and during that wait they forget their ideas or decide not to express them (Forsyth, 1999).

Nominal Group Technique

The nominal group technique (NGT) helps members generate ideas and air their opinions, but it minimizes the blocking and loss of effort seen in brainstorming groups by reducing interdependence among members and increasing the structure of the idea-generation stage. NGT involves a pre-discussion phase when participants, working individually, generate ideas or solutions. If, for example, a class were asked to weigh the pluses and minuses associated with using discussion methods, the instructor would ask students to take 10 minutes to develop two lists of pros and cons. Then, in a round-robin discussion, these individual comments would be pooled in a group discussion. Each unique addition to the pool of strengths and weaknesses would then be examined, clarified, and rewritten as necessary. At the session's end, the instructor could rank the five most important considerations and then summarize the group's final opinions (Gustafson, Shukla, Delbecq, & Walster, 1973).

Agenda-Based Discussions

Most professors are veterans of meetings that are structured around an agenda that outlines the session's business. Classroom discussions can also use this method to structure the movement from one topic to another, particularly if a number of issues must be reviewed in a limited period of time. The agenda should be circulated prior to the class so that students can prepare for each item appropriately. The agenda may also identify individual students in the class who will be asked to make reports or presentations on particular subjects. An agenda also lets the professor organize the various phases of a class that involve a mixture of lecture, discussion, and student reports (Sunwolf & Siebold, 1999).

Discussion Leader Skills

Rogers (1961), perhaps understating the point, suggested that "a wide range of ingenuity and sensitivity is an asset" (p. 288) when teaching a student-centered class. But most professors are fully capable of conducting such sessions, even though their leadership skills may have atrophied from prolonged exposure to poor role models: departmental chairs, deans, and committee chairs who *ran* their meetings but did not *lead* them. In consequence, teaching professors may need to review their leadership skills and bolster their repertoire of effective behaviors in the two basic categories that comprise effective leadership: task orientation and relationship orientation (see Table 3.2; Conyne, 1999; Fujishin, 2001; Posthuma, 1999).

Task Leadership

Task leadership concentrates on the problem at hand. Defining problems for the group, establishing communication, providing evaluative feedback, planning, motivating action, coordinating members' actions, and facilitating goal attainment by removing barriers are key aspects of leading discussions. Professors leading discussions are responsible for facilitating effective group process, where *process* refers to all the members' various actions during the meeting. At the start of the class, the professor must remind students about the function and objectives of the discussion. By keeping one eye on the content of the discussion (points raised, ideas offered, questions resolved) and one eye on process (who is talking most, how involved students are, where the discussion is headed) the professor works to make the session move along smoothly. To achieve this goal, professors should monitor the amount of time spent on each topic and encourage resolution when appropriate. Group discussions can bog down if members are not reminded of time constraints, and professors can win many friends and admirers by keeping meetings interesting, lively, and fast-paced. The professor can also work to improve communication among

TABLE 3.2
Discussion Leadership Skills

Type of skill	Example
Task behaviors	
Directing	"I would like to discuss Jan's point further." "Let's move on to the next question."
Gate-keeping	"Ed, you've been quiet; do you have anything to add?" "Let's hear from some else for a change."
Group and individual mirroring	"The group seems to be focusing on . . ." "I hear you saying that . . ."
Informing and con-tributing	"According to a study conducted by Wortman . . ." "That study has some methodological problems . . ."
Observing process	"Why do we drift off into tangents whenever the question of ethics comes up?"
Opening	"Here is the question that I would like us to consider today."
Paraphrasing	"Let me see if I can say Jim's idea in a different way . . ."
Questioning	"Let me follow that point up with another question." "Does anyone have any ideas why a person would react that way?"
Restating and clarifying	"Let me see if I understand your point: You are saying . . ."
Summarizing	"Let me sum up."
Time-keeping	"We need to finish up in the next 10 minutes or so." "We have plenty of time, so let's not cut our discussion short."
Relationship behaviors	
Approving	"That's a great point . . ." "Jill made a good point there . . ."
Confronting	"Do you realize that when you make statements like that you are offending other members of the class?"
Energizing	"We still have 20 minutes left, and we are making great progress. Let's continue to nail these points down."
Expressing feelings	"I'm not happy about the way this discussion is going." "How are you people doing right now?"
Negotiating	"Can we come to a consensus on this issue?"

members by providing clear transitions from topic to topic (especially when a change in topic also involves a change in function), summarizing and synthesizing the points made in discussion, providing feedback to discussants, and drawing out reticent members through questioning. Hence, skilled discussion leaders must be fully involved in the content of the discussion but must at the same time remain mindful of the group process; they must be members of the group at all times but also observers.

Relationship Leadership

Classes discussing an intriguing theory, finding, or issue in the field of psychology are focused on the task at hand: weighing evidence, generating new ideas, critiquing positions, and so on. But classes also have an interpersonal, socioemotional side as well as a task side, and these personal and interpersonal processes express themselves more robustly in student-centered classes than in lecture classes. In consequence, the professor must meet not only students' intellectual needs, but also their socioemotional needs. They must teach students psychology, but also boost their confidence, increase the class's cohesiveness, resolve interpersonal conflicts, establish leader–follower rapport, and illustrate concern and consideration for group members (Forsyth, 1999).

Rogers's (1961) approach to teaching and therapy was based, fundamentally, on creating a strong interpersonal relationship with students and clients. As Rogers explained, the effective therapist (or teacher) should show

> deep respect and full acceptance for this client as he is, and similar attitudes toward the client's potentialities for dealing with himself and his situations; if these attitudes are suffused with sufficient warmth, which transforms them into the most profound type of liking or affection for the core of the person; and if a level of communication is reached so that the client can begin to perceive that the therapist understands the feelings he is experiencing and accepts him at the full depth of that understanding, then we may be sure that the process is already initiated. (pp. 74–75)

Lowman's (1995) findings, which were discussed in chapter 2, similarly suggest that good discussion leaders are warm, open, emotionally stable, and supportive of students. Gibb's (1973) studies of group climate in instructional groups also stress the importance of the interpersonal side of discussion. Gibb noted that discussions should be cooperative endeavors built on openness and trust rather than competitive debates emphasizing strategy, one-upmanship, and verbal manipulation of others. When the members of the learning groups he studied felt personally threatened, their satisfaction with the group plummeted along with their involvement and learning rate. Gibb suggested that a defensive climate can be made more supportive if members do not evaluate but merely describe; if control over others is treated as an unimportant issue relative to sharing information and solving problems; if group behavior seems spontaneous rather than strategic; and if empathy, equality, and provisionalism replace gestures of neutrality, superiority, and certainty (see Table 3.3).

TABLE 3.3
Characteristics of Defensive and Supportive Classrooms (Gibb, 1973)

Characteristic	Defensive climate	Supportive climate
Evaluation versus description	People in the group seem to be judging your actions.	People in the group are trying to share information and ideas.
Control versus problem oriented	Others are seen as manipulative, attempting influence.	Others seem to be focused on the problem at hand.
Strategy versus spontaneity	Members seem to plan out their "moves," interactions, and comments.	Interaction seems to flow smoothly with little strategic control.
Neutrality versus empathy	People in the group seem to react to you with aloofness and disinterest.	People in the group seem to identify with your ideas and interests.
Superiority versus equality	Others seem condescending, acting as if they are better than you are.	Group members treat one another as equals.
Certainty versus provisionalism	Some people in the group seem to feel that their own ideas are undoubtedly correct.	People in the group are not committed to any one viewpoint, for they are keeping open minds.

Distributed Leadership

Different classes need varying amounts of task and relationship leadership. An introductory course, particularly at the beginning of the semester, will likely require both structure and support, whereas advanced classes (i.e., senior capstone classes, graduate seminars) should function well with only minimal leadership infusions. Indeed, when appropriate these skills should be shared with the class—particularly if students will move into a small-group discussion format later in the course where they will need to act as leaders themselves.

Preparing the Class for Discussions

Because students often expect to hear lectures rather than take part in discussions, they need a period of orientation to this method of instruction. Discussions are complex social events, and so students may not know how they are supposed to act, particularly if they are used to listening rather than relating (Meyers, 1997). In many cases, too, students are confused about the discussion's purposes and may not feel that the opportunity for student-to-student communication is worthwhile. Because "ambiguity and lack of clarity tend to be associated with increased anxiety and diminished productivity and learning in a variety of settings" (Bednar & Kaul, 1978, p. 733), professors should dispel students' uncertainties by clarifying the class's purposes and procedures. In therapeutic groups this ambiguity is often minimized by pretraining the participants: providing them with a general orientation to the rationale and procedures to be used during the therapeutic encounter (Forsyth, 1991). Classes, too, may profit from a similar review of the purposes, procedures, and rules of discussion (Kramer & Korn, 1999).

Set the Goals

Groups founder when their members do not know what goal they are collectively pursuing. Larson and LaFasto (1989), in their study of effective and ineffective groups, nearly always found "a clear, elevating goal" in the productive groups and a loss of direction and ambiguity in the unproductive groups. Because clear goals stimulate increases in effort, better process, more accurate monitoring of the quality of the discussion, and increased commitment to the group (Weldon & Weingart, 1993), students should be regularly reminded of the purposes of the discussion, both in general and in particular. For example, students have a difficult time bringing the theoretical and empirical material to bear on the issues under discussion. Discussions of various psychological topics—adjustment, addiction, intelligence, motivation, and so on—often consist of students relating their personal experiences: brother Frank's memory problems after a car accident, aging Aunt Edna's increasing dementia, Geraldine's increased commitment to her sorority after the initiation, and so on. Students must therefore be regularly reminded to weave content into their discussion by backing up their contributions with theoretical principles and allusions to empirical studies. Students can even discuss discussion, with the goal of identifying the purposes and principles that should apply to their own class interactions.

Set the Ground Rules for Discussion

The first few discussions of any class are often cumbersome events characterized more by self-protective disinterest than by active involvement. By the third or fourth session, the class will have developed a fairly clear structure of norms, roles, and intermember relations, but in the early sessions members are not sure how they should relate to one another. This temporary social uncertainty presents the professor with a golden opportunity to shape the group's structure. For example, if members initially feel that the teacher should "run" the class's discussion, the professor can dispel this preconception from the outset by defining his or her role as a process facilitator rather than a process controller. To avoid creating the norm "Rogers is in charge of the class," Rogers (1961) refused to take the initiative from the very moment his classes convened. For example, in one course's very first session, he suggested that the members introduce themselves, but he did not orchestrate that process. He did not nod to the student on his left or say "I'll start with myself." The students, after a period of uncertainty, all began to introduce themselves. The professor also can make certain that the class's discussion ground rules are clear. Must students raise their hands to be recognized? Will the material discussed be on the exams? Will grades be assigned based on participation? These sorts of questions should be clearly answered.

Set Responsibilities

Recommendations on discussion as a teaching tool tend to focus primarily on the discussion leaders, as if they alone determine the class's destiny. Clearly, such an assumption overlooks the fact that the students can make or break even the most elaborately planned, carefully orchestrated discussion. Thus, participants should not simply sit back and listen to the group discussion, secure in the belief that the possible failure of the class could be blamed on the professor or other participants. Rather, class members should do all they can to make the discussion a positive, productive experience by preparing, communicating carefully, and cooperating with each other.

The kind of preparation required before a discussion depends in large part upon the function of the session. If students must engage in critical analysis of complex issues, they must have carried out the required readings *before* they offer their comments in class. Preparation is sometimes not required when students are discussing personal experiences, but they may nonetheless need to spend some time organizing their thoughts prior to the discussion. Some professors encourage preparation by asking students to write short papers before class or giving them 5 minutes at the beginning of class to write a brief statement pertaining to the topic (Clarke, 1988). Responsibilities can also be more specifically defined by rotating roles among the class members through the term. Some professors, before each discussion, select students to act as the timekeeper, recorder, and even devil's advocate. When the discussion focuses on content, individual students can also be selected to make presentations.

In some cases, students take their responsibilities more seriously if they are graded on the quality of their contributions. Some professors use a system for grading participation that combines ratings given by the students to each other and the professor's rating of each student's contributions. Other systems, described by B. G. Davis (1993), involve giving students cards after they have made particularly noteworthy contributions, which students can redeem for bonus points. Davis noted, though, that grading discussions can be problematic, because such evaluations are often too "subjective and not defensible if challenged" (p. 80). Grading discussion may also inhibit the discussion process, as students become too grade-conscious to risk making comments that others may evaluate negatively.

Set Standards

The success of any discussion is heavily dependent upon students' ability to communicate effectively with one another. If the discussion shoots off on tangents, members ignore one another's comments, and ideas are poorly presented, students will no doubt leave feeling "another wasted class; we accomplished nothing." In contrast, if students communicate effectively, then they will walk away from the class with a sense of progress and self-satisfaction. Most researchers (e.g., Davis, 1993) recommend that students be apprized of the principles that guide discussions, including:

- Make your statements brief and clear.
- Try to add your own comments, suggestions, statements, and questions at the "right" point in the discussion; timing can be critical.
- Make long verbal presentations to the group interesting by using imaginative phrasings, colorful analogies and similes.
- Actively listen to what others are saying.
- Ask for clarification of statements that you do not understand.
- Draw silent participants into the discussion through questioning.
- Explore rather than avoid sources of disagreement and tension.
- Follow the course of the discussion carefully, keeping in mind the points that have been made while anticipating profitable directions to follow. (Forsyth, 1982, p. 425)

Poe (2000) added that students should be reminded about the importance of courtesy prior to discussions of touchy topics, those that "provoke an emotional response in both students and instructors" (p. 18). Such discussions can be upsetting for some students but very irritating as well when students disagree very strongly with the opinions expressed by their peers. Poe recommended mentioning the types of topics to be discussed in the class during the first week of class and warning students about upcoming discussion topics so students can "come to class more emotionally prepared" (p. 19).

Start Slowly

Never, as Kramer and Korn (1999) warned, surprise students with a day of discussion. When, after a month of lecturing, the professor unexpectedly says, "What do you think about that idea?" students are often slow to respond in a productive way. They recommended holding a relatively extensive training session with students before actually engaging in a discussion, particularly if students are not familiar with discussion. Similarly, Bligh (2000) recommended gradually working up to a full class discussion by first attempting subcomponents of discussion: "Start with simple tasks in small groups for short periods of time, and then gradually increase their respective complexity, size, and duration" (p. 4).

A Word of Caution About the Backlash

Mann and his colleagues (1970), in their analysis of professors who used discussion methods, reported that students enjoyed the discussion approach initially but that before too long, they began to rebel. This backlash stemmed, in part, from the deliberate ambiguity of a discussion approach: The material is not neatly packaged for learners and so they must themselves create meaning in the flow of ideas and opinions. The conflict was also fanned by the type of tests the professors gave their students. When students were given content-based tests, they began pressuring their professors to drop the discussion method and revert to lecture-based procedures. Discussions are also easy targets for criticism because they intentionally amplify students' voices. Students in lecture halls may also be angry, disappointed, and dispirited, but the conflict never has the chance to surface.

This backlash, even if unpleasant, is nonetheless predictable. Conflicts are so ubiquitous in groups that Tuckman (1965), in his classic theory of group development, included a storming stage in his model: a period when tensions erupt in the group, distracting the members from their concentration on the task at hand. Ironically, even Rogers (1961) reported that some of his students reacted negatively to his use of discussion, for they wanted him to give well-organized lectures on his theories so that they could memorize the essential ideas and parrot them back to him on the examinations. Tenenbaum (1961), who was a student in a Rogers seminar, remarked, "We are Rogers-centered, not student-centered. We have come to learn from Rogers" (p. 302). If students were shocked when Carl Rogers taught through discussion, then any professor who uses student-centered methods is going to surprise, and possibly irritate, a few students.

How did Rogers, the master of the nondirective method, respond to this conflict? Tenenbaum (1961) reported that when the students argued vehemently for more structure and help, Rogers answered "I see you feel strongly about this." In another instance Rogers modified his method and agreed to give a lecture. He read verbatim from his notes—which he provided full-text to students—and so the result was "dull and soporific to the extreme" (p. 304). Students did not ask for any more lectures.

SMALL GROUP DISCUSSIONS

An active, energetic discussion conducted by a skilled professor is unmatched in its educational impact. But when classes are large, some of the benefits of full-class discussion are lost. Discussions in large classes can become unwieldy, for when too many students become too expressive, the skills of a ringmaster rather than a discussion leader are needed. One of the key benefits of discussion is the opportunity it gives students to express themselves and so become actively involved in the exploration of the psychological topics. A class-wide discussion, however, limits the number of students who can offer comments during the discussion. In all but the smallest of groups, communication rates are usually unevenly distributed among members. Some individuals initiate far more comments than others, and they are also the targets of more comments (e.g., Goetsch & McFarland, 1980). Even in groups with as few as 10 members, the discussion is best considered a series of monologues rather than an interactive dialogue. As Fay, Garrod, and Carletta (2000) reported, in five-person groups, interaction is more evenly distributed across members, and interactants are most influenced by the people they talk to the most. In 10-person groups, communication becomes centralized in certain dominant figures, who influence the more reticent members. If, as Mathie et al. (1993, p. 185) argued, "active learning requires that all students have the opportunity for the complete experience," then full-class discussion sessions do not often qualify.

What's the solution? Break classes down into even smaller groups for discussions and group-based activities.

Small Group Discussion (SGD) Methods

SGD, like full-class discussion, can be used to share information, stimulate critical thinking, and double-check comprehension. SGD is particularly useful, however, as an interpersonal arena where students can express course concepts and terms in their own words, work closely with other students, and clarify their personal values though social comparison and exchange. Because the professor is not present in the group, the discussion topics must be chosen with care and students must be ready to explore them without close faculty supervision. In many cases discussion topics that work well with a skilled, informed moderator do not yield a productive discussion when used in leaderless groups. In general, small group discussions are most effective when the group's task is a structured one, when students are practiced in collaborative work, when goal of the discussion is clear to them, and they are well prepared.

Start Simple

Bligh's (2000) advice about discussion groups—start simple and gradually increase complexity—is particularly important to heed with SGDs. He reported that he has had the most success when he has gradually moved his students from individual work to dyads to short-term, informal discussion groups, and then to small groups. The tasks themselves should also be relatively simple ones, initially. Begin with discussions of personal experiences (e.g., Have you ever been the victim of racism or sexism? What are the key sources of stress in your life? What are your sleep habits? What type of parenting style did your parents use, and what style will you use?) or the development of lists (e.g., List all the causes of stress in a college student's life) before moving on to more complex discussions of social issues or applications of text and lecture material.

Selecting Group Goals

What will students be doing in these groups? Will they share personal opinions? Answer multiple-choice items pertaining to the text? Debate fundamental psychological issues? Dissect case studies and recommend courses of action? Develop new measures of psychologically interesting variables and propose ways to test hypotheses about behavior?

The category "small group discussion" includes a wide range of learning experiences and activities, but McGrath's (1984) taxonomy of small group tasks organizes the many different uses of groups into the four categories shown in Table 3.4: generating, choosing, negotiating, or performing. When groups work at generating tasks, they strive to concoct the strategies they will use to accomplish their goals (planning tasks) or create altogether new ideas and approaches to their problems (creativity tasks). When choosing between options, groups make decisions about issues that have correct solutions (intellective tasks) or problems that can be answered in many ways (decision-making tasks). When groups are negotiating, they must resolve differences of opinion among the members regarding their goals or their decisions (cognitive-conflict tasks) or resolve competitive disputes among members (mixed-motive tasks). The most behaviorally oriented groups do things. Executing groups compete against other groups (contests) and perform (presentations).

Duration

Most SGDs exist for only a portion of a single class session, with some meeting for just a few minutes as students discuss a specific issue or collaborate to solve a few structured problems. Other SGDs, though, may meet regularly during the term both in class and outside of class. Benjamin (1991), for example, described his use of small group sessions as adjuncts of lecture classes. He lectures twice a week to students in a large-class

TABLE 3.4
Four Types of Tasks That Can Be Performed in Small Groups
(McGrath, 1984)

Group goal	Examples
Generating: concocting strategies to use to accomplish the group's goals (planning tasks) or creating altogether new ideas and approaches to problems (creativity tasks)	Developing a measure of a personality trait Designing research procedures Generating examples that illustrate concepts Writing questions pertaining to course material
Choosing: making decisions about issues that have correct solutions (intellective tasks) or problems that can be answered in many ways (decision-making tasks)	Reviewing cases and making diagnoses and recommendations for treatment Completing test questions as a group Identifying solutions to social issues
Negotiating: resolving differences of opinion among the members of the group regarding their goals or their decisions (cognitive-conflict tasks) or resolving competitive disputes among members (mixed-motive tasks)	Discussing ethical dilemmas pertaining to human and animal research Discussing social issues and controversial ideas Debating pro–con issues
Performing: competing against other groups (contests) and carrying out a performance of some kind	Competing against other groups in contests Planning and performing skits illustrating psychological concepts Presenting panel sessions and group reports

session, but once a week students meet to carry out group discussions and activities in smaller groups. These groups are coordinated by graduate student teaching assistants, and their tasks are relatively structured ones, but they nonetheless give students the opportunity to express themselves and form connections with other students:

> Many remark about actually being able to express their own ideas in a class. Some talk about how it helps them to meet other people in class. One couple who met in a small group announced their wedding to the group on the final day of the course. However, matchmaking is not one of my course objectives. (Benjamin, 1991, p. 71)

Such groups, because they exist long enough for meaningful relationships to develop among members, are likely to be more cohesive and influential. They are also likely to be more frequently marked by conflict. When Wall and Nolan (1987) asked their students who met for the semester in small groups, "Did your group experience any conflict?" the students identified 424 instances of interpersonal irritations. Professors must monitor the interpersonal side of long-term groups carefully, because in some cases conflicts arise that are so great that educational outcomes are threatened.

Closing Summaries

In a full-class discussion, the session ends when the moderator recaps the issues raised, identifies critical points, and ties the material to other course resources, such as readings or lectures. SGDs, in contrast, are more difficult to close because the groups may have reached very different solutions using different procedures. A typical method, having one person from each group make a brief report, works so long as the number of groups is not too great. Bligh (2000) wrote: "Of all teaching methods, stand-up reports by a nominated group member 'of what we discussed,' are rated most unfavorably. They are liable to be repetitious" (p. 213). Bligh preferred to monitor the groups and extract key points that can be reviewed in a full-class session or have each group write their answers on a transparency that he has prepared in advance that asks key questions about the issue under discussion. Another effective method involves asking groups to summarize their discussion in a table or graphic form on a large sheet of newsprint that can be presented to the entire class.

Forms and Variations

Buzz Groups

Buzz groups, named for their distinctive bee-like clamor, are highly structured, problem-focused, and short-lived SGDs. Bligh (2000) advocated using these groups periodically to break up extended lectures, even in large classes with theater-style seating. He created such small groups early in the term by asking students to spend a few minutes writing out their thoughts on a discussion issue. He deliberately gave the students more than enough time to complete the individual portion of the task, and in many cases they spontaneously began to form groups with people sitting nearby. He then asked the groups to continue their discussions but limited the groups to three members to control the noise level. This method, when based on two-person groups, is sometimes termed Think-Pair-Share.

Bligh found that students develop a clearer understanding of definitions, concepts, and issues when they have been given the opportunity to discuss such ideas with other class members:

> A concept such as "conditioning" can be explained in ordinary language using words such as "rat," "lever," "reward," and so on. But the concepts of "extinction" and "higher order conditioning" can only be understood if the term "conditioning" is understood first. Experimentally I have found that if these terms are introduced in a lecture, 80% of the students will know the meaning of the word "conditioning" immediately after the lecture, but only 20% will know the meaning of

"extinction" and "higher order conditioning" . . . However, if there is a buzz group after the word "conditioning" has been taught, but before the terms "extinction" and "higher order conditioning" are presented, post-test scores for the latter are very much improved. (Bligh, 2000, p. 36)

Problem Analysis and Decision-Making Groups

A number of professors structure the small group's interaction and learning by presenting students with a case, problem, or decision to analyze and resolve. Case study groups in business classes, for example, provide students with information about a fictitious company and students must decide its mission, organization, marketing, and management (Ginsberg & Morecroft, 1997). Guided design discussion groups in engineering classes spend a semester immersed in detailed information about a mechanical, chemical, electrical engineering problem and its possible solutions (Wales & Stager, 1978). Problem-based learning is an increasingly popular teaching method in medical education, where students are provided with problems and cases to diagnose and treat (Albanese & Mitchell, 1993). The techniques are all based on developing an intriguing problem that students, by working as a team, can solve by applying course principles, gathering relevant information, and weighing alternatives. The success of a problem-based SGD depends, ultimately, on the features of the problem itself. The most educationally influential problems have the following characteristics:

- *Engaging*: Because students must spend considerable time on the issues they are examining, the case, problem, or issue should be an intriguing one; practical, realistic problems are particularly motivating.
- *Multifaceted*: A good problem is one that has no obvious, simple solution. It should be ill defined and require that students research facts, gather information, generate solutions, choose alternatives, and reach a consensus.
- *Multistaged*: Problems should be relatively complex and include a series of interlocked stages. The first stage should be related to recently learned material but should be open-ended or controversial. Once the group makes an initial decision, it must then acquire additional information and make a series of subsequent decisions.
- *Nondivisible*: The task should a unitary, nondivisible one that calls for collaboration and interdependent action rather than the pooling of individual efforts. When students are assigned divisible problems (e.g., interview projects, research papers, chapter reviews), they often cut the task up into components

and assign each one to an individual member. Nondivisible problems (e.g., community-based projects, program evaluations, research studies), in contrast, are harder to solve piecemeal so students must work together to complete them.

- *Significant:* The problem should raise issues that are central to the learning objectives of the course.
- *Resources:* The best problems can be solved only by consulting with archival and text material rather than simply through the exercise of logic and reasoning. The problem should force students to identify and locate the information they need to resolve the problem.

McBurney (2000) used problem-based SGDs in his research methods courses. He noted that his students often responded negatively to discussions: "I have seen students put down their pens, ostentatiously fall asleep, or walk out" when he stops lecturing and entertains discussion (p. 135). Because the problems he uses are closely linked to the course material—and require an application of that material to work them out—student interest remains high. McBurney hands out the problems, which vary in length from a paragraph to several pages, one or more weeks in advance of their analysis. Students generally work in pairs, and he requires a written paper that includes a summary of the problem, suggested solution and justification for that decision, and analysis of the alternatives that were rejected (see McDade, 1995).

Peer Instructional Groups

Some SGDs promote student-to-student instructional activities. Writing groups, for example, involve systematic cross-critiques by students who provide feedback about writing style, grammar, and meaning. Supplemental instruction groups are voluntary meetings held outside of class, taught by students (often for pay), which use discussion methods to review course content. They are similar, in many respects, to SGD models that use advanced students as mentors or tutors for students in introductory classes. These mentors, who are supervised by the course instructor, lead discussions, provide general advising, stimulate debates, and encourage students to extend their own learning. These mentors provide each student with a tangible, personal link to the university by answering academic and non-academic questions (Kochenour et al., 1997).

The Jigsaw method, developed by Aronson, Stephan, Sikes, Blaney, and Snapp (1978), is one of the best-known examples of peer instruction. Before the group sessions, a unit of study is broken down into various subareas, and each member of a group is assigned one of these subareas; students must then become experts on their subjects and teach what they learn to other members of the group. For example, in a class studying learning, the professor might separate the students into three-person groups, with one member being assigned classical conditioning, one operant conditioning, and one social learning theory. In developing an understanding of their assigned topic, the students would leave their three-person groups and meet with their counterparts from other groups. Thus, everyone assigned to study one particular topic—such as classical conditioning—would meet to discuss it, answer questions, and decide how to teach the material to others. Once they had learned their material, these students would then rejoin their original groups and teach their fellow members what they had learned. Thus, the Jigsaw class uses group learning and student-to-student teaching techniques. Carroll (2001), when using this method with college learners, required that the groups sign a contact and scheduled each step in the project so that no student can fail to do his or her share (see Perkins & Saris, 2001).

Team Activities

Many SGDs use team-based approaches to teach course content and the interpersonal skills needed to work well with others. Although cooperative interdependence, taken in isolation, promotes achievement, teams further motivate students by establishing a supportive, achievement-oriented atmosphere; ensuring a high degree of interaction by linking students' outcomes; and heightening group cohesiveness. The Teams/Games/Tournaments (TGT) technique, for example, evolved from the old idea of spelling bees, but it emphasizes group interaction and student instruction (DeVries, Edwards, & Fennessey, 1973). First, students are assigned to four- or five-person teams. Next, the groups work on material the teacher has recently presented to the class, completing problems designed to test and extend their understanding of the information. At the end of the week the class plays in a tournament; students compete with representatives from other teams for points. In TGT the teams should include members of varying levels of ability.

Team techniques capitalize on the self-correction processes operating in interacting learning groups, in which members have the opportunity to teach one another by detecting, correcting, and explaining the sources of comembers' errors. The team procedures also seem to strike a responsive motivational chord in most students, who often become dedicated learners as they strive for personal and group achievement. A desire for group success sometimes becomes so strong that it is not unusual for formerly bored students to seek out teachers after class to ask for extra materials in the hopes of improving their inputs to the group. These team techniques have also been used effectively in reducing out-group rejection in heterogenous classrooms by promoting cross-group interactions. Whereas rejection of a student on the basis of race, color, creed, nationality, religion, or age is possible in the traditional classroom, such discrimination becomes self-defeating when the other student, as a teammate, possesses valued information and skills.

ACTIVITIES

The 1984 National Institute of Education report, *Involvement in Learning*, Chickering and Gamson's (1987) *Seven Principles for Good Practice in Undergraduate Education*, the Center for Postsecondary Research and Planning's *National Survey of Student Engagement* (2000) project, and the National Conference on Enhancing the Quality of Undergraduate Education in Psychology (Mathie et al., 1993) all agree on one point: Student achievement is enhanced by the use of active, experiential methods in college teaching. Lectures on such topics as schedules of reinforcement, image memory, depth-of-processing, group polarization, or dream symbolism, even when delivered by a brilliant teacher, may be confusing for students until they actually experience a fixed-interval or variable-interval schedule, complete a computer-based version of Sperling's 1960 study of cued image memory, listen to a list of words after noting which ones are self-relevant, make riskier decisions in groups rather than when alone, or record three dreams and review their meaning. Active learning methods, when they work effectively, help students apply concepts to their own lives, get them involved in the learning process, and challenge them to think about themselves. As Rogers (1961), writing rather forcefully, concluded, "Neither the Bible nor the prophets—neither Freud nor research—neither the revelations of God nor man—can take precedence over my own direct experience" (p. 24).

Types of Activities

Mathie and her colleagues (1993, p. 185) identified several types of active learning methods, including simulations, demonstrations, discussions, debates, games, problem solving, experiments, writing exercises, and interactive lectures. Ideally, active learning methods should involve the entire class rather than just a subset, and they work by recreating, in vivo, a psychologically interesting process, event, or outcome. Simulations, for example, ask students to imagine that they are facing a particular situation (e.g., the board of directors of a company, therapists making a diagnosis) and to make decisions about how to deal with problems in that situation. Demonstrations recreate psychologically interesting phenomena in the classroom, and replications involve reproducing the methods and results of studies with students. Table 3.5 presents examples of learning activities, all

TABLE 3.5
Examples of Activities Used to Teach Psychological Concepts

Topic and authors	Description
Research design and analysis (Lutsky, 1986)	Students are given a data set containing a number of psychologically interesting variables and asked to test a hypothesis using the data set and write up their findings.
Sampling distribution of the mean (Dyck & Gee, 1998)	Bags of M&M candies are distributed to all students, who count the blue M&Ms in their bags; 15 samples of 5 bags are selected randomly to generate a distribution and mean.
Research and scientific method (Bates, 1991; Gross & Bernstein, 1999; Kalat, 1999)	The professor performs a series of demonstrations of telepathy or other psychic phenomena before asking students to generate explanations and ways to test their explanations.
Observational research methods (Zeren & Makosky, 1986)	Teams of students develop their own methods for time sampling, event sampling, and trait ratings before applying their systems to the same taped interaction.
Research ethics (Beins, 1993)	Students participate in a replication of Forer's 1949 study of the Barnum effect before discussing their reaction to being deceived.
History of psychology (Brooks, 1985)	Students are assigned a set of important historical figures in psychology and they must write, cast, and perform a skit, play, or scene in which these figures act in ways that are consistent with their theoretical orientations.
Neuroanatomy and localization of function (Wilson & Marcus, 1992)	Students who have already dissected a sheep's brain are taught to reconstruct one out of clay.
Neuronal functioning (Hamilton & Knox, 1985)	Thirty volunteers who are assigned such roles as activating stimulus, action potential, synaptic knob, and axon role-play the knee-jerk reflex.
Split-brain and hemispheric specialization (Morris, 1991)	Two volunteers, seated side-by-side, with one arm held at their sides and the other arm crossed over their partner's arm, demonstrate hemispheric dominance, motor and sensory neural pathways, and coordination problems.
Eye structures and color perception (Blair-Broeker & Bernstein, 1999)	One volunteer is asked to name objects (e.g., colored markers, books) and their colors as they are moved from their peripheral field of vision to the center of their visual field.
Taste and smell sensation (Beins, 1999)	Students consuming jelly beans with their noses blocked or unblocked guess the beans' flavor.
Sensory and perceptual phenomena, including illusions (Wagor, 1990)	Students develop and demonstrate in class an activity that illustrates a sensory or perceptual phenomenon.
Classical conditioning of a startle reaction (Vernoy, 1987)	Students hold 14 balloons as the professor pops one after another with a foot-long needle; students flinch when the professor pokes but does not pop the 15th balloon.

Table continues

TABLE 3.5 (*Continued*)

Topic and authors	Description
Cognitive processes and memory (Gronlund & Lewandowsky, 1992)	Teams of students develop commercials for products and services that demonstrate one or more cognitive principles examined during the course, including chunking, serial position, repetition, and rehearsal.
Cued and free recall of long-term memory (Miserandino, 1991)	Students are asked to recall the names of the seven dwarfs from the movie *Snow White* before they take a recognition test including distractors and correct answers.
Memory errors in eyewitness testimony (Gee & Dyck, 1998)	Students watch a short scene from the movie *Robocop* before taking an unannounced 15-item quiz on its content.
Cognitive development (Balch, 1986)	Volunteer students videotape children performing three Piagetian conservation and moral judgment tasks and present the tapes during a summary class session.
Adolescent development (McManus, 1986)	In lieu of a major term paper, students meet regularly with a teenager (recruited by the professor from local schools) and summarize their case study in a written report.
Parenting and child development (Bernt, 1999)	Students ask parents to describe their parenting strategies and the traits they hope to foster in their children through open-ended interviews and checklists.
Issues in personality theory and research (Beers, 1986)	Working individually and in teams, students generate three test questions weekly, classifying their own and others' questions according to Bloom's taxonomy (see chapter 1).
Abnormal psychology and treatment (Scogin & Rickard, 1987)	Students are assigned to an inpatient psychiatric facility for 25 hours of volunteer staffing during the semester.
Psychological disorders and treatment (Rudisill, 1999)	Students assigned different psychological disorders role-play a group therapy session, after which they discuss possible DSM diagnoses for each participant.
Aggression and media (Lloyd, 1999)	Students watch television programs that vary in their violent content, code the contents of each, and compare the programs in an in-class discussion.
Personal reactions to social psychology (Snodgrass, 1985)	Students keep a log of their reactions to all class exercises and materials, with time allocated to log notations in class prior to class discussions.
Social behavior in anonymous circumstances (Dodd, 1985)	Students are asked what they would do if they could do anything they wanted but would not be identified or held accountable and their anonymous responses are classified.
Self-concept and depth of processing (Forsyth & Wibberly, 1993)	Students' incidental memory of a word list reveals their tendency to remember a larger proportion of self-schematic words.
Various topics selected by students (Fish & Fraser, 1993)	Students are required to complete a project of their choosing for presentation during a psychological science fair held in a public location.

drawn from Ware and Johnson (2000a, 2000b, 2000c) and Benjamin et al. (1999).

Design Issues for Activities

Using activities in class (and outside of class, for that matter) raises a number of issues. As Rosenwein (1983) and Weber (1983) explained, activities consume time, equipment, money, and personal energy. Because they are involving and experiential, they may also convince some students that psychology lacks scientific substance. Also, activities do not always turn out as planned, students are often skeptical about the usefulness of such activities, and sometimes the activities can lead to unintended side effects such as personal stress and conflict. As Mathie et al. (1993) noted, students must sometimes be able to take part in other activities if they feel uncomfortable participating in the active learning procedure.

Active learning methods also falter in their purpose if the students never really grasp the pedagogical purposes of the activities. Students often enjoy the active-learning, experiential phase, but then they fail to make the connection between the experience and the psychological concept. To help them make this connection, the professor may need to add descriptive, analysis, and application phases to complete the learning cycle. These phases include the following:

- *Experiential phase*: Students perform an active learning exercise individually or in small groups.
- *Descriptive phase*: Students describe their personal feelings, thoughts, and reactions through open-ended discussion or structured questioning, information-exchange procedures, or a written assignment.
- *Analysis phase*: The professor helps students conceptualize their experiences by guiding their analysis of underlying concepts that give meaning to the event.
- *Application phase*: Students identify ways in which they can apply their newfound knowledge in their own work, family, and other interpersonal settings.

These activities, too, sometimes require the withholding of information from students or actively misleading them. Such deception should be undertaken with as much caution as the use of deception in research. One should, before using a technique that involves deception, review the costs and benefits of the exercise. Will students gain an understanding of the material that cannot be gained through nondeceptive methods? By actually experiencing the phenomena, will students better realize how psychological principles apply to them? But will the students, once deceived, become wary of future class activities? Will they even show reluctance to accept the validity of material presented in class? Do the benefits outweigh the costs?

OTHER STUDENT-CENTERED METHODS

Discussions, small group discussions, and activities are only three of the many student-centered teaching methods used by teaching psychologists and summarized in Table 3.1. Although space limitations prevent a complete review of the many other valuable methods, examples from the primary categories are discussed briefly in the final sections of this chapter.

Composition

The psychologist's defense against writing assignments—"I teach psychology, not English, so why should I assign writing activities?"—is a weak one. Many students certainly do need help with their writing, for despite years of schooling they still have many problems with grammar, punctuation, sentence structure, and vocabulary. But writing assignments are not just exercises in grammar and grading; they are exercises in learning.

Writing as a Learning Process

Psychologists know so much about psycholinguistics, language, and memory that they should well understand the close link between composition and knowledge. Yet many psychologists view writing as only a means of assessing a students' understanding of course material, and overlook the profound impact that the writing process has on understanding itself (Boice, 1982). As writer and professor of English composition Donald M. Murray (1985) explained:

> Meaning is not thought up and then written down. The act of writing is an act of thought. This is the principal reason writing should be taught in the academy, yet, ironically, it is this concept that is most often misunderstood by academicians. They give writing assignments based on the assumption that writing begins after thinking is concluded, and they respond to those assignments as if the etiquette of language were more important than the thinking represented by the language. (p. 3)

Granted, students who just *write* a formulaic paper will experience few of the benefits of the experience, but students who *author* a paper become an "authority" on the subject. They must create, comprehend, analyze, synthesize, and evaluate as they fill the blank page or screen with text. They must identify their topic and the goals they hope to achieve. They must then plan out the paper, breaking down this complex process into manageable pieces that can be tackled in sequence. The writer must then generate the text: the words, phrases, sentences, and paragraphs that will communicate the content to a reader while conforming to the rules and etiquette of language. The good writer must also review and rewrite the text, making certain that the words convey the meaning clearly and, ideally, creatively.

Writing, then, is a profoundly active learning experience, for when people write, they identify and define problems, evaluate evidence, analyze assumptions, recognize emotional reasoning and oversimplification, consider alternative interpretations, and reduce their uncertainty (Wade, 1995). Indeed, in many cases writers do not understand a concept clearly until they must organize their thoughts on the topic and communicate those thoughts through composition. As a result, authors are often surprised by the ideas they themselves write, for understanding emerges during the struggle to make points clear to others (D. M. Murray, 1985). Rogers (1961) related this experience with writing when he was preparing for a 2-hour session with Harvard educators. Although he had been asked to prepare a demonstration of "student-centered teaching," he realized that spending "two hours with a sophisticated group to try to help them formulate their own purposes, and then respond to their feelings as they did, would be highly artificial and unsatisfactory" (p. 273). So he instead sequestered himself and wrote down his thoughts on "what my experiences had been with teaching, as this term is defined in the dictionaries, and likewise my experience with learning" (p. 274). The resulting paper was thought-provoking, even for Rogers himself.

Types of Writing Assignments

McGovern and Hogshead (1990) related an apocryphal story of the senior psychology major who, in her final semester, finally had the time to take an elective in an upper level English literature course. The English professor, after reading the student's first two papers, took her aside to explore the source of her weak writing. The professor traced her deficit back to the dearth of writing assignments in her psychology courses. One psychology professor required her to write two short papers, and her experimental methods instructor required her to write an APA-style research report, but what of her other 45 hours of course work in psychology? No papers, no essays, no writing.

Professors who wish to add just one element of student-centered instruction to an otherwise professor-centered approach should start by asking students to write. These writing assignments may include the traditional favorites, term papers and essay tests, but Walvoord (1982) wisely recommended giving shorter but more varied and frequent, writing assignments. For example:

- *Freewriting:* Experts on teaching composition agree that students need to write on a regular basis without having to worry about how their text will be judged. They therefore recommend that students spend time each day writing a paragraph or two about something. They should write quickly, without editing or rereading, and not worry about style or technique (see Hinkle & Hinkle, 1990).
- *In-class writing:* To help students find the time, some professors stop class for 5 minutes from time to time for unannounced periods of freewriting.
- *Journals:* Journals are dated, autobiographical notes that offer personal commentary on daily or weekly experiences. When Hettich (1990) used journal writing in psychology classes, he distributed a set of guidelines for journal writing that stresses the value of connecting class material to everyday personal experiences. Students, when they evaluated the impact of the experience, felt that it increased their level of critical thinking, provided feedback about comprehension, and served as a means of self-expression.
- *Activity-based reports:* Writing assignments can be used to cement the connection between an experiential activity and the underlying psychological principle it addresses. If students must reflect on the meaning of the activity in a written assignment, the educational impact of activities and demonstrations will be enhanced.
- *Abstracts:* Because published abstracts rarely contain sufficient information for their use in papers (and they are copyrighted), students should abstract articles themselves by describing the (a) theoretical background and hypotheses; (b) procedures used to test the hypotheses; (c) results; and (d) applications. They should be urged to never copy the abstract in the original article, although they can quote clever or essential portions of the article so long as they include page numbers and the quote doesn't exceed 50 words. Writing abstracts of course and text material also improves students' performance (Radmacher & Latosi-Sawin, 1995).
- *Literature reviews:* When students write detailed reviews of the published literature on psychological topics, they learn a number of scholarly skills. Poe (1990) offered suggestions for helping students write literature reviews by breaking the project down into discrete components, and Froese, Gantz, and Henry (1998) taught students to use meta-analytic strategies to help them narrow and integrate their papers.

- *Research articles:* Students, working individually or in teams, can in some cases collect the data they will need to generate a report of an empirical investigation. In such cases students can develop their project into an APA-style paper complete with abstract, introduction, methods, results, discussion, and references (Snodgrass, 1985).
- *Research proposals:* When students do not have time or opportunity to collect data, they can generate a proposal for a study or series of studies. Procidano (1991), who linked this type of paper to the course goals, reported that students valued the assignment as an opportunity to design their own studies and think creatively.
- *Reviews:* Students can write book and article reviews modeled after those published in *Contemporary Psychology.* They should be reminded to not abstract the book, but instead review the purpose, the ideas, and conclusions critically. The best reviews are those that aspire to literary as well as scholarly excellence.
- *Alternative genres:* Although most of psychology's text is scientific writing, students can use alternative genres—poetry, fiction, letters—to communicate information about psychology. Dunn (2000), for example, asked students to write letters to peers in other sections of her statistics classes to help them learn to express statistical concepts in their own words.
- *Open assignments:* Students can be given unstructured, free assignments to write about anything that interests them, so long as they connect the essay or paper to the contents of the course. They will often need guidance in selecting and narrowing down a topic, but their papers are generally more interesting because they presumably pick topics that they want to know about rather than topics their professor wants to read about.

McGovern and Hogshead (1990) described a number of other types of assignments used by psychologists in their classes and identify a host of resources for psychologists who are interested in adding more writing assignments to their courses.

Coaching and Grading

When students write, they are learning to use "the traditions of language to discipline their thinking and to make that thinking clear to others" (D. M. Murray, 1985, p. 52). Unfortunately, many students will need coaching on the process of writing and feedback about the quality of the writing they generate. The professor must, as Walvoord (1982) suggested, "make writing assignments meaningful, establish a wholesome and stimulating writing environment for their students, coach pupils in the writing process, respond accurately and specifically to student papers, communicate clearly with students about their writing successes and failures, and help students improve writing *as they learn* and *in order to learn*" (p. 3). How can the teaching psychologist enact Walvoord's charge?

- *Clarify the assignment:* Nodine (1999) noted that students need to learn about writing assignments as much as they need to learn about writing per se. Telling the students to "write a 5–10 page paper on one of the topics covered in this unit" is likely to frustrate students and disappoint professors. Instead, the assignment should explain the paper's purpose, the audience for the paper, the genre, voice, typical length, style, degree of documentation expected, and deadlines.

- *Challenge myths and misunderstandings about writing:* Boice (1994) noted that many students misunderstand the process of writing. They feel that writing is a private, secretive process that requires huge blocks of time. Others feel that writers must be first moved by the Muse, and so they procrastinate too long before beginning. Most also fail to recognize the amount of planning, research, and drafting that is needed to generate a final paper. These myths should be discussed and replaced with more accurate information about writing.

- *Provide students with some guidance on the process of writing:* Some students will need to know about the importance of selecting their topic, planning their draft, library research, drafting, reviewing and revision, and preparation of the manuscript final draft. D. M. Murray (1985) recommended spending class time discussing "The Writing Process" so that students can share their ideas with one another.

- *When giving feedback, focus on content first, then mechanics:* Willingham (1990) recommended establishing a hierarchy of comments, and putting content above mechanics. Psychology professors may be able to edit a paper as deftly as a composition teacher, but their initial focus should be on ideas, thoughts, and conclusions in the paper. By circling misspellings and crossing out extra commas, professors may send the signal "I have read this paper," but may also convey to students that form is more important than substance.

- *Offer specific comments:* Willingham (1990) and Handelsman and Krest (1996) recommended offering specific, but not too specific, suggestions. Vague complaints, such as "Think more about what you're saying here," "Rephrase," "Vague," and the

TABLE 3.6
Handelsman and Krest's (1996) Ten Most Common Problems in Students' Writing and Examples of Feedback

Frequent problems	Example of comment
The significance of the topic, issue, or paper is exaggerated	"My first impression was that this paper was about stereotypes rather than a study of student attitudes. How about starting closer to your topic?" (p. 23).
Key details are omitted or ideas are not linked to the paper's overall themes	"Readers who have not read Smith's article may not understand the basis of this argument" (p. 23).
Too much detail about specific studies or examples is included	"Omit these details that readers don't need" (p. 23).
Large portions of the paper consist of summaries of studies with no interpretative framework provided	"How do these two paragraphs tie into each other, and into the rest of the paper?" (p. 23).
Original sources are quoted extensively	"Paraphrase these quotations, and explain their significance" (p. 23).
Only one ideological or theoretical position of many is examined	"What are the distinctions between behavioral and psychodynamic approaches?" (p. 23).
Conceptual distinctions are examined, but their implications are not discussed	"I need less definition of the principles and more about how they apply" (p. 23).
The paper draws conclusions that overreach the paper's contents	"I don't understand how you came to your conclusions. Your reasoning is the most interesting, creative, and important part of your paper! Please share your thinking with me" (p. 31).
No conclusions are offered	"After all your good analysis, I'd love to hear your personal conclusion; what is your judgment on the ethics of deceptive research?" (p. 31).
The writing is stilted or mechanically inadequate	"Watch out for passive voice throughout the paper" (p. 31).

favorite "awk" do not point students to the specific problems with their text. More specific comments, such as "This sentence is too long and wordy," "Help the reader connect the ideas you are discussing in this paragraph to the ones you discussed in the previous one," and "I'm confused by the way you are using the word 'reward'" provide students with more direction for the next draft. (Table 3.6 suggests other wordings for feedback from Handelsman & Krest, 1996.) Rewriting the section entirely for the student, though, should be avoided. Students should not be able to revise their papers by typing in the professors' comments directly into the previous draft.

- *Comment kindly*: Comments that are too harsh will likely not be heeded, so they do not help students revise their work. The best comments are ones that are written as if the professor is giving comments to a peer. Rather than bluntly criticizing the paper, skillful reviewers first comment on the paper's strengths before identifying weaknesses. Negative comments, too, should be conversational in tone, and can often be phrased as questions rather than declaratives (Willingham, 1990).
- *Bolster students' motivation to write*: Writing, as Bruning and Horn (2000, p. 28) explained, is a difficult task that requires "extended periods of concentration and engagement in which writers must marshal all of their cognitive, motivational, and linguistic resources." Bruning and Horn's suggestions for augmenting students' motivation to write, summarized in Table 3.7, include nurturing their writing self-efficacy, assigning interesting topics, giving feedback carefully, and modeling positive attitudes about writing.

Finding the Time

Adding writing requirements need not generate stacks of to-be-graded papers so tall that one's own writing, research, and mental health suffer. In many cases the papers need only be checked off as completed, rather than assigned a grade. Wade (1995), for example, assigned eight papers a semester, and students must complete six of the eight to pass the course. She comments on the papers, but she does not give them grades. Students can also revise their papers if they are unsatisfactory, or replace them with a paper on a different topic. Some composition teachers save time by giving feedback to their students orally. They may, for example, give students an in-class writing assignment and then hold short feedback sessions at the front of the class with individual students. They may also walk around the classroom reviewing students' journals or brief papers (e.g., summaries, lab reports) informally, giving feedback as necessary. Some also tape-record their comments for students or, time allowing, meet with students individually or in small groups (D. M. Murray, 1985; Walvoord, 1982).

Time can also be saved by shifting the locus of evaluation elsewhere: to a set of guidelines, to peers, or to the students themselves. Some professors, before students begin their work, develop and review with students a set of numbered orienting guidelines and frequent mistakes. This structuring information reduces the number of mistakes students make and speeds up the feedback process; if students violate an element of the guidelines, their error can be noted by referring to its number. Many teachers make use of peers. Students can comment on each others' early drafts,

TABLE 3.7
Factors in Developing Motivation to Write

Cluster	Related motivation-enhancing conditions
Nurturing functional beliefs about writing	• Creating a classroom community supporting writing and other literacy activities • Displaying the ways that teachers use writing personally • Finding writing tasks that assure students of success • Providing opportunities for students to build expertise in areas they will write about • Using brief daily writing activities to encourage regular writing • Encouraging writing in a wide variety of genres
Fostering student engagement through authentic writing goals and contexts	• Having students find examples of different kinds of writing (e.g., self-expressive, persuasive, entertaining) • Encouraging students to write about topics of personal interest • Having students write for a variety of audiences • Establishing improved communication as the purpose for revision • Integrating writing into instruction in other disciplines (e.g., science, math, social studies)
Providing a supportive context for writing	• Breaking complex writing tasks into parts • Encouraging goal setting and monitoring of progress • Assisting students in setting writing goals that are neither too challenging nor too simple • Teaching writing strategies and helping students learn to monitor their use • Giving feedback on progress toward writing goals • Using peers as writing partners in literacy communities
Creating a positive emotional environment	• Modeling positive attitudes toward writing • Creating a safe environment for writing • Giving students choices about what they will write • Providing feedback allowing students to retain control over their writing • Utilizing natural outcomes (e.g., communication success) as feedback sources • Training students to engage in positive self-talk about writing • Helping students reframe anxiety [and] stress as natural arousal

Note. From "Developing Motivation to Write," by R. Bruning and C. Horn, 2000, *Educational Psychologist*, *35*, p. 28. Copyright 2000 by Lawrence Erlbaum Associates, Inc. Adapted with permission.

provided they receive some guidance in how to present their comments and suggestions. Writing groups are based on the same principle, and work effectively as long as students are not competing for a limited number of high grades. Some professors also ask students to critique their own papers, and to turn in with the paper a brief synopsis of their view of the work's strengths and weaknesses (Willingham, 1990).

Presentations, Panels, and Seminars

In some classes the students do more of the things traditionally associated with teaching—such as structuring content, providing information, and leading discussion—than the professor. The instructor organizes the class and supervises sessions, but students control much of the content and process. In such classes students make formal and informal presentations, including didactic overviews of specific topics, summaries of research studies, discussions of their own personal research, and reviews of the text material. Students may also be organized into panels ranging from 2 to 10 members, with each participant in the panel responsible for a portion of the class content (Benz & Miller, 1996). In a seminar course professors may lecture or lead discussions occasionally, but their influence and input is no greater than that of each student. Seminar sessions often begin with a student presentation of a paper, followed by general discussion coordinated by the professor. In other cases, however, a number of subtopics or key readings are reviewed, with particular students coordinating each subtopic's or reading's analysis. In the most student-centered form, a specific student or group of students takes on the instructional activities typically carried out by the professor, including reviewing the topic, identifying key points to be covered, selecting general readings and those assigned to specific students, and developing any teaching methods that might be used for that week.

Seminars are often used with advanced students, such as graduate students, who already have a strong background in the topics or issues that will be covered in the course. Bligh (2000) wrote:

> Don't use the seminar method with inexperienced undergraduates. It's a postgraduate method.... It assumes the language of the subject. More than the ability to solve standard problems, it assumes the capacity to pursue a line of reasoning. It demands a balanced knowledge of the subject and its associated values. The fears of participation must have been overcome. (p. 255)

Seminar students should be advanced students who are prepared to engage in self-directed learning, and they would likely be frustrated by too much structure, direction, and input from the faculty. Seminars also promote the development of the skills needed in a scholar, with a particular emphasis on the development of communication skills needed when discussing psychological issues with colleagues. The professor remains available to students as necessary by moderating the discussion, clarifying issues, and interceding to correct errors in interpretation, but the students are the primary teachers in seminars. In consequence, the success of this approach depends, to a large extent, on the motivation, skills, and experience level of the student organizers. If they are unskilled in making presentations, inarticulate when discussing complex issues, insufficiently prepared, uninterested in the course itself, or do not understand their responsibilities, then little learning may occur. The results may be as bleak as those described by a seminar veteran interviewed by Sykes (1988):

> I've taken six seminar courses, and in every one of them it's been almost impossible to learn a god damn thing. On the first day of class, the professor announces that everyone will write a paper. Sometimes he says that since the first paper writer will need about three weeks to get ready, there won't be a class for those three weeks. After that, all of the class periods will be spent having people read the papers aloud, with discussion to follow. . . . You can learn more in two hours' random reading in the library than you can in a semester-long seminar. (pp. 76–77)

Projects, Independent Study, Research

Some student-centered learning methods ask students to take an active role in the creation of psychological knowledge rather than the inspection and analysis of the existing stock of knowledge. By carrying out projects, independent studies, theses, dissertations, and other types of research, they not only learn the field's theories, concepts, and findings, but also must take part in creating this content. They do psychology, rather than merely study it.

The types of projects students undertake in psychology parallel the field's basic journals. Just as the vast majority of journals publish empirically based studies, most projects are field or laboratory studies of psychological phenomena that test some hypotheses about cognition or behavior. Of these studies, some are applied projects that are driven by practical problem, whereas others originate in some purely theoretical issue that requires data for its resolutions. Less frequently a project will focus on reviewing the literature with the goal of organizing prior work in a coherent, *Psychological Bulletin*-style framework. And even rarer still is the theoretical précis, in which students strive to develop *Psychological Review*-like theoretical models. In some cases, such as honors theses, Master's theses, and dissertations, the student is the primary intellectual owner of the project: If a publishable product resulted, he or she would be first or sole author. In most cases, however, a student works closely with professors on their projects rather than initiating a completely distinct, independent study. Professors in psychology are always working on a long-term project of some kind—a study, a literature review, grant-sponsored research, a book—and invariably students can play significant roles in these undertakings (Plante, 1998).

Students, both undergraduate (Horner, Stetter, & McCann, 1998) and graduate (Zanna & Darley, 1987), require considerable supervision throughout the course of their projects. When the general public and the media complain about the easy teaching schedules of college faculty who spend 6–12 hours in a traditional classroom setting each week, they overlook the large chunk of time professors spend helping students identify, plan, conduct, and write up their projects. Effective supervision requires frequent communication between the professor and student, including face-to-face meetings, electronic mail connections, the exchange of papers and guidelines, and the development of feedback and reports. Students appreciate the support they are given by faculty who are available, empathic, and who take a positive approach when mentoring and supervising (Avery & Gray, 1995), but faculty often find that the demands of multiple students carrying out diverse projects can drain them of the time they need for their own work (Zanna & Darley, 1987). Horner et al. (1998) offered a number of suggestions for adding structure and efficiency to this sometimes unstructured, time-consuming supervisory process, including using a syllabus, requiring a research log and prospectus, group meetings, e-mail communication, and oral summations. Students should also be encouraged to turn their experiences on their project into a written report of some kind. S. F. Davis (1999), for example, encouraged his undergraduate students to take part in regional undergraduate student conferences and provided them with support as they develop their conference materials. He also required an APA-style paper from all students who receive course credit for their independent study work.

Field Placements, Internships, Practica, Service Learning

A number of student-centered activities—field work, internships, work-study, practicum placements, service learning, and so on—integrate academic study with work experiences in nonacademic settings. These programs integrate the values of a traditional college course with the experiences gained in vocational settings such as businesses, mental health agencies, community organizations, or schools. With varying degrees of faculty assistance, students choose a placement service site where they can take on the responsibilities of a clerk or intern. They carry out duties for their on-site supervisor, all the while attempting to apply their knowledge of psychological processes to the tasks and problems they confront.

Graduate-level training in clinical and counseling psychology relies heavily on the internship model for helping students develop their professional skills as therapists. When students are placed in mental health settings, they have the opportunity to become familiar with the breadth of clinical and social service programs available in their communities, to apply knowledge and skills gained in their courses to work with clients, and to learn firsthand about the issues and concerns professionals face as they provide mental health services. Students in such programs sometimes attend regularly scheduled weekly seminars or practica meetings where their treatment choices are reviewed, cases are examined, assigned readings on clinical practice and professional issues are considered, and they take part in clinical skills training exercises.

Service learning is another widely adopted model used to integrate academic preparation with practical experience. Students in courses with a service-learning component, like those in traditional internships, work for as many as 10 to 20 hours a week in a community setting. Service-learning courses require that the service component provide a public good for the community, and that the community is fully involved in the students' educational experience. The service component must also be closely integrated into a content-based course dealing with some aspect of psychology. Unlike a traditional internship where the student works for several hours a week at a school, hospital, or business and then writes a short report of the experience, students in service-learning courses must actively integrate their hands-on learning experiences with the content of their discipline. This integration can occur through student-centered methods such as discussion or in more traditional lecture classes, but this reflection process is usually structured by a supervising faculty member (see Bringle & Duffy, 1998; Zlotkowski, 1998).

Student-Centered Methods: Conclusions

Many professors avoid using student-centered teaching methods and are wary of their limitations and problems. How can discussions be controlled so that the key ideas that must be covered in the course emerge, as if spontaneously, during the natural give-and-take dialog between professor and student? When students work in small groups how can their relative contributions be balanced so that all do their fair share of the work? How can the time be found to grade all the writing that students should be doing? What will grades be based on? What if the demonstration fails and students are left bewildered and the professor embarrassed?

Professors' distrust of student-centered methods may also spring from their distrust of groups in general. Teaching psychologists, as psychologists, may not be able to completely escape their discipline's paradigmatic preference for individualistic variables and methodologies. When they look at a group of students discussing an idea or working on a project, they see first the individuals in the group—their personalities, skills, and abilities —and only grudgingly take notice of the group and its emergent properties. They are so focused on individuals rather than the group that they fail to recognize the important interpersonal processes students are experiencing and the group skills they are learning.

But student-centered teaching has much to recommend it. In theory, the method seems well suited for helping students achieve fundamentally important educational goals, including

- a more comprehensive understanding of the field, its concepts, its issues, and orientations;
- higher order cognitive skills, including critical thinking, analysis, synthesis, and evaluation;
- self-directed involvement in the learning process;
- fluency in the expression of significant issues and ideas in psychology;
- interdependence among students and increased faculty–student contact;
- allocation of responsibility to students for their educational direction and outcomes; and
- opportunities to clarify and reconsider personal opinions, attitudes, values, and ethics.

And empirical research, although less than definitive in either design or results, has suggested that student-centered methods, depending on their quality, are equal to lectures in terms of their efficiency in delivering course content, and perhaps even superlative in terms of their impact on critical thinking skills. Bligh (2000), for example, after reviewing 123 empirical comparisons of discussion methods and other types of teaching, including lectures and supervised readings, concluded that discussion is as effective as lectures and supervised readings.

Given these strengths, it is difficult to argue with Rogers (1969) when he concluded, "If we are to have citizens who can live constructively in this kaleidoscopically changing world, we can *only* have them if we are willing for them to become self-starting, self-initiating learners" (p. 126). And such learning is most easily achieved "in a growth-promoting, facilitative, relationship with a *person*."

4

TESTING: STRATEGIES AND SKILLS
FOR EVALUATING LEARNING

I often say that when you can measure what you are speaking about and express it in numbers you know something about it; but when you cannot measure it, when you cannot express it in numbers, your knowledge is of a meager and unsatisfactory kind.

—Lord Kelvin
Popular Lectures and Addresses (1891, p. 80)

Developing effective ways to assess student learning is an elemental component of good teaching. Just as researchers must carefully define the theoretical construct they wish to measure, weigh the relative benefits of open and closed response formats, generate items that accurately assess the construct in question, and psychometrically evaluate the adequacy of the measure, so professors must identify the instructional goals they wish to assess, choose between choice-type and supply-type items, write items that test students' attainment of the specified course goals, and then evaluate the adequacy of the test with item analysis.

* * *

Tests, quizzes, and examinations are as central to teaching as the lecture, the discussion, and assigned readings. Their practical function is obvious: Professors, as agents of educational systems that are based on credentialing only those students who achieve the standards set by the college or university, use tests to acquire the information they need to appraise their students' learning. When the term ends and the dean's office asks who deserves credit for having mastered the course, tests provide answers —answers that are ostensibly based on fair, objective standards. Tests are also motivators. A high score on a test is a concrete, clearly definable goal that can be more motivating than the more illusory goal of knowledge, wisdom, or learning. A high grade on a test is a reinforcing event, just as a failing grade is a punishment, and so the delivery of grades by professors often increases the frequency of studious behaviors and decreases the occurrence of behaviors that undermine performance. Tests also keep students on-task by breaking up the relatively long, 3–4 month performance period into more compact segments. Tests and the grades they generate also provide students with feedback about their progress, helping them to close the too-wide gap between perceptions of learning and actual learning. When students review tests, they may even learn from their mistakes, making testing—and subsequent review—an important teaching tool. Testing also provides professors with feedback about *their* performance: "Classroom assessment helps individual college teachers obtain useful feedback on what, how much, and how well their students are learning. Faculty can then use this information to refocus their teaching to help students make their learning more efficient and effective" (Angelo & Cross, 1993, p. 3; see Walvoord & Anderson, 1998).

These useful functions are all generic reasons for measuring student's performance; they apply to all professors, whether they are teaching English, music theory, management, or physical education. But teaching psychologists test for one more reason. They measure students' accomplishments because they are psychologists, and that is what psychologists do: They develop measures of psychologically interesting phenomena. Teaching psychologists, when they develop, distribute, and interpret the results of classroom examinations, are drawing on disciplinary traditions that date back to Binet's tests of intelligence (Binet & Simon, 1905), Thurstone's (1928) indexes of attitudes, Stevens' (1951) psychometrics, and a century of experience in assessing individual differences in personality, temperament, and adjustment. They take, as a given, Thorndike's (1918) principle of measurement: "Whatever exists at all exists in some quantity. To know it thoroughly involves knowing its quantity as well as its quality" (p. 16).

Teaching psychologists, as psychologists, have far more expertise in testing than professors in other disciplines. The skills and methods needed to construct a good classroom test are the same skills and methods needed to develop a measure of personality, an index of adjustment, a survey of opinions, or a behaviorally anchored rating scale. But because most psychologists are trained in measurement, they have little excuse for using inadequate measurement methods in their classes. The philosophy professor who measures a semester's worth of learning with the question "What does it all mean?" or the chemistry professor whose eyes glaze when asked, "What was the Cronbach alpha for the five true–false items you used to measure knowledge of Boyles law?" can be forgiven for psychometric naiveté, but psychologists who fill their exams with questions like "List Piaget's four stages of cognitive development"; "Psychology is the scientific study of cognition and: (a) life, (b) behavior, (c) nutrition, (d) motorcycles"; and "True or false: IQ stands for intelligence quotient" have no excuse. In fact, teaching psychologists, as psychologists, are obligated to develop and administer valid and reliable tests of students' knowledge. The American Psychological Association's (1992) *Ethical Principles* requires that psychologists "refrain from misuse of assessment techniques, interventions, results, and interpretations and take reasonable steps to prevent others from misusing the information these techniques provide" (p. 1603).

PLANNING A TEST

The tasks of "professoring" are often described with quaint euphemisms. As if professors were intellectually rich philanthropists, they "give lectures to their students." They "train their graduate students," as if advanced scholars learn best through regimented, structured teaching. They "hold office hours," as if they were jurists or monarchs holding court. And their tests? They "make them up," as if they were writing a piece of fiction, penning poetry, or cooking up a good excuse for some indiscretion. Certainly test construction has its creative aspects, but for the most part the task calls for careful planning, deliberation over choices, and the analysis of available data. Tests are not *made up* like stories, poetry, or excuses, but *constructed* like houses or intricate machines.

Identifying the Instructional Objectives

Just as a "psychological test can be only as good as the ideas of the psychologist who constructed it" (Cattell, 1986, p. 10), so a classroom test is only as good as the conceptual objectives that it measures. As Mager (1962) explained:

> Tests or examinations are the mileposts along the road to learning and are supposed to tell the teacher and the student the degree to which both have been successful in their achievement of the course objectives. But unless goals are clearly and firmly fixed in the minds of both parties, tests are at best misleading; at worst, they are irrelevant, unfair, or useless. To be useful they must measure *performance in terms of goals.* (p. 4)

Mager championed the use of behaviorally oriented learning objectives that clearly communicate the professor's instructional intentions about the test's content. Such objectives should also tap a range of cognitive outcomes while remaining congruent with the broader methods and objectives of the course, the department, and the discipline of psychology. Instructional objectives should therefore be behaviorally oriented, content-oriented, and domain-extensive.

Behaviorally Oriented

Learning objectives, when properly specified, should please the Skinnerian who wants to know what students will *do* to demonstrate their learning. It is not enough to say that students will "appreciate the differences between schools of thought in psychology" or can "grasp the pitfalls associated with the analysis of nonorthogonal factorial designs." Such general verbs as *know, understand, appreciate, grasp the significance of, believe,* and *examine* should be replaced with *list, identify, construct, solve, select, compare, contrast,* and *classify*.

Content-Oriented

When students ask "What is on the test?" they are asking about its content: the topics, concepts, and skills examined by the instrument. Descriptions of test content such as "know all boldfaced terms in the text" or "be clear on the accomplishments of the great psychologists of the past" should be replaced with more specific statements, such as "distinguish between punishment and negative reinforcement" or "be able to link the following terms with the theorist who first coined them."

Domain-Extensive

As chapter 1 noted, psychology courses help students reach a variety of learning outcomes. Much of the course may focus on lower order cognitive outcomes, such as learning facts and information about the field, but most professors also hope to teach higher order cognitive skills, including problem solving, evaluation, and critical thinking. Examples of the types of verbs that can be used to specify learning outcomes at each of Bloom's cognitive domains follow (Bloom et al., 1956).

- *Knowledge:* define, enumerate, identify, itemize, list, name, outline, quote, recall, recite, recognize, record, reiterate, repeat, replicate, restate, state
- *Comprehension:* convey, discuss, delineate, describe, explain, express, identify, locate, recognize, rephrase, report, reword, show, tell
- *Application:* act out, calculate, compute, carry out, demonstrate, employ, illustrate, implement, interpret, perform, role play, use
- *Analysis:* analyze, break down, chart, compare and contrast, diagram, differentiate, distinguish, dissect, inspect, relate, test
- *Synthesis:* combine, collect, compare and contrast, create, design, develop, formulate, integrate, plan, prepare, propose, reconcile, reunite
- *Evaluation:* appraise, critique, gauge, evaluate, estimate, judge, rate, review

Goal-Congruent

Objectives should be congruent with the larger purposes of the class. If a course is skill-focused, then the objectives should identify those skills. If the course syllabus claims that students will learn critical thinking skills, then the objectives should define those skills in behavioral terms. Objectives that focus on trivial minutia, outcomes that are too advanced for most of the students in the class, or—worse yet—ideas that the field of psychology has long since abandoned should be replaced with ones that are consistent with psychology's central concerns.

Preparing the Test Specifications

Many measurement experts recommend controlling the content of the test by using a table of specifications (TOS). A TOS ensures that the exam adequately samples the unit's learning objectives, both in terms of content and cognitive outcome (Gronlund, 1998; Nitko, 2001). Consider, as an example, the first test in an introductory psychology course that covers the history of the field, research methods, physiological psychology, and sensation and perception. Although these general topics could be broken down into subtopics to increase the specificity of the content, the TOS in Table 4.1 identifies four major topics to be tested. It also adopts a simplified version of Bloom's taxonomy (Bloom et al., 1956): knowledge, application, and conceptual as column headings. The result is a 4 × 3 table that specifies 12 types of outcomes that the examination should assess.

Types of Items

Student achievement, like any psychological variable, can be measured in a variety of ways: behaviors can be recorded, either by mechanical devices or trained observers; students can be questioned, during interviews and oral examinations; their products, including papers, projects, and per-

TABLE 4.1
An Example of a Table of Specifications (TOS) for a 50-Item
Examination, With Cell Entries Indicating the Number of
Items on the Test Corresponding to Each Category

| | Learning outcome | | | Total number of items |
Topic	Knowledge	Application	Conceptual	
History of psychology	4	4	4	12
Research methods	4	5	5	14
Physiological psychology	6	3	3	12
Sensation and perception	6	3	3	12
Total number of items	20	15	15	50

formances, can be judged and critiqued. But by far the most frequently used method is the so-called paper-and-pencil test, which comes in two basic varieties: *choice-type* (CT) items that ask students to select the answer they feel is correct from ones that are provided by the tester and *supply-type* (ST) items that require students to generate their own answers. Multiple-choice, matching, and true–false items are all CT items, whereas completion, short-answer, and essays are ST items.

CT and ST items offer several unique advantages and disadvantages in terms of assessment. Some are purely practical ones. It takes longer, for example, to score the results from an ST test than a CT test. Other advantages and disadvantages, in contrast, are psychometrically significant: They influence the resulting test's reliability and validity.

Skills Assessed

The simpler forms of CT items, such as true–false and matching items, are best suited for testing lower order outcomes, such as the recognition of terms and facts. Multiple-choice questions *can* be crafted that measure higher order cognitive outcomes, such as analysis, synthesis, and evaluation, but these items tend to drift toward lower order outcomes (Martinez, 1999). Instructional objectives that focus on creativity, analysis, evaluation, and expressive skills are usually assessed with ST items such as unrestricted essays.

Comprehensiveness

Multi-item CT tests are generally more comprehensive, in that they widely sample the domain under study. The number of ST items that can be asked and answered during the time available for testing can be increased by asking shorter, more highly structured questions such as short-answer questions or fill-in-the-blank.

Objectivity of Scoring

CT tests yield the same score no matter who scores them, provided the scorer uses the key appropriately. ST items that ask for specific types of information, such as lists of stages or names of theorists, can also be scored objectively, but scorer characteristics (such as background, mood, and preferences) can influence the scoring of essay items.

Fidelity

Scores on CT tests accurately indicate the number of items a student answered correctly, but this score can overestimate achievement because students earn credit for correct guesses. Scores on ST tests are not influenced by guessing, but they can be inflated by bluffing, impressive penmanship, or a pleasing writing style. Haladyna (1994) notes that guessing will rarely raise a student's score on multiple-choice tests. Even if the test contains only 10 items, the probability of earning a passing grade through guessing is very small.

Writing and Reading

Only ST items provide students with the opportunity to express their understanding in their own words, but such tests may consistently underestimate the achievement of students who know the material well but do not possess advanced verbal skills. Both types of items are influenced by reading skill, but CT items put more reading demands on students in terms of amount and precision.

Feedback

Both types of tests provide students with useful information about their performance. CT items, in particular, can pinpoint specific areas of weaknesses; students who misunderstand certain topics but grasp others can be identified by analysis of the profile of their scores. ST items, because of the limited scope, yield less information about specific strengths and weaknesses, but they do provide an opportunity for the instructor to comment directly on the quality of the students' writing skills. Such items are also particularly useful for identifying errors in step-by-step problem-solving questions, as when students must show the steps they follow when solving a statistics problem.

Pedagogical Implications

Martinez (1999) reviewed a number of studies that suggest that students study differently for ST tests than they do for CT tests. When students anticipate multiple-choice tests they focus on details, but when they prepare for ST tests they focus on general concepts and connections between ideas. ST tests, because they involve writing, may also require more elaborate processing of course information during the test itself, and therefore trigger increased comprehension as a side effect of the testing process.

Cheating

If students want to cheat, test format alone will not prevent them. Short-answer ST questions can be copied from one test-taker by the next, just as the answers to CT tests can be easily copied from a distance. Students have less success copying long-answer essay questions from one another, but these tests are nonetheless vulnerable to cribbing. ST tests are also very vulnerable to leakage: If a professor uses the same questions in multiple sections, students in one section can easily remember the few questions on the ST test and pass them on to students in the next section.

Practical Concerns

CT tests are more efficient ways to measure outcomes because they can be scored rapidly by individuals with little advanced training or by automated scoring systems. In consequence, they can be used in any size class. ST items must generally be graded by knowledgeable or trained scorers, although the use of scoring rubrics can decrease the time needed for scoring. Still, most professors find the task of grading the essay tests of 100 students to be a daunting one. ST items can be constructed more quickly than CT items, particularly CT items that tap higher order learning outcomes. CT items, however, can be reused in some cases, and test banks of items can also be used to reduce the amount of time it takes to write items. Such tests can also be administered via computer or the Web and scored immediately.

Reliability and Validity

No psychologist should be surprised when told that a classroom test, like any decent psychological instrument, must have two basic qualities: reliability and validity. Tests should be dependable, stable indicators of learning, and this reliability should be indicated by the consistency of the students' scores across time and across the test's components. If students have learned the intricacies of experimental design; the functions of various structures of the brain; the nuances of psychoanalytic, humanistic, and behavioral approaches to therapy; or the steps to follow when calculating and interpreting a correlation coefficient, then a test that reliably measures that learning should yield nearly the same results each time the students take it so long as the period between tests is not so great that students can no longer recall the material. Also, if a number of questions are asked about the material, then students' answers across the questions should be relatively consistent; if students demonstrate a clear understanding of neuronal functioning in answering Item 2's query about serotonin, then they should not miss Item 16 that asks about the relationship between depolarization and action potentials.

Because tests with more items tend to be more reliable, CT tests are usually more reliable than ST tests. Cronbach's alpha coefficient, a commonly used index of reliability, is associated with the length of a test, and in consequence simply adding more items to a test tends to increase its reliability (Cortina, 1993). CT tests, because of their length, can also include several questions about a single topic, so their internal consistency increases because students who correctly answer one question dealing with a topic tend to get the other questions pertaining to that topic correct as well. ST tests' reliability is diminished not only by the limited number of questions asked but also by inconsistencies between different graders reading the same essay (low interrater reliability) and variations in a single grader's reaction to essays caused by fatigue, halo effects, order effects, and so on (intrarater reliability).

Validity describes the extent to which the test measures what it is supposed to measure. Although Cronbach and Meehl's (1955) conceptualization of validity has been changed and revised in recent years, their basic assumption—that scores on a measure must be linked to a theoretically meaningful construct—is still accepted by most contemporary psychometricians (Messick, 1995; Shepard, 1993; Zimiles, 1996). The subcomponents that are most relevant to classroom tests are content, criteria, construct, and face validity.

Content Validity

One of the key elements of validity is content validity: the extent to which the test adequately samples the behavioral outcomes, content, domains, and goals specified in the instructional objectives. A poorly prepared test may suffer from construct invalidity to the extent that its items are concentrated on certain topics to the exclusion of others, may focus on lower level learning outcomes, or may ask students questions about trivial aspects of the course content.

CT tests generally include many more items than ST tests, so their content validity is higher, *unless* the items do not adequately represent the domains identified in the TOS. Messick (1995) termed this type of invalidity *construct underrepresentation* because the assessment does not adequately sample the material identified in the instructional objectives.

Criterion Validity

Well-designed CT and ST tests yield grades that are correlated with other indicators of student achievement (concurrent validity) and are useful in predicting achievement-related outcomes (predictive validity). These types of tests even predict one another, for the correlation between ST and CT items when completed by the same students tends to be as high as the reliability of the instruments will allow (Haladyna, 1994).

Construct Validity

An achievement test's construct validity depends on the extent to which the items on the test measure the learning objective specified by the instructor. If the TOS stresses higher order outcomes but the test includes only fact-oriented selection type items, then the test's construct validity is low. Conversely, if the learning objectives stress the acquisition of factual information, then an ST test may not be valid. In general, if one of these types of formats best suits the learning objectives of the class, that method should be used as the assessment. If, for example, the learning objectives state that "Students should be able to state and defend their personal position in the therapist-facilitated memory retrieval controversy," then an essay test will likely provide the most direct measure of this objective, whereas a multiple-choice test will only serve as a proxy for the desired outcome.

The construct validity of both types of items can also be plagued by two types of problems identified by Messick (1995): construct-irrelevant difficulty and construct-irrelevant easiness. When a multiple-choice test, for example, demands a higher level of reading skill than the text requires, slower or poorer readers are penalized—the test measures both knowledge of psychology and reading skill. Similarly, students who have little experience in expressing themselves through their writing and students for whom English is a second language are at a disadvantage in ST tests. Construct-irrelevant easiness factors include any characteristics that make the items easy to answer by students who have not learned the material. Multiple-choice tests, for example, are easier for students who are testwise (skilled in the tricks of such testing procedures), just as essay tests are easier for the glib and garrulous. These factors contribute to invalidity by giving students higher scores than they deserve.

Face Validity

A well-constructed CT or ST test has face validity: "The test 'looks valid' to the examinees who take it, the administrative personnel who decide on its use, and other technically untrained observers" (Anastasi, 1988, p. 144). Face validity, however, can be undermined by the use of general, vaguely worded, or creative ST questions that seem only remotely related to the course material. Such items as "In what ways is the nervous system like e-mailing and the endocrine system like postal mailings?" "Use your knowledge of psychology to critique the social welfare system," "Discuss how painters use perceptual cues in their work to create depth and definitions," or "Ralph Waldo Emerson once wrote: 'A foolish consistency is the hobgoblin of little minds.' Drawing on social psychological studies of counterattitudinal behavior, do you think that most people take Emerson's argument to heart?" may be excellent indicators of student performance, but students may feel that such items are too general and grading methods too subjective for them to accurately indicate their learning. Similarly, a CT test that includes tricky, trivial questions or inadequately samples the content domain may give the impression that it, too, has low validity. Most students also have idiosyncratic personal theories about the validity of both types of tests, and may strongly believe that one type is a more valid indicator of their achievement than another (Dweck, 1999).

Even though face validity is not a true form of validity, it nonetheless influences the testing process in many ways. When students take a test with high face validity, the intent of the questions is obvious to them, and in consequence they may be more likely to interpret the questions as the instructor assumed they would (Bornstein, 1996). Perceptions of face validity are substantially influenced by performance outcomes—students who do well on a test are convinced that it is more valid than students who perform poorly—but even when many students are disappointed by their grades, the postperformance review session will be more constructive when the relationship between the test's contents and the course objectives is patently obvious (Forsyth, 1986).

Selecting the Measure

The great debate in testing circles pits the multiple-choice test against the essay test. The multiple-choice testers staunchly defend their method as most efficient and accurate, and stress the importance of reliability and validity to support their claims. The ST testers ridicule the trivia of multiple-choice tests that amount to little more than "multiple-guess tests" and claim that the essay is the supreme measure of achievement of college-level learning (Traub, 1993). Although both sides can marshal strong arguments in their favor, Haladyna (1994, 1997) found little evidence to support the rejection of CT items for achievement testing. First, the greater reliability of multiple-choice tests speaks strongly in their favor, particularly because reliability is highly correlated with validity (Meyer et al., 2001). Second, multiple-choice tests suffer from fewer validity problems, such as construct underrepresentation, construct-irrelevant difficulty, and construct-irrelevant easiness (e.g., Lukhele, Thissen, & Wainer, 1994). Third, empirical evidence has indicated that well-designed multiple-choice tests are highly correlated with test scores generated by essay tests—although the magnitude of those correlations is suppressed by the low reliability of the essay tests (e.g., Bridgeman, 1992). Last, empirical studies do not support the claim that selecting the correct answer from a list of possible answers requires fundamentally different cognitive processes than writing down the correct answer (Bennett et al., 1990; Bennett, Rock, & Wang, 1991). Haladyna (1994) concluded that "under most circumstances the multiple-choice format is more effective than the essay format for measuring knowledge" (p. 34).

MULTIPLE-CHOICE ITEMS

In nearly all respects the role of question-asker is more enjoyable than the role of question-answerer. Those who ask the questions can pick and choose which topics, issues, and concepts they will explore with the answerer, who has little time to reflect on the answer and even less power to control the kinds of questions asked. In consequence, and as Ross, Amabile, and Steinmetz (1977) confirmed when they randomly assigned participants to one of these two roles, answerers usually leave sessions feeling more "relief than pride" (p. 493), but questioners depart feeling more confident of their own knowledge of the topic.

The question-asker role does have one major drawback, however. Questioners must develop the questions, and in some cases these questions are difficult to construct—particularly when they are based on a multiple-choice format. These types of items usually have two parts: a stem and a set of choices or alternatives. The stem is usually a question or an incomplete statement; one of the alternatives is considered the correct answer, and the others function as foils. A quiz may contain as few as five items, but full-fledged tests generally contain 30 to 50.

Crummy multiple-choice items are easy to write. Take a definition from the textbook, state it as the stem of the item leaving out the term itself, and then list the term and several other terms and the question is written. Writing *effective* multiple-choice items, in contrast, takes time, effort, and the judicious application of item-writing rules. Haladyna and Downing (1989a, 1989b) identified these rules by reviewing the recommendations of 45 experts and by searching the published literature for studies that confirmed or disconfirmed the rules. They discovered that the majority of the rules have never been empirically tested, and that the experts did not always agree in their recommendations. Still, the following rules offer useful guides for professors as they develop their items. (See Haladyna, 1994, 1997, for a more comprehensive listing of the rules.)

Don't Measure Trivia

Avoid simple recall and recognition questions that people who memorize the book and lecture can answer. When the test asks students to define terms and identify which psychologist developed which theory, or checks the accuracy of their memory for examples that were used in class or in the text, students will quickly learn that they should study specific facts and details. The test developer should avoid asking too many questions about relatively minor aspects of psychology's vast corpus of theories, facts, and concepts. For example, the following question is an excellent one for a trivia contest, but its focus is too narrow for a test:

> The working title for the book, *Unobtrusive Measures* (Webb, Campbell, Schwartz, & Sechrest, 1966) was _____.
> a. *The Bullfighter's Beard*
> b. *Oddball Measures*
> c. *Other Measures*
> d. All of the above

If you tell students you want them to think, but then test them on rote memory or trivial items, they will stop thinking.

Write Items That Measure Higher Order Learning Outcomes

If the TOS requires items dealing with higher order thinking, then basic knowledge and factual items must be supplemented by conceptually challenging items like those in Table 4.2. These questions are difficult to write and require careful posttest analysis to check their validity, but including them on exams rewards students who learn the course material thoroughly and thoughtfully.

Use Multiple but Credible Alternatives

The ideal multiple-choice test offers test-takers a choice between one correct answer and several plausible, attractive, but undeniably incorrect options. When students answer the question, those who have not achieved the designated learning objective will not be able to tell the correct answer from the incorrect ones, and so their choices should be distributed relatively evenly across the foils. An unprepared student will, some small percentage of the time, choose the correct answer by chance, but on a multi-item test the influence of guessing will be negligible. Each of the offered distractors, therefore, should be chosen by some of the students who miss the question. An obviously incorrect distractor—one that is humorous, strange, or improbable—weakens the validity of the question. But distractors should be wrong, so that when students who miss the item review the test, their suspicion that the question unfairly included several correct alternatives will be disconfirmed by the hard evidence of their notes and the readings.

Effective alternatives parallel the structure, tone, and length of the correct answer. If the correct answer includes 10 words, the distractors should include about that many.

> Evidence indicates that people who see cars collide overestimate the speed the cars were traveling before they collided if they are asked the question:
> a. "How fast were the cars going when they hit each other?"
> b. "Did you hear a horn honking before the cars collided?"
> c. "How fast were the cars going when they slammed into each other?"
> d. "Can you estimate the speed at which the cars were traveling?"
> e. "Were the cars going more than 5 miles an hour?"

Good foils are also as specific as the correct answer, although in some cases a more technically phrased distractor will capture the interest of the poorly prepared. Statements that are factually correct but irrelevant to the issue posed by the item's stem also make effective foils.

TABLE 4.2
Examples of Multiple-Choice Items Associated With Each Level in Bloom's Taxonomy (Bloom et al., 1956)

Level of learning goal	Example items
Knowledge: remembering information	Which cognitive skill is included in Bloom's taxonomy of educational outcomes? a. problem solving b. comparison c. critical thinking d. performance e. analysis Which is true? a. Recently researchers have identified a nervous system located near the stomach (the enteric system). b. When a neuron fires, a small electrical spark jumps the gap between the axon and the dendrite. c. Information enters and leaves the neuron through the axon. d. Electrical activity plays no role in neural transmission process. e. Nerve cells have no nucleus.
Comprehension: understanding ideas, concepts, theories, and so on	You are reading a research report in which the author has performed a factor analysis, described in part with the phrase "varimax." This phrase tells you the analysis used: a. a principle components extraction method b. an orthogonal rotational procedure c. an oblique rotational procedure d. a principle axes extraction method Assume that research indicates that viewing violent TV is positively correlated with aggressive behavior. Given this correlation, which statement is the MOST accurate? a. Watching violent TV causes aggression. b. Increases in violent TV are associated with increases in aggression. c. Decreases in violent TV are associated with increases in aggression. d. Legislation should be passed to control TV violence. e. Aggressive individuals seek out violent TV programs.
Application: applying material in new contexts or situations	In our classroom, students noticed the buzzing sound caused by the TV monitors on 8 of 10 class days. As a psychologist I must conclude that the buzzing sound: a. is greater than the absolute threshold for sound. b. does not lead to a JND. c. has been muted by perceptual adaptation. d. is detectable at a subliminal level.

Table continues

TABLE 4.2 (*Continued*)

Level of learning goal	Example items

	The department decides that all graduating seniors must take a standardized psychology test before they can graduate. The average score on the test is 2000, and the standard deviation is 200. Assuming scores are normally distributed, your score of 2200 indicates that you:
	  a. scored better than 55% of the students, but worse than 45%.
	  b. should not graduate because you have too low a score.
	  c. are average in psychology.
	  d. outscored a substantial number of the others (approximately 84%) who took the test.
	  e. are slightly below average, by the 20% percentile mark.

Analysis: identifying elements and relationships	If you wanted to kill someone, what part of the brain should you damage?
	  a. corpus callosum
	  b. amygdala
	  c. prefrontal lobe
	  d. brain stem
	  e. femur
	  f. cerebellum
	
	Which one fits in least well with the others?
	  a. operant
	  b. unconditioned response
	  c. shaping
	  d. reinforcement

Synthesis: integrating elements	Sensory is to motor as ＿＿ is to ＿＿.
	  a. axon; dendrite
	  b. afferent; efferent
	  c. brain; spine
	  d. out; in
	
	Synthesizing the findings of Asch and Moscovici, we can conclude that group change generally results from:
	  a. strong, determined leadership
	  b. the majority influencing the minority
	  c. mutual influence between the majority and minority
	  d. the minority influencing the majority

Evaluation: gauging value, quality, worth and usefulness	The most central element in operant conditioning is the:
	  a. reflex
	  b. stimulus
	  c. response
	  d. reinforcement
	  e. UCS
	
	Which type of test format is best for measuring achievement of students in psychology classes?
	  a. essay
	  b. short-answer
	  c. multiple-choice
	  d. true–false

Traditional wisdom on the number of distractors stresses the need to have at least three decoys so that students who must guess have only a 25% chance of getting the question correct. This logic, however, underestimates the odds of an individual repeatedly guessing correctly on item after item. Sechrest, Kihlstrom, and Bootzin (1999) recommended using just three options if the fourth and fifth options are implausible, anyway.

Control Difficulty Through Judicious Choice of Content

In some cases the questioner may be tempted to increase the difficulty of the item by making it more complicated, rather than rewriting the item so that only students who have a clear understanding of the material answer it correctly. The questioner might, for example, make an item such as "Which heuristic prompts individuals to estimate probabilities by taking stock of information that is immediately accessible in their memories?" into:

> The _____ allows the individual to base rough estimates of frequencies or probabilities on cognitive information gleaned from that which is activated in working memory.
> a. confirmatory heuristic
> b. representativeness heuristic
> c. availability heuristic
> d. anchoring-adjustment heuristic
> e. distancing

This item is unnecessarily complicated, and will likely stump some students who have achieved a relatively in-depth understanding of this concept.

Don't Use Trick Questions Deliberately

A valid but difficult question is not a "trick" question. Valid questions include distractors that students who have only a superficial understanding of the material will find appealing, so they trick students only in the sense that people who do not know the material are prompted to miss the item. True trick questions, in contrast, are items that mislead students who actually know the material, with the result that students who have accomplished the level of understanding specified in the instructional objective are seduced into selecting one of the distractors. Using the cues that test-wise students rely on when taking tests, such as "If you must guess, pick the longest answer," to mislead them could turn a question into a trick question, as does deliberately spelling words incorrectly so that technically they are incorrect. Roberts (1993) identified a number of other ways questions can trick students.

Keep the Stem, Responses, and Structure Simple

The KISS principle (Keep it Simple, Stupid) applies to multiple-choice items. The item should focus on a single concept, and the options should be similar to one another in terms of structure and content. The question should not unfairly favor the superior reader or native English speaker, so wordiness, flowery language, elaborate set-ups, and verbosity in general should be minimized. Haladyna (1994, p. 66) argued that the "vocabulary should be simple enough for the weakest readers in the tested group." The following item violates this rule:

> Warr and his colleagues' model of job satisfaction argues that certain aspects of the workplace function to create feelings of job satisfaction in workers. If these aspects are present in the workplace, people will be dissatisfied, but if they are present in sufficient amounts then motivation and satisfaction will be high. If some of these elements are too strong, though, they reach toxic levels that can undermine satisfaction. What is the name for Warr's approach?
> a. Vitamin Model
> b. List Model
> c. Warr Model
> d. Commandments Model
> e. Circumplex Model

The simplicity rule also suggests that intricate, intertwined options—which are typical of advanced tests in some fields—should be avoided.

> Psychology is the scientific study of:
> a. cognition
> b. behavior
> c. mental illness
> d. adjustment
> e. trivia
> f. both a and b
> g. both b and c
> h. both d and e

This item should be rewritten to eliminate the two-choice responses and ensure that only one of the options is clearly correct.

Match Item and Instructional Complexity

Test questions should not use language, terminology, or writing styles that differ too greatly from the language and difficulty level established during class lectures, discussions, and readings. If, for example, the professor has introduced the concept of shaping very informally and stressed examples over definitions, students who understand the concept many not realize that the stem "The selective reinforcing of closer and closer approximations to the desired operant response" is completed by that term. Similarly, professors who set the level of difficulty of their lecture so that even their less well-prepared students can understand the material or who use a lower level text should not then use test items written in technically specific language or ones that require a much more thorough understanding of the material than the treatment in class suggested. For example, after discussing Pavlov's dogs and a few other examples of conditioning, the professor shouldn't then ask this question on the next test:

A CS–US pairing will be most easily established when the:
a. CS and US are presented simultaneously.
b. US precedes the CS (backward conditioning).
c. CS precedes the US and overlaps with it.
d. CS begins and ends before the US begins (trace conditioning).
e. CS begins at least 30 seconds before the US but continues until US onset.

Favor Question Over Completion Formats

Haladyna and Downing (1989b) and Statman (1988) recommended using question-type stems rather than completion-type stems. Students have been asked questions about the material throughout the class, so they spend less time deciphering the item's purpose and more time identifying the answer. With a question, the bulk of the verbal material is concentrated in the stem, so that the student knows what concept is being assessed without reading through the options. Completion items, Statman suggested, require more concentration as students iteratively review the fit between the stem and each option, so performance may diminish when students are distracted or anxious.

When _____ processing occurs information is processed rapidly, effortlessly, involuntarily, and unintentionally.
a. bottom-up
b. controlled
c. explicit
d. top-down
e. automatic

They would suggest that the stem of this previous item be rephrased into the question "What term is used to describe a cognitive system that processes information rapidly, effortlessly, involuntarily, and unintentionally?" Also, if a completion item is used, the blank should appear at the stem's end (or beginning) to reduce the amount of time the reader spends testing the fit between the stem and each option. If the tester is wedded to the question "When _____ processing occurs information is processed rapidly, effortlessly, involuntarily, and unintentionally," he or she should at least rephrase it so the blank begins or ends the phrase: "When processing is rapid, effortless, involuntary, and unintentional it is described as _____" or "_____ processing is rapid, effortless, involuntary, and unintentional."

Use Negations, All of the Above, and None of the Above Items Sparingly

Some material lends itself to negatively worded questions. Theoretical models that include a number of components, such as Erikson's theory of conflict and identity, Kohlberg's stage theory of moral development, the big five personality models, or Bloom's taxonomy of educational outcomes are ripe for such items, because students' memory of the entire set can be easily assessed by asking "Which one of the following is NOT one of . . . ." For example:

Which one is NOT one of the "big five" personality traits?
a. introversion
b. neuroticism
c. Type A/Type B
d. agreeableness (warm-cold)
e. intelligence (or openness to experience)

Most assessment writers are leery of such items, for they worry that students may overlook the question's negative frame, and pick an option that matches the model, theory, or concept. They suggest that such items be placed together in a special section of the test with a notice that the items are asking students to identify exceptions rather than confirmations. The word *not* should be accentuated, say by bold print or all capital letters.

The testing experts are also suspicious of the usefulness of "none of the above" and "all of the above" as options. The "none of the above" option, when it is the correct answer, is selected by students who know that all the other options are incorrect *and* by clueless students who are totally baffled by all of the issues and concepts noted in the distractors. Nitko (2001) recommended that if "none of the above" is the correct answer on a test item, then it should also be used as the incorrect option in a relatively easy question early in the test and the distractors should include concepts even the least prepared students will recognize.

"All of the above" options can also introduce error into the measurement process if students answer the question by picking an option before reading the "all of the above" option that occurs as choice d or e.

The correlation between two variables will be small when:
a. a third, unmeasured variable is suppressing the relationship between the two variables.
b. the variables are related in a nonlinear fashion.

    c. the range of one or both variables is restricted.

    d. the two variables are unrelated to one another.

    e. all of the above.

Presented with a question such as this, students may read option a, recognize that it is correct, fill in the circle on their answer sheet, and move on to the next question without noticing that all the other options are correct, too. To prevent this possibility, (a) the test instructions should emphasize the importance of reading the entire question and alternatives, (b) these items can all be collected into a specific section, (c) the phrase *all of the above* can be emphasized, or (d) the "all of the above" alternative can be shifted to the first choice by phrasing it as "all of the following are true." "All of the above" items in which this option is the correct one can also be transformed into a multiple true–false format as described later in this section (Haladyna, 1994). In any case, if the "all of the above" option is used, the test must include items in which it is the correct answer and items in which it is the incorrect answer.

Convert True–False Items

Some experts recommend converting true–false items into multiple-choice items.

Multiple True–False Formats

A multiple true–false item asks a series of true–false questions about a specific topic (Frisbie, 1992). For example:

> For items 1 to 5, mark on your answer sheet A if true or B if false.
> When will the correlation between two variables be small or zero?
> 1. When the variables are related in a linear fashion.
> 2. When a third, unmeasured variable is suppressing the relationship between the 2 variables.
> 3. When the range of one or both variables is restricted.
> 4. When the two variables are not related to one another.
> 5. When no causal relationship exists between the two variables.

The format does not protect against guessing, but more items can be asked because the questions can be answered quickly. Increasing the length of the test should reduce the impact of guessing on performance.

Double True–False Format

An innovative method of testing with true–false items involves presenting two statements and asking respondents to indicate if one or both are true. For example:

Consider these two statements:
X. Some people don't dream.
Y. Dreaming is related to memory processes.
a. both are true
b. both are false
c. X is true, Y is false
d. X is false, Y is true

Bundled True–False Format

True–false questions can also be asked by bundling together a group of true statements and a single false one, or a group of false statements and one true one. For example:

Which is true?
a. Human infants cannot see until they are 1 to 2 weeks old.
b. Human infants, unlike the offspring of other species, are born without any innate reflexes.
c. During the first year of life the number of neurons in a human infant's brain doubles.
d. The placenta protects the infant from such harmful substances as alcohol or cocaine.
e. Babies form an emotional bond with their caregivers during the first year of life.

Minimize Distractions

A funny distractor added to more serious options or a question with a touch of humor can relieve the tension associated with exams, but humor can lead to some not-so-funny outcomes. When the small group of students who move through multiple-choice tests so rapidly that you wonder if they are even reading the questions reach the humorous questions, their guffaws disturb those moving along at a more subdued rate. Some students, too, take umbrage over the items, for they are deadly serious about their performance and expect the professor to be just as businesslike (Renner & Renner, 1999). Rosenfeld and Anderson (1985) discovered that men performed more poorly on tests with humorous alternatives, whereas women excelled on such tests. A cautious tester avoids funny questions, as well as other types of distracting materials. Outlandish or famous names for people or places in examples, for example, should be avoided:

When Mr. Mxyspitalik's son Obiwancanobe makes up his bed, Mr. M.
pays him $1. Mr. M. is using:
a. punishment
b. positive reinforcement
c. negative reinforcement
d. classical conditioning

Instead, just ask "A father who gives his son $1 when the son makes his bed is using _____."

Also minimize distractions during the test process, including ones that are generated by the test itself. When the test mislabels the options (including, for example, two option bs), misspells key terms (e.g., "An interactionist stance on the nuture/nature debate," or "Bandana's research dealing with social learning theory"), uses an incorrect word that escapes the detection of the spell-checker (e.g., "Stress can be reduced through mediation" versus "Stress can be reduced through meditation"), or bad grammar ("When the student fails they tend to focus on external causes"), or grammatically clumsy matches between the stems and the options, students must refocus their attention on the content of the question, and some cannot tolerate the increased cognitive load.

Break Any Rule You Want

Haladyna (1997) offered one final rule for test-writers to consider and possibly heed: His Rule 99 "states that since most of these rules do not have the common ground of expert agreement and research, *break any rule you want*" (p. 92). Rule 99 is a reminder that some perfectly good test questions do not adhere to the general rules-of-thumb for test-question writing. These rules, then, are actually general guidelines rather than inviolate principles, and in some cases a question-writer must break them to create the most effective question for measuring student learning.

A Note on Test Banks

Rather than writing their own questions, many professors rely on the publishers of textbooks to provide a test bank filled with items they can swap into their own tests. Some publishers will even generate a test for a professor, who then only needs to duplicate enough copies for their classes. Such test banks can help, for they take away much of the pain of preparing items and can save enormous amounts of time. But the banks also have shortcomings that must be considered:

- *Factual and trivial focus:* Because multiple-choice questions that measure lower level learning, such as the memorization of facts and basic comprehension, are easier to write than conceptually challenging items, such items tend to make up the bulk of the items in the bank. Also, because of the large number of items needed, in many cases authors of the banks generate questions about relatively trivial material in the chapter. Faced with the task of generating hundreds of items, the writer may end up asking questions about captions, citations, footnotes, and specific examples.

- *Content validity:* Using a bank exclusively will violate most professors' TOS. Test banks typically do not evenly sample the contents of the text, because definitions and facts are oversampled and complex relational material is undersampled. The bank does not, of course, include items pertaining to material that was covered only in class, so students who attend class regularly will notice that discrepancy between course content and test content.

- *Pretesting:* In most cases the items have not been pretested. Test bank authors must sometimes generate the items during the relatively short space of time between the preparation of the manuscript in final form and its publication, so they rarely have the time or the students they need to check the items. They are untried until you test them on your students.

- *Difficulty and discriminability:* Test bank items tend to be too easy. When Scialfa, Legare, Wenger, and Dingley (2001) examined the psychometric performance of more than 4,000 items from test banks written for introductory psychology tests, they discovered that approximately 70% of the students passed each item. Nor did the items discriminate well. When they subtracted the proportion of high-scoring students who got the question correct from the proportion of low-scoring students who got the question correct, the average for this index was only .36. They concluded that 20% of the items are too flawed to use on a test. Some items can, however, be salvaged by revising them.

- *Poor construction:* Some banks include finely crafted items composed by authors with years of experience in teaching and testing, but others are compiled by inexperienced authors who violate many of the rules of good item preparation. The first test bank I ever wrote was rife with flaws, for I developed it when I was a first-year graduate student who had never even written a test before.

- *Random sampling:* Some test banks permit testers to sample items randomly from the bank. Such tests are more likely to be low in content validity unless the sampling considers the requirements of the TOS. Such methods also increase the likelihood that the answer for one item is "given away" by the stem of some other question because most banks contain multiple items for each concept.

- *Leakage of items:* Problems arise when different instructors have different procedures about releasing test bank items to their students after the test is given. A professor who reviews each item after its use and recycles the good ones each term will likely not want students to keep copies of the items because such copies are likely to be passed to incoming students. But if other professors in the department who use the same text have their graduate teaching assistants just download 50 items from the publisher-supplied test bank for each examination, they will likely not worry about the dispersion of previously used items in the testing population.

In sum, test banks should be used cautiously, for they do not free instructors from their professional and ethical obligation to administer psychometrically sound tests to their students. Ethics of assessment do not include a special rule for professors that says "you should use appropriate measures except when you can blame crummy items on the text publisher or item-bank author." If the test bank is not adequate, then it should not be used to create a test.

ESSAY TESTS

Like fall afternoon football games and fraternity parties, the essay test is a classic element of the traditional college experience. Students dread, but expect to take, essay tests at various points during their academic careers, and college book stores still sell those quaint collections of pages stapled at the seam called "blue books," although they aren't books and in many cases they aren't blue.

Types of Essay Tests

Essay tests come in two basic varieties: extended response (ER) essays and restricted response (RR) essays. These two categories, however, are fuzzy sets rather than discrete classes because they are based on variations in essays along such continua as breadth, directiveness, writing demands, and higher order cognitive demand. The ER asks students a question that is sufficiently general that they must interpret the meaning of the question, organize their thoughts on the matter, and then present those thoughts in appropriate detail. ERs provide few hints about the direction the essay should take, and they also require a command of the language as well as the content. The RR is narrower, in that it focuses on a specific instructional objective and so requires a more specific answer. The question gives students more directions about the type of information they should provide or skill they should demonstrate, and so the need to plan, organize, and deftly execute the writing is reduced.

Consider, for example, a professor who uses an essay test to measure students' knowledge of the psychological and physiological mechanisms that govern food intake (e.g., Woods, Schwartz, Baskin, & Seeley, 2000). If she uses an ER type item, she may simply ask, "Discuss the psychological, neurological, and hormonal factors that combine to regulate food intake." Or, if she trusts her students to understand the need to demonstrate their knowledge despite the vagueness of the question asked, she might just ask "Why do people eat?" She may, however, wish to restrict the range of responses by revising the question to ask:

> Humans need to take in sufficient quantities of food to offset the energy spent during daily activities.
> a. Describe the process of energy homeostasis as it would occur during a typical 24-hour period.
> b. What role does the liver play in this process?
> c. Critique the glucose monitoring model of hunger and contrast it with an explanation that stresses the importance of environmental stimuli.
> d. Discuss the impact of adipose mass on energy homeostasis, and extend your analysis to outline a weight-regulation program that is consistent with studies of adipose-signaling processes.

Or consider a methods class instructor who wishes to examine his students' understanding of experimental design, and so asks this ER item: "Design and describe a study that tests the hypothesis that 'Failure leads to a loss of self-esteem, unless the task being attempted is a very difficult one.'" If, however, he wishes to structure the task, he might instead ask:

> Consider this study: I decide to investigate the relationship between performance, test difficulty, and self-esteem. So, I bring in 48 men and women to the lab and have them work on a bogus task. After the task, I tell 12 that they succeeded and that the test was difficult; 12 that they succeeded and that the test was easy; 12 that they failed and that the test was difficult; 12 that they failed and that the test was easy. I then measure their self-esteem on a scale from 1 to 10 where 1 means "I am not worthy" and 10 means "I am very, very pleased with who I am."
> a. Explain what type of study this is and justify your answer.
> b. Identify the key variables under study, and label them as dependent, independent, etc.
> c. Are there any flaws with the study?
> d. What do you think the results will be? Please graph them.

Both types of questions in these examples demand higher order thinking, but the ER requires more original and critical thinking than the RR. The RR, however, clarifies the topics that must be covered, decreases the amount of time students will need to generate an answer (and thereby frees up time that can be used for answering additional test questions), and simplifies the grading of the responses. Indeed, the instructors may wish to tell students how many points each component of the RR item is worth in determining the overall grade.

Suggestions for Writing Essay Tests

As with multiple-choice items, superficial essay questions are easy to write. Ask students to generate a list, such as "What are Freud's psychosexual stages of development?" Or ask a very general question, such as "Summarize and identify weaknesses in Watson and Clark's (1992) tripartite model of anxiety and depression." Writing *effective* essay items, in contrast, takes time and effort, although there are fewer items than on a CT test.

Use Essays to Measure Higher Order Outcomes

Essays are ideal tools for measuring higher order learning outcomes, so given the amount of time they take to grade, they should be used for that purpose. They should not, therefore, ask students to recall information or define terms but instead to think critically about issues, apply psychology to specific issues, identify possible solutions to problems, express their ideas in their own words, and explore their own position on controversial issues. When words such as *analyze, apply, appraise, compare and contrast, create, critique, demonstrate, develop, discuss, formulate, gauge, evaluate, estimate, integrate, judge, rate, relate, review,* and *use* appear in the item, then their focus is likely more appropriate than when such words as *define, describe, identify, list, recall,* or *repeat* are used.

Focus the Questions on Objectives

Comedian Bill Cosby reports that when he was asked "Why is there air?" on an earth science test, he answered "To blow up basketballs." Then there is the student who, when asked the question "Why?" on his philosophy test answered only "Why not?" And the student who, when asked by his physics professor "How would you discover the height of a tall apartment building using a barometer?" answered "I would find the building superintendent and tell him 'I'll give you this swell barometer if you will tell me the exact height of the building.'" Good answers, yes, but ones that failed to demonstrate students' achievement of the course objectives.

The possibility of receiving such answers can be minimized by wording items carefully so that students cannot satisfy them with any odd consortium of ideas they muster on the fly. Items should pertain to the course's instructional objectives, or at least students must know that their answers should pertain to those objectives. Assessment experts therefore recommend that if wide-open, unrestricted essay questions are asked, the instructions on the test should remind students that to receive credit, their answers must demonstrate an understanding of the course material. Such instructions protect against students who answer an item such as "Evaluate dual-process models of attitude change" by writing "I don't like them." Vague, ill-defined essay questions can also be honed by providing a stimulus for students to react to in their answers. Rather than ask "What are the strengths and weaknesses of the Boulder model of therapist training?" briefly describe a fictitious graduate program and ask students to critique its adequacy in terms of the Boulder model. Rather than ask "What types of learning, memory, and behavioral problems result from injury to the brain?" describe a series of sensory-motor impairments caused by physical injury and ask students to identify the possible brain structures that are responsible for each one. Rather than have students write a results section, give them a draft of one and ask them to revise it.

Clarify Procedures and Standards

Some students perform poorly on essay tests, not from a lack of knowledge of the issues addressed by the question, but from a lack of knowledge about essays themselves. So rather than assume that everyone has been trained by some previous professor in the elements of writing an essay, review with your students the basic elements of a good essay, including (Hairston, Ruszkiewicz, & Friend, 1999, p. 160):

- A clear thesis statement in the first paragraph, or better yet, in the very first sentence. Don't worry about crafting a dramatic introduction—there isn't time.
- Logical organization with a single key idea developed in each paragraph and with clear transitions between points.
- Adequate support and evidence for each point, drawn from course readings and lectures.
- Your own views or analysis when the question asks for them. Remember, though, to justify your ideas with evidence and support.
- A conclusion that ties together main points and summarizes their importance, even if you have time for only a sentence or two.
- Clear prose free of major grammatical and mechanical errors.

Students should also be informed about time and page limits and the procedures that you plan to use in grading their papers.

Require Students to Answer the Same Questions

Many instructors give students the option of selecting which items they will answer on the essay test. They may, for example, ask four ER items but let students select which two they will answer during the 50-minute testing period. Another instructor may ask 12 RR items and let students select which 10 they will answer. A choice of questions protects students from the grade-fatal consequences that occur when they cannot answer, even partially, an essay question that comprises 10% to 50% of their grade. A choice among items functions as a kind of mini-portfolio, in which students can control the work that they present for grading. The method may also reduce their pretest anxiety by limiting the chance that a topic overlooked during their preparation will doom them to failure. Psychometrically speaking, however, this practice limits the validity of the assessment. The grades are based on different, nonparallel forms, so score-based comparisons can no longer be drawn between students (Wang, Wainer, & Thissen, 1995). The practice also undermines the content validity of the measure. If the test adequately samples the domain of content identified in the instructional objectives, then students should be able to answer all of the items. Essay tests themselves tend to be lower in content validity, and providing options lowers that validity further. Students who realize that they have a choice may also be less thorough in their preparation, choosing to omit an entire topic from review because they know they can side-step it on the assessment. The only exception to the general recommendation against letting students make choices is when the essay test has a large writing-skill component. In such cases, when the students' ability to express themselves eloquently will have a large impact on their grade, then perhaps they should be able to choose a topic that excites their creative muse.

Many professors deal with the problem of gaps in students' preparation causing irreparable harm to their scores by giving students a set of possible essay questions in advance of the test day (B. G. Davis, 1993). The actual test will contain some, but not all, of the questions, and students will not be able to use any previously prepared materials during the test. Such methods may encourage more thorough preparation and the formation of collaborative learning cells.

Take-Home and Open-Book Essays

When time is limited and the questions asked are numerous and complex, the essay test that is supposed to be a power test becomes a speed test. Converting the exercise into a take-home test addresses this problem but raises other difficulties. On the one hand, take-home essays may not only test student achievement but also stimulate learning. The process of putting into words answers to complex questions often improves comprehension, and this process will be far more profound when it takes place at a slower pace as students work on the items using text, lecture, and library materials. Indeed, Onifade, Nabangi, and Trigg (1998) reported that students who had previously taken a series of take-home quizzes got higher scores on an in-class exam than did students who took the same series of quizzes in class. Take-home tests may also have more external validity, in that such testing conditions more closely approximate the actual work conditions that students will confront in their careers. As Walvoord (1982) pointed out, essays written in class are at best first drafts only. Students also report experiencing less anxiety about their tests when they know that they can take them home (e.g., Weber, McBee, & Krebs, 1983).

Take-home tests have limitations, however. Marsh (1984) found that his students did not study as much for take-home tests as they did for in-class examinations, and this lack of preparation may undo any gains in learning that the take-home format stimulates. Take-home test scores may also be distorted by cheating. Onifade and his colleagues, for example, found that students tend to collaborate with other students on their take-home essays even when the instructions for the test explicitly forbid such group efforts (Onifade, Nabangi, Reynolds, & Allen, 2000).

Allowing students to use the text and other course materials during the exam—the so-called open-book test—also creates benefits and costs. An open-book examination confirms the test's emphasis on higher order learning skills and comprehension by giving unrestricted access to the specific facts of the course. However, when students know that they can consult their materials, they may not study as diligently. Even more problematic, they may not use their materials appropriately during the test. As Boniface (1985) discovered, during open-book tests students who made more extensive use of materials generally got lower grades, and these students were the same ones who had lower scores in previous assessments. B. G. Davis (1993) related the strategy of allowing students to prepare limited amounts of material to use during the test, say by restricting them to an index card or a single page of notes.

A Note on Time

Even when professors are committed to giving essay exams, their classes may be so large that they cannot act on their assessment principles. The feasibility of giving an essay exam depends on factors such as the grading skills and experience of the professor, the nature of the questions (extended or restricted response formats), and the type of grading rubrics used. In classes with 30 or more students, however, the time needed to grade an ST test becomes too great, particularly when papers must be graded in a fixed period of time. In small class of 10 or fewer, time favors the ST test, because the CT test takes longer to prepare. But once a class becomes too large (more than 50), professors should explore other ways of assessing students' ability to express themselves (e.g., writing assignments, projects).

Scoring Essay Tests

Grading essay tests is similar to conducting a content analysis that will assign numeric identifiers to qualitative data. Just as coding procedures reduce the extent to which subjective impressions of the data determine that identification process, scoring rubrics reduce the impact of rater biases on the grades assigned to the essay. One general type of rubric, *analytic scoring*, specifies the elements that the answer must contain in order to receive maximum credit. These elements are derived from the points iden-

TABLE 4.3
Example of an Analytic Scoring Rubric for a Restricted Essay Item
Dealing With Hunger and Food Intake

Item	Points	Elements of successful answer
1. Describe the process of energy homeostasis as it would occur during a typical 24-hour period.	2	Defines the concept of homeostasis as it applies to fluctuations in energy levels from high to low in relationship to activity, ambient temperature Notes that stored food reserves provide energy for processes, with intake of food monitored and regulated by neural, hormonal, and biological mechanisms
2. What role does the liver play in this process?	2	Summarizes briefly Laghans's (1996) work that suggests that when the liver detects too low a level of useable, energy-producing fat, it signals the decline to the brain via the vagus nerves
3. Critique the glucose-monitoring model of hunger and contrast it with an explanation that stresses the importance of environmental stimuli.	4	Describes the concept of glucose monitoring Notes weakness of the model (e.g., too slow to adjust, humans eat at fixed times independent of blood glucose levels) Summarizes evidence supporting the concept of cue-dependent food consumption
4. Discuss the impact of adipose mass on energy homeostasis, and extend your analysis to outline a weight-regulation program that is consistent with studies of adipose-signaling processes.	6	Discusses the notion of a set-point and the implications of adiposity levels over time Describes a diet program that includes changes in activity level, reconditioning of responses to food-related cues, and administration of drugs that control food intake processes

tified in the item, in the case of a restricted response item, or from the points made in a model answer written by the grader or culled from the pool of essays generated by the class. Table 4.3 illustrates an analytic scoring approach for the question about energy homeostasis.

Rather than break the answer down into component parts or rate the essay on dimensions, a *holistic scoring* rubric assumes that the whole of the essay is greater than the sum of its parts. The scorer uses this procedure to assign the essay to one of a series of graded categories that range from low to high in quality. The number of categories generally corresponds to your university's grading system, such as 4 (A), 3 (B), 2 (C), 1 (D), and 0 (F), or just pass/fail in certain situations, and ideally the attributes of the typical paper in each category are described in a scoring key like that shown in Table 4.4.

TABLE 4.4
Example of a Holistic Analytic Scoring Rubric for a Restricted Essay Item Dealing With Hunger and Food Intake

Characteristics	Grade
Elaborates extensively in answering all the elements of item. Demonstrates clear and consistent use of the language, offers examples when relevant, or uses citations appropriately to support theoretical points with empirical evidence. The essay is unified and coherent, and conveys information in a precise, lively, or original way. The mechanics, spelling, and grammar are superior.	4
Develops ideas efficiently, answering at least generally all the elements of the item clearly and concisely. The answers indicate that the material is clearly understood, and in several cases additional examples or material are used to support arguments. Errors in understanding are minimal, although in some cases details and implications are not presented. The writing is above average in quality, showing some energy or originality, and mechanics are not problematic.	3
Answers the basic question asked but does so without providing extra detail, depth, or analysis. The basic issues appear to be understood, but the answer rarely takes material beyond the descriptive level or relies heavily on the wording used in the text, readings, notes, or item itself. The organization is clear enough to follow without difficulty, although there are a number of errors in mechanics, spelling, and so forth.	2
Offers some material relevant to the item, but the content is sparse and the answer itself is very short. The answers are vague or incomplete, and errors suggest that portions of the content are not clearly understood. Some key points are omitted, and much of the analysis deals only with generalities. The response is not well organized, with little flow from one idea to the next. No citations are given to support the points made, and very rarely is evidence used to buttress a theoretical point. The mechanics are poor in places.	1
Fails to indicate that the author understands the issues. Very little information is presented, the answer is too short, and errors in interpretation outnumber correct interpretations. The writing is difficult to follow and contains severe composition errors.	0

Holistic scoring takes less time, in most cases, than analytic scoring, particularly when essays are lengthy and the item is an unrestricted one. Such items are difficult to score using analytic methods because students' responses may be so diverse that required elements cannot be specified in advance. Analytic scoring, which narrows the criteria to be used, is likely to be more reliable and valid, particularly because inconsistencies in the application of standards across students can be quickly detected and corrected.

No matter what type of scoring system is used, other standard practices, most of which are designed to increase validity by minimizing scorer biases, should be used during the grading process. They include

- preparing a scoring rubric (like those shown in Tables 4.3 and 4.4) or a model solution,
- reading over a sample of the answers before beginning grading,
- masking the students' identities,
- grading only one item at a time (grade all Item 1s, then all 2s, and so on),
- avoiding contaminating evaluations of subsequent questions by masking scores during the grading process (e.g., record scores on a separate sheet of paper),
- if at all possible, doing all grading (of any one item) at a single sitting,
- re-grading a sample of the papers as needed to prevent rater drift,
- varying the order of the grading by shuffling papers before next scoring, and
- not letting style and writing quality overly influence the grading process.

Ideally, too, students should be provided with some kind of feedback—in addition to a grade or the analytic-rubric's points—about the quality of their work.

TEST ANALYSIS

Loevinger (1998, p. 347) described her years of work devising a test of ego development as a "life sentence," for she created, administered, tested, and revised the instrument over and over again in what seemed to be an unending iterative process with no parole in sight. Similarly, teaching psychologists will spend their entire academic careers constructing, analyzing, and revising their tests. Because each new class reveals fresh insights into psychological processes, the tests must be adapted to include new items pertaining to that material.

General Review

In the best of all possible worlds, tests and final exams are written weeks before they are to be given, with ample time for the departmental staff to desktop publish them and duplicate the number of copies needed. In reality, of course, deadlines creep up and tests are generated at the last minute, leaving little time to catch errors, correct formats, or even carry out a thoughtful review the questions. But professors who are giving a test in a new area, with items they have never used before, should leave time to carefully review the test before it is duplicated and administered. They should also seek out colleagues' comments, if time allows. A fresh set of eyes often identifies errors and limitations that escaped the developer's review, and seasoned colleagues can use prior experiences in teaching the course to catch problems in the test. But even this process may need to be structured to increase its usefulness. Because colleagues are sometimes reluctant to comment negatively, or the request gets lost in the mountain of other to-be-done tasks, ask them specific questions about the exam such as:

- Given your experience with the class and the unit the test covers, does the test cover the content adequately?
- Is the balance between fact questions and higher order, conceptual questions about right?
- Would you flag the five most problematic items on the test (ones that seem too picky, poorly worded, trick questions, etc.) and annotate them as needed?
- Is the test too easy or too difficult? Are any specific items too difficult to include? Were you uncertain of the answer to any of the items?
- Will students have enough time to complete the test?
- Does the test match up well with the usual types of assessment methods used in the department?
- Does the test seem to be a fair one?
- Will any phrases or wordings irritate or be more difficult for individuals from various ethnic, gender, and racial groups?
- Would you please mark any typos or errors that I overlooked in my own proofreading?
- Would you please make editorial suggestions or reword as needed?

Analysis of Choice-Type (CT) Tests

The accurate evaluation of a test's reliability and validity requires data, and so test-developers must conduct their work postmortem (as it were). And because even the most skilled question-writers sometimes generate items that fail to perform as they are designed, test analysis is required whenever new items are used or old items are administered to populations of students unlike those tested in the past. Such an analysis generally begins with a review of descriptive statistics and reliability before turning to the more conceptually intriguing question of validity and item discrimination.

Descriptive Statistics

Descriptive statistics provide an overall indication of how well students performed on the test and serve as indicators of any unrecognized instructional problems. Consider, as an example, a test covering 5 basic topics with 8–12 items written per topic and each item worth 2 points (so a score can range from 0 to 100). When administered to 275 students, the mean score on the test was 68.47 and the mode and median were both 68. The standard deviation was 14.84, and scores ranged from 36 to 100. The convergence of the mean, mode, and the median at 68 suggest that the scores are normally distributed, but the kurtosis (deviation from standard normal distribution) of −.82 indicates a slight flattening of the distribution. Inspection of the frequencies (which are presented in chapter 5's Table 5.1) also reveals a negative skew (−.12) caused by the relatively larger number of low scores.

Reliability

Few students would appreciate taking the same test twice so that test–retest reliability can be calculated, so most estimates of reliability use internal consistency as an indicator of stability. A split-half procedure, for example, divides the test in half (usually combining odd- and even-numbered items rather than the first half and the second half) and then correlates the two halves. This index underestimates reliability because reliability is positively associated with length, so a correction factor (Spearman-Brown) is often applied to correct this estimate. The Kuder-Richardson formula and Cronbach's alpha offer other ways to calculate reliability. The Cronbach alpha coefficient for the sample test was .83, which is considered adequate although not that impressive given the large number of items on the test and the range of students' scores.

Item Analysis

The heart of a test evaluation is the analysis of each question's performance as an indicator of student achievement. The developer crafted the items to discriminate between students who have achieved an important instructional objective and those who did not, but items do not always reach this standard. Some are so easy that incapable students answer them correctly. Some are so hard that not even the students who have mastered the objective answer them correctly. And some items are neither too hard nor too easy, yet they do not discriminate between the incapable and the capable. Many of the students who have mastered the material get them wrong, and many of the students who have not prepared adequately answer them correctly.

Various indexes of item difficulty, or p, exist, but the most frequently used indicator is the proportion of students who answered the question correctly. A p of .50 means that half of the class got the item correct. A p of 1.0 indicates everyone answered the question correctly, and question with a p of 0.0 was never answered correctly. Psychometrically speaking, the ideal test question has a difficulty of .50, although as Sechrest et al. (1999) noted, such a test may be too demoralizing for students. They recommend questioning any item with p above .80 or below .20, and feel that the average of p should be about .70. Such a test would yield an average score of about 70% correct.

Many different indexes of discrimination have also been developed, but most use the relationship between the individual item and the total score. These procedures assume that the total score, although possibly distorted by the inclusion of invalid items, is a reasonably accurate indicator of overall performance. Each individual item should correlate significantly with this overall score, with Sechrest et al. (1999) suggesting the liberal standard of .20. This information can also be obtained by applying a variation of the known-groups scale validation procedure to the data. Students are first separated into three or more groups on the basis of their score: for example, the top 25% of the scorers, the middle 50% of the scorers, and the lower 25%. Their performance on the specific item in question is then reviewed to determine if the proportion of high scorers who answered the question is greater than the proportion of low scorers who answered it correctly.

Table 4.5 presents this information for the second item listed in Table 4.2 asking about overall understanding of neural information transmission ("Which is true? a. Recently researchers have identified a nervous system located near the stomach [the enteric system] ...."). Inspection of the right-most column reveals the desired decline in correct answering moving from the top-scoring students (89%) to the middle range students (46%) to the lowest scoring students (13%). The table also provides the data needed to calculate the item discrimination index, or D-score, by subtracting the proportion of high-scoring students who answered correctly from the proportion of low-scoring students who answered correctly. Hence, scores of 1.0 indicate maximum discrimination, of 0.0 indicate no discrim-

TABLE 4.5
Item Statistics for Second Item Listed in Table 4.2
(the correct answer is a)

Level of overall performance	Number of students at each level who selected this alternative					Proportion correctly answering item
	A	B	C	D	E	
High (top quartile)	34	1	3	0	0	.89
Middle (middle 2 quartiles)	27	15	14	1	2	.46
Low (lowest quartile)	5	19	13	0	2	.13
Totals	66	35	30	1	4	.48

ination, and −1.0 suggests the item has been coded incorrectly, because every high scorer missed it and every low scorer got it right. The D-score for this item is .76.

Table 4.6 presents the item-analysis data for the following three items:

Item 1. Which one does not fit with the others?
a. Peripheral nervous system
b. Central nervous system
c. Enteric system
d. Endocrine system

Item 2. Which is true?
a. Smell is the only sensory system that is not routed through the thalamus before it projects to the cortex.
b. The sense of taste depends on four basic tastes: sweet, spicy, spoiled, and slimy.
c. Taste preferences are genetically determined, and so are constant across the world's cultures.
d. Sound perception is made possible by rods and cones located in the cochlea.
e. All of these statements are true.

Item 3. Don studies the impact of music on behavior. He exposes one group of 12-year-olds to Dave Mathews' music. He exposes a second group of 12-year-olds to Britney Spears's music. He then measures their musical ability when they are 14. Don is conducting _____ research.
a. correlational
b. biological
c. survey
d. experimental
e. parapsychological

Items 1 and 2 demonstrate the relationship between the difficulty of the item and its power to discriminate among students. Item 1 is a difficult one, with a p of .34. It discriminates well among students, overall, but its

TABLE 4.6
Item Statistics for Three Items That Vary in Difficulty and Discrimination

Level of overall performance	Number of students at each level who selected this alternative					Proportion correctly answering item
	A	B	C	D	E	
Item 1						
High (top quartile)	1	0	10	27	0	.71
Middle (middle 2 quartiles)	6	5	33	15	0	.25
Low (lowest quartile)	2	1	31	5	1	.13
Totals	9	6	74	47	1	.34
Item 2						
High (top quartile)	37	0	0	1	0	.97
Middle (middle 2 quartiles)	45	1	4	8	1	.76
Low (lowest quartile)	20	1	2	13	4	.50
Totals	102	2	6	22	5	.74
Item 3						
High (top quartile)	14	0	0	24	0	.63
Middle (middle 2 quartiles)	23	0	0	34	2	.58
Low (lowest quartile)	15	2	0	17	6	.43
Totals	52	2	0	75	8	.55

D-score is lowered by the high proportion of high-scoring students who missed it. Note, too, that option b was chosen rarely, and that one student in the class mistakenly coded e, even though no option e was offered. This item could be improved by editing it, but the large proportion of errors among high-performing students suggests that an instructional intervention is needed: more time thoroughly discussing the nature and functioning of the enteric nervous system.

Conversely, the D-score for Item 2 is lowered by the ease of the item ($p = .74$). Virtually all the high scorers answered the question correctly, and half of the low scorers did so as well. This item could be improved by checking the distractors for flaws in content and design. Distractor b ("The sense of taste depends on four basic tastes: sweet, spicy, spoiled, and slimy"), for example, was not plausible. A revised version should replace *slimy* with a clearly incorrect, but believable, alternative (e.g., tangy, fruity, juicy).

Note, however, that a rarely chosen alternative is not necessarily a bad alternative. In some cases distractors may be checks of very basic instructional objectives, so when students avoid them they are demonstrating mastery of these objectives. In the case of distractor c in Item 2, for example, in-class and text discussion of norms about foods, coupled with students' overall awareness of cultural variations, were sufficient to teach them that the statement, "Taste preferences are genetically determined, and so constant across the world's cultures," is not true. If the testers' goal is to maximally discriminate among students, then this distractor should be revised, but if the testers' goal is to measure students' achievement of course learning objectives, then this distractor should be retained. The item statistics also confirm the usefulness of distractor d. Although this distractor seems to be too implausible—almost a throwaway option to pad out the question—a substantial number of low-scoring students thought that the rods and cones, which are needed for vision, are located in the cochlea, which is the organ responsible for detecting sound.

The statistics for the third item indicate that this item was appropriately difficult, but it only weakly discriminated among students. The item contains irrelevant information about the specific types of music played in each condition, which could have distracted some of the high-performing students. Posttest discussion of the item with students also revealed that they were confused by the absence of information about random assignment of subjects to conditions, which they considered (with good reason) to be a necessary condition for an experiment. The item should be reworded to state that, "Don, at random, exposed some 12-year-olds to one type of music . . . " to make it clear that the study was an experiment and minimize distractions. The item also needs better options because more than 90% of the choices were concentrated on only two of the alternatives.

Dropping Items

In some cases, item analysis will indicate that an item performed so poorly that it should not be used in the assessment. Items with extremely low p-scores, for example—ones that 90% of the class missed, for example —are sometimes, but not always, candidates for deletion. If the instructor feels that the item measures a key (although obviously very challenging) aspect of the class and the question suffers from no major design flaws, then retaining the item is completely appropriate. But if inspection of the item's content suggests that the question was badly worded, focused on a trivial aspect of the course, or was a trick question, then a question missed by nearly the entire class should be dropped. Questions with suspicious D-scores should also be considered as candidates for deletion. A D-score near 0.0 or, even worse, a negative D-score (indicating that more of the low-scoring students answered it correctly than did the high-scoring students), should trigger a careful inspection of the item's design and its possible elimination.

Dropping items, even when done with care, creates a number of procedural problems. If the question listed two alternatives that are arguably correct, then the tests should be rescored to give credit to those students who selected either option. But skipping a question altogether (for example, basing grades on only 48 of the 50 questions on the test) is often viewed, with some justification, as unfair by the students who managed to answer the faulty items correctly. A less preferable alternative involves simply adding the points the invalid items contributed to total scores to all students' tests, in effect changing the invalid items into bonus items. These procedures should be carried out before the tests are returned to students to reduce confusions.

These procedures can also be avoided (in all but the most extreme cases) by including several extra items on each examination. Just as some standardized tests include a few uncounted items that are examined for possible inclusion on future administrations, a class-based test can include extra items so that faulty items can be deleted without distorting the numerical requirements of the grading system.

Criterion Validity

Students' grades are typically based on several tests, rather than just one, as well as other types of classroom-based assessments: lab work, written assignments, attendance, participation in discussion, term papers, and so on. When the intercorrelations among these various indices of achievement are examined, patterns of high and low correlations provide evidence of concurrent and discriminant validity. For example, the correlations between scores on the test examined here (see Table 4.5) and two other examinations administered in the class were .70 and .73. The test was not as highly correlated with students' scores in their labs $r = .28$. These grades were based on attendance, quizzes, and four response-restricted writing assignments.

Power and Data Limitations

Just as the power of any research study depends on the number of individuals who participated, the usefulness of detailed statistical information about a test depends on the number of students who took it and the number of items on the test. A class with 100 or more students will yield useful psychometric information, but it is unlikely that a class of 10 will. Item analysis procedures are correlational techniques, so they must be interpreted cautiously when the sample size is low (fewer than 50). Most item analyses also assume that the test is a reliable one, and this assumption is not always born out by the data. The classroom exam, even though it examines multiple topics, is assumed to be unidimensional—a single, unified scale rather than a collection of theoretically and empirically distinct subscales. If the reliability is low, this assumption is not justified, so the total scale score should not be used to create the known groups (high-performing and low-performing students) for the item analysis. Preliminary work may be needed to identify a subset of reliable and valid items, which can then be used to create the aggregates needed for the subsequent item analysis.

Analysis of Supply-Type (ST) Tests

A detailed statistical analysis of an ST test is usually not appropriate. As previously noted, statistical exploration requires an adequate number of students and an adequate number of items, but essay tests generally contain few items and they are usually not given in large classes. In consequence, ST tests require a more qualitative rather than quantitative approach.

Rater Reliability

Essay tests cannot be dropped off at the campus testing center for machine scoring (yet). Instead, they must be hand-graded by the professor or a well-trained and knowledgeable assistant, and these graders may not apply scoring standards consistently as they work their way through the papers. Even when they use a scoring rubric, they may drift over the course of the grading period. For example, after reading a particularly good essay, a scorer may think that the mediocre essay that follows is particularly weak. As a check for intrarater reliability, the raters should regrade a sample of the essays and check for agreement in the two sets of scores. If the scores do not match, then the grading system should be revised and the entire set regraded. If several individuals grade the examinations, then interrater reliability should be checked because one grader may apply a different set of standards than another. These variations will not be detected until scores are compared on a sample of the tests that both raters grade.

Item Analysis

ST items must pass the same standards as CT items. They must not be too difficult or too easy. They should discriminate between those students who have reached the class's instructional objectives and those who have not. They should also be related to each other because scores on each item will be added together to yield a total score. Their success in reaching these standards can be checked by inspecting the spread of scores across items and students. The information needed to carry out the analysis is illustrated in Table 4.7, which presents the data from 10 students who took a 10-question test. Each entry in the matrix reflects the score, on a 4-point scale generated using a holistic rubric, of each student on each item (although the scorer gave one student a bonus point and another partial credit).

The information in Table 4.7 is only heuristic, given the small number of data points. That said, the mean on the exam was 28.8, or 72%, and the standard deviation was 7.2. Scores ranged from 16 (40%) to 40

TABLE 4.7
Example of Score Distribution on a 40-Point Examination

Student	Item 1	2	3	4	5	6	7	8	9	10	Total points	Percent
Kellie	5	4	4	4	4	4	3	4	4	4	40	100
Hope	4	2	3	4	4	4	3	4	4	4	36	90
Felinta	3	4	3	3	4	4	3	4	4	4	36	90
Shauna	4	2	3	3	3	2	3	3	4	4	31	77.5
Aimee	4	3	3	3	4	2	1	2	3	4	29	72.5
Kelly	3	2	2	3	4	2	2	3	2	4	27	67.5
Joshua	3	0	3	3	3.5	3	2	1	2	4	24.5	61.3
James	2	2	3	2	1	2	3	2	3	4	24	60
Jennifer	1	0	4	2	1	2	3	4	3	4	24	60
Ian	1	1	2	1	2	0	2	3	2	2	16	40
Item mean	3.0	2.0	3.0	2.8	3.1	2.5	2.5	3.0	3.1	3.9	28.8	72
Item SD	1.3	1.4	0.7	0.9	1.3	1.3	0.7	1.1	0.9	0.6	7.2	
p-score	.70	.30	.80	.70	.70	.40	.60	.70	.70	.90		
D-score	.60	.75	.40	.60	.60	.80	.60	.40	.60	.20		

Note. The p-score is the percentage of students who received scores of 3 or 4. The D-score for the item (discrimination) is estimated by subtracting the proportion of students who received overall scores of 0 or 1 (D/F range) from the proportion of students who received overall scores of 3 or 4 (A/B range).

(100%). If for the sake of illustration students are assigned a letter grade based on the percentage of points they earned, and these assignments are based on a simple 10% rule whereby 90–100% = A, 80–89% = B, and so on, then the distribution of grades would then be 1 F, 4 Ds, 2 Cs, no Bs, and 3 As. The difficulty of each item is indicated by the average of students' scores. For example, Item 2 was the most difficult one on the test (M = 2.0), whereas Item 10 was the easiest (M = 3.9). If a p-score-like index is required, then the proportion of students who received scores in the 3 and 4 range could be calculated, yielding .30 for Item 2 and .90 for Item 10.

A D-score-like index of discrimination can also be calculated by subtracting the proportion of students who received overall scores of 0 or 1 (D/F grade range) from the proportion of students who received overall scores of 3 or 4 (A/B range). This index indicates that Item 2, despite its level of difficulty, discriminated well. One high-scoring student missed it, but so did all of the low-scoring students. The very easy Item 9, however, did not discriminate among students. Inspection of the content of the item reveals the problem, for the item asked: "Give an example of classical conditioning, being sure to identify each component in the model." High scorers all described original applications, but nearly all of the low-scoring students earned full credit by describing Pavlov's original dog-conditioning paradigm. The item should be reworded so that students must generate a novel example rather than repeat one that they learned from class. The remaining items are adequate, for no item was consistently missed by high-scoring students yet answered correctly by the students who got lower scores.

TEST ADMINISTRATION: PRACTICAL SUGGESTIONS

When it comes to assessment, the devil is in the details. A temperament that leans toward compulsivity and an excess attention to details —so often a liability in everyday affairs and interpersonal relations—is a bonus when developing, administering, and analyzing tests. This style demands that care must be taken, not only in the construction of the test, but also in the way the test is administered to students.

Order of Items

Just as the order of items in a public opinion poll can influence results (e.g., Schwarz & Hippler, 1995), so the order of test items may influence students' responses. The easy-to-hard rule of thumb favors ordering questions so that students gain confidence early on the test, thereby reducing the impact of test stress on their responses. The cluster rule, in contrast, recommends grouping the items by topic, so that in general the questions follow the sequence that they were examined in the lecture or text. The format approach recommends placing together all items of the same type and layout (e.g., negatively worded items, ones with "all of the above" options). All these suggestions seem reasonable, and argue for a hybrid approach that organizes questions within topic clusters, with easier items appearing first (particularly at the beginning of the test).

Preparing the Examination

If your staff takes your collection of test items and turns it into desktop-published examination booklets overnight, then you need not worry about the following recommendations. But if you play an active role in the creation of the test document you may want to:

- Create the answer key for the exam several days before the test day so that any errors can be corrected before tests are duplicated.
- Check and recheck item numbering and the lettering of alternatives.
- Format the alternatives consistently throughout the examination. If you use two columns for four alternative items, then a consistent style (e.g., the a and b alternatives appear in the

left column and c and d in the right) should be used throughout.

- Avoid items that continue from one page to the next.
- Maintain tight test security prior to the test.
- Line up extra students and colleagues to serve as proctors in large classes.
- Prepare two versions of the examination as a safeguard against copying (chapter 6 offers other suggestions for reducing cheating).

Preparing for Exam Day

Murphy may have had test day in mind when he made up his law: "Anything that can go wrong, will go wrong." Whole pages left out of the question booklet. Too few answer sheets. No #2 pencils. No pencil sharpeners for the #2 pencils. Avoid these surprises, if at all possible, by taking some precautions.

- Count the exam booklets before you go to class the day before the test, even in large classes.
- Arrive for class early and plan to stay late.
- Have a few extra test copies prepared in case you must replace ones with missing pages, illegible print, and so on.
- Take too many bubble sheets (a.k.a. Scantrons or answer sheets).
- Remind students in large classes to bring both pencils and identification with them.
- Review test decorum rules with students prior to exam day and at the beginning of the examination (e.g., Can they leave when they finish? Should they raise their hands if they have a question or get up from their seats and find a proctor? How much can they spread out?).
- If possible, close off an entire row of seats in the class with "reserved" signs for your use in seating students who arrive late, for students who behave in suspicious ways when they take the test, or for students who need more room.

Instructions for Exams

Do not assume that students will know how to take the test. Include, at least on the first test, detailed instructions that cover such points as type of pencil to be used (#2), how their name and identification number should be indicated, and whether they can leave once they complete the examination. Students will want to know if they can write notes to themselves on the test booklets and if they must return the booklets at the end of class. If the test booklets are to be retained, take steps to make certain that students do not take extra copies when they are distributed.

The instructions should also briefly review any special conditions pertaining to the test. On a multiple-choice test, for example, students should be told whether incorrect answers will be counted against them. If they are not, then students should be encouraged to complete all items, even if they must guess. Instructions for essay tests should describe the length and time limits, and remind students that grading will be based on their ability to demonstrate their grasp of psychology in their answer and the quality of their writing. The instructions for take home essay tests should describe the types of materials students can use, but they should clearly note that the project is to be done without help from others.

The Challenge of Assessment

Measurement, as Stevens (1951, p. 1) explained, "is the assignment of numerals to objects or events according to rules." This deceptively simple definition conveys little of the time, energy, and care that go into good assessment. Teaching psychologists, if they comply with the demands of their dual roles as psychologists and teachers, must bring the psychometric skills that would inform assessment in general to the development of instruments for classes. As psychologists, they must make sure their tests meet the field's standards for tests in general, which are very stringent. And as professors, they must use assessment to measure accurately their students' achievements as well as their own; for if students' scores are strikingly low or high, then the professor must carefully diagnose the course to determine whether the level is set incorrectly, inadequate methods are being used, or if the fault or credit lies in the preparation of the students. Professors must also give feedback to students with the same sensitivity that they would respond to a client or a research participant. Students are often preoccupied with their grades, and so it is important to deal directly with the issue of testing. The next chapter examines the use of test results for grading students and the ways that grades can be used to help students reach their educational goals.

5

GRADING (AND AIDING): HELPING STUDENTS REACH THEIR LEARNING GOALS

For some individuals ... a realization occurs, whether suddenly or gradually, that they are less or will be treated as less than they have learned to expect of and for themselves, and that the frustration of these ingrained expectations is due to the possession of an attribute that functions as a social stigma. Defining themselves as persons who will run in a particular race, they come to find that they have been partly disqualified and involuntarily re-identified in terms of their disqualification. The new category to which they find they belong separates them from those whom they thought they were like, and brings them together with those from whom they previously differed.

—Erving Goffman
"Normal Deviants" (1967, p. 267)

Feedback is an essential component of virtually all performance situations. Few achievements can be evaluated without reference to some standard that defines which outcomes are correct, successful, or satisfactory. Grading systems provide that clarity, for they assign a judgment of worth to individual students' achievements. This feedback helps students assess their performance, reset their goals, and possibly increase their effort. Giving students feedback is, however, psychologically, procedurally, and interpersonally complicated, and for a system of performance evaluation to be fair it should be coupled with resources that students can use to improve their evaluation.

* * *

Psychologists are wary of using labels to describe people, but their work often requires it. The clinician must decide if her client's symptoms are sufficiently grave to warrant a diagnosis of depression, anxiety, or one of the other 300 or so recognized disorders. The researcher, as scientist, relies on classifications to make distinctions among individuals and often sorts subjects into groups before determining how this classification predicts their reactions. The personnel psychologist, through assessment and interview, determines who is trustworthy, management material, or a possible perpetrator of workplace violence. The school psychologist must determine

171

if the child he is testing should receive the educational adjustments associated with such categories as learning disabled, emotionally disabled, attention deficit disorder, and so on.

Teaching psychologists must also classify, but they categorize their students rather than their clients, employees, or subjects. Sometimes students are judged as failing, passing, or as demonstrating mastery of a topic. But far more frequently, professors' classifications grade students' achievement along a 5-point continuum from A to F. Exceptional students receive As, good students Bs, students doing satisfactory work get Cs, weak students Ds, and the worst students receive Fs. Only the F label is acronymic: F stands for Failure.

These grades serve a variety of useful functions. As noted in chapter 4, tests and the grades they generate are motivational. Most students, when asked what their primary goal is in taking a class, mention a specific grade or the completion of the course with a passing grade before they mention the material they will learn (Covington & Wiedenhaupt, 1997). Students carry out the required work in a class to raise or maintain their grade point average (GPA), rather than achieve more nebulous learning goals (Polczynski & Shirland, 1977). Grades on tests, quizzes, and other assignments also function as feedback, and so help students calibrate their perceptions of their work. Educational systems are cybernetic: They require constant infusions of feedback to function effectively, and grades provide that feedback.

Grades are also the gold standard for judging performance in the classroom. Verbal judgments such as "nice job" or "excellent work" or "inadequate" are open to interpretation, but a letter grade is readily understood by professors, students, parents, and employers. C is average, middle-of-the-road; Bs and Ds identify work that falls above or below this norm, respectively; and As and Fs are reserved for exceptionally good or bad work, respectively. Grades also legitimize the educational process itself. Just as laypersons are more impressed when such symptoms as difficulty sleeping, negative affect, self-blame, and low energy are labeled "depression" rather than "feeling blue," so stakeholders in the educational process consider grades to be objective, meaningful ratings of student achievement. Like HMOs that question the value of therapy for clients who are not given a diagnosis from the *Diagnostic and Statistical Manual*, parents, teachers, and employers question the value of a educational experience that is not graded (Dreeben, 1972).

These benefits come with a cost, however. Grades are massive extrinsic rewards, so they shift the locus of students' motivations from the intrinsic side to the extrinsic side. Students who are intrinsically motivated "experience interest and enjoyment, they feel competent and self-determining, they perceive the locus of causality for their behavior to be internal, and in some instances they experience flow" (Deci & Ryan, 1985,

p. 34). Students who are extrinsically motivated, or "grade-grubbers," value only the grade and the rewards it brings. When grades, rather than learning, become the goal, students sometimes feel as though they can negotiate for grades in the same way they might barter for a better deal on a used car.

Grades fail as feedback mechanisms if they do not provide the kind of clarity students need to understand their performance (Cronbach, 1977). When students check their posted grade and read "64%, D," all they know is they failed to learn a third of the material covered on the test, but they do not know which items gave them problems or how they can improve their scores in the future. Grades are essentially summative: They scale the quality of performance in terms of the success in reaching criteria or in terms of performance quality relative to others. But students need formative evaluation: specific, useful, and focused information about strengths and weaknesses that they can use as feedback to reshape their learning activities.

The value of grades as standards can also be questioned. Although As, Bs, Cs, Ds, and Fs are the Eurodollars of higher education, these classifications are not equivalent across professors, courses, and universities. Grade inflation in recent years has contributed to an increase in the frequency of higher grades, so a B average of the 1960s is not the same as a B average in the 2000s (Goldman, 1985). Specific professors grade more leniently than others, just as some are more casual, calculating, consistent, or even careless than others. Indeed, in many cases grades are based not on how much psychology was learned but on altogether irrelevant criteria. Although college professors are not likely to use grades the way my sixth grade teacher did—Mrs. Floyd would lower our grades in subjects that were most important to us if we challenged her authority in class—they sometimes let personal biases influence the grading process (Tabachnick, Keith-Spiegel, & Pope, 1991). This ambiguity means that the grades, because they are not determined wholly by objective factors, can unfairly classify people and their products. Just as many psychologists worry about the use of labels for identifying people and their psychological health, so educators worry about grading students and their accomplishments. When students are given grades of D or F, for example, these labels can leave them feeling inferior to other students, undermine their self-efficacy, and further erode motivation. These students, before the test, believed they were ready to join the race for learning, but when they got their low grades realized that they had been disqualified (Goffman, 1967). They belonged, they were told, to a lower class of students, and their membership in that category might even influence their professor's perceptions of them. The student who asked so many penetrating questions in the first few weeks of class but earned a D on the first test is transformed instantly from a "curious seeker" into a "clueless loser."

Are these problems with grades so substantial that the question, "Shall we get rid of grades?" should be answered in the affirmative? Ebel (1974) said no, arguing that these limitations of grading can be addressed, in large part, just by doing a better job grading students. Grading systems, whether intricate or simple, comparative or criterion-based, quantitative or qualitative, or old-fashioned or high-tech, must reliably connect specific grades to specific levels of achievement. Grading systems should also provide students with the information they need to identify the causes of their good and bad performances and possible remedies should their performance be inadequate. Instead of just telling students they failed, they should be told why they failed and what they can do to avoid failure in the future.

GRADING SYSTEMS

Some students are convinced that their professor tosses a dart at a target for each student on the roster, and only if the dart lands in the bull's-eye is an A awarded. Contrary to this myth, however, most professors carefully track student performances and use some sort of grading system to rate these performances. These grading systems, as systems, accept information about student performance, combine that information in ways that are specified by the rules of the system, and then generate grades as output. But the rules of the system vary from professor to professor. Some use *criterion-referenced systems* (or task-referenced, absolute standards) that compare the student's performance to some benchmark. Others use *norm-referenced systems* (or group-referenced, relative grading, grade curving) that compare students to each other (Glaser, 1963). And still others use systems that combine elements of criterion-referenced grading or norm-referenced grading.

Criterion-Referenced Systems

Dr. Criter, after completing a 3-week unit, administers a 50-item test to her 275 students. The items are all deemed psychometrically adequate, so she calculates the percentage of questions each student answered correctly and charts the results as shown in Table 5.1 (and discussed briefly in chapter 4). But before she returns the marked tests to students she must decide what grade to assign to each score. Is a 68% score a C or D? Is an 88% an A or B? And which score is so low that the student should fail?

If she uses a criterion-referenced method, she will base grades on preset standards that define the quality of performance that each grade designation—A, B, C, D, or F or, in some cases, pass or fail—requires. If, for example, she uses the *fixed-percent method* with 10% cutoffs, her grading scale may allocate an A only to those students who answer at least 90%

TABLE 5.1
Example of Score Distribution on a 100-Point Examination

Score	Frequency	Percent	Cumulative frequency	Cumulative percent
36	2	0.73	2	0.73
38	2	0.73	4	1.45
40	3	1.09	7	2.55
42	3	1.09	10	3.64
44	7	2.55	17	6.18
46	7	2.55	24	8.73
48	10	3.64	34	12.36
50	13	4.73	47	17.09
52	8	2.91	55	20.00
54	6	2.18	61	22.18
56	5	1.82	66	24.00
58	8	2.91	74	26.91
60	9	3.27	83	30.18
62	16	5.82	99	36.00
64	11	4.00	110	40.00
66	8	2.91	118	42.91
68	20	7.27	138	50.18
70	12	4.36	150	54.55
72	15	5.45	165	60.00
74	12	4.36	177	64.36
76	12	4.36	189	68.73
78	16	5.82	205	74.55
80	8	2.91	213	77.45
82	8	2.91	221	80.36
84	12	4.36	233	84.73
86	7	2.55	240	87.27
88	12	4.36	252	91.64
90	7	2.55	259	94.18
92	7	2.55	266	96.73
94	4	1.45	270	98.18
96	2	0.73	272	98.91
98	2	0.73	274	99.64
100	1	0.36	275	100.00

of the questions correctly. She then relaxes this standard for each lower grade, so that an 80–89% score earns a B, 70–79% a C, and 60–69% a D. Those students who did not manage to answer 60% of the items correctly are given a grade of F. The distribution of grades, as Table 5.2 indicates, would then be 27% Fs, 23% Ds, 24% Cs, 17% Bs, and 9% As.

Dr. Criter uses criterion-reference grading because it bases students' grades on their personal accomplishments, independent of the performance of others in the class. If all of the students reach all of the course objectives that she measures on her exam, then every one of them can earn a high grade in her class. But should they all fail to reach her standards, then all will receive low grades. The criterion-referenced method also automates a decision that most professor dislike having to make: who will pass and who

TABLE 5.2
The Impact of Different Grading Methods on the Test Scores Shown
in Table 5.1

Example	Criteria for A, B, C, D	Percentage of students earning each grade				
		A	B	C	D	F
10%	90/80/70/60	9	17	24	23	27
15%	85/70/55/40	15	35	28	21	1
20% Cs	90/80/60/50	9	17	48	14	12
Normed	88/74/60/50	13	27	33	15	12
Bell-curved	98/83/53/38	1	19	60	19	1

will fail. It does so by providing clear standards for each grade. Dr. Criter can tell her students, in class and on the syllabus, precisely what scores they must earn to receive particular grades. Although students who earn grades such as 88s or 89s on examinations may feel that they are "close enough" to the A criteria to deserve that grade—and they may carefully review their tests searching for the points they need to reach the criterion —Dr. Criter can stand firm against their entreaties, supported by her standards.

These advantages of criterion grading are offset by certain liabilities. The method assumes that the items on the test measure the key learning objectives for the course. A score of, say, 90% is persuasive evidence that the student has mastered 90% of the course's objectives only when the test measures those objectives. As Nitko (2001) argued, if you have not defined the unit's content domain "and have not built the assessment to sample the domain, then you cannot use the percent grade to accurately estimate the student's status on a broader domain" (p. 363). Although the specificity of the percent grades suggests that students' learning has been measured precisely, given the error in measurement, a score of 90 is only an estimate of actual mastery.

Criterion-grading systems also depend, fundamentally, on the boundaries for each grade, and in some cases only convention or habit can explain why a particular set of cutoffs is imposed on students. As Table 5.2 indicates, Dr. Criter's standard of 10% may be defensible given the difficulty of the material, the level of the students, and the quality of the instruction, but it produces far more failures than the second example in Table 5.2, which uses a more lenient 15% rule. And why are the intervals for each grade equal? The third example in Table 5.2 illustrates how a grading scale that expands the cutoff for Cs from 70–79% to 60–79% will also redefine the criteria for Ds and Fs. If Dr. Criter discovers that too many students fail when using the criteria she set on the syllabus, she may find herself in the uncomfortable position of having to change her standards—which undermines one of the key strengths of criterion-referenced grading.

Norm-Referenced Systems

Dr. Norm uses a norm-referenced approach that compares students to one another rather than to some pre-established criterion. Dr. Norm, like Dr. Criter, sets cutoffs for each type of grade, but he bases these cutoffs on the number of students who will qualify for each type of grade. Rather than assigning a grade of A to students who "learned most of the material presented in the course," Dr. Norm thinks an A should indicate students who "learned significantly more of the course material than the average student."

Dr. Norm scores the exam by ordering the students from the lowest scoring to the highest scoring (see Table 5.1) and sets his cutoffs depending on a relative standard. If he decides that approximately 15% of the class should receive As, 30% receive Bs, 30% Cs, 15% Ds, and 10% Fs, he adjusts the cutoffs to create clusters of this size. This method, applied to the example test, yields the cutoffs shown in the fourth example of Table 5.2: 100–88 is an A, 86–74 is a B, 72–60 is a C, 58–50 is a D, and below 50 is an F. Even though the specific cutoffs can be determined only after the test because the distribution of grades depends on the difficulty of the test and the average skill level of the students who take it, the percentage of students in each grade category can (and should) be defined in advance of the testing.

Norm-referenced grading is sometimes described as *grading on a curve* because it is based on the distribution of grades within the population and such distributions often display the characteristic bell-curve shape. But Dr. Norm's grades need not be normally distributed in order for him to use this method, and he does not have to base cutoffs on the standard deviations or the distribution mean. If Dr. Norm did adjust the test according to a bell curve, then he might decide that all students within a *SD* of the mean should receive Cs; those 1 *SD* above and below the means Bs and Ds, respectively; and those 2 *SD*s above or below the mean As and Fs, respectively. The cutoffs, as the last example ("bell-curved") in Table 5.2 indicates, would therefore be 98, 83, 53, and 38. He may, however, increase the "curve" of this relatively stringent grading scheme because so few students qualify for A grades. He might, for example, set the interval for a C grade around .5 or .7 *SD* rather than 1 *SD* to decrease the size of the C range and increase the proportion of other grades.

Normative grading's greatest strength is its flexibility. Even when nearly all the students unexpectedly get very high or low scores, analysis indicates the items have low reliability and validity, and the test is a poor indicator of the unit's learning objectives, norm-referenced methods offer a way of assigning grades by rewarding students who outperform their peers. Normative approaches also mesh well with students' natural tendency to evaluate themselves through comparison with others. Professors who do not use normative grading methods and insist that students need only worry about their ability to reach the criteria set for the course often find that students demand information about the mean, spread, and so on. As social comparison theory suggests, individuals spontaneously evaluate their own abilities and attitudes by comparing themselves to others, and the need for comparison data is particularly strong in testing settings (Festinger, 1954).

But norm-referenced methods can be criticized for not basing grades on students' mastery of the material in the course. Most people, on hearing a student earned an A in a psychology class, would assume that the student learned a prodigious amount of psychology, but norm-referenced grading does not guarantee that interpretation. All that is known for certain is that the A student outperformed many others, but the entire class may have learned very little in an absolute sense. The method, at least as typically operationalized, also requires that some students be given low grades, even if they have learned a substantial proportion of the course material. Students who have the bad luck to end up in classes with a large proportion of high achievers will get lower scores than those who have the good luck to end up in classes with weaker students. Natural variations in the composition of the class may also require changing the cutoff levels for grades from class to class and from test to test. As Ebel (1988) suggested, when one teaches a course composed of excellent students, fairness dictates using smaller deviations from the mean when setting grade cutoffs. Similarly, the cutoffs for grades will need to be adjusted for each test, because they tend to vary in degree in difficulty. A score of 88 may earn a student an A on Test 1, but if Test 2 is easier and more students perform well, an 88 becomes a B. Standards will also shift as the composition of the class changes over the course of the term. If students who are performing poorly drop out of the class after the first or second test, the overall level of ability of the class will increase accordingly, making it harder for students to distance themselves from the ever-increasing mean for the class.

Many educators also feel that the norm-referenced grading methods increase competition among students for grades and prevent them from using collaborative learning procedures. Although introducing competition among students is a popular way to prompt them to expend greater effort, competition focuses students' attention on winning, to the extent that they eventually conclude that "learning something new" is not nearly as important as "performing better than others" (Ames, 1987, p. 134). Failure in a competitive setting also undermines self-esteem and prompts students to blame their failures on lack of ability, rather than on lack of effort. Ames (1987), after thoroughly reviewing the literature, recommended excising all forms of competition from the college classroom by using criterion-based grading schemes (rather than norm-referenced schemes), by not posting grades and not grading on a curve, and by stressing the cooperative nature of learning.

Norm-referenced grading methods, in sum, are interpersonal rather than personal. Whereas criterion-referenced methods evaluate students relative to the course's learning goals, a norm-based approach evaluates them by comparing them to other students. Students who earn Ds or Fs in criterion-referenced classes are told, in essence, that they did not learn very much of the material covered on the test. The grades of D and F students in norm-based classes, in contrast, tell them that they are inferior to many of their peers.

Variations and Issues in Grading

Many professors avoid the limitations of criterion- and norm-referenced grading systems by using hybrid methods. Some, too, reduce the evaluative impact of grades by using pass–fail grades or considering how much progress students made during the term and then giving higher grades to the "most improved" rather than the "most successful." Some of these variations, and other issues pertaining to grading, are considered below.

Curving Grades

Even though *grading on the curve* generally means to use a norm-referenced approach, many students think that "curving" means adding points or softening designated cutoffs so that their grades are raised. When they ask, "Will you be curving the grades?" they generally want to hear answers such as, "Yes, I'm changing the curve so that an 85% will be enough for an A" rather than "Yes, the grades are curved such that 68% of the class will receive Cs."

Norm-referenced grades are always curved, but criterion-referenced graders sometimes curve their grades when they discover that their test is so hard that very few students will get high grades. Faced with too many low scores and recognizing that the scores may reflect problems with the test and their teaching rather than the low ability of their students, they abandon their commitment to their preset standards and fudge the scores by lowering the cutoffs or adding points to all students' grades. In some cases the criterion-grader may revert to normative methods by considering the distribution of grades and adding the points needed to shift the distribution of scores upward so that a reasonable number of As and Bs result. They may, for example, feel that the distribution of grades for the test summarized in Table 5.2, in which half of the class received Ds and Fs, is too harsh and add points to limit the number of low grades. The number of points added might also be determined by the highest scorer's grade. If the best score in the class is only a 95%, then all students are given 5 percentage points so that the top score is then a perfect 100%. With this method, the top scorer is said to have "set the curve" for the class. A more subtle approach to curving involves adding points to offset items on the test that were too difficult (say, missed by 80% of the class or more) or were psychometrically inadequate.

Gap Grading

Some faculty modify their norm-referenced cutoffs to take advantage of natural breaks in the distribution of students' scores. Although they may have a general idea about how many As, Bs, Cs, Ds, and Fs they will give to students, they modify these percentages to maximize the distance between adjacent grade categories. They may, for example, initially decide that scores of 90 or more will be As because this cutoff gives 20% of class As. But further inspection of the distribution of scores may reveal a gap just below this cutoff: 2 students got 89s, but then the next highest score was an 86 earned by 8 students. In such a case, the professor may drop the curve down so that the 89s receive A grades as well.

Gapping serves one valuable purpose: It reduces the number of borderline students in class (McMillan, 1997). These students, if they understand the fundamentals of psychological measurement, can reasonably argue that the assessment they have just taken is not so precise that their scores do not contain several points' worth of measurement error. The professor can argue that their score might overestimate their true score and so they deserve an even lower grade, but students assume that the error goes in their favor rather than against them. Gapping, however, is very subjective and likely capitalizes on chance variations in grade distributions (Jacobs & Chase, 1992). Gaps are also rare in larger classes. The scores for the 250+ class shown in Table 5.1, for example, reveal very few gaps, and so this method of sculpting the class curve would not be very effective with these scores.

Grading by Growth

Davis (1993) described the issues that complicate grading methods that consider how much a student improves over the course of study. Such methods are norm-referenced, but the norm is based on the individual student's average scores rather than comparison to the class average. Students who begin with low scores but show gains by the term's end are rewarded with better grades than students who show little improvement or declines in scores. As Davis noted, such practices can result in unfair grades, particularly when students who earn the highest scores in the class on all tests get lower grades than students who start off with low scores and end up with mediocre ones. Many professors, however, take growth into account by awarding bonus points to students who show steady improvement over the course of a semester.

Minimal and Developmental Objectives

Gronlund (1998) recommended using criterion-referenced grading methods when deciding who passes and who fails a course, but then applying norm-referenced methods when assigning the grades of A, B, C, and D to those who pass. Gronlund based this recommendation on the distinction between minimal objectives and developmental objectives. Minimal objectives are ones that the student must complete in order to receive credit for having taken the course. To pass a course in statistics, for example, the student must be able to perform certain basic calculations and conduct a number of specific tests. These minimal requirements do not change relative to the capability of other students in the class, for they represent the basic information students must know in order to take more advanced classes. Developmental objectives, in contrast, are typically higher order outcomes that some students, but not all, will be able to attain. Students' success in reaching these objectives will be determined by comparisons among students.

Pass–Fail and Mastery

In some cases, the 5-category system of A, B, C, D, and F is collapsed into the dichotomy of pass and fail (P and F). This practice is often used in advanced courses, such as independent studies or the dissertation research, where students are expected to be self-motivated. Students at many universities can also choose to take some of their regular courses on a pass–fail basis. Pass–fail grading reduces the burden on the professor to evaluate, critically, the student's work, for the only question asked is "Should the student get credit for taking the course?" Pass–fail grading may also undo some of the damage that grades can do to students' intrinsic motivation. When students are not working toward a grade, they feel they are free to explore more controversial topics, carry out more creative and unusual projects, and enjoy learning for learning's sake (Zlokovich, 2001). Then again, they may do only the minimal amount of work needed to pass the course, knowing that a P produced by A-quality work is equal to a P produced by D-quality work.

Mastery learning is, in some respects, a form of pass–fail grading. This approach to teaching, as described by such educators as Bloom (1976) and Block (1974), assumes that students should not stop their studies until they have mastered the essential elements of the course. Instead of rewarding them with a C or D for learning only a portion of the required material, students should be given the resources and time they need to reach a basic level of achievement of all material. Those students whose work exceeds these basic standards can receive special recognition in the form of grades of A and B, but those who do not reach the level of competency required for credit receive no grade.

Ory and Ryan (1993, p. 125) described an advanced criterion-referenced method that bases grades on the mastery of key elements rather than a fixed percent of items correctly answered. To use their method, one must first review the items on the exam and identify those "items a student with 'average' knowledge of the course material will get correct. . . . This total number is the cutoff score for a grade of C, assuming a grade of C represents average competency." One then identifies which items students must answer correctly to earn a B, and how many they must answer correctly to earn an A, and then set the cutoffs appropriately. Last, one sets the cutoff for passing with a D by reviewing all the items to "determine how many of these items should be answered correctly by a student to minimally pass the exam." When applied to the example test, review of the items might identify 25 items that the average student should answer correctly. This review also identifies 8 items that B students must answer correctly and 9 questions that A students must answer correctly. And what is the minimal number of items that must be answered correctly just to pass? If we assume it is 15, then the percent cutoffs for grades A–D would be 84, 66, 50, and 30, respectively. This approach has fairness on its side, but it assumes that each question corresponds to an objective and that the professor can objectively identify which objectives, when passed, qualify a student for the A-list, the B-list, and so on.

Extra Credit

Faculty are far from unified on the issue of extra credit. Such opportunities, because they are not based on criteria set in the syllabus or on comparison of performance to other students' achievements, step outside both criterion- and norm-referenced grading systems. Students view extra credit as a second chance to earn a good grade, but faculty worry that it can "encourage a lax or irresponsible attitude and that it is unfair when offered only to selected students" (Palladino, Hill, & Norcross, 1999, p. 57).

Psychology faculty use extra credit more than professors in other disciplines, but only because they often entice students into research by giving them extra credit for participating (Hill, Palladino, & Eison, 1993). This practice, although a traditional one in many departments, raises both ethical and instructional issues. If students can earn extra credit only by acting as research participants, then they are being unfairly coerced into research. Most institutional review boards (IRBs) therefore require that students be provided with other ways of earning credit that are equally effortful. Educationally, if students receive extra credit by taking part in studies then they should learn something from that experience. Instructors may assume that researchers are providing educative materials to their participants, but researchers may not do so.

Palladino et al. encouraged faculty to exercise caution when allowing extra credit. They suggested (paraphrased from Palladino et al., 1999, pp. 59–60):

- making extra credit available to all students in the class;
- selecting extra credit assignments that are pedagogically sound and clearly connected to the course;
- providing several choices of extra credit opportunities;
- discussing the rationale for extra credit with students;
- setting clear limits on the amount of credit that can be earned;
- using extra credit only when this practice is consistent with overall grading practices; and
- avoiding the use of extra credit altogether by turning any activities that once could earn extra credit into required, scored, aspects of the class.

Computing Final Grades

Grades must be assigned after each test, homework, exercise, and project, *and* at the completion of the term. This final assignment of grades is the most important step in the grading process, but also the most complicated because it requires the creation of a composite score that accurately integrates all the scored assessments completed by the students. Although professors who give only mid-term and final exams have a relatively easy time of it, those who use many different types of assessments, of varying complexity and importance, must integrate this information so that the final scores are consistent with their assessment plans. Computers, and the spreadsheet and grade book programs they support, make this task easier (as chapter 7 notes), but the process nonetheless requires a series of decisions, and these decisions must be made thoughtfully because they directly influence the grade that will be entered into students' permanent records.

Checking Records

The calculation of final grades requires a complete, error-free set of class data. If students completed make-up examinations, turned in homework late, left assignments under doors, or faxed in papers after hours and these offerings wandered into the wrong files, stacks, or office, then they must be tracked down, graded, and entered into the database. But data also may be missing because students did not take the exam, turn in the paper, or complete the assignment. In such cases the professor must decide if the missing value will be replaced with a zero, if the student will be assigned a "no grade" or "incomplete" (if the professor's university permits such forms of grading), or if some other replacement method will be used (Brookhart, 1999).

Aligning Metrics

No researcher would create an index of personality by adding together responses to three items that used a 6-point Likert-type scale and three items that used a 10-point scale. Similarly, if professors used different metrics for their various assignments—grading some as pass or fail, others as percentage scores ranging from 0 to 100, and others as letter grades—these components must all be converted to some common scale so that they can be combined in a composite score. Many professors avoid this step by using a common metric for all assignments, but others deal with the problems associated with varying metrics by using letter grades to calculate final grades. They convert all the student's scores to letter grades and average the grade points from each element (e.g., A = 4, B = 3, C = 2, D = 1, F = 0) to yield a final score. This procedure results in a loss of precision, which can be partially—but not completely—minimized by using pluses and minuses.

Assigning Weights

The various activities, assignments, tests, and quizzes given in the class may not be equal in terms of their impact on final grades. If, for example, the syllabus explains that grades on the four major tests in the class will determine 80% of the grade with the remaining 20% coming from completion of four written assignments, then the composite score must reflect that scheme by weighting these components appropriately. These weights, too, should reflect the overall instructional objectives for the course. In general, components that are the most reliable and valid indicators of achievement should be weighted more than components that are not as reliable, valid, or focused on the course's learning objectives. Weights should also reflect the emphasis that the component received during the class, so that tests on topics that were reviewed at length are weighted more heavily than tests on topics that received only cursory attention in class.

Creating the Composite Score

Once the data are properly organized and coded, graders multiply each scored element by its weight before summing these products to generate a composite score. If, for example, a class's assessments include three tests, six homework assignments, a term paper, and student participation in four studies as subjects, and these activities are weighted as 60%, 12%, 20%, 8% of the grade, respectively, then their scores (on a common metric) would be weighted by these percentages and summed. Grades are then awarded to the students using their a priori grade boundaries based on percentage of total points earned, relative standing in the class, or some hybrid system.

Criterion-referenced graders can also use the *total-points method* of grading to avoid the complexities of varying metrics and weights (Nitko, 2001). At the beginning of the semester (preferably), they decide the maximum number of points to award students for each scored assignment and test (e.g., each test is worth a possible 100 points, but homework is worth only 10 points). They then set the number and type of these elements so that the total number of possible points equals some reasonable amount; for example, 100 points for each of 3 tests, 10 points for each of 6 homework assignments, 100 points for the term paper, 10 points for each study students take part in as participants (and briefly describe in a short written paper) up to a maximum of 4, yields a possible 500 points. Naturally the points assigned to each element should reflect the importance of the element as a determinant of the students' grades, because these points determine the element's weight. This system's major advantage: Students can calculate grades using mathematics no more complicated than addition. They need only add up their points and compare them to the standard stated in the syllabus. If they need a total score of 90% of the material to receive an A, the syllabus can translate that percentage into points (450 in a 500-point system) and define the grade cutoffs for them.

Criterion-referenced graders also need not worry about the impact of differing variances in the components of their assessments, but norm-referenced graders must take an additional step if the scores on the various tests and scored activities have different ranges. This step is necessary to control the impact of score variance on final grades. Imagine, for example, a norm-referencer who gives three tests to a class. The mean for all three tests is 70, the *SD* for first two tests is 10, and the *SD* for the third test is 30. When a composite score is created from these three tests, the score on the third test—because of its wider range—will have a greater impact on students' rankings. The professor should convert the scores to standard scores before combining them or be content with the unexpected large weight associated with the third test.

GIVING STUDENTS FEEDBACK

Grades are key cogs in the self-regulation/learning system (Husman & Lens, 1999; Karoly, 1993). Few people can decide, using only their own good judgment, if their achievements, their learning, or their teaching are superlative, complete, or noteworthy. Instead, most must compare their outcomes to official standards that define what is "correct," "successful," or "satisfactory" and then, if necessary, take steps to decrease the discrepancy between those standards and their outcomes. In the case of learning, these official standards are grades, which professors must relay to students so students can assess their performance, reset their goals, and possibly increase their effort. Grades also serve as reality checks. Vast numbers of undergraduate psychology students want to become clinicians and psychiatrists with private practices, but only a small proportion of them have the drive, the intellectual skills, and the self-control needed for success in the arduous training that will qualify them for those careers. Receiving a C in General Psychology provides them with the feedback they need to set achievable goals.

But giving students feedback is procedurally, psychologically, and interpersonally complicated. Students should be informed of their performance as soon as possible, but this feedback process should be a discreet one that respects their privacy. When the feedback is negative, students may also need help coming to terms with their failure. They may, for example, prefer to blame a poor performance on the quality of the instruction they have received rather than on themselves, and such perceptions may prevent them from adjusting their studying to enhance their grades. Some students also need to be reassured that, even though they did not perform well on the examination, they should not abandon their quest to achieve a good grade in the class. Others, in contrast, may need to consider other options, such as withdrawing from the course before they fail it.

Providing Summative Feedback

Students seek, and sometimes even appreciate, detailed, formative feedback about their specific strengths and weaknesses but only after they are informed of their overall score and grade. Indeed, students begin seeking feedback about their scores even before they leave the classroom after the exam. Some, while dropping off their test, cannot help but ask what the answer was to a particularly bothersome item. Others gather in clusters outside the room, sharing opinions about specific items and the answers they gave. Some professors help their students quench their thirst for immediate feedback by letting them keep copies of the exam questions and providing them with solution sheets or sample answers. Others post the scores by social security number on a bulletin board near their office when the grading is completed. Many universities and colleges, however, have banned this practice because the use of social security numbers for such purposes without the student's written consent is prohibited by federal law. Some professors therefore ask students to provide code names to be used for posted grades, or they use social security numbers only after students sign a waiver consenting to such use.

Other professors prefer to discuss the test's characteristics, and provide students with their scores, during a class session. During this review, the instructor can present the class with general information about the reliability and validity of the exam, a histogram of grades, the connection between the items and the course objectives, and review any problematic items that many students missed as well as items that the class mastered surprisingly well. Such sessions are complicated when classes are large and the professor returns students' papers to them individually. If classes are extremely large, some other method of feedback must be used, such as displaying students' grades on the classroom projection system or circulating a few dozen copies of the grade sheet during the first few minutes of the class. These methods are allowable so long as students' anonymity is protected by listing only their identification numbers or codes.

These sessions must be handled carefully because reviewing a test with a class, en masse, can be an unpleasant experience for both the students and the professor. Tests are very important events in the lives of students, and a low score on one can trigger a complex of affective, cognitive, and behavioral reactions. Students who receive a score that is lower than they expected may question the validity of the score, in general, or the items themselves. Snipers, the most rebellious cluster of student types identified by Mann and his colleagues (1970) in their analysis of student types in college classrooms, are particularly likely to express their displeasure during such sessions. Others may become very upset and angry about their grades, and will display these emotional reactions openly in class. Schweighart Goss (1999) offered suggestions for dealing with such students, including meeting with them in private, allowing them to express concerns without challenging them, and responding professionally and unemotionally despite their hostile manner. Research on emotional reactions to assessments has suggested that such student reactions are normal ones, particularly when students set high standards for themselves and the grade is very discrepant from their usual level of performance (e.g., Forsyth & McMillan, 1981b).

These sessions generally go more smoothly if they focus squarely on summative feedback rather than formative feedback. The professor can ask and answer such questions as "How well did the class perform?" "Were any of the test questions too hard or too easy?" "Did the test indicate that many of students in the class misunderstood some key concept, study, or finding?" but he or she would do well to avoid such questions from students as "On question 12, why wasn't option B considered correct, too?" and "Did we ever cover that stuff that question 45 asks about in class?" Rather than respond defensively or angrily to such pointed remarks, one should instead note that the available data confirm the validity of the test and that students with specific questions should raise them during office hours.

Studies have also indicated that the intensity of the emotional reaction will abate rapidly over time as students regain their composure, so a short "cooling-off period" between the time the feedback is given and any discussion of the feedback will dramatically reduce the tension (Forsyth, 1986). This post-test feedback moratorium can be established by providing summative feedback to students via e-mail and posting the analysis of the test's general characteristics to the course Web page. Alternatively, when a portion of a class session is spent discussing the test, ban any requests for individualized, follow-up discussions for at least 24 hours. Tell students that they are welcome to discuss their grade during office hours or after class—and even require students with Ds and Fs to contact you—but ask them to wait 24 hours before they approach you.

Providing Formative Feedback

Ebel (1974, p. 2) wrote "grades provide a concise summary of . . . a vast amount of specific detail. Often that summary is all that is wanted." But in many cases, too, students need to know more than just their percentage score and grade. They need to know which items they missed, why their essay answers were marked down, and, most important, they need to identify the learning objectives that their test indicates they have not yet mastered. They also need to understand the meaning of the score in terms of their overall expectations for the class.

Test-Review Sessions

Formative feedback must be tailored to the individual student, so these sessions must be conducted in small groups or one-on-one sessions. They generally have three components: (1) an *individual review* period during which students work alone, reviewing the items they missed, and comparing their solutions to the key; (2) a *tutorial review* during which any questions that the student missed and does not understand are discussed; and (3) a *diagnosis review* that involves identifying any systematic types of errors committed by the student. Although general tendencies cannot always be identified, in some cases the pattern of students' errors will indicate that they missed mostly items that were covered only in lecture or only in the text, items that required particular cognitive skills (e.g., applying course materials to novel examples), or particular types of items (e.g., analogy items, definition items).

If possible, these sessions should be delegated to teaching assistants, not because they are time consuming (they are) and not because they are unimportant elements of teaching (they are very valuable pedagogical tools), but because the sessions are often more effective when students meet with another student rather than their professor. Students who cannot bring themselves to confess their confusion about a topic that the professor has examined for 30 minutes in class can disclose their concerns more freely with a third party. Students who also want to use the session to merely ingratiate, manipulate, or irritate also take less pleasure and time in these machinations when the target is a TA rather than their professor.

Written Feedback on Essay Tests

Professors who use supply-type tests—essays, short answer questions, research papers—can provide students with information about their work by sharing their grading rubric, but they should also provide formative feedback as well. Some professors relay their comments to their students orally, during one-to-one or small group sessions, but the most common method is the tried-and-true comments-in-the-margin technique. As noted in chapter 3, these comments have more value as formative feedback if they are content-focused rather than mechanics-focused, specific rather than vague, constructive rather than bluntly critical, and heartening rather than discouraging.

Challenges of the Score

Review sessions will often result in students challenging the validity of a particular item or the fairness of an essay's scoring. These challenges can be handled during a negotiation session with students, but Schweighart Goss (1999) and Whitford (1992) recommend using a more formal procedure to structure these disagreements. Schweighart Goss (1999) asks students to complete a form to identify the troublesome item and the basis for their challenge of it. She also informs students that she will reread any essay item that students feel was unfairly graded, but because she provides students with a written commentary on each question, few choose this option. Whitford (1992) asks students who feel that a question has been unfairly scored to

> write their name, student number, and section on a piece of paper, then the offending item number. Next, I tell the students to look up the answer in the text or lecture notes and write a minimum of a paragraph explaining why their answer is better than my choice. Then, finally, I ask them to bring the paper to my office during office hours and we will discuss the question. (p. 55)

Whitford notes that, in most cases, the students cannot generate a persuasive paragraph because their answer is wrong. These students, by reviewing the material, relearn the concept correctly. Very few students have a good argument to support their solution, and in these cases Whitford awards them credit for their answer.

Grading Fairly

Students often assume that any low grade is an unfair one. Like most people, they do not believe that negative information is accurate, but wholeheartedly accept the validity of positive feedback. The student who fails the test says, "What an ambiguous, invalid test." The A student replies, "I thought it was an excellent, comprehensive exam" (Snyder, Shenkel, & Lowery, 1977; compare with Johnson et al., 1985). College students often have been highly successful in academics in the past, so low grades often take them by surprise. Redding (1998) relates the comment of one of his students who rejected the validity of his low score: "Remember that we are highly successful college students. . . . We do not need to be told how to write or be given low grades!" (p. 1227).

Whitley et al. (2000) and Rodabaugh (1996) agreed that students' reactions to their grades are determined, in large part, by the grades themselves: Students feel that grading that yields a high score is fairer than grading that yields a low score. But the researchers also noted that students' perceptions of their professor's *interactional fairness*—the extent to which the professor's interactions with students are impartial, respectful, supportive, sincere, and appropriate—also influence how they react when graded. Faculty who extend special privileges to certain students, treat students rudely, show little concern when students experience problems, change key aspects of the course without warning or explanation, and act in sexually provocative ways are not considered to be interactionally fair teachers. Students' judgments also take into account their estimates of the professor's *procedural fairness* and *outcome fairness*. Professors who design fair tests, who give appropriate amounts of work, and regularly give students feedback about their progress are considered to be fair in the procedural sense, whereas those faculty who base their grades on well-defined objective standards that are neither too difficult nor too easy are considered to be fair in the outcome sense. Whitley and his colleagues (2000) offered additional suggestions to faculty who wish to maximize one, two, or all three of these forms of fairness in their teaching.

HELPING STUDENTS LEARN

Sometimes being a psychologist is a bad thing. For instance, when the man next to you on the long plane trip follows up your ill-considered disclosure of your profession by seeking your advice on his mental health, his boss's mental health, and his partner's mental health. Or when the cold-calling journalist from the local newspaper reaches you by phone with one of those out-of-the-blue questions like "What can you tell people to help them keep their New Year's resolutions?" or "How can people best cope with the stress of holiday shopping?" or "What's the best color to paint a bedroom?" and then distills your 30-minute conversation into a one-line dopey quote that your delighted colleagues post by the photocopier.

But being a psychologist comes in handy when students, learning that they are not performing well in your class, meet with you to explore the causes of and solutions to their academic difficulties. Professors in other disciplines must confront such situations equipped with only the lessons their own experiences as students and as teachers of students provided them. But psychologists understand studying and learning. They also know how to help people change their behavior, even though they recognize how difficult such change is to accomplish and the complexity of the processes involved.

Developing Academic Skills

Pastorino (1999) recommended taking into account students' backgrounds before delving too deeply into the analysis of their academic shortcomings. Struggling graduate students, for example, likely have the basic academic skills needed for success, so their difficulties must spring from some other source. Similarly, the problems of transfer students, nontraditional students, English-as-a-second-language students, and students who are working full- and part-time jobs may not be caused by their lack of motivation, poor study habits, or the quality of their academic preparation but by life circumstances that are negatively affecting their academic work. But many students who are new to college suffer from a basic lack of academic skills. They thought they knew how to take notes, read a text, write papers, and prepare for an examination, but in point of fact their skill levels are not sufficient for college-level work. So in addition to teaching them psychology, one must also sometimes teach them how to study, how to read critically, how to take notes, and how to prepare for tests.

Study Skills

Even though those individuals who sit in our classes are usually called *students*, they do not always know how to study and to learn. As Gardiner (1998) discovered when he surveyed nearly 800 college students, only 14% reported having received any formal instruction on studying. In consequence, their idea of studying may amount to little more than skimming the textbook and reviewing their notes the night before the examination. If the test is easy and the students are gifted, those steps may be sufficient to earn them a high score on the exam. But most students will need to spend a great deal of time actively engaging the material by:

- *Organizing*: Students, when studying a unit of material, should have clear goals about the major topics that will be covered. They should be taught to examine the outline that begins each chapter and review the summary that appears at the end of the chapter. For lectures, they should study the general outline and notes until they understand why each subtopic is included in the overall topic.
- *Preparing materials*: Students should spend a significant portion of their outside-of-class time preparing the materials and resources they will use in their review sessions. These materials should include personalized outlines of the texts and lectures, copies of any e-mailed instructional materials, detailed notes from lecture, and so on.
- *Reviewing*: Students frequently complain "I read the book and came to class!" yet they cannot remember the information later. They failed to consolidate the material by organizing the information they extracted from the text and lecture. They should be encouraged to develop a systematic approach to reviewing lecture and text material, and use their approach consistently. Bjork (2001) offered a number of useful suggestions for studying, all drawn from studies of cognitive psychology and memory.
- *Self-testing*: Students should test their understanding prior to the professor's test. Self-testing provides them with the diagnostic information they need to identify topics that they have mastered, and others that they must continue to review.

Students should also realize that they will need to spend significant amounts of time studying. When the Center for Postsecondary Research and Planning surveyed more than 60,000 first-year students and seniors at colleges and universities, they discovered that very few followed the general formula of 2 hours or more spent studying for each hour spent in class (National Survey of Student Engagement, 2000). Nearly half of the students surveyed averaged only an hour studying outside of class for every in-class hour, and only 15% of the students carrying a course load of 15 or more hours spent more than 26 hours per week studying. Ten percent reported studying less than 5 hours a week—total! Seniors spent no more time studying than did first-year students, although the quality of their studying may have been superior.

Reading Skills

Students tend to be inefficient readers. They assume that they can read a textbook chapter much like they read a magazine article or a novel, so they watch television with their text open in their lap or fall asleep reading their book in bed. Unfortunately, most textbooks must be studied, rather than merely read. Active reading involves, at minimum, three components: previewing contents, reading, and deliberately committing critical information to long-term memory. Instead of just reading and re-reading chapters, student should first read the chapter summary, study the organization of topics, and generate an outline of the major topics the chapter covers. Only then should they read the text itself, in a situation where they can monitor their understanding of the material, remain alert, and take memory-enhancing notes. They should also be reminded to

- read assignments prior to any lectures or discussions that will cover the topics, and be careful to allocate enough time to complete that task. If a chapter is too long to complete in one sitting, students should read the chapter by breaking it up into chunks.
- take advantage of the pedagogical features of their texts. If the book contains outlines, chapter previews, or summaries, students should study these sections as they develop their overall conception of the material. They should also learn to make use of the headings and subheadings, which may be based on an implicit outline format that students fail to recognize.
- generate a verbal interpretation of any information presented in the text's charts and graphs.
- underline, highlight, or star key points, spend extra time reading complicated or detailed sections of the text, and pay special attention to expository elements embedded in the text such as lists, summaries, transitions, and pointer words ("More important," "Unfortunately," and "First of all," "Second," and so on).
- use a general reading system, such as SQ3R. This approach to active reading involves *Surveying* the chapter content, formulating a *Question* for each major topic or section, *Reading* the text for information that answers the question, *Reciting* the answer several times (aloud or in writing), and *Reviewing* the material without referring to the text or notes.

Taking Notes

Note taking is a demanding cognitive task, for it requires listening to and understanding the information presented by the lecturer, separating the key points from background information, and then writing down that material in a form that will serve as a mnemonic for retrieving the information from long-term memory. Advanced students may already know how to take effective notes, but first-year students and those with weaker academic backgrounds may need help. Training may include hints such as the following:

- Students should use a note-taking system, such as Pauk's (1993) Cornell System of note taking that describes ways to organize each page, special steps to take when recording definitions, spacing needs, and summaries.
- Effective note takers prepare for each lecture by taking notes on the readings before class, acquiring any lecture outlines that the professor has made available on the Web or at the bookstore, and reviewing the notes from the previous class session. If the notes from the readings already cover the in-class points, students can take fewer notes while concentrating on the lecturer's presentation.
- Students should use the outline presented in class to structure notes, but supplement that outline by listening to the lecturers' points and then summarizing them in their own words.
- Recall of information presented in lecture is highly dependent on the completeness of the notes that are taken (Aiken, Thomas, & Shennum, 1975). Notes should be detailed enough so that they can be understood when reviewed weeks later, but they should not be verbatim transcriptions of the lecture. Good note takers wait to write down phrases and partial sentences after listening to the entire idea that the lecturer is presenting (Bjork, 2001). Notes should include diagrams, stories, examples, jokes, and other supplemental material presented by the lecturer.
- Students, if they ask, should be allowed to tape-record lectures. They can then use the recordings to flesh out their classroom notes.
- Taking notes results in some improvement in encoding, but most of the memorial benefits come from reviewing the notes after they have been written: The notes must be studied outside of class for memory consolidation to occur. Pauk (1993), for example, stressed the steps that occur after recording the notes, including reducing (questioning), reciting, reflection, recapitulation, and review.
- If time allows, students should enter all classroom notes into a computer file as soon possible after class.
- Students should be encouraged to build networks of note takers who share notes throughout the term. If the members of the group are similar in the note-taking ability, they can ro-

tate the note-taking responsibility among members of the coterie, leaving the others free to listen attentively to the lecture.

Preparing for Tests

College is full of surprises for some students; the ones who forget about tests until they notice that the students around them, instead of talking before class, are busy cramming; the ones who study topics that interest them, and skip all those that they find boring; the ones who ask, as the test is being distributed, "What chapters does this test cover?" Skilled students, in contrast, encounter few surprises when they take tests. They have such a firm grasp on the overall set of material the test covers that they could list, on a blank sheet of paper, all the major headings, subheadings, key theorists, and important studies and terms without prompting. Realizing that their professor will eventually ask them questions about the material they are studying, they generate their own sample test questions as they study. If permitted, they make use of questions asked on their professor's old exams, and they take all the practice quizzes they can. They also adapt their preparations to fit the type of test they will be taking. If the test will use a choice-type format such as multiple choice, they review all of the material thoroughly, being careful to not overlook any important topic. If the test will use a supply-type format, such as essays, they worry less about comprehensiveness and more about depth of understanding.

But academically skilled students are not just better at preparing for tests; they are also better at taking tests. They focus their attention on the test itself, and use all the recommended strategies for testing success. They read questions completely and carefully. They ask questions about confusing items. They skip "stumpers" and come back to them. They double check their work, if time allows. They avoid careless errors. When taking choice-type tests, these "test-wise" students use a set of heuristics that helps them identify the answers to questions even when they have failed to master the learning objective that the question addresses (Millman, Bishop, & Ebel, 1965). And when taking supply-type tests, they bluff when they do not know the answer (Gronlund, 1998). They carefully restate the question in their answer, add some factually correct but irrelevant information, and include such phrases as "This question is an important one if we are understand the nature of society and our relationship to it," "Psychologists have been studying this fundamental issue for many years," or "This question lies at the heart of many important and time-honored debates in the field of psychology." Expert graders do not give students points when they use such tactics exclusively, but they often reward students whose essay combine comprehensive content with skillful packaging.

Resources

One need not face the task of tutoring students on study skills alone, however. Many excellent books on college-level study skills are available, and students who have poor study habits should be urged to order them and review them. Most schools also offer academic support for students, from workshops on study skills to entire "Introduction to College" classes that cover the basic ingredients for academic success. Other resources can also be utilized, including the English department's writing clinic, the university's counseling center, or tutorial programs coordinated by Psi Chi or your department's psychology club chapter (Pastorino, 1999).

Developing Self-Regulation Skills

Some students fail, not because they lack the academic skills needed for success, but because they cannot bring themselves to exercise those skills on a regular basis. They know how to study, take good notes, and read, but they do not. They have the time they need to complete assignments and make every session of class, but they never get around to doing their homework and they skip classes. They have plenty of potential, but they do not realize it because they are poor self-regulators.

One of the profound differences between high school and college is the level of self-regulation college requires. In high school, parents, teachers, and administrators regulated many aspects of learning for students. In college, these external sources of self-control are relaxed, and the students themselves must take responsibility for nearly all the tasks associated with learning. Some students may rise easily to the challenge, but others may need to learn about, and practice, the self-regulatory skills Zimmerman (1998) identified in his studies of successful athletes, writers, musicians, and students. The following recommendations are "practical techniques that the resourceful acquire and hone to a fine degree" (Zimmerman, 1998, p. 79):

- *Goal-setting*: identifying desired outcomes and end-states, including the topics to be covered in a review session, lists of chapters to be read and reviewed, and learning activities to complete before an examination
- *Task-strategies*: developing and using personalized strategies for studying, such as compressing all the unit's notes into a single page, developing extensive outlines of text material, or developing examples for concepts reviewed in class
- *Imagery*: creating images that capture the essence of material, as well as enhancing motivation by imagining oneself taking and acing the upcoming examination
- *Self-instruction*: talking to oneself about the material to be

learned, as well as reviewing material aloud, urging oneself on (e.g., "let's do it!"), and prompting or praising oneself

- *Time management:* developing schedules for daily and weekly studying, attending classes, completing homework, and non-school activities
- *Self-monitoring:* keeping track of progress toward one's goals, including keeping a personal grade book; counting all pages, articles, or books read; and updating a graduation worksheet
- *Self-evaluation:* developing and taking self-quizzes covering material to be learned, reviewing papers carefully prior to turning them in
- *Self-consequences:* establishing contingencies of self-reward and self-punishment, such as making social contacts, television, music-listening dependent on meeting study objectives
- *Environmental structure:* controlling the area where one studies to maximize stimulus control over learning and minimize distractions
- *Help seeking:* seeking support from others, such as attending review sessions, forming study groups

When Zimmerman and Martinez-Pons (1986) interviewed students in both undergraduate and graduate courses, they found that the successful ones used these techniques regularly.

Professorial Social Support

Professors can help their students overcome their academic difficulties by giving them instrumentally tinged social support: advice, ideas, and suggestions for improving their study and self-regulatory skills. But students may also need social support. Wills (1987), for example, reported that when people experience negative events that leave them emotionally shaken, they gain little from informational support. Harlow and Cantor (1995), in their studies of college students coping with social and academic setbacks, found that students seeking self-improvement seek the counsel of those they admire (*idols*), but when they are struggling to cope with the emotional consequences of a failure they turn to *encouragers* and *confidants*. Students need to be "shown the ropes," but they may also need a "shoulder to cry on."

Emotional Support

Some students may need help managing the emotions they experience in the academic settings in general, and in testing and grading situations in particular (Halamandaris & Power, 1999). Stress levels surge just before and during exams, and then ease off afterwards (Jemmott & Magloire,

1988). But they rise, once again, when students learn whether they have passed or failed the exam. Studies of the psychology of success and failure confirm what every professor knows: Students experience a range of emotional reactions after they succeed on or fail exams. Students who fail, relative to successful students, describe themselves as less relaxed, satisfied, content, elated, and pleasantly surprised, and more unhappy, tense, incompetent, inadequate, upset, depressed, guilty, and hostile (Forsyth & McMillan, 1981a).

Test Anxiety

If students' emotions are particularly intense, distracting, and negative, they may be experiencing test anxiety. In many cases students experience test anxiety simply because they have not studied for the exam. Such students *should* be worried that they might fail, given that they have not prepared properly (Naveh-Benjamin, McKeachie, Lin, & Holinger, 1981). But in some cases, students' claim of anxiety is a legitimate one, characterized by high levels of tension, pronounced worrying, intrusive thinking, and physiological interferences. If students agree with the following types of statements about their reactions to tests, they may need help learning ways to control their test-related anxieties (Sarason, 1984, p. 932):

- I feel distressed and uneasy before tests.
- I find myself becoming anxious the day of a test.
- Before taking a test, I worry about failure.
- During tests, I think about past events.
- Irrelevant bits of information pop into my head during a test.
- During tests, I find myself thinking of things unrelated to the material being tested.
- I get a headache during an important test.
- My stomach gets upset before tests.

Test anxiety responds well to treatment, but professors should help anxious students by referring them to counseling rather than by attempting treatment themselves (Zeidner, 1998).

Motivational Support

When students perform poorly on examinations, the wind goes out of their motivational sails. They may still value a good grade and mastery of the material, but their score lowers their expectations. In consequence, their self-confidence may wane and they may consider giving up their goal rather than redoubling their efforts to reach it. They may also engage in self-protective strategies that buoy up their sense of self-worth, while undermining their chances for success in the future (Covington & Beery, 1976). They may blame their failure on external factors—bad luck, an unfair test, the professor's lack of instruction skills, or the opacity of the text—rather than personal limitations and lack of effort (Forsyth & McMillan, 1981a, 1981b). They may also engage in self-handicapping. Rather than working hard to overcome factors that stand in the way of success, they protect their self-esteem by deliberately seeking out impediments: They skip class, take drugs, binge drink, and so on (Jones & Berglas, 1978). Because these defensive machinations can have ruinous effects on students' learning, professors must sometimes intervene to steer students away from these motivational pitfalls (Forsyth & McMillan, 1991; McMillan & Forsyth, 1991).

Emphasize Growth and Change

Students who think that achievement outcomes are stable rather than unstable overreact to a failure. Because they assume that scores are relatively fixed, they doubt that they will ever rise above their current level of performance (Dweck, 1999). These students may therefore benefit from information about the degree of inconsistency seen in students' grades. As Wilson and Linville (1982, 1985) discovered, first-year students who are told that most college students' grades steadily rise over the course of their college career were less likely to drop out at the end of their second year and achieved greater increases in their grade point averages.

Provide Differentiated Feedback

Give students a ray of hope to brighten the shadow cast by an F by complimenting something about their work. Even a student with a low score on a test will have answered something correctly, and this success should be mentioned. Be careful, however, to highlight the student's ability to answer these items rather than mentioning the ease of the items.

Encourage Psychological Controllability

Students who feel that they can control their academic outcomes show no loss of motivation even when they fail repeatedly. Those who feel that their outcomes are unrelated to their efforts tend to give up rather than persevere after a failure (Dweck & Leggett, 1988). Professors should therefore stress the extent to which educational outcomes are caused by factors students control—time spent studying, note taking, diligence, preparation—rather than factors beyond their control—test difficulty, native ability, academic background. In one study, researchers succeeded in shifting the failure attributions of a group of low-scoring students away from external, uncontrollable factors (such as "difficult test") to internal, controllable causes (such as "effort" and "motivation") through a brief counseling intervention. On subsequent tests and on the final examination, students in the experimental condition earned higher grades than the control students who received no attributional information. Indeed, at the end of the course, the students in the experimental condition earned Cs, but most of the students in the control group received Ds and Fs (Noel, Forsyth, & Kelley, 1987).

Encourage Behavioral Controllability

Interventions that give students a sense of control can be strengthened by actually giving students control over their learning. Professors can, for example, hold workshops on study skills, time management, and effective reading; hold question-and-answer sessions after class periodically during the term; provide students with additional resources to use in their studying, such as computerized tutorials, downloadable copies of annotated notes, and study hints; and allow students to take a role in designing evaluation procedures. Students' sense of autonomy and control should prosper if they know what steps they can take to improve their outcomes.

6

MANAGING: FOSTERING ACADEMIC INTEGRITY, CIVILITY, AND TOLERANCE

Proctors are to watch students actively throughout the examination and be on guard for the following: eyes roving, lips moving, left arm not covering paper, bending down to tie shoe lace or pick up fallen object, blowing nose, yawning or sneezing too loudly, reaching into pocket, crumpling scratch paper into a ball, stretching legs too far out, studying nails or insides of wrists. Impress upon students the importance of high ethical standards: When they cheat they are cheating themselves. If they are caught cheating, the proctor must be blamed for lax supervision.

—Bel Kaufman
Up the Down Staircase (1964, p. 260)

Professors do not just walk into a classroom and teach the students they find there; they must also create and manage that classroom. Even though their top priority is promoting students' learning and achievement, they must also enforce basic principles of academic integrity, civility, and tolerance. When students violate principles pertaining to academic integrity, the professor must intervene with sanctions for the violators and rewards for those who conform. Teaching is also a profoundly interpersonal activity, and so like all interpersonal activities it can be disrupted by conflict, crises, misunderstandings, and antagonisms. Some of these problematic aspects of teaching are inconsequential, but others can significantly disrupt the learning experience unless handled swiftly and carefully.

* * *

Many employees dream of the day when they will be promoted to a management position. Once they gain this lofty post, they expect their days will be far more meaningful, for they'll spend their time directing the activities of the people who work in their unit; they'll be leaders, organizers, resource persons, and motivators. But most new managers are surprised when they discover the host of job duties that comprise their new position. Luthans and his colleagues documented the real work of the manager in various types of organizations: attending meetings, processing paperwork, resolving conflicts, inspecting facilities, filling in as needed, developing procedures, answering the phone, chewing out workers, politicking, contacting vendors, and so on (Luthans, 1998; Luthans, Hodgetts, & Rosenkrantz, 1988).

New professors, too, expect that 90% of their time will be spent teaching students, but they soon discover that they must also spend a good deal of time managing the details of that teaching: completing paperwork, updating their grade books, keeping up with course correspondence, ordering supplies and textbooks, supervising student workers, monitoring students' compliance with university regulations, reporting burned out lights in the classrooms, and so on. Some of these tasks and issues are mundane, routine ones that are easily and swiftly handled, but others demand as much energy and attention as teaching itself (Emmer & Stough, 2001). The classroom, as a complex interpersonal setting, is governed by implicit and explicit rules of conduct and decorum, and the professor-as-manager must sometimes take steps to make certain students abide by those rules. The professor must also deal with the interpersonal and personal conflicts that inevitably arise when people with varying skills, interests, and motivations join in a shared pursuit. When students are disrespectful, angry, intolerant, or troubled, the teaching psychologist must intervene to help them regain the emotional and behavioral stability they need to succeed in their studies.

MANAGING ACADEMIC INTEGRITY

A college or university, like any complicated social system, is governed by sets of norms that regulate the actions of the individuals in that system. Prescriptive norms define the socially appropriate way to respond in class—the *normal* course of action most people display in the situation—and proscriptive norms describe categories of actions that are prohibited or at least frowned on and so should be avoided if at all possible. For example, some of the prescriptive norms of a college classroom are "Listen to the professor," "Sit in the available chairs," and "Take notes," whereas the proscriptive norms are "Do not ask stupid questions" and "Do not talk on your cell phone in the middle of the lecture."

But norms are not merely base rates that define what is expected; they also include an evaluative component. People who violate norms are not just acting atypically; they are being "bad" and hence open themselves up to condemnation by others. This condemnation can include hostility, pressure to change, negative sanctions, and punishment, but the reaction depends on the importance of the norm, the magnitude of the discrepancy, and the characteristics of the person who violates the norm. If the norm reflects current social standards pertaining to minor aspects of conduct, violations are often overlooked, particularly if a prestigious or powerful person is doing the violating. But some norms are considered so essential to the integrity of the classroom that their violation will be roundly and quickly condemned (Sabini & Silver, 1978). Such norms comprise the classroom's moral code. They include such norms as "Do not cheat," "Do not plagiarize," "Do not help others cheat," and "Do not abuse library books and other academic materials." Individuals who break moral norms risk severe penalties if their violation is proven, but because the consequences are so severe, in many cases accusers must present evidence that substantiates the charge.

Variations and Violations

Standards of morality pertaining to lying, stealing, or breaking promises apply to all members of the university community. Classrooms have an additional set of standards, however, standards that are designed to guard against students being (a) credited for learning they did not achieve and (b) gaining advantages or privileges that they do not deserve. Every university or college likely has a list of the specific actions that violate these two principles, but most such lists include:

- *Cheating on tests:* Using information from books, notes, other people's tests, other people themselves, or some other source when these materials are not permitted.
- *Plagiarizing:* Presenting another person's words or ideas as one's own by copying verbatim another author's wording, attempting to paraphrase another's work but failing to change the wording sufficiently, or discussing material drawn from another source and failing to cite the origin of the words or ideas.
- *Collusion:* Working with other students on projects that are explicitly defined as individual projects.
- *Falsifications:* Fabricating explanations for missed work or making false claims in an attempt to secure an unfair advantage in a testing situation.

But the number of ways that students can cheat is limited only by their ingenuity, and each day they develop and implement entirely new methods. For example:

- *"Razoring":* Students in classes where grades are based on relative performance destroy reference materials, often by slicing out key pages from books and reserve readings with a razor.
- *Signaling:* Cooperating students send answers back and forth during the exam using a signaling system, such as notes on a shared eraser, hand signals, facial cues, and so on.

- *Creative cribbing:* Instead of using a bit of paper with critical bits of information jotted on it, creative cribbers write codes on the paper covers of notebooks, on their skin (wrists, hands, ankles), on the back pages of the blue books they will use for essay tests, on their clothing (e.g., the bills of caps, shirt cuffs), on food wrappers (e.g., on the inside of a gum wrapper), and on food items themselves (e.g., on a stick of gum, which is then eaten to destroy the evidence).
- *"Headphoning":* Students record audio information about course material (on a cassette, a CD, or MP3 file) and use headphones to listen to the recording during the test.
- *Stealing and switching:* As students pass in an assignment, the perpetrator steals one of the papers printed in a font he can duplicate. He explains after class that he left his paper back in his room, and he needs to just run over and pick it up. He retypes and replaces the cover sheet and turns in the other students' paper as his own.
- *The bomb scare:* Unprepared students call in a bomb threat for the building where the final examination is given. A less dramatic approach: Unprepared students go to class before the professor and write on the board "Due to illness, class and test canceled for today." By the time the professor arrives, many students have already departed, and the test must be rescheduled.
- *The lost test:* The student, sensing failure, asks several questions of the professor during the examination so that the professor will remember that she was in class that day. She then leaves the class without turning in her test, and contacts the professor when grades are posted complaining that her test was lost. She has studied the test thoroughly since the exam date, and willingly takes the test again and aces it.
- *"Ghosting":* A skilled student who is not registered for the class (a "ghost" or "ringer") comes to class on test day and takes the test with another student or lets that student copy his answers.
- *Mourning:* The student claims she must attend the funeral of a family member but will be able to take the examination a few hours after the class does; a friend in the class steals a copy of the test and the mourner studies it before taking it.
- *Scouting:* When quizzes are administered at computers, one student (the scout) quickly completes the test, fails, but gets his score and item-by-item feedback. He passes this information on to the students seated around him. Next time

someone else in the clique becomes the scout so others can get 100s.

- *Claiming disability*: A student requests an adjustment in the testing procedures or a learning situation by claiming a disability that is not substantiated.
- *Hacking*: A student breaks into computer databases and alters records of performance.

These sorts of actions violate a number of principles that most professors hold sacrosanct. Academic dishonesty opposes higher education's fundamental mission, which is the creation of knowledge and the dissemination of knowledge to others. Those who cheat or plagiarize not only fail to expand the scholarly stock of knowledge, but they also fail to even learn what is already known. Such actions also suggest that grades and test scores are all that matter, when in fact it is the learning that matters most. Cheating and plagiarizing are also unfair to the professor and to other students. When students cheat, they increase their individual scores even though they have not achieved the learning that their scores suggest. When grades are based on normative evaluation systems, their cheating unfairly lowers the grades of students who did not cheat. In consequence, students who do not cheat may be tempted to cheat themselves when they see others cheat successfully. Cheating and plagiarism are also specialized cases of a class of behavior that is widely condemned as immoral: the lie. When students cheat and plagiarize they are lying to their professor by claiming "I wrote this," "I answered this question," or "I learned the material you asked me to."

Maintaining Academic Integrity

Surveys of college students, like those described by Davis, Grover, Becker, and McGregor (1992), McCabe, Treviño, and Butterfield (2001), and McCabe and Treviño (1997), indicated that cheating is no rare avis: Three in four students reported having engaged in relatively serious forms of academic dishonesty, such as using crib notes, copying off of someone else's examination, working with others on projects that were supposed be done by individuals only, and plagiarizing. When asked if they cheated in a particular class or during a given semester, 20–30% of the students surveyed reported committing an infraction, and some students reported having cheated repeatedly in the same class throughout the term (Stearns, 2001; Ward & Beck, 1990). Nor is cheating limited to undergraduate students. Wajda-Johnston, Handal, Brawer, and Fabricatore (2001) found that more than half of the graduate students they surveyed admitted plagiarizing (by inadequately paraphrasing the sampled text rather than copying entire sections), and one in four reported working collectively on individual assignments. Whitley's (1998) meta-analytic review refined these estimates somewhat by suggesting that men cheat more, as do students whose time is more limited—say by a job or by participation in extracurricular events —and students who are younger. Students who are members of sororities and fraternities also cheat more frequently than other students (McCabe & Bowers, 1996).

Human beings in general, and college students in particular, have a great capacity for moral goodness, but in many educational settings students fail to fulfill that potential. What can be done to encourage more positive forms of behavior and discourage antisocial actions (Davis, 1993; McBurney, 1999; McCabe et al., 2001)?

Clarify and Review What Is Acceptable and Unacceptable

The words *cheating* and *plagiarism* are ominous but indefinite in meaning. Students who tell themselves "I do not cheat" may nonetheless do things that their professor considers cheating only because they did not think their actions fell in the value-laden category of "cheating." Students may not realize that a take-home test should be completed when they are alone if the test's instructions do not explicitly state: "This test must be completed by single individuals, without any discussion, help, or communication from others." They can justifiably claim that the old tests given them by friends are legitimate study aids, for they did not know that the tests were stolen from the classroom by students who skirted the professor's test-security procedures. They may even feel that glancing at another student's test paper is only "checking their own answers" rather than cheating, particularly if they claim that they didn't change their own answers after their visual incursion into their neighbor's test. Students should therefore be given guidelines that turn gray ethical areas to black and white.

Reviews of standards pertaining to plagiarism are particularly useful because psychologists themselves do not always agree on the proper rules of citation and referencing (Roig, 2001). Although most students realize that copying an article out of a journal or purchasing a paper online and turning it in instead of writing their own paper is plagiarism, some do not think that taking a few sentences from someone else's work qualifies as plagiarism. Students are also surprised to learn that even when only the ideas, and not the words, are presented, a reference to the source of the ideas is still required. Students should be referred to the *Publication Manual of the American Psychological Association* (American Psychological Association, 2001), which explains:

> Psychologists do not claim the words and ideas of another as their own; they give credit where credit is due. Quotation marks should be used to indicate the exact words of another. Each time you paraphrase another author (i.e., summarize a passage or rearrange the order of a

sentence and change some of the words), you will need to credit the source in the text. (p. 349)

In courses with large amounts of writing, the professor may also want to assign an activity that requires students to identify instances of plagiarism, paraphrasing that retains so much of the original phrasing that it remains plagiarism, allowable paraphrasing, and failures to reference the source of ideas. Davis (1993) offered a number of useful activities that can be used to help students learn about plagiarism, as well as suggestions for syllabus sections that define plagiarism clearly. Prescribed behaviors should also be reviewed, if appropriate. Some universities, for example, require that students must report all honor violations, so students in such institutions should be reminded of their responsibilities. They should also be urged to take steps to reduce the possibility of cheating by others by safeguarding their work from theft.

Establish a Code

What is wrong with taking a few answers from another student? Working together on a project that the professor said was to be individual work only? Borrowing the words of another author and using them to make a point in one's own paper? If students are simply given a list of banned behaviors, with no explanation for why these behaviors are untoward, then their compliance may be minimal. Academic integrity experts therefore recommend making cheating a moral issue by developing an honor code or set of academic integrity principles (e.g., McCabe et al., 2001). Whitley and Keith-Spiegel (2001), for example, suggested that an academic integrity policy should specify clearly the

- reasons for the policy by examining the values of the university and arguing that cheating and other forms of academic dishonesty are inconsistent with those values;
- types of behavior that are forbidden;
- responsibilities of all parties, including students, faculty, and administrators;
- procedures that will be followed when a student is suspected of academic dishonesty; and
- penalties that can be imposed for various types of offenses.

Faculty themselves should be familiar with their college or university's ethics policy, if one exists. Although many professors prefer to handle cases of cheating themselves, say by conducting their own investigations and lowering grades if warranted, their institutions' ethics policy may not permit this approach. In many cases such policies explicitly require that all instances of suspected violation be handled formally, using specified procedures, rather than informally by the professor. Faculty, too, are limited in terms of the severity of the sanction they can impose. Whereas individual faculty members can only fail a student in individual classes, more formal procedures can recommend expulsion of the student from the university.

Encourage the Internalization of Academic Integrity Codes

Evidence has indicated that fewer students cheat on campuses that have a well-conceived honor code, but the codes' impact depends in large part on the extent to which students have accepted the academic values it expresses (Jordan, 2001; McCabe et al., 2001). If students do not personally accept the moral claim of the rules prohibiting cheating or plagiarism, then they will likely look to the situation to define what is right or wrong and will disobey a moral rule if everyone else is doing it, if no one can detect the violation, or if the potential benefits are substantial. Steps should therefore be taken to increase the extent to which students internalize the code:

- Involve students in the discussion and development of a classroom policy. Just as managers have discovered that people are more likely to comply with workplace policies if they had a hand in developing those policies, so professors will find that students will be more likely to endorse and comply with ethical standards if they contribute to the development of the standards.
- Give students the opportunity to endorse, formally, their adherence to the code.
- Encourage the development of mastery goals that focus on learning and development rather than on extrinsic goals such as grades, GPA, and the dean's list (Jordan, 2001).
- Encourage the development of a full range of attitudes and values pertaining to academic integrity. Individuals who are generally opposed to cheating, but who have yet to formulate a position on specific types of cheating (such as cribbing or buying term papers), are more likely to cheat than those who have action-specific attitudes (Homer & Kahle, 1988).
- Increase the accessibility of anticheating attitudes by mentioning them prior to each test and when making assignments. Evidence indicates that individuals sometimes act in ways that are inconsistent with their values only because they act without considering their personal position on the matter (Langer, 1989).

Eliminate Temptations

Milgram (1963, 1974), in his famous obedience studies, found that everyone wilted when pressured. Every single one of the thousand people he tested obeyed initially by delivering painful shocks to a helpless victim, and 65% were completely obedient. Similarly, studies of cheating have suggested that nearly everyone, if subjected to strong, focused situational pressure that demands cheating, will cheat (Forsyth & Berger, 1982). Given the power of the situation to compel even the best-intentioned student into cheating, testing situations and assignments should be designed so that acting dishonestly is difficult and risky, and acting honestly is simple and easy. When giving a test in class:

- Ask students to sit with an empty seat between them if possible. If necessary, break up clusters of friends or have students sit in assigned seats.
- Reserve one row of a class for students who are tardy, who ask frequent questions, or who engage in suspicious behavior and must be moved.
- In crowded classes, make up at least two versions of the test by reordering the items. Have the versions printed on different colored paper and interleave the tests prior to class so that no student is seated beside another student taking the same test version. As students work, visually inspect each row for adjacent students with same-colored tests and move them if necessary.
- In theater-style classes, count out the number of examinations needed for each row prior to class. When passing out the exams, hold back a question booklet for each empty seat. If a student in the last seat in the row does not get a test, ask the students in the row "to check to make sure they didn't accidentally get two copies."
- In large classes, ask students to display a photo ID when they drop off their test. If very cautious, ask each student to sign an attendance list and their question booklet upon leaving the room.
- If the college honor code does not limit proctoring, observe students carefully as they complete the examination, moving to the rear of the room frequently. In large classes, additional proctors will reduce cheating, particularly during the end of the period when attention is diverted to the collection of the tests.
- Guard exams prior to test day by asking a particular staff member to photocopy them and notify you immediately when they are ready. Lock the exams away or keep them with you before the test day.
- Change the content of the exams as frequently as you can, given time limitations and the need to verify the psycho-

metric adequacy of items by first using them in testing settings.

- Periodically exchange tests and test banks with professors who teach at other universities.
- Collect all blue books at the start of class and redistribute them at random (Davis, 1993).

When assigning papers, reports, and other written assignments, consider taking some of the following steps:

- Consult with students on their topics rather than allowing them to pick freely the subject of their paper (since their choice might be based on papers available to them from non-personal sources, such as Web sites).
- Explicitly ban the use of papers written for other classes if you do not permit such recycling.
- Change the nature and topics of required exercises and papers routinely so that students are not tempted to use papers written by other students who took the class in a previous term.
- Require students to complete a series of steps as they develop their papers. McBurney (1999), for example, recommended having students submit short paragraphs describing their papers, a list of references they plan to consult, and an outline before turning in their drafts. These stages help students begin their work, and they also create a paper trail that confirms that their work is original.
- Ask students to save early drafts of their papers on a computer disk and to turn in the disk with their final paper.
- Consider letting students work in three-person groups on take-home papers to reduce the temptation to collaborate secretly.

Be Alert to and Investigate Possible Instances of Cheating

Sometimes faculty look the other way when their students cheat (Tabachnick et al., 1991). When Keith-Spiegel, Tabachnick, Whitley, and Washburn (1998) asked them why, most traced their leniency to evidentiary concerns: They did not think they had the proof they needed to make a strong case against the student. Other inhibiting factors, identified through factor analysis, included emotional consequences such as stress and lack of courage, concerns about the amount of time and effort the process would take, fears of retaliation and legal entanglements, and various denials that rationalized not intervening, such as assuming that the student would fail even if he or she were not confronted.

Inaction, however, leaves the cheater's unfairly high grade intact, reinforces students' beliefs that they can get away with cheating, and might even instill the implicit norm "cheating is allowable," so professors should:

- Announce, prior to class, that you will be asking people to move during the exam when you see any sign at all of test copying. Note that in many cases the people being asked to move are innocent of copying, but are being moved away from the individual who is suspected of copying.
- During the examination, when observing suspicious behavior, announce to the entire class the reminder about cheating while staring directly at the possible cheater.
- Establish a clear policy pertaining to attendance on exam days and deadlines for papers, and require documentation of students' excuses for missing tests or deadlines (Caron, Whitbourne, & Halgin, 1992).
- Use statistical or computer-based detective methods to detect cheating and plagiarism, if possible, and warn students about these procedures. Bellezza and Bellezza (1995), for example, describe a technique that tests for unlikely coincidences in answer patterns of students, and several computer programs and Web sites (e.g., Scrutiny!) allow instructors to search for statistical evidence of cheating and plagiarism.
- Assemble as much evidence as possible pertaining to the incident. Describe the incident in writing and send a copy of the report to your chair. If proctors witnessed the infraction, have them write and sign a statement describing the incident. Statements can also be obtained from students in the class.
- Respect the suspected student's rights to due process by following your institution's academic integrity guidelines scrupulously. If those codes prohibit you from handling the infraction personally (by giving a cheater a zero on a test), then turn the matter over to the office that handles such matters.

Reduce Pressures That Sustain Cheating

Some students may cheat as a last resort, feeling that it is the only way they can pass the class or test. Indeed, one of the best predictors of cheating is level of preparedness, with unprepared students cheating more than prepared ones. One could therefore eliminate all cheating by giving all students As, but less extreme interventions may be just as effective, such as:

- Make certain that the demands of the course are appropriate for the types of students you are teaching.

- Use clear grading criteria and communicate those criteria clearly to students.
- Test frequently so that students' grades are not based on just one or two major assignments.
- Give students sufficient time to complete their work.
- Accept valid excuses for missed work and absences.
- Consider letting students prepare one page or index card of notes for their use when taking tests.
- Do not let norms that encourage cheating (e.g., "Everybody cheats around here," "The only way to pass this class is to cheat") develop in the classroom. Even students with well-internalized values may cheat if the norms of the situation prevent them from acting on the basis of their values.

Maintain Rapport With Students

McBurney (1999) predicted that a professor who enjoys a sense of rapport and relationship with his or her students—say by acting positively toward them and treating them respectfully—may be rewarded with fewer problems pertaining to cheating in their classes. Stearns (2001), supporting McBurney's suggestion, found that students who admitted cheating in a particular class were also more likely to report less liking and respect for their professor. Although the students who cheated may have derogated their professor after the fact so as to rationalize their untoward actions and reduce their sense of guilt, their negative opinion of their professor may have contributed to their cheating. Students who like and respect their professor, but then cheat in his or her class, could resolve this attitude-behavior inconsistency by derogating the professor, by claiming they had little choice, or telling themselves that their cheating had yielded no negative consequences, but these modes of dissonance resolution require far more cognitive ratiocination than a single behavioral change: not cheating.

Model Integrity and Fairness

Social learning theory, with its emphasis on learning through observation, suggests that professors can influence students by modeling actions and expressing values that are consistent with high standards of academic integrity (Bandura, 1969, 1977). A professor who prepares diligently for classes, develops sound methods for testing students' achievements, treats students and teaching assistants fairly, and enthusiastically supports the academy's emphasis on scholarship provides students with an admirable ideal to emulate. But if students are taught by a professor who seems to be cheating—not by plagiarizing others' words or stealing answers from another student's test but by treating students unfairly, by teaching badly, or by acting inappropriately—then they will likely learn a different lesson.

Professors who want students to obey the rules should obey the rules, too. The ethics of psychologists, when they take on the role of teacher, are discussed briefly in the next section.

The Ethics of Psychologists Who Teach

Academic integrity applies to professors as well as to their students. The university that asks its students to abide by shared rules pertaining to cheating and plagiarism likely also asks the faculty to make certain their actions are consistent with the academy's standards for scholarship, teaching, and service. But psychologists who teach, if they are members of the American Psychological Association, are also bound by that association's *Ethical Principles of Psychologists and Code of Conduct* (APA, 2002). This code sets forth a set of basic ethical principles that define the professional responsibilities of psychologists, in general. The introduction states that psychologists are obligated to "comply with the standards of the APA Ethics Code and to the rules and procedures used to enforce them" and that psychologists should consult with their colleagues or other appropriate authorities when they are "applying the Ethics Code to their professional work." The code's list of principles define the aspirational goals of the psychologist and stress such values as competence, integrity, responsibility, respect and concern for others, and social responsibility. The code also contains a set of enforceable standards of behavior that, if violated, can lead to formal sanctions, including expulsion from the Association. Although the Ethics Code focuses primarily on the complex ethical issues that face therapists, many of its rules and principles are relevant to teaching psychologists. *Principle C: Integrity*, stresses the importance of dealing with others fairly and honestly, and warns against "unwise and unclear commitments." *Principle E: Respect for People's Rights and Dignity*, states that psychologists, when teaching, "respect cultural, individual, and role differences . . . and consider these factors when working with members of such groups." The rules themselves offer relatively clear standards for professional conduct in a variety of areas related to teaching, including testing, relationships with students, and competence. Examples include (paraphrased):

- *Conflicts between ethics and organizational demands* (1.03): When the demands of the professors' college or university conflict with this Ethics Code, "psychologists clarify the nature of the conflict, make known their commitment to the Ethics Code, and to the extent feasible, resolve the conflict in a way that permits adherence to the Ethics Code."

- *Informal resolution of ethical violations* (1.04): When possible, teaching psychologists resolve ethical issues involving their colleagues informally, so long as "an informal resolution appears appropriate and the intervention does not violate any confidentiality rights."
- *Reporting ethical violations* (1.05): When necessary, teaching "psychologists take further action" in their attempts to resolve ethical problems, including "referral to state or national committees on professional ethics, to state licensing boards, or to the appropriate institutional authorities."
- *Cooperating with ethics committees* (1.06): Teaching psychologists are obligated to "cooperate in ethics investigations, proceedings, and resulting requirements of the APA," and their failure to do so itself constitutes an ethics violation.
- *Improper complaints* (1.07): "Psychologists do not file or encourage the filing of ethics complaints that are made with reckless disregard for or willful ignorance of facts that would disprove the allegation."
- *Unfair discrimination against complainants and respondents* (1.08): Teaching psychologists "do not deny persons employment, advancement, admissions to academic or other programs, tenure, or promotion, based solely upon their having made or their being the subject of an ethics complaint."
- *Boundaries of competence* (2.01a): Psychologists teach only within the "boundaries of their competence;" they teach in new areas only after first undertaking appropriate study, training, supervision, and consultation from people who are competent in those areas.
- *Maintaining competence* (2.03): Psychologists who teach "undertake ongoing efforts to develop and maintain their competence."
- *Personal problems and conflicts* (2.06b): When teaching psychologists "become aware of personal problems that may interfere with their performing work-related duties adequately, they take appropriate measures."
- *Unfair discrimination* (3.01): Teaching psychologists "do not engage in unfair discrimination based on age, gender, gender identity, race, ethnicity, culture, national origin, religion, sexual orientation, disability, socioeconomic status, or any basis proscribed by law."
- *Exploitative relationships* (3.08): Teaching psychologists do not exploit their students because they "have supervisory, evaluative, or other authority" over them. (See also Standard 7.07, *Sexual relationships with students and supervisees*.)

- *Maintaining confidentiality* (4.01): "Psychologists have a primary obligation and take reasonable precautions to protect confidential information obtained through or stored in any medium."
- *Minimizing intrusions on privacy* (4.04b): Teaching psychologists discuss confidential information about their students "only for appropriate scientific or professional purposes and only with persons clearly concerned with such matters."
- *Use of confidential information for didactic or other purposes* (4.07): Teaching psychologists do not disclose confidential information about their students in their "writings, lectures, or other public media " unless "the person or organization has consented in writing" or unless "there is legal authorization for doing so."
- *Descriptions of education and training programs* (7.02): Teaching psychologists develop and disseminate accurate descriptions of their educational programs' "content (including participation in required course- or program-related counseling, psychotherapy, experiential groups, consulting projects, or community service), training goals and objectives, stipends and benefits, and requirements that must be met for satisfactory completion of the program."
- *Accuracy and objectivity in teaching* (7.03a, b): "Psychologists take reasonable steps to ensure that course syllabi are accurate regarding the subject matter to be covered, bases for evaluating progress, and the nature of course experiences" and also "present psychological information accurately."
- *Assessing student and supervisee performance* (7.06a, b): Psychologists collect information about the quality of their teaching by using "a timely and specific process for providing feedback to students and supervisees." They also evaluate their students fairly, basing these evaluations on students' "actual performance on relevant and established program requirements."
- *Sexual relationships with students and supervisees* (7.07): Teaching psychologists "do not engage in sexual relationships with students or supervisees . . . over whom" they have "evaluative authority."
- *Plagiarism* (8.11): "Psychologists do not present portions of another's work or data as their own, even if the other work or data source is cited occasionally."
- *Publication credit* (8.12a, c): "Psychologists take responsibility and credit, including authorship credit, only for work they have actually performed or to which they have substantially

contributed. . . . Except under exceptional circumstances, a student is listed as principal author on any multiple-authored article that is substantially based on the student's doctoral dissertation."

- *Test construction* (9.05): Teaching psychologists use "appropriate psychometric procedures and current scientific or professional knowledge for test design, standardization, validation, reduction or elimination of bias, and recommendations for use."

- *Obsolete tests and outdated test results* (9.08a): Psychologists who teach "do not base their assessment or intervention decisions or recommendations on data or test results that are outdated for the current purpose."

Do teaching psychologists agree with, and conform to, the requirements of their ethics code? Tabachnick and her colleagues (1991) examined this question by surveying 482 members of APA who listed an academic department as their address or belonged to Division 2 of APA: Teaching of Psychology. They asked these individuals to rate 63 behaviors listed in Table 6.1 in terms of their ethicality, and to indicate if they performed the identified behavior with any regularity.

Tabachnick et al.'s results suggested that teaching psychologists' ratings coincide with some, but not all, of the APA principles. Sexual harassment, teaching while under the influence of drugs, claiming credit for students' work, falsifying information, accepting a bribe from a textbook publisher, insulting students, expressing racist or antigay beliefs in class, becoming sexually involved with a student, ignoring cheating, using biased grading methods, showing films that have little educational worth, accepting gifts from students, and revealing confidential information to colleagues were all rated as unethical by at least half of the respondents, and these were also the behaviors that they reported rarely, if ever, performing. Many respondents, however, were relatively tolerant of a number of teaching practices that violate APA standards, such as failing to keep up with the field's discoveries, teaching material that they have not yet mastered, teaching when too distressed to be effective, teaching without preparing—and many of the respondents admitted they did such actions on occasion. As regards sexual involvement with students, most respondents felt faculty should not date or have sex with their students, reveal their sexual inclinations to students, or even fantasize about students in sexual ways. Students, by the way, tend to agree with faculty on this matter. Keith-Spiegel, Tabachnick, and Allen (1993) found that a majority (54%) of the students they surveyed thought faculty should not date students and 70% evaluated student–professor sexual relationships negatively.

Faculty–student sexual relationships are controversial ones. These re-

TABLE 6.1
Teaching Psychologists' Judgments and Self-Reports
of Various Types of Behaviors

Behavior	Rating	
	Unethical	Self-report
Making deliberate or repeated sexual comments, gestures, or physical contact that is unwanted by the student	94.6	0.0
Teaching while under the influence of cocaine or other illegal drugs	83.0	0.0
Accepting undeserved authorship on a student's published paper	82.4	0.0
Including false or misleading information when writing a letter of recommendation for a student	81.3	0.4
Accepting for yourself a publisher's monetary rebate for adopting their text	79.7	0.4
Teaching while under the influence of alcohol	79.3	0.6
Insulting, ridiculing, etc., a student in the student's presence	73.4	0.8
Teaching that certain races are intellectually inferior	73.2	0.8
Accepting for your department a publisher's monetary rebate for adopting their text	71.2	1.0
Becoming sexually involved with a student	71.0	1.4
Ignoring strong evidence of cheating	69.3	2.7
Telling a student: "I'm sexually attracted to you"	68.9	0.2
Teaching that homosexuality per se is pathological	64.3	3.3
Allowing a student's "likability" to influence your grading	63.3	9.7
Insulting, ridiculing, etc., a student in the student's absence	61.4	10.4
Using films, etc., to fill class time (and reduce your teaching work) without regard for their educational value	53.5	2.7
Accepting a student's expensive gift	52.3	1.4
Telling colleagues confidential disclosures told to you by a student	52.1	3.3
Assigning unpaid students to carry out work for you which has little educational value for the student	49.4	5.4
Criticizing all theoretical orientations except those you personally prefer	47.5	8.7
Dating a student	45.6	5.1
Privately tutoring students in the department for a fee	45.4	0.0
Using a grading procedure which does not adequately measure what students have learned	45.2	13.9
Taking advantage of a student's offer such as wholesale prices at parents' store	43.8	0.4
Inadequately supervising teaching assistants	43.2	7.9
Giving easy courses or tests to ensure your popularity with students	39.8	3.3
Ignoring unethical behavior by colleagues	36.3	28.8
Using cocaine or other illegal drugs in your personal (nonteaching) life	30.7	7.2

Table continues

TABLE 6.1 (*Continued*)

Behavior	Rating	
	Unethical	Self-report
Teaching where there's no adequate grievance procedures for students	30.5	9.5
Selling unwanted complimentary textbooks to used book vendors	29.7	39.6
Grading on a strict curve regardless of class performance level	28.2	8.1
Teaching content in a nonobjective or incomplete manner	27.6	20.6
Omitting significant information when writing a letter of recommendation for a student	25.7	17.5
Requiring students to use aversive procedures with rats, pigeons, etc.	24.3	5.3
Becoming sexually involved with a student only after he or she has completed your course and the grade has been filed	20.7	3.5
Engaging in sexual fantasies about students	20.3	25.5
Having students be research subjects as part of a course requirement	18.7	39.0
Teaching in buildings which could not accommodate physically challenged students	17.8	35.5
Teaching full time while "moonlighting" at least 20 hours per week	17.2	10.2
Allowing students to drop courses for reasons not officially approved	16.8	16.6
Giving academic credit instead of salary for student assistants	16.0	35.7
Teaching in classes so crowded you couldn't teach effectively	16.0	23.5
Being sexually attracted to a student	15.4	38.5
Failing to update lecture notes when re-teaching a course	14.5	35.6
Using profanity in lectures	14.3	20.3
Engaging in a sexual relationship with another faculty member within your department who is of higher or lower rank than you	14.1	3.1
Selling goods (e.g., your car or books) to a student	12.4	4.7
Teaching material you haven't really mastered	10.8	38.4
Engaging in a sexual relationship with another faculty member within your department who is of the same academic rank as you	10.0	2.6
Teaching in a setting lacking adequate ethnic diversity among the faculty	9.5	64.0
Teaching when too distressed to be effective	8.9	21.1
Teaching a class without adequate preparation that day	8.5	40.8
Using school resources to create a "popular" psychology trade book	7.9	3.1
Encouraging competition among students	6.8	36.1
Lending money to a student	6.6	12.2
Using school resources to prepare a scholarly textbook	5.8	25.0

Table continues

TABLE 6.1 (*Continued*)

	Rating	
Behavior	Unethical	Self-report
Hugging a student	5.6	34.6
Asking small favors (e.g., a ride home) from students	5.2	25.9
Helping a student file an ethics complaint against another teacher	5.0	5.6
Accepting a student's inexpensive gift (worth less than $5)	4.8	44.6
Teaching ethics or values to students	3.9	79.5
Accepting a student's invitation to a party	3.1	51.5
Encouraging students to participate in your research projects	2.9	39.7

Note. The entries for the column labeled Unethical indicate the percentage of respondents who indicated the action was "unquestionably not ethical." The entries for the column labeled Self-report indicate the percentage of respondents who reported engaging in the behavior "sometimes," "fairly often," or "very often." Adapted from "Ethics of Teaching: Beliefs and Behaviors of Psychologists as Educators," by B. G. Tabachnick, P. Keith-Spiegel, and K. S. Pope, 1991, *American Psychologist, 46*, pp. 510–511. Copyright 1991 by the American Psychological Association. Adapted with permission.

lationships run the risk of violating any number of APA standards, include those pertaining to sexual harassment, maintaining objectivity in evaluating student's performances, avoiding dual relationships, and the exploitation of those who are in positions of lower status. Such relationships also create ripples of ethical uncertainty within departments and programs, for faculty who are not involved in the relationship but are aware of it must debate the need to discuss this personal, but potentially unethical, behavior with their colleagues. Such relationships can also undermine the primary mission of the professor: to teach. As Kitchener (2000) noted, "if the psychologist removes him- or herself from the role of educator or supervisor in order to avoid the multiple roles, the student is denied the opportunity to have the person as a mentor or instructor" (p. 151).

But even though Tabachnick et al. report a high level of consensus for cases that clearly violate APA standards pertaining to exploitative relationships, they also found that respondents were largely divided on other issues related to sex. Some respondents felt that sexual fantasies about students, sex with colleagues, and sexual relations with former students were completely unethical, but many others felt that they were ethical under many circumstances. This diversity of opinion is to be expected given individual variations in moral thinking, values, and philosophies. Although the Code of Ethics warns against relationships between professor and student for as long as the professor can determine the student's evaluations and outcomes, many psychologists may not feel that such relationships are exploitive. Questions of morality must be discussed and debated, and as the APA Code of Ethics requires, psychologists must be tolerant of cultural and individual differences in attitudes, including those that have a moral content. Moreover, involvement in the relationships of others violates APA's Principle E, which requires members to respect the privacy, dignity, and autonomy of others.

Faculty must, however, exercise caution and sensitivity in such matters. Psychologists who teach are likely bound by a number of codes of ethics, and these codes' mandates may not converge in a tidy set of dos and don'ts. As professors, some may wish to heed the ethical code of the American Association of University Professors or the Society for Teaching and Learning in Higher Education (Murray, Gillese, Lennon, Mercer, & Robinson, 1996). As psychologists, they may base their actions on the standards set by the American Psychological Association's (2002) Code of Ethics or their state licensing standards. But as employees of their college and university, and as members of the community, they are also bound to act in ways that are consistent with their institution's regulations and their community's standards. Although particular classes of actions, such as sexual relationships with students, may not be inconsistent with one code of ethics, these actions may be condemned by another. The professor who cites the APA Code of Ethics to support his or her actions may quickly discover that the college's administrators base their appraisals on an altogether different code. If local norms condemn certain behaviors, considering them tantamount to moral turpitude, then faculty would be well advised to conduct themselves accordingly. At minimum, any professor who is considering questionable behaviors should discuss the matter with colleagues and supervisors.

CLASSROOM MANAGEMENT

Movies and television programs often juxtapose scenes from raucous high schools with images of idealized college classrooms. Teachers in high schools are shown struggling with unruly adolescents who talk constantly to friends and show little respect for the teacher. Professors' classrooms, in contrast, are veritable temples of learning, with stylishly dressed students seated in elegantly appointed lecture halls listening respectfully to their teachers' every word. Unfortunately, not all college classes reach Hollywood's high standards. Faculty, particularly when facing large classes, must contend with a variety of classroom incivilities (Boice, 2000): Students arrive late and the leave early. They don't pay much attention during class, preferring instead to banter with friends even after pointed warnings. As attention ebbs at the end of class, the sound of zipping book bags drowns out the lecturer's summary. And of course students read newspapers, answer cell phone calls, and fall asleep. What can professors do to maintain control in their classrooms?

Civility in the Classroom

Carbone (1998) provided case studies of three professors' approaches to classroom management. One professor establishes the norms that pertain to his classroom on the first day of class, and maintains them with zeal throughout the term by publicly embarrassing any rule-breakers. He informs students that if they must leave class early or will be late arriving, then they should not come to class that day. When asked about his approach, he explains, "As an instructor I'm not afraid to act as a policeman and squash that type of behavior" (p. 78). A second professor uses a laissez-faire approach. He pays little attention to attendance, comings and goings, and ignores as best he can side conversations, asking only that people who talk consistently sit at the back of the room. He concludes, "They're paying for it, they're grown-ups. They can come if they want to" (p. 78). A third professor permits students to come late and go early, but requires that they submit a written request for each occurrence. She also intervenes if students talk excessively in class, but rather than publicly questioning them, she asks the offenders to meet her after class.

These professors have very different standards about classroom civility: One expects that students will come to class prepared to learn and creates a uniformly attentive classroom by pressuring inattentive students to either act appropriately or to skip class; one is willing to put up with disruptions to learning to maintain rapport with his students; and one maintains control through an elaborate hall-pass system. Each approach is defensible, but the wide range means that teaching professors must make certain to create the type of classroom norms that they most prefer at the start of the term, and then reinstate these norms whenever students stray too far from the desired standard.

Creating Classroom Norms

Classrooms, as groups, rapidly develop a set of norms that will become powerful determinants of members' actions. If the classroom is set in a university or college where most professors set the same standards for their classes, then the class norms will likely reflect the university's norms. But when diversity is the rule rather than exception, professors should encourage the formation of the types of classroom norms they prefer. Suggestions for professors include the following:

- State the classroom rules clearly in the syllabus and reiterate them as needed.
- Link classroom rules to a more general framework of social and moral principles that provides an overall rationale for the class's procedures. Students can be reminded, for example, that the classroom's highest priority is learning, and that all

other concerns must be set aside during the time spent in the classroom.

- Stress the need for cooperation and teamwork, particularly in larger classes where the actions of a minority can substantially disrupt the quality of the experience for the majority. Remind students of the importance of putting their personal, individual needs aside for the good of the collective.
- Share responsibility for maintaining norms with the students. Remind students they are collectively responsible for maintaining classroom norms, and so attentive students should feel free to tell talkative students to be quiet.
- Compare the classroom to other types of social aggregates, such as audiences, congregations, and mobs. Inform students that the classroom is similar to an audience at a theatrical performance, where patrons can be seated only between acts but different from a movie audience where viewers can come and go as they please.
- Use rituals to start and end each session. For example, begin class each day by standing silently at the lectern until the class quiets or use the same stock opening phrase (e.g., "Good morning scholars!"). End class abruptly, rather than gradually, with a strong summarizing phrase or a ritual closing phrase, such as "And so ends the lesson," or "How time flies."
- Reduce pluralistic ignorance by making the amount of conformity to the preferred standards salient to students. Note, for example, that virtually all the students in the class are happy to comply with norms pertaining to attendance and attention, and stress instead the unexpected and atypicality of noncompliant actions.
- Nip emergent norms in the bud. New norms can pop up in a group at any time, and when these norms are not conducive to learning, they should be eliminated quickly. For example, never tolerate the "there are only 5 minutes left so I'm going to get ready to leave" habit. If students get noisy, stop class, remind them you are aware of the time remaining and that you will end class on time, but that you must have their attention during the class's final minutes so you can complete the day's teaching.

Using Social Influence

Even in classrooms with well-ensconced norms of civility and attendance, students will sometimes slip up and violate established standards. Students must modify their behavior from class to class in order to match the unique normative demands of each professor's classroom, and if something else requires their attention—such as studying, socializing, or working—then actions appropriate for one classroom may be displayed in a different classroom. In such cases the professor may need to intervene more directly by using informational, normative, or interpersonal influence (Forsyth, 1999). A professor may

- move from the dais and stand close to students who are talking among themselves;
- use the classroom and the students in the classroom frequently as examples of psychological events (e.g., find drowsy students to check for REM, discuss the physiological reactions of students who are acting in amorous ways in class, violate the personal space of students who are talking);
- ask students who are not paying attention simple questions: ones that they can easily answer with a personal opinion or by restating a point just made in class;
- reward students on days when they remain attentive to the very end of class by praising them and thanking them effusively; and
- monitor the classroom carefully and focus attention on students and clusters of students who are not acting appropriately. In extreme cases, subgroups of students who develop their own norms about proper decorum will need to be dismantled by reseating them in different parts of the class.

Controlling Attendance Patterns

Norms pertaining to attendance in classes are particularly varied. Many professors feel that college students should be free to choose when and if they attend class, so they do not take attendance or penalize students for absences. Other professors feel that the classroom experience is so essential to learning that they require students to attend. Required attendance raises a number of logistical problems, particularly in large classes, which can be partially solved by considering the following suggestions offered by Carbone (1998, pp. 80–82) and other veterans of large classes.

- Collect homework as students enter the classroom and accept no papers once class begins.
- Give relatively easy tests during class to create a record of attendance.
- Make a seating chart and have an assistant check it each session.
- Ask students who must leave early or will arrive late to notify you in writing.

TABLE 6.2
Four Basic Ways to Deal With Classroom Conflicts

	Negative	Positive
Active	**Fight:** dominate the situation, stress authority and rules, display anger, apply pressure, permit no discussion of issues, show no concern for students' outcomes	**Cooperate:** share ideas, discuss issues, collaborate in search for a win–win synthesis, negotiate, show high concern for principles and for students' outcomes
Passive	**Avoid:** withdraw, adopt a "wait-and-see" attitude, deny and evade the problem, exit the situation, minimize own losses, show low concern for principles and for students	**Yield:** admit mistakes and make concessions, smooth emotions by giving in, show low concern for principles and high concern for students

- Reward students who leave class early after getting permission by acknowledging their use of appropriate procedures.
- Make each class session so educationally rewarding that students will want to attend.

Modeling Respect

Boice (2000) pointed out that students are not the only ones who sometimes act uncivilly in the classroom. During his observation of hundreds of classes, Boice recorded many instances of faculty treating students coldly, abruptly, or "with unmistakable rudeness and condescension" (p. 84). He concluded that professors are often partners with students in producing incivility, and suggests that faculty can reduce rudeness by remaining positive and approachable.

Managing Conflict

Nearly all classes experience periods of conflict. As the term wears on, networks of likes and dislikes will enfold the students, and tensions will arise as individual students and cliques rival for the professor's blessing. When exams approach, evaluation apprehension will mount, and the post-exam class is often one marked by debate and argument even in classes that had previously been remarkably placid. Many classes, too, move into a period of conflict, or "storming," at some point in the semester, often as a result of students' struggle against what they perceive to be the professor's authority (Tuckman, 1965).

Table 6.2 describes passive methods (avoidance and yielding) and active methods (fighting and cooperating) for dealing with such conflicts. The passive methods involve downplaying and minimizing the conflict

(Thomas, 1992; van de Vliert & Euwema, 1994). The professor may, for example, apologize for the conditions that created the conflict and offer to resolve the problem by making the changes the students request: points can be added to grades, assignments that were viewed as too demanding can be dropped, and so on. Alternatively, the professor can simply explain that the issue is obviously a controversial one that is causing strong feelings, and ask students to discuss the matter with him or her privately. In many cases students will not accept such an invitation, so the conflict is effectively avoided. The professor may, however, quash the conflict by citing principles or standards set on the syllabus, invoking privilege, or explaining the nature of classroom power differentials to students. ("If you don't like it, tough." "If you don't agree with this policy, there's the door.") The professor may, however, seek an integrative solution to the problem by discussing the problem with the class, inviting students to express their views—presenting concerns pertaining to the issues and then searching for a solution that satisfies all concerned parties (Fisher & Ury, 1981; Fisher, Ury, & Patton, 1991). Negative methods (avoidance and fighting) tend to be viewed as more disagreeable and unjust, whereas the positive methods (yielding and cooperation) are viewed as more agreeable and fair (Jarboe & Witteman, 1996; van de Vliert & Euwema, 1994). Avoidance, fighting, and yielding are also only temporary solutions, for they quell conflicts at the surface without considering the source. Cooperation, in contrast, is an active, positive method that yields immediate and long-term benefits for the class (Deutsch, 1994; Thomas, 1992).

Most classroom conflicts, once resolved, leave behind little in the way of hard feelings or nagging worries. In rare instances, however, these conflicts can be more intense and more intractable. They can escalate from simple disagreements over the interpretation of an example, vague challenges to authority, deliberately ill-timed and provocative questions, or disputes over a grade into full-fledged arguments and rebellions. The cooperative spirit that a classroom needs to function effectively can be replaced by tensions, hostility, and competitive maneuverings that are so distracting that they interfere with the class's progress toward its learning goals. Such conflicts may require the application of more strategic, and more prudent, conflict management methods, including private meetings with students, clear documentation of the incident, the introduction of third-party mediators, and counseling. Steps to consider include:

- meeting with disaffected students in your office but keep the door open or alert colleagues with nearby offices;
- allowing students to express their concerns and focus on helping them clarify their feelings, thoughts, and position by using basic skills of empathy, reflection, and reframing;
- stating your interpretation of the problem in writing, includ-

ing your preferred resolution to the problem, and deliver this interpretation to the student in class or through e-mail;

- keeping a file of dated notes pertaining to the incident;
- keeping colleagues informed about the problem and seek their input; ask them to mediate, if appropriate; and
- referring the students to your superior, to counseling, or to an ombudsperson if available.

In extreme cases, as when a student or group of students disrupts class so thoroughly that instruction cannot continue, check with your college's administrators to determine what options are available to you. Some institutions, recognizing that other students' right to receive instruction is violated by the disruptive student, permit professors to expel miscreants from their classrooms. But if the disruptive student does not obey such an order, then even more extreme steps must be taken such as adjourning the class or contacting campus police. In any case, the intervention must be consistent with standards and procedures adopted by your institution. The intervention must also be lawful. One should not, for example, physically touch a student to assist him or her in leaving your class.

Managing Diversity

As noted in chapter 1, the "traditional college student" is disappearing. In the 1950s men outnumbered women on college campuses 2 to 1. In 1987 the numbers of men and women in college were nearly equal, but by the turn of the century 2 million more women than men were students. Women began to outnumber men in graduate programs in 1984, and from 1987 to 1997 the number of male full-time graduate students increased by 22%, compared to 68% for female full-time students. During this period the number of older students increased as well, so that, at present, nearly 20% of college students are ages 25 or older. Members of minority groups in the United States are also attending colleges in increasing numbers. These groups, just 16% of the students in 1976, are now more than 27%. These percentages include 11% African American, 6% Asian and Pacific Islander, and 10% Hispanic. Another 3% of students on campus are international students (National Center for Education Statistics, 1999).

Diverse, multicultural classrooms offer many advantages over homogenous ones. Because of psychology's historical roots, the field implicitly takes a White, male, and Western perspective on psychological issues. "Even the rat was white," as Guthrie (1997) aptly puts it. This narrow view can be revised and enlarged when students with different backgrounds, life experiences, and cultural outlooks offer their interpretations of psychology's theories and methods. Diversity in groups also tends to promote creativity and enhance innovative thinking, so any collaborative, active learning experiences should be particularly dynamic when members bring very different opinions and ideas to the task (Jackson, 1992). A diverse classroom can also become a laboratory for learning about diversity itself. For many students, college will be their first contact with people who differ from them in culture, race, ethnicity, and religion. The diverse classroom gives them the opportunity to interact with people who are outside of their usual circle of friends and family (Triandis, 1995).

Diversity can, however, lead to complexities: conflict over values, disputes over the fairness of traditional procedures, and misunderstandings (Jackson, May, & Whitney, 1995; Moreland, Levine, & Wingert, 1996). Because segregation is still pervasive in most communities, students may be uncomfortable interacting with people who are not "their own kind." Diverse groups are often less cohesive than homogeneous ones, for differences in values, background, and interests create barriers that students cannot cross. In some cases, too, students may be prejudiced, and these attitudes may surface in their comments, actions, and demeanor. When diversity increases, so does the need to monitor relationships among individuals and intervene to correct any problems that arise. As Chism (1999) explained, all students, irrespective of their background, personal or social qualities, and abilities should (a) "feel welcome" in the classroom, (b) "feel that they are being treated as individuals," (c) "feel that they can participate fully," and (d) "feel they are being treated fairly" (p. 221).

Nontraditional Students

Like all "non" categories, nontraditional students are a diverse group themselves, including part-time students returning for a single class each semester, college graduates returning to take more courses, and older students who are restarting their educational careers after a long hiatus. These students are mature adult learners, so their motivations, strengths, and limitations are different from those of the college student fresh out of high school (Graham & Donaldson, 1999; Pratt, 1992). Nontraditional students have already sharpened their self-regulatory skills, so they tend to be responsible, self-directed, goal-oriented learners. They therefore prefer student-centered learning over purely lecture-centered classes and readings of authoritative sources. These individuals' life experiences are often myriad and much more varied than those of the other students in the class, so when discussions turn to such topics as mental illness, interpersonal conflicts, drug use, religion, parenting, management, and values these students are a rich source of insight and examples. They tend, however, to be more concrete, practical learners, and so must learn to tie their own experiences into psychology's theories and perspectives—just as more theoretically oriented instructors must learn to recognize the pedagogical value of sharing students' unique experiences with the class.

Nontraditional students are sometimes rusty when it comes to performing routine academic tasks, so they may initially need to be given more time and support. They may also lack confidence in their abilities and experience the self-consciousness that comes from being different from the average student in the class. In most cases, however, nontraditional students' serious work ethic and problem-solving skills more than compensate for their academic greenness (Allen, 2000).

Ethnic, Gender, and Cultural Diversity

The modern college campus and classroom bring together men and women of varying ages, religions, races, cultures, and lifestyles, and the result is often a vibrant, unique learning experience that profoundly changes students intellectually and attitudinally (Alwin, Cohen, & Newcomb, 1991; Newcomb, Koenig, Flacks, & Warwick, 1967). Yet college campuses, once oases in a sea of American prejudice, frequently serve as venues for ethnic, racist, and sexist conflicts. In some cases, students express their prejudices against others openly in class, as when the White racist openly denounces African Americans or the sexist expresses reactionary opinions pertaining to the role of women in contemporary society. In most cases, however, bias is more subtle (Kleinpenning & Hagendoorn, 1993). Whenever a nontraditional student offers his or her opinion during discussion, the younger students glance at each other and roll their eyes. None of the students in the class speak to the student who is physically challenged and uses a wheelchair. The White students in the class keep to themselves by forming interpersonal networks that exclude all the Hispanics, Asians, Native Americans, and African American students.

Instructors should monitor their classes for evidence of intergroup conflict and dispel it as needed by following the recommendations of researchers in the field of prejudice reduction (e.g., Cook, 1985; Devine, 1989; Gaertner & Dovidio, 2000; Wright, Aron, McLaughlin-Volpe, & Ropp, 1997). First, status differences between students should be minimized by insisting that all members of the class treat one another in respectful ways. Second, when possible, collaborative activities should be used to create informal, personal interaction among students. Third, the professor should respond actively to any instances of intergroup bias because ignoring this problem can be misinterpreted as approval. As Blanchard, Tilly, and Vaughn (1991) discovered, when students believe that their campus tolerates the unfair treatment of others, they are more likely to express racist opinions themselves—to the point of condoning the harassment of people in other racial groups. Fourth, because situations that require cooperative interdependence in the pursuit of common goals tend to reduce prejudice, professors with diverse classes should use noncompetitive grading procedures when possible.

Professors, too, should monitor their own behaviors for evidence of unintentional bias. A prejudiced psychologist is an oxymoron, but biases produced by years of living in a prejudiced society may nonetheless surface when psychologists are interacting with their students. Hall and Sandler (1986), for example, reported that male faculty sometimes treat female students differently than male students (Sandler, 1988). Some make blatantly sexist remarks about women and their role in contemporary society. More frequently, however, classroom sexism takes the form of discounting women rather than singling them out for ridicule, or using patterns of language that exclude them, such as "mankind" or "when the experimenter ran subjects, he . . ." Professors may also treat students differently depending on their ethnicity and race because they themselves are not sufficiently experienced with multicultural environments. Some professors may use dated terms to describe members of a group, thereby unintentionally insulting the members of the group. More likely, however, they will use examples, ideas, stories, and illustrations drawn from their particular social background, so students who share that background feel included but students who do not feel left out. Every example may refer to Johnny or Jill instead of Rafael or Zhakima or Lakeish. Unwarranted generalizations may be offered about activities and interests that are more prevalent in one group rather than another: Rap music may be denounced, inner city neighborhoods called *ghettos*, and social organizations characterized as gangs. Davis (1993) and Allen (2000) offered a number of excellent suggestions for increasing one's sensitivity to issues of diversity in the classroom.

Students With Disabilities

Students with disabilities are also headed off to college in ever-increasing numbers. The innovations in helping students with disabilities are based on changes in federal law that prohibit the exclusion of people with physical and psychological impairments from any postsecondary education programs that receive any form of federal funding. Physical impairments include sensory losses, such as total or partial blindness and deafness, physical conditions that limit mobility (e.g., cerebral palsy, multiple sclerosis), and chronic diseases (e.g., diabetes, seizure disorders, AIDS) that will influence students' attentiveness, stamina, classroom behavior, and so on. Mental impairments include learning disabilities (e.g., dyslexia, expressive dysphasia, aural receptive dysphasia), processing impairments caused by injury to the brain (e.g., traumatic brain injury), and some psychological disorders (e.g., depression, schizophrenia, adult attention-deficit disorder).

Institutions that receive federal funds are legally required to facilitate the full participation of students in all aspects of campus life. They cannot, for example, put in place admissions standards that are biased against students with disabilities or deny housing to students because of their disability. Psychologists, if teaching at such institutions, are also legally and ethically required to provide to students with disabilities the resources they need to succeed in their courses. Instructors should willingly arrange their classrooms to take into account the special needs of these students, say by providing extra space for any special equipment (calculators, computers, tape recorders) the students may require. They should also permit people who are not registered for the class but who are assisting the student, such as note takers or interpreters, to attend class. Guide animals, too, cannot be excluded. They should also adjust the content of curricula and course content, activities, and testing procedures as necessary for qualified students with disabilities. These modifications are termed "adjustments" or "accommodations," and they can include substitution of courses, elimination of requirements, adjustment in the length and type of examinations, and the substitution of one type of activity or assignment for another.

Faculty should ask students with disabilities to contact them at their earliest convenience to discuss accommodations. My university, for example, asks that all faculty insert the following paragraph in their syllabi for all courses:

> Section 504 of the Rehabilitation Act of 1973 and the Americans with Disabilities Act of 1990 require Virginia Commonwealth University to provide an "academic adjustment" and/or "reasonable accommodation" to any individual who advises us of a physical or mental disability. If you have a physical or mental limitation that requires an academic adjustment or an accommodation, please arrange a meeting with me at your earliest convenience.

Students with disabilities are not obligated, however, to identify themselves to their instructor by any deadline, so in some cases students seek accommodations late in the term.

Most institutions have policies in place that determine how students with disabilities can certify their need, and thereby qualify for accommodations, adjustments, and support services. The institution can, if it deems necessary, refuse to make accommodations in curriculum areas that it considers essential to the program of instruction.

Managing Students' Stress

Stress is a part of every student's daily life. Each day brings an avalanche of minor hassles, including broken down cars, parking tickets, overdue library books, and shortages of cash. Many students are experiencing developmental changes, not to mention significant changes in their connections to their families, roommates, and partners. Then there are the academic stressors: excessive homework, difficult or ambiguous assignments, classrooms filled with environmental irritants, and overall time pressures (Towbes & Cohen, 1996; J. J. Wright, 1967). Most manage to cope with this stress, but those who do not should be advised, counseled, and referred to treatment if their problems warrant it.

When to Refer a Student for Counseling

Some students, often during class or office hours, will express a self-diagnosis and ask if they should be concerned about their problem. These self-diagnoses spike immediately after a lecture on psychopathology, for more than a few students will become convinced that the list of symptoms of one of the disorders describes them perfectly. Other students may become concerned about their sleep habits, their drinking, the drugs their family doctor prescribes them, their conflicts with roommates, their problems relating to their mother, their intrusive thoughts during exams, and so on.

In some cases the students are overreacting. Not realizing the intensity of the emotions, thoughts, or behaviors that characterize psychological disorders, they mistake their relatively transient disturbances for symptoms of psychological dysfunction. In other instances, however, students report and even display significant disruptions in mood, thought, and action. When talking with the student, the professor may note that their behavior is inappropriate: flat and unchanging, hostile to the point of fury, or depressed and listless. They may also act in odd, atypical ways. Some reveal their anxiety by crying uncontrollably. Others may act erratically in class, asking odd questions and expressing thoughts that you, and other students, find incomprehensible. Their attention to their clothes and appearance may decline noticeably, and they may also show signs of drug abuse. In such circumstances, the professor should help the student seek counseling.

How Should You Refer a Student?

Students often seek out their psychology professor when they become concerned about their mental health, for they often assume that all psychologists are trained therapists who can help them. But teaching psychologists' primary mission is teaching, and they risk becoming involved in a dual-role relationship if they also become a student's therapist. Concerned professors should, instead, use their best judgment to determine if the student's problems are so substantial that he or she would benefit from counseling, and then refer the student to the appropriate campus service agency.

Referral involves more than simply saying, "You should get some help." Rather, the referral should take place in the context of a consultation with the student, during which the professor shows appropriate interest and concern for the student's well-being. During this meeting the professor should try to gauge the severity of the problem and help the student separate distress caused by academic concerns from distress caused by personal difficulties. If the root cause of the student's problems is academic, then the professor should recommend strategies the student can use to deal with them. If it is personal distress, however, the professor should suggest ways the student can deal with his or her problems. The professor may ask about family or friends, and ask if the student has let them know about the problems. He or she may also want to discuss more formal methods of dealing with the problem, including treatment. These options should be discussed as matter-of-factly as possible. A recommendation to visit a counselor can be normalized by avoiding a medical model mentality that describes the process as *treatment* or the problem as a *disorder*. Moreover, if the students are psychology majors, the referral can be framed as an informal assignment that will give the student "a firsthand look at the way a counseling center operates." Students can be reassured that psychologists themselves turn to counselors whenever they must deal with significant life events, such as divorce, crises in their careers, and so on.

You may need to take additional steps in extreme cases. You may, with the student still in your office, call the counseling center personally and make an appointment for the student. You can also walk the student to the center. Colleagues can also be contacted, as well as the police, if the student threatens suicide or violence. In most cases, however, all students need is a sympathetic listener who is experienced in working with students and their problems.

7

INNOVATING: USING TECHNOLOGY CREATIVELY IN TEACHING

It's not the motorcycle maintenance.... It's all of technology they can't take.... They talk once in a while in as few pained words as possible about "it" or "it all" as in the sentence, "There is just no escape from it".... The "it" is a kind of force that gives rise to technology, something undefined, but inhuman, mechanical, lifeless, a blind monster, a death force.... I just think that their flight from and hatred of technology is self-defeating. The Buddha, the Godhead, resides quite as comfortably in the circuits of a digital computer or the gears of a cycle transmission as he does at the top of a mountain or in the petals of a flower.

—Robert M. Pirsig
Zen and the Art of Motorcycle Maintenance (1974, pp. 14–16)

The nature of college teaching is being reshaped by technology as more campuses are upgrading their older versions of Professor 1.0, jumping to the faster, slicker, but buggier Professor 2.0. Not so long ago, professors punctuated their lectures with chalk marks on a blackboard, guided students' discussions from the front of the classroom, insisted that the papers they assigned be typed, and assessed learning with paper-and-pencil tests and quizzes. Professors still use these tools in classes today, but they have integrated new technologies—e-mail, Web sites, online discussion forums, multimedia programs, quiz-giving programs, and the like—in their teaching. These tools offer professors the means of solving certain problems in their teaching, although in doing so they often create new ones.

* * *

Claude Monet's canvases changed the world's conception of beauty (Stokes, 2001). Linus Pauling, by integrating physics, mathematics, and chemistry in his theoretical models, earned the 1954 Nobel Prize in chemistry (Nakamura & Csikszentmihalyi, 2001). Novelist John Irving, who claims his work improved once "I began to take my lack of talent seriously" (1996, p. 34), received the Academy Award for best screenplay in 2000 (Amabile, 2001). Charles Darwin, at a time when most scientists were focused on classifications of organisms and the analysis of their structures,

233

reshaped modern scientific thinking with his sweeping theory of natural selection (Gruber & Wallace, 2001).

Monet, Pauling, Irving, and Darwin are all recognized as brilliant innovators: creative individuals who did things differently than had been done before. Working in fields that had traditions, methods of operation, and standard procedures, each one sought novel, original, and unexpected alternatives, ideas, and explanations. Not eccentrics or dogged nonconformists or dreamers, these innovators, through hard work guided by their own particular vision, created practical, satisfying, and ultimately successful art, science, and literature.

Many teaching psychologists are innovators, as well, who constantly strive to solve the problems they face in their teaching with new, untried solutions. For centuries professors only lectured and led discussions, but innovators after Gutenberg added required readings. In the 1800s cutting-edge instructors began to use the latest innovation in visual-aid technology: the blackboard. One student of the time remarked, "on entering this room, we were struck at the appearance of an ample Blackboard suspended on the wall, with lumps of chalk on a ledge below, and cloths hanging at either side. I had never heard of such a thing before" (cited in Rocklin, 2001, p. 1). Inventors tinkered with projection systems for classrooms throughout the early 1900s until, in 1947, Fitzgerald patented what he called the "overhead projector," which he designed to help "teachers, lecturers, and sales people" display transparent images to large audiences.

The innovative professors of the present century continue to use blackboards and overheads, but they are also trying out new technologies and tools in their search for better ways to teach. Some of these innovations are refinements of tried-and-true methods, such as dustless whiteboards, hybrid computer projectors, and books that can be read from a computer's screen. Others, in contrast, use information technologies to fundamentally reshape the way professors teach and students learn. These professors, in the language of Sternberg and Lubart's (1996) investment theory of creativity, believe that even though many of these technologies are still unproven, their potential is so great that they are worth buying into despite their cost in terms of time, effort, and currency. They are hoping to "buy low" now in the hopes that the value of these innovations will soar in the future. We survey these new developments below, as well as consider some suggestions for implementing them in the classroom now rather than later.

INNOVATIONS IN TEACHING

Who has not noticed the influx of technology-based influences into teaching: course Web sites; online study aids, such as text outlines, lecture notes, and e-mails from the professor offering information about the day's lecture or discussion; PowerPoint presentations with animated models of the interneuronal transmissions at the synaptic cleft, 3-dimensional brain images, and diagrams of stimulus-response contingencies with colorful arrows instead of drab, black-and-white ones; lectures by psychologists at distant universities streamed via the Web to students' desktops; computer-based learning exercises that help students learn, at last, the difference between punishment and negative reinforcement; library research assignments that can be done online rather than in the library; computerized assessments that give immediate feedback and recommendations for areas to study further; and threaded discussions of key course topics with links to specific pages in the text and lecture files.

These innovative presentational modes and information delivery methods, and those summarized in Table 7.1, are making their way into contemporary educators' classrooms (and virtual classrooms). Some of these methods let professors enhance their classroom instruction by helping them integrate graphic information, such as photographs and graphs, into their lectures. Others allow students to use different sensory modalities in their learning by supplementing a textbook's verbal information with auditory or visual information. Others use content provided by the professor, by other students, or retrieved from some distant source. Although some of these high-tech methods are clearly creative and unprecedented, others are ideas, products, or processes that have been updated or merely renamed. McKeachie, for example, first used distance learning back in the early 1950s, when television was first invented. He taught a 1-hour televised course on psychology on Sundays, broadcasting from a studio in Detroit (Herman, 2000).

Why are professors increasing their reliance on these new instructional mechanisms? Some, one suspects, use them because they are explorers rather than innovators. They are curious about the methods and want to try them out in their classes. Others use them only because they are obedient to the law of the hammer: Give a child a hammer and he or she will realize everything needs pounding. These professors, once they go online, think everyone and everything should be online. But true innovators consider and sometimes adopt these methods because they are not completely satisfied with the ways they teach. They have recognized a problem—or number of problems—and they are turning to technology for solutions to them. They may, for example, realize that they are supposed to be teaching students to be life-long learners, yet they are not teaching the methods students will need to find information once they leave college. These innovators may worry, too, that their methods are too passive and professor-focused, yet with very large classes they do not feel that discussion methods will succeed. They may feel that they are not connecting personally to their students in the classroom, and wonder if a cyberprofessor will

TABLE 7.1

A Sampling of Technologies That Can Be Used in Teaching

Technology	Characteristics	Applications
Multimedia	Presentations of information and explanations that combine two or more modalities, including visual, verbal, auditory channels	• slides and overheads • in-class PowerPoint presentations • instructional videotapes
Hypertext	Electronic documents that allow readers to dynamically adapt the information's presentation to meet their needs. Readers can navigate the document and expand and collapse portions of the document to display varying levels of detail.	• e-books • Web documents with hyperlinks • interactive study guides (e.g., CyberPsych, Psyk.trek)
Instructional software	Computer programs that integrate text and graphical information in tutorials, simulations, statistical displays, and so on.	• Hypercard applications • PsychSim (Ludwig, 1996) • Web pages with imbedded interactivity
World Wide Web	A network of linked text, graphic, and data files typically accessed through programs called browsers.	• hypertext web pages • virtual psychology research laboratory • online discussion forums • e-learning platforms, such as Blackboard.com
Networks	Systems of interconnected computers, including the Internet (which is a network linking computers across the world) and intranets (local area networks)	• e-mail • online searchable databases • shared electronic programs and resources
Distance learning	Using such communication technologies as televised broadcasts, two-way satellite hook-ups, streamed audio downloads, and telephone conferencing for instructional purposes when students and professors are in different locations	• Zimbardo's Understanding Psychology series • online real-time conferencing telecourses
Digital archives, databases, and libraries	Information reduced and stored in digital form on computers that can be accessed through networks, the Web, or direct computer-to-computer connections	• university "card catalogs" • PsycINFO • libraries of e-books • student information systems

be more approachable than one in an office located in some hard-to-find building on campus. Technology, as noted below, may offer ways to solve these and other problems.

Transmitting Knowledge

The professor's primary and most obvious goal is the communication of information about psychology's theories, theorists, researchers, and findings to students. Teaching technologies address this goal in two basic ways: (a) by providing professors with new ways to communicate course content efficiently and accurately and (b) by empowering students by giving them unprecedented access to information about psychology.

In-Class Presentation Tools

Even the most orally fixated professors must, from time to time, display an image, spell a name or term, illustrate a model, graph data, work out a statistical formula, or outline the lecture's key points in the class. They do so by using a range of tools, including the lowly chalkboard, the slightly less lowly whiteboard, the overhead projector with its transparencies, slides packed into a carousel tray, and computers hooked to projection systems that throw the screen display on a large screen. All these methods work, although their functionality depends on the size of the class, the complexity of the images, and the amount of material to be displayed.

Chalkboards and their marker-based variations remain one of the best tools for displaying text and personally generated graphic material to class. Chalkboards do not need electricity, they do not break down, and their contents can be edited on the fly with little more than a piece of chalk and an eraser or bit of sleeve. Another bonus: The lights in the classroom need not dimmed for a chalkboard to work, so students' expressions (and sleepiness) can be monitored with greater accuracy. Some professors are artists at the chalkboard, expertly leading students through a maze of terms, formulas, computations, and diagrams from the class's start until its final minute.

But board work is labor intensive and ephemeral; the contents disappear at the class's end, and so must be replicated the next time the class meets. The chalkboard's flexibility can also invite such disorganization that an hour's lecture results in an uninterpretable tangle of terms, names, phrases, and sketches that range from the illegible to the misspelled. Last, the line made by a piece of chalk is not thick enough to be seen from any great distance. Even bold, large lettering is hard to see from 10 rows away because of the limits of human vision. People may be able to feel a bee's wing falling on their cheek from a height of half an inch or taste the sweetness of a teaspoon of sugar in two gallons of water (Galanter, 1962), but they cannot see PIAGET and JUNG written in chalk from a distance of 30 feet or so.

The overhead projector (OHP) and slide projector (SP) solve some of these limitations. Professors can prepare their materials in advance, and so satisfy their personal need for order, artistry, or information. The slides also structure the course of the presentation, for they give students and presenter a running outline to follow. The OHP can also be used as a chalkboard, in that unexpected terms can be added and the prepared transparencies can be annotated during the presentation. Slides, because they are more difficult to prepare and cannot be revised easily or annotated during lecture, are generally used only for fixed types of images, such as illustrations from textbooks. OHPs and SPs, because of their low cost, are also relatively plentiful in college classrooms, and they are portable. They are also simple machines, so they need less maintenance than computer systems and are less likely to fail in the middle of class.

Computerized projection (CP) systems, which typically consist of computers connected to liquid crystal display panels, interactive whiteboards, large monitors, and/or digital projectors, offer maximum control over the nature of the display and maximum potential for calamity. Microsoft's *PowerPoint*, Corel's *Presentations*, and other similar software packages let professors develop slides using their computers, sequence these slides to create a presentation or "slide show," and then save these shows for display to their classes. The software automates the process, to a degree, by offering users templates that regulate the colors of the background and fonts, the format of the text material, and the location of any graphic materials. The software lets the user insert all types of material in a slide, including pictures, animations, video and audio clips, and the material can be edited easily so that revisions are simple. The following are suggestions for using CP systems and other types of presentational methods:

- At least initially, use the presentation design templates provided by the software. Over time, add interesting backgrounds and vary formats to increase visual interest.
- Configure the size, color, and font of the type to match the requirements of the classroom or lecture hall; many of the figures and slides provided by textbook publishers are too small to be used in large classrooms.
- Use the software's tools to create bulleted lists so that elements in the lists can be displayed one at a time. Otherwise you risk the possibility of students writing down the information on each screen and then daydreaming until the next screen is displayed.
- Do not put too much information on a single screen.
- Try, whenever possible, to add visual information to text in-

formation on a screen. If the entire presentation is text, consider using an overhead projector rather than a computer-based system.

- To add material during class, open a word processing program and type the material into a temporary document using a large font. Use the pen tool only as a last resort or to underline and circle material on the slide.
- Save classroom presentations in Web-based formats and upload them to the class Web site for students to retrieve. If your presentation-building program does not have this capability, get a new one or reinstall the old one and be sure to include "HTML tools."
- Use authoring software to generate a print-version of the presentation, turn the pages into transparencies, and take them with you to class until the projection system in the room demonstrates itself to be 100% reliable.

CP systems, although of great potential use to the professor, have clear limitations. Building a presentation takes time, particularly for the novice. The files that contain the shows are portable in that they can be saved on diskettes or network drives and shown elsewhere, but only thieves consider the equipment itself to be mobile. Because these shows are computer-based, any problems that affect the operation of a computer (viruses, slow processors, conflicts) can influence their operation. The equipment that runs the show is also complex enough that small problems, such as an overlooked setting or a jack inserted in the wrong outlet on the projector, can bring the presentation to a standstill.

Web Sites

Most universities provide faculty with space on the university Web server that they can use to create personal home pages, pages for their research and professional work, and pages for their classes. Because Web pages are hypertext documents, they can contain a mix of text and graphic information. They also, in most cases, allow the viewer to interact in certain ways with the material on the page. Even the simplest page has clickable links, which are images or text areas that, when selected by the user (who usually clicks on them with the cursor), direct the browser to download a page located elsewhere on the Web or to move to a different part of the current document. More sophisticated pages let visitors interact more extensively with the ideas and materials by running small programs and scripts.

Web sites provide faculty with another means of communicating information about psychology to students. Although the most basic Web site for a course contains only the syllabus information, professors can post all sorts of course materials to the Web: copies of all handouts, lists of terms, lecture notes, annotated lecture notes, feedback about quizzes and exams, discussion questions, and so on. Professors can also post more detailed analyses of psychological topics to the course page, so that students who want to know more about a particular topic can review it when online. Web sites can also be created and edited relatively quickly, so professors can keep students informed of the most recent research findings. Whereas the information in the text is likely 2 to 3 years old, Web sites are updated constantly.

One of the most important areas of a professor's course page is the Web links: clickable lists of other pages on the Web that students can visit to download more information. Although students can browse the Web themselves and use search engines such as Google and HotBot to locate more information about topics that interest them, professors can help by pointing them to particularly informative pages. Many of the pages on the Web also contain large amounts of questionable material, so by posting links on their pages, professors can be certain their students are referred to reputable sources of information. Possible sites for the Web links section include research laboratories located throughout the world that are investigating psychological topics, archives of research papers, sites maintained by mental health agencies and research foundations such as the National Science Foundation and NIMH, the Web pages of the American Psychological Association (APA), and so-called megasites: sites that index the most information-rich sites on the Web that deal with psychological information.

E-mail

The Internet allows individuals with accounts on computers that act as mail servers to send and receive messages electronically. E-mail therefore provides the professor with yet another means of conveying information about psychology, and announcements about the course, to students. Like a Web page, an e-mail message can provide additional information about ideas discussed in class, suggestions for further readings, reminders about upcoming topics, and new questions for students to ruminate over in preparation for the next class. Students must visit Web sites before they can be influenced by the information they contain, but e-mails are sent directly to students, increasing the chances that they will read the information. Indeed, Forsyth and Archer (1997) found that of all the technology-based elements used in teaching a section of introductory psychology, students most appreciated the heavy use of e-mail by the instructor. The following ideas suggest ways to use e-mail effectively:

- Require all students to use e-mail and to register their account number by the end of the first week of the semester. If only some students use e-mail, any teaching done with this tool will discriminate against the unwired.

- Send messages to students regularly. These messages should contain not only information about class logistics, but also content information that is assessed on the class tests.
- Use e-mail to provide the class with global, summative feedback after examinations to avoid negative experiences in the classroom.
- Use the features of your e-mail program to streamline the e-mail teaching. For example, use the software to create a distribution list that can be used to send all students in a class an e-mail simultaneously. Require students to use particular headers, and sort incoming mail with this header into separate files.
- Use sophisticated e-mail programs, such as LISTSERV, if classes are large, if students are encouraged to post messages to the entire class, and if an archive of e-mail messages is needed.
- If you ask students to turn in assignments via e-mail, require that they paste them directly into the body of the e-mail or that they write them using a popular word-processing program and attach them to an e-mail message. In large classes use either method, but not both.
- Install and regularly update a good antivirus program, and regularly check Web sites that provide information about viruses. Do not delegate this task to anyone else.

Computerized Instructional Packages

Professors and software publishers have created topic-specific educational programs that "teach" the students who run them by providing information dealing with psychological topics. Some are primarily linked files of text information, which students read before they answer some questions that check on their understanding of the material. Students can, for example, run programs that teach such concepts as operant and classical conditioning, neuronal structures, schedules of reinforcement, and Piaget's theory of development by presenting text material, graphics, and interlinked topic lists. These programs are interactive; they allow students to control the pace of their movement through the topics. Most programs also ask students to respond to questions as a check of their comprehension, and will move students to different material depending on their responses. These programs are available from publishers, who often provide them as supplements to students who buy the linear printed text. Some professors, who are familiar with the programs that are used to author such packages, construct their own programs to suit their specific teaching needs. Depending on design and availability, students can install these programs on their own computers, use them in computer labs located on campus, or run them directly off the Web.

E-Books

Publishers of textbooks are gradually transitioning from print to hypertext. Most readers still prefer the simplicity of a traditional book (Harris, Harris, & Hannah, 1998), but e-books are improving rapidly as designers work to reduce the discrepancy between reading a traditional book and a computer screen. E-books that are little more than text poured into computer-readable files are difficult to wade through, but reader-friendly designs that emulate the look and feel of a book with pages, graphics, and indexes offer alternatives to traditional textbooks. Publishers of enhanced e-books, by building useful tools into the reader software, may make it easier for students to remember the information contained in their texts. Many programs already include notepads, bookmarks, search options, and pop-up dictionaries, and these tools will likely be supplemented with embedded simulations, animations, charts, and other informative graphic material.

Thinking Skills

Professors are not, in the language of the Web, just "content providers." They do not merely stream psychological information to their students, but they also teach students how to process that information more systematically, logically, scientifically, and thoroughly. They do not teach only memorizable facts and concepts, but also the conceptual skills needed to solve problems, make decisions, interpret statistical data, evaluate conflicting positions on issues with policy implications, and so on. Students develop these higher order conceptual and analytic skills gradually during the course of their undergraduate and graduate careers, but the acquisition of such skills can be accelerated through structured problem-solving activities, participation in simulated and real research, the analysis of data, and analyses of controversial issues in psychology.

Simulations

Computer-based learning tools facilitate the development of conceptual skills by creating virtual problems, cases, and laboratories. One specialized type of instructional program, *interactive simulations*, illustrates psychological processes and applications in virtual reality. These programs create hypothetical situations for students and then guide explorations of these situations. One program, for example, teaches students to distinguish among myriad psychological disorders by asking them to play the role of a clinician who must diagnose a client. The students are given case records for hypothetical clients and must seek information from a set of demographic variables, medical history, reason for seeking treatment, and so on. Another program is based on the well-known artificial intelligence program Eliza, and simulates a nondirective, client-centered (Rogerian) therapist who responds to the typed statements made by the students. Then there is the digital brain program that asks students to explore localization of function by implanting electrodes at various central nervous system sites, and the digital rat program that mimics the responses of a rat on variable and fixed ratio and interval schedules.

Other instructional programs simulate the scientific side of psychology and its procedures by allowing students to replicate laboratory research or carry out entirely new studies in a virtual psychology laboratory—often with the students themselves serving as participants. One of these *research simulations*, for example, utilizes Craik and Tulving's (1975) levels of processing paradigm by asking students to process words presented on the computer screen at structural, phonemic, semantic levels of processing. After the trials, students are asked to recall as many words as they can. Then participants are given a recognition task, and finally shown graphs of the results. Another simulation replicates Sperling's (1960) classic memory study by flashing letters on the computer screen, and then asking students to recall as many letters as they can. It also incorporates cued recall to test Sperling's hypothesis pertaining to duration of image memory. A third simulation replicates Asch's (1946) study of impression formation by asking students to form impressions of a person who is described with a string of adjectives that includes either the word *warm* or the word *cold*. Participants then complete the same measures Asch used, and their responses are compared to his original findings.

When students carry out experiments or simulations on the computer, they participate in the production of information. They can better experience the steps required in approaching a problem as a psychologist might, and can be guided by the computer through to a final conclusion. In addition, computers, more than any other media, can combine visual, auditory, verbal, and graphical data. A skilled psychologist must, for example, be able to clearly grasp the meaning of graphic representations of theories and data, and computerized instructional packages can help students hone these skills. These problems are also very involving for students, because they must respond to the situations created by the computer.

Statistical Analyses

Statistical programs, such as SPSS and SAS, give students the chance to study psychological data and draw their own inferences from the results of their statistical analyses. Before the widespread distribution of statistical programs, students spent considerable time collecting data and performing calculations by hand. Much of the learning focused on the nuts and bolts of statistics rather than on the inferences that could be drawn from the data. Now, by using computer programs such as MEL LAB (Hinds, Schneider, & St. James, 1990), data can be collected rapidly and saved to files that can then be examined using statistical packages. Johnston (1989) quotes one teacher of statistics who concludes:

> The computer allows us to decrease the amount of time that we would spend number crunching, and it gives us that time to use in more profitable ways. We can do more sophisticated kinds of experiments, we can collect more data, we even analyze the data in more sophisticated kinds of ways, and it doesn't take as long. (p. 2)

Internet and Web Resources

Professors can also take advantage of the Internet's vast resources to create active learning experiences that promote the development of analytical, creative, and practical thinking (Sternberg, 1997c), critical thinking, and information-gathering skills. For example:

- Many sites on the Web invite students to take part in research studies online. These studies expose students to some of the diversity of empirical work that takes place in psychology and provide actual experience with the research process and educational interaction with researchers.
- Students can find and retrieve a great deal of information about psychological topics from the Web. The main PsycINFO database maintained by APA, for example, contains more than 1.5 million references to psychological literature from 1887, including journal articles, books, book chapters, technical reports, and dissertations.
- Class discussion of controversial issues can take place in virtual discussion rooms made possible by conferencing software and through e-mail. The anonymity of these communication methods can sometimes increase the intensity of students' comments, but it also encourages more thorough analysis of emotion-laden issues. Students who are reluctant to discuss issues of the genetic bases of intelligence, prejudice on their campuses, political attitudes, and addictive behavior may express themselves more openly when exchanging ideas via computer.
- Students can study controversial topics in psychology by visiting Web sites developed by individuals who take widely differing views on such topics as nature–nurture, the accuracy of retrieved memories, and the genetic bases of intelligence.

Language Skills

As noted in chapter 3, when people write, they confront one problem after another, and successful problem resolution requires creativity, planning, monitoring, comprehension, and even empathy (for the reader). Skill in writing is also related to skill in reading, such that individuals who can use language well to express themselves can also read and easily understand the meaning in others' words (Fitzgerald & Shanahan, 2000). Technology, once again, proves useful in teaching language skills to students.

Word-Processing Programs

Some of the most difficult and time-consuming aspects of writing and composition are made easier, and partially streamlined, by the use of word-processing programs. When students complete a paper using a word processor, they can turn it in electronically, and professors can add running comments using the editor function. Students can also revise their documents more easily, and professors can verify changes by using the comparison functions of the programs. The grammar and spelling tools in these programs help students catch any distracting grammatical errors and typos, and the built-in thesaurus and dictionary also help students express themselves more clearly.

E-mail and Conferencing

Electronic forms of communication encourage students to express their understanding of course material in their own words—a form of learning that is sometimes overlooked in traditional classrooms. When appropriate, students can be asked to answer questions via e-mail, and these responses can be shared with all members of the class. Students can also express their opinions, ideas, and insights in online discussion sessions. These discussions can be asynchronous, as when students post comments to online bulletin boards and forums, or in real time, as when all students who are communicating through widely dispersed computers post their comments to chat room-like message areas. Forum-type software, such as newsgroups, Yahoo's groups, and Blackboard.com's Forum area, generally promotes a more thoughtful analysis of issues because it gives students the opportunity to plan, compose, and revise their text before posting it. All these methods, as noted below, also create connections between students, increasing the collaborative nature of their learning.

Collaborative Learning Skills

Bill Gates (1999), in his book *Business @ The Speed of Thought*, offered rules for using technology to improve business practice. Nearly all of his rules stress the tremendous potential of technology for creating connections between people. He insists, for example, that all employees use e-mail to communicate with one another. He also recommends reviewing digital documents online so that workers can share their interpretations, and creating virtual teams using networking software. These insights apply equally well to teaching, for computer-based technologies increase, rather than decrease, interaction among students and faculty. When professors encourage their students to e-mail and confer online, students can interact with their instructor and other students in the class 24 hours a day, 7 days a week. In consequence, the "total communication increases and, for many students, the results seems more intimate, protected, and convenient than the more intimidating demands of face-to-face communication with faculty" (Chickering & Ehrmann, 1996, p. 2). This increased availability must, of course, be managed. Just as many professors prefer to keep their home telephone numbers private, many carefully restrict their virtual availability so their time is not drained away by demands to be constantly online.

Information technologies also increase the effectiveness of some of teaching's most conventional practices, such as office hours, the guest lecture, and study groups. Because many students cannot attend office hours held on campus, virtual office hours can be held at night and on weekends in a discussion area of the Web. Students can visit the site before their professor does, post their question, and then return for the answer when the professor has had a chance to respond. When students post questions when their professor is "in the room" (online), then they can have their queries answered immediately. Technology also creates greater connections among scholars and students. When students raise questions that go beyond their professor's interests and expertise, then the professor can involve other experts and scholars in classes. Students can also join together in small groups, or virtual learning teams, which can complete problem-based assignments using shared electronic files, Web-based whiteboards, and Web-conferencing.

Motivation

Students learn more easily when they have identified their educational goals, value these goals, and are confident that they can achieve them. Information technologies can increase students' motivations by influencing all these aspects of motivation. In traditional classes, the instructor typically decides what topics will be covered and in what depth. In contrast, in classes that take advantage of computer-based learning tools, students gain more control over their learning experiences. Students, with the help of the faculty, can create personalized educational experiences that match their unique interests, needs, and goals. When a particular topic interests them, they can delve deeply into the subject. If they feel challenged by a concept or topic, they can re-run programs and move through them slowly. If they are visual learners, they can study multimedia presentations that combine graphics, images, and text information. If they are text learners, they can spend their time studying information-dense Web sites and e-books.

Students can also control *when* they will learn in classes that use technology. Provided students can gain access to the Web and class resources, they can learn at any time and anywhere a computer can be located: Dorm rooms, private residences, or the library at 11:00 p.m. all become classrooms when teaching is asynchronous. Many students are also interested in using new technologies simply because they are new and cutting edge rather than old-fashioned. Forsyth and Archer (1997), for example, reported that some of the students they surveyed expressed a fear of technology, but the majority rated such technologies as e-mail, Web resources, simulations, and tutorials very positively. They also found that students who expressed positive attitudes about these tools tended to use them more, and these students also earned higher grades in the course.

Learning and Study Skills

The professor, while pursuing such worthy goals as relaying information to students and stimulating their conceptual growth, sometimes takes for granted the development of skills needed to learn. Knowing all the current facts, theories, and models of contemporary psychology may be sufficient to earn students As in their classes, but what happens when psychology's stock of knowledge changes? Students must not only learn but also learn *how* to learn.

Many of technology's earliest and best developed applications to teaching and learning are designed to help students study more effectively, both by providing study tools and by structuring their methods of studying. Many computer-based learning programs, for example, are tutorials that can trace their ancestry back to Skinner's early vision of a teaching machine that shapes students' behavior through reinforcement (Benjamin, 1988). These tutorials usually segment material into modules, and students must demonstrate proficiency on a quiz before they are given credit for completing the module. Other tutorials are sophisticated nonlinear hypertexts with various tools added for students: self-quizzes, search boxes, indexes, pop-up dictionaries, libraries of additional titles, or animated professors who provide comic relief. These tools all structure students' learning, but at the same time teach them how they should study the material.

The Web also offers extensive information about studying and learning. Many universities' academic support units create virtual workshops on study skills, and students can visit these pages to get basic pointers on how to use the library, how to take notes, how to study effectively, and so on. Many textbook publishers have also built Web sites to support their textbooks, and these sites offer students a wide array of tools to help them study: practice quizzes, glossaries, learning objectives, informational supplements, and so on.

Computer Literacy Plus

E-mail, Web sites, computerized tutorials, multimedia presentations, and other technologies are useful to professors because they provide the means of achieving basic educational goals, including sharing knowledge of the field, stimulating critical thinking, developing language skills, promoting collaborative learning, motivating students, and helping them strengthen their study skills (see Table 7.2). But technology also yields several other beneficial side effects, including increased computer literacy and solutions to such everyday tasks as tracking students' performances and reducing cheating.

Computer Literacy

Many postsecondary educators now stress the importance of helping students become "life-long learners": scholars whose college experiences equip them with the skills they need to grow intellectually after they graduate. Although graduates may continue their learning by returning to campus for public lectures or visiting the public library, in all likelihood most will rely on information technologies such as e-mail and the Web to search out the information they need. Although technologically based psychology classes do not explicitly teach networking, use of e-mail, or word-processing, students may learn these skills in order to accomplish the course's content-based goals.

Reducing Paper Flow

Professors can stem, at least partially, the flow of paper during the course of the term by posting all necessary course information at the course Web site. When students lose their syllabi, need another copy of the learning objectives for Test 2, or miss your riveting lecture on Sternberg's (1999a) seven types of creativity, they can access the material (and probably print it out on paper) via the Internet.

Grade Books

Many commercial software packages can be purchased that create electronic grade books, although most textbook publishers willingly provide such supplements to instructors who adopt their products in their classes. Because psychologists are already adept at using spreadsheets and statistical

TABLE 7.2
Learning Goals and the Technologies That Facilitate Their Attainment

Outcome	Instructional issues	Examples
Knowledge	How can the content of the field be communicated effectively to students, and how can students acquire information about psychology themselves?	• PowerPoint • Web pages • e-mail • computerized instructional packages • e-books
Thinking skills	How can professors shift the focus of their teaching and of their students' learning away from facts and information to conceptual and analytic skills? What can be done to make learning more active rather than passive?	• interactive simulations • research simulations • statistical programming with SPSS, SAS, etc. • computer searches of databases
Language skills	What can be done to enhance students' ability to read and understand text, compose research papers and reports, and express their own viewpoints about psychology and its applications?	• word-processing programs • Internet conferencing and discussion forums • e-mail discussion groups
Collaborative skills	How can professors establish interpersonal connections with their students and increase opportunities for interactions among students?	• e-mail • electronic document sharing • online office hours • virtual study teams
Motivation	What can professors do to increase their students' motivation to learn about psychology?	• engaging Web links • multimedia instructional programs
Learning and study skills	How can professors help students learn how to learn and study more effectively?	• computerized tutorials • online guides to academic success • self-quizzing programs

packages such as SPSS, they can also use these programs to manage their grades.

Feedback to Students

Some Web-based teaching portals, such as WebCT and Blackboard, automate a number of time-consuming tasks, such as administering and grading quizzes and disseminating the results to students. Because students can track their performance carefully throughout the semester, they can make informed decisions about their learning goals and the amount of time they need to invest to reach them.

Research Pool

The Web can also be used to manage the department's research participant pool. A local coordinator can require that all students who wish to take part in research as participants register via e-mail, and in many cases premeasures can be taken via Web-based forms. The pool can also be coordinated by using a commercial service provider, such as Experimetrix.com. This site manages all aspects of the participant pool by registering participants, providing online sign-ups for all approved studies, recording all participations and credit, reminding students of their appointments (via e-mail), and generating a list of students and their credits at the end of the term.

Academic Integrity

The Web raises new problems for professors who are concerned with cheating and plagiarism. Students can communicate with each other at all hours of the day, increasing the chance that they will collaborate on take-home tests. Students, when writing papers, can cut chunks of text from online dictionaries and information sites, and paste that information directly into their papers. They can also download entire papers from the Web, particularly when their assignment does not specify a topic.

Technology offers partial solutions to these problems, however. When students submit their paper as files, these files can be reviewed using plagiarism-detection programs that search for identical strings of words. Various Web sites offer specialized cheating detection services. Turnitin.com, for example, lets professors check the integrity of every document students submit. Once registered with the site, students turn in their written papers by submitting them to the turnitin.com portal. The site's software then checks for plagiarism by comparing the student's work to a database of documents submitted by students at all other registered universities. The site also checks the work against text material available on the Web, and flags cases of identical strings of words. Anti-plagiarism Web sites suggest using common Web-based search engines to locate plagiarism as well as other useful tips for faculty who are concerned that their students are not turning in original work.

Coping With Curricular Demands

Technology offers a way to cope with transitory changes in curriculum and course content. Psychology, like all the sciences, is expanding so rapidly that its courses are becoming overcrowded with content. Many colleges, too, are asking that first-year courses such as general psychology not only satisfy the field's needs but also promote other valued educational outcomes, such as communication, critical thinking, computer literacy, and ethical thinking. Although technology is not the panacea for this complex conundrum, the demand to cover more areas in the same amount of time can be met, in part, by using e-mail, Web materials, and other information technologies.

EVALUATING INNOVATIONS

Creative innovators rarely keep their achievements to themselves. Once they find that their methods are effective, they try to influence the social field and encourage others to adopt their approach. Early users of the overhead projector and the blackboard, for example, eventually convinced others to use these innovations, and soon they became standard features of the college classroom. Innovative technologies such as distance learning, computer instruction, and smart classrooms have not yet made that transition from "interesting idea" to widespread acceptance. The innovators are convinced they are on to something, but many others are skeptical. As Deloughry (1995), writing in the *Chronicle of Higher Education* put it, "the question of whether information technology can improve the productivity of professors is one that often sours stomachs in higher education" (p. A17).

Computer-Based Methods and Learning

Are high-tech teaching methods fulfilling their promise by "revolutionizing the way students learn" and "transforming the academy?" The evidence of their effectiveness in teaching psychology is mixed (Chaparro & Halcomb, 1990; Forsyth & Archer, 1997; Kulik, Bangert, & Williams, 1983; C. Kulik & Kulik, 1991; J. Kulik & Kulik, 1987; Niemiec & Walberg, 1987). On the one hand, evaluations of the impact of technological innovations in such courses as experimental psychology (Chute, 1986; Goolkasian, 1989; Monahan, 1993; Perone, 1991), introductory statistics (Marcoulides, 1990), and educational psychology (Grabe, Petros, & Sawler, 1989) suggest that students learn more when traditional instructional methods are supplemented with computer-based instruction. Duncan (1991), for example, augmented her instruction with technology during only one segment of her course on experimental design. Students' scores were higher on the test that covered that segment. Petty and Rosen's (1990) students had higher test scores in an experimental design course when they used computer tutorials and simulations, and students also reported increased enjoyment with the course. Marcoulides (1990) found that students in an introductory statistics course performed significantly better on a statistics achievement test when using computer-based teaching aids as compared to those in a lecture group without such software. On the other hand, Welsh and Null (1991) reported that traditional teaching methods in research design were more effective than the computer-based methods available at that time.

Several studies have also reported increased performance through the use of computer-based tutorials. Chaparro and Halcomb (1990) found that in a general psychology class, those students who used the computerized tutorial, Self-Test and Review (STAR), performed better than those students that did not use the tutorial. Grabe, Petros, and Sawler (1989), in an educational psychology class, gave students access to a computer-based tutorial for half of the chapters covered in the course. They found that students performed better on material from chapters covered by the computer-based tutorial. They also found that when given free access to computerized study materials, those students who utilized those materials performed better on two of four examinations than students who did not utilize the computer-based tutorial. However, Sawyer (1988) found that computer-based study guides did not improve performance over traditional student workbooks.

Researchers have also begun to examine the impact of computerized learning laboratories on achievement. These laboratories bring together a number of learning technologies, including tutorials, access to the Web, e-mail, and simulations. Goolkasian and Lee (1988), for example, reported that 70% of their students agreed that the laboratory experience helped them learn the course material more easily. Worthington, Welsh, Archer, Mindes, and Forsyth (1996) and Forsyth and Archer (1997) compared the learning rates of students who took part in a 1-hour computer-based laboratory to those of students who attended only a traditional lecture class. Worthington et al. found that students who took part in the computer labs scored better on the final examination, in part because they were more likely to correctly answer questions about topics that were covered in both the lecture and lab. Forsyth and Archer (1997) examined the relationship between students' grades and the extent to which they actively used the various computer-based learning tools that comprised their learning lab. They reported that students who used the technology had higher grades than those who did not—but only if their academic preparation was weak. Stronger students (with higher grade point averages) who used technology achieved slightly higher scores on tests than those who did not use technology (76.3% vs. 74.5%). Weak students who were technology users averaged 71.1%, but weak students who did not use the technology scored 62.4%. Nearly two-thirds of the students who did not re-enroll at the school the next semester were low technology users.

Investigators have made only a small dent in the heap of unanswered questions pertaining to technology and learning, but much of the existing evidence suggests that computer-based instructional components increase learning when they supplement traditional teaching methods. These studies must, however, be interpreted with caution given the design issues that arise when evaluating the efficacy of these multifaceted interventions (Duncan, 1993). Consider, for example, a simple comparison of a lecturer who teaches classes in a traditional manner and a series of computer-based multimedia programs that are designed (by that same lecturer) to teach students the same material. What conclusions can be drawn from this study if the students in the computer-based learning group outperform those in the lecture group? Not much, unless drastic steps were taken to control the content differences between the groups, the mix of visual and verbal information, the amount of time students spent on the learning, and so on. Analysis should focus, as Mayer (1997) suggested, on other questions, such as "Do instructional lessons that contain verbal information and visual information (whether delivered via computer or by a skilled lecturer) facilitate more learning than instructional lessons that first provide verbal information and then provide visual information?"

Costs of Technology

A thorough evaluation of the value of computer-based instruction methods must consider not only the impact of these methods on learning, but also the costs associated with developing a working, reliable, high-end class, course, or professor. Although many people assume that technology is a low-cost panacea that will, in time, replace professors, others recognize that computers will only add to the complexity and cost of higher education.

Time

Most professors find that technology steals away the time they need to spend on their other teaching, research, and service duties. Although technology promises to save professors time in the long run—once all the e-mail, Web materials, and automated quizzing tools are put in place—in the short term, technology requires a substantial time investment. Many professors, too, report that the long-term time-saving claims of technology are exaggerated; they note that teaching psychology to 300 students who meet for 3 hours a week in a large auditorium is an extremely time-efficient strategy, and that technology only adds more chores to this task.

Courses that are taught entirely online are particularly time consuming in comparison to onsite, face-to-face classes. One psychologist who teaches the department's statistics course remarked that his online course:

> requires far more time than teaching in a classroom. . . . For an online
> class, I probably spend triple the time I spent per week when I taught

in a conventional classroom. . . . I came to somewhat despise the course because I couldn't get away from it. . . . Every time I turned around there was a question, a comment, a concern, or an issue for me to address—and I had obligated myself to a 24-hour turnaround. (cited in Chamberlin, 2001, p. 65)

Reliability

Psychologists are familiar with the laws that govern many psychological processes: Weber's law of perception, the law of effect, Michel's iron law of oligarchy. But innovative technologies do not comply with these laws. Rather, they follow Murphy's and Parkinson's laws: "Anything that can go wrong, will go wrong," and "Work expands so as to fill the time available for its completion." Computer-based technologies continue to evolve, but even the newest technologies are not glitch-free: software still has bugs (although now they call them "exceptions," "glitches," and "exploits"), machines break down, and unanticipated limitations to very expensive, complicated systems surface only after they are implemented. When professors and students come to rely heavily on technology, and that technology crashes, then their teaching and learning comes to a standstill. As Levinson and Grohe (2001) warned, "If you choose to be an early adopter and are not capable of implementing the system, you could have a disaster on your hands, with a technical mess, a poor instruction program, and a very unhappy, divided staff" (p. 58). They noted that the cutting edge is often the bleeding edge.

Funding Costs

The cost of information-based technologies is dropping faster than any other technology in history, but networks, servers, personal computers, projectors, and so on are all costly items to purchase and maintain. These items and their support mechanisms rarely replace existing systems, so they increase costs rather than decrease them. Many universities reduce their costs by shifting the burden to their students by requiring them to purchase computers, but some students may not be able to afford them. Many faculty are willing to increase their use of appropriate technologies, but are frustrated by the lack of resources in terms of money for software, hardware, technical support, and release time.

Costs for Students

These innovations may increase how much students learn, but at what cost for the learners? Although computers are often considered to be a basic tool any student needs, students who cannot afford their own computer will need to spend much of their time in a computer lab somewhere on campus. Computers increase the cost of attending college and contribute to the gulf between students from economically prosperous families and those who can barely make ends meet. In the long run, technologies should save students time and effort (and some money) by making course resources available for their use on their desktops: fewer trips to the library, less time in line at the bookstore, and no more time wasted tracking down their hard-to-find professors. But professors who use technology usually require more verifiable work be done outside of class, so students' workload may increase rather than decrease. When Web sites can track students' movements through the pages, noting which ones they visited and how long they spent on each one, when students must take a quiz and earn a 90% or better to move to the next online reading or are required to post at least three comments per week to the class forum, students may need to put in the 10–15 hours of outside preparation for each class each week professors expect.

BECOMING THE WIRED PROFESSOR

Sternberg (1997a, 1999b) argued that intelligent people meet the challenges they confront by using all three of their basic types of intellect. They use their synthetic skills to help them identify approaches and methods that more conventional thinkers either overlook or fail to consider. Their analytic skills then allow them to select, from the many ideas they discover, the ones that are most worth pursuing. Their practical-contextual ability provides them with the drive and good sense they need to put their idea into operation. Professors who want to upgrade their classes to take advantage of these innovative, computer-based tools, but who are not familiar with these technologies, will need to use all of their intelligences as they transform themselves from novice (newbie) to expert (oldie). They should also heed the recommendations of early adopters of these new teaching methods, such as Chamberlin (2001), Ralston and Beins (1999), and White and Weight (1999).

Ponder and Plan

The most skilled, successful innovators begin the problem-solving process, not by immediately leaping into action, but by first studying and conceptualizing the issue as a whole. Whereas novices often skip this step and immediately start clicking buttons and pulling down menus, experts say they begin by "thinking things over," "stepping back and taking a second look," or "turning the problem over in their mind." Aspiring high-tech professors may, for example, first review their teaching thoroughly, identifying goals, satisfactions, and problems. They may then imagine ways to use technology to solve problems, or at least reduce the length of the

"Things I Like Least About Teaching" list. They may also review their existing technology skills, and identify areas that they wish to improve through study and practice. This review increases the likelihood of a successful project by channeling the problem-solvers' efforts into more useful directions. This review also helps innovators get over any anxieties or misgivings they may have about their decision to use technology. Few individuals are truly computer-phobic, but some individuals consider technology to be a major cause of stress in their lives. Researching technology demystifies it, turning it into just a tool that is hard to use but even harder to break.

Bent (1997) described how he mindfully studied his problem—how to develop a Web site to complement his course—before he plunged into building the actual site. He first identified six specific goals for his site that included providing readings for his students, locating and making available resources that are not available in most libraries, linking to existing Web resources, and so on. He next considered his audience, and deliberately chose to design his site for his own local students. He also ruminated about how he could organize the 40 or so documents (files) that he wanted to post so that students would find them maximally useful, and he spent time surfing the Web for resources that were relevant to his own site.

During this planning phase, Bent (1997) gradually made decisions about the site's configuration, structure, and appearance. He wanted it to be simple, so that his students with slower, older machines could move through it quickly. He also wanted students to read the text—that was the point, after all—and so he decided that he needed to control the way material would appear on the page. Rather than wide lines of text in a hard-to-read font, he decided to enlarge the font and the margins so that the texts would be easy to read online. He also decided to emphasize local links on his site rather than connecting his pages up to distant resources that he could not monitor closely. He developed, in other words, a set of opinions about how a Web site should be designed to maximize learning and became personally committed to this conception.

Practice

Ericsson and Lehmann (1996) reported that most experts become experts through sheer practice. Every grand master, maestro, and gourmet chef was once a novice, but through weeks, months, and years of practice, they acquired the behavioral and information skills that others now admire. Professors then, to become experts with technology, must use it extensively in all aspects of their teaching, research, and service. Most already have basic computer skills; they can use e-mail, word process a document, navigate their operating system such as Windows, and use a Web browser.

They should, however, learn to use fully the features built into these programs and add a few new skills to their repertoire.

Word-Processing Programs

Professors who wish to hone their information-technology skills should learn to type well and quickly with one of the newest versions of standard word-processing programs, such as Microsoft's Word or Corel's WordPerfect. Students will be submitting papers written in these programs, and professor's who use some archaic or unusual word processor will have so many problems just opening documents that they will soon abandon the effort. In addition to using the program to generate papers and course materials, professors should explore the more advanced tools in the program that can be used to create different colors of type, different fonts, tables, graphics, and links. Most programs can generate and modify the Web's most popular document type (those that are based on an HTML, or hyper-text mark-up language, format). They also accept plug-ins (secondary programs that interface with the primary program) that permit you to create documents formatted as portable document files, or PDFs.

Mail Programs

The skilled user of technology needs to use a modern e-mail program —one that downloads messages from the mail server to the local computer rather than one of the older programs typically found on many college and university mainframe computers. Use all the features of the e-mail program, including tools for organizing messages, sending out messages to multiple recipients, and checking spelling. Join a moderated LISTSERV discussion group or two (but save the message that explains how to remove yourself from the list), and learn how to send attachments.

Browsers

The modernized teaching professor should be adept at using a Web browser for routine tasks, such as locating information about psychology on the Web, downloading materials from the campus library, searching databases of abstracts and articles, and buying good books on a commercial bookseller's site. But to extend these skills, try the following:

- Get a free account on one of the .com sites, such as Yahoo, and spend some time configuring your personal page. Use the online calendar and note space, for example, and upload a set of "favorite links" to Web sites you visit frequently.
- Download and install all the "plug-ins" needed by the pages you visit. Shockwave sites and files saved in the PDF format,

for example, will not run or cannot be read unless you install their plug-ins.

- While visiting pages, occasionally press the "reveal source" button on your browser to look at the code (usually HTML and Java) that generated the page.

Web-Authoring Programs

Many programs generate files that can be posted on and downloaded from the Web. Some require no more skills than a word-processing program —indeed, Web pages can be written using a simple text editor or the word-processing program you already use. Others, such as FrontPage and Dreamweaver, are more sophisticated and complicated to use, but they also have more functionality. In other words, one can build more interactive, interesting, and involving pages with them. These programs also ease one of the major headaches of Web page writing: transferring files from the computer where they were developed and tested to the computer that is connected to the Internet.

Professors need not learn to author Web documents, however, to use the Web in their teaching. They can, instead, make use of portals developed by commercial educational-support providers, such as WebCT or Blackboard. These companies build and market Internet software that allows professors to post their files and other materials to a pre-built Web template. In many cases these sites allow faculty to upload their material directly to the site, even if it is saved in a word-processing format. These sites also offer tools that faculty can use to make the site more interactive. Blackboard users, for example, can post information into one of five categories: announcements, course information, staff information, documents, or assignments. They can also develop and post a set of external links and administer tests to students online. Students' tools include a personal folder for their papers and their grades, as well as communication tools: virtual classrooms where students can talk synchronously and a bulletin board where they can post messages for classmates to read when they log on. Those who are interested in using such tools should spend some time experimenting with them to learn their uses and weaknesses.

Network

Creative innovation is a surprisingly interpersonal process. Although many people intuitively assume that people who generate new ideas and innovations do so through hours spent working alone, in many cases these creative individuals were part of a network of other creative individuals. Monet, for example, was sustained in his work by the ideas and support of his colleagues in the loose gathering of artists known as the impressionists

(Forsyth, 1999). Pauling prospered scientifically by maintaining relationships with scientists in other disciplines and by working closely with his students (Nakamura & Csikszentmihalyi, 2001). Innovations in technology also require collaboration with experts and with colleagues.

Find a Local Expert

Even when faculty are willing to increase their use of appropriate technologies, they may not have the technical skills needed to integrate technology in their classrooms. So they must turn to the technology experts in such offices as "IT: Information Technology," or "Media-Support Services," or "Instructional Development Center." The individuals in such offices are a rich resource of technical information, for they actually understand what terms like "band-width," "parity," "vertical risers," and "tcp/ip stack" mean. They also know how to get the equipment to work. The skills of a field anthropologist, however, are sometimes needed when learning to decipher their colorful local dialect. D. M. Murray (1985) described how many professors still feel about technology staff when he wrote: "They spoke a private language that I could not understand, and it was so filled with offensive jargon that I did not want to understand it" (p. 70).

Find a Colleague

Some faculty do not feel confident in their use of computers and high technology. Whereas such individuals may be willing to work with colleagues in an informal, information-sharing setting, they would be less likely to work with experts in computing. New information and technology flow best from colleague to colleague rather than from tech experts to professors. Virtually all recommendations for increasing the use of technology in teaching argue in favor of discipline-based programs rather than centralized, technology-based programs.

One of the best places to find a colleague, and an expert, is in a local workshop on teaching technologies. These sessions are often, ironically, examples of poor teaching. In some cases they feature talks by experts who string together three letter acronyms ("TLAs") like RAM, ROM, URL, GIF, JPG, PDF, HTM, and FTP in sentences like, "Unix is case-sensitive so be certain to use only lower-case when labeling all GIFs, j-pegs, and HTML files" and "After FTPing the file up make sure you issue a 555 command if the page includes executables." They sometimes use sophisticated PowerPoint or Web-based presentations but invariably something glitches and the audience leaves wondering, "Why bother?" Or they use a "hands-on" approach by putting faculty in front of computers, but the faculty ignore the presenter and spend the session reading their e-mail. These presentations are, however, good places to meet colleagues who are also learning to use the technology and connect to the experts who can offer advice about specific problems.

Increment

Innovations are not always the result of radical plans that replace the status quo with something completely unprecedented. In many cases they reflect modifications and improvements of existing systems; they can be incremental changes rather reconstructive ones (Sternberg, 1999a). An incremental approach suggests adding to your existing teaching methods gradually as you acquire and implement new skills. Begin, for example, by creating a Web version of your syllabus using your current word-processing program and move it to your institution's Web server. Then add more files as they become available. Eventually you should (a) link them together to create a Web site; (b) add sophisticated features, such as graphics and interactive elements; and (c) develop assignments that are based on these materials. And rather than agreeing to shift an entire course to an online one—with the only contact between professor and students occurring over the Internet—first experiment with computer-enhanced courses that make use of technology, but do not rely on it exclusively to mediate the relationship between professor and student.

Upgrade

It has been said that when it comes to the future, there are three kinds of people: "Those who let it happen, those who make it happen, and those who wonder what happened" (Richardson, cited in Percy & Leight, 2001, p. 13). Although the potential of innovative teaching methods such as e-mail and the Web is only beginning to be realized, the investment in time taken to learn these tools will likely be justified in the long run. Professor 2.0 offers many advantages over the well-worn Professor 1.0: If you are teaching today the same way you did 10 years ago, you should consider an upgrade.

8

EVALUATING: ASSESSING AND ENHANCING TEACHING QUALITY

Reduce teaching to intellect and it becomes a cold abstraction; reduce it to emotions and it becomes narcissistic; reduce it to the spiritual and it loses its anchor to the world. ... Good teaching cannot be reduced to technique; good teaching comes from the identity and integrity of the teacher.

—Parker J. Palmer
The Courage to Teach (1998, pp. 4, 10)

Lines on a vita can be counted to gauge research productivity, outside experts can provide commentary on the impact of one's scholarship, peers can attest to the critical contributions made in service, but how can one's teaching effectiveness be measured? Courses vary dramatically in size, level, and content, and professors' approaches to their classes run the gamut from formal lecture to open-ended discussion, structured to unstructured, cautious to risky, slow- to fast-paced, and practical to theoretical. Yet, most colleges systematically evaluate the quality of the instruction their professors provide by surveying the students themselves. These student evaluations of teaching, or SETs, if reliable and valid indicators of teaching, can be used to guide faculty development and personnel decisions. But if these inventories are used as the sole source of information about teaching and without considering their construct validity, then they can be transformed from useful resources into obstacles to overcome.

*   *   *

The professor's world is an evaluated one. Just to join it, one must pass a succession of tests, graded papers, and oral examinations that culminates in the defense of the dissertation. To land that first job in academia, prospective faculty members are interviewed, quizzed, and critiqued by search committees, deans, department chairs, and the faculty. The articles professors write, if published in the best journals, are often written, reviewed, and revised again and again until they are eventually deemed acceptable. If professors are practicing psychologists, they must take and pass a licensing exam. Their grant proposals are sent to banks of experts who scrutinize their ideas before deciding if the proposals warrant further review, let alone funding.

This evaluative edge extends to the classes professors teach. Most colleges and universities evaluate the quality of instruction by regularly reviewing the adequacy of course offerings; tracking retention and graduation rates; and monitoring the quality of the library, technologies, and other resources students will use to reach their learning goals. Most universities also collect data about each teaching professor's competence in the classroom. In many cases the term's end turns the assessment tables on professors; they grade their students' learning with final exams, but the students grade their instructors' skills with "student evaluation of instruction" forms. Professors typically pass through a relatively detailed review each year when administrators make decisions about wage and salary increases, but the most elaborate evaluations are saved for promotion and tenure decisions.

All this evaluation is needed to sustain personal and professional standards. After all, psychologists are supposed to be "fully trained, keep up-to-date, and be good at what they do. Otherwise they should stop doing it" (Swenson, 1997, p. 64). *Personal evaluation* double checks individuals' subjective, and potentially biased, assessment of their adequacies. *Summative evaluation* serves the profession's and institution's purposes, for through evaluation they ensure that they live up to their obligations to serve students, parents, and the public. This evaluation also functions as feedback to professors as they refine their skills and extend their expertise; it is through practice paired with *formative evaluation* that the unskilled become skilled, novices become experts, and rookies become pros.

Few would argue against evaluation, in general, but the specifics of how, when, and for what purpose are more often points of critical debate. Many universities, for example, rely heavily on one particular source of information when evaluating faculty—students' ratings of their teachers' skills—and many faculty feel that these data are too distorted to be useful. The audience for the evaluation must also be considered when designing the feedback system, for the kind of information that will help instructors improve their teaching may be different from the kind of information that administrators need to make decisions about salary, promotion, and tenure. This chapter considers these issues, but interested readers may wish to also consult Braskamp and Ory (1994), Cashin (1995), and a November 1997 *Current Issues* section of the *American Psychologist* featuring papers by Greenwald and Gillmore, d'Apollonia and Abrami, Marsh and Roche, and McKeachie.

STUDENT EVALUATIONS OF TEACHING

Dr. Greenwald was surprised when he opened the envelope that held the summary of his student ratings of his instruction for his undergraduate course in social psychology (Greenwald, 1997). He expected they would be good, because when he taught the course just the year before he got glowing marks from his students—the best evaluation he had ever earned. But this year's evaluations were not positive. In fact, they were the most negative reviews he had ever received. The shift was enormous—it spanned 2.5 standard deviations—even though he had used the same teaching and testing methods in the two classes. And he himself had not changed, had he? Wasn't he the same Dr. Greenwald who taught the course just the year before? Had his teaching skills suddenly eroded, or was the problem the source of the evaluation: Can students accurately judge their professors' instructional skills?

Most colleges systematically review the performance of their faculty, and each college's approach to this task is based on local norms, procedures, and historical precedent. But most colleges, despite their uniqueness, rely heavily on one key source of data: student evaluations of teaching, or SETs. These surveys yield a great deal of useful information about teaching, but many faculty question the meaning of the scores themselves. The most vehemently debated issue concerns the reliance on students' opinions and perceptions when evaluating teachers, but a number of related issues must also be considered, if only briefly: Are general impressions of teaching effectiveness more accurate than ratings of specific aspects of teaching? Does the use of student evaluations contribute to grade inflation? Should these ratings be used to make decisions about wages, tenure, and promotion?

Reliability of SETs

Reviews of the vast research literature dealing with SETs—estimated by Cashin (1995) at well over 1500 studies—generally agree that students' evaluations of a given instructor are reasonably stable across different rating forms, times (e.g., mid-term vs. end-of-term rating periods and immediately after class vs. delayed postclass follow-up), and courses taught in the same year. Test–retest reliabilities are high, as are internal consistency estimates of multi-item scales, even with scales with as few as five items (Marsh, 1982). Ratings also do not change much with the passage of time; when researchers tracked down students one year after they had completed the target course, they found that these retrospective ratings correlated .83 with the ratings students gave at the end of the course (Overall & Marsh, 1980). Interrater reliability is also high. Sixbury and Cashin (1995), for example, found that the median intraclass correlations across all items of a SET survey ranged from a low of .69 for a 10-student class to a high of .91 for a 40-student class.

The Structure of SETs

Most SETs include global summary items and specific items. The global items ask students to rate the general quality of their instructor, the course, and their learning with such questions as "On a scale from 1 to 5, how would you rate this instructor?" The specific items focus narrowly on the elements of good teaching, including knowledge of the subject, enthusiasm for the material, respect displayed to students, and so on. The forms may also invite students to express their evaluation of the course in their own words with open-ended items such as "Why did you rate this instructor as you did?" In many cases, too, professors can select the items they wish to have included on the evaluations from a bank of items or devise their own unique queries about their teaching.

Do these items capture the meaning of effective teaching? Some investigators, noting the complex, multifaceted nature of the teaching process, have argued in favor of a complex, multidimensional inventory (Braskamp & Ory, 1994; Centra, 1993; Feldman, 1989). Marsh and Roche (1997), for example, argued against the use of global items because teaching is too complex and multifaceted to be measured with a single item such as "How effective was your instructor?" They based this conclusion on more than 2 decades of work by Marsh and his colleagues with the Students' Evaluations of Educational Quality (SEEQ) inventory of teaching effectiveness (e.g., Marsh, 1982, 1983, 1984; Marsh & Hocevar, 1991; Marsh & Roche, 1993). This measure asks students to rate specific characteristics of the class and the instructor—such as degree of organization, skill in stimulating discussion, rapport with students—but factor analysis of these items yields the following key components of effective teaching:

- *Organization of presentations and materials:* use of previews, summaries, clarity of objectives, ease of note taking, preparation of materials
- *Group interaction:* stimulating discussion, sharing idea/knowledge exchange, asking questions of individual students, asking questions to entire class
- *Breadth of coverage:* contrasting implications, conceptual level, and giving alternative points of view
- *Learning/value of the course:* challenge to students, value of material, amount of learning, increase in understanding
- *Rapport, or student–teacher relations:* friendliness toward students, accessibility, interest in students
- *Examinations/grading:* value of examination feedback, fairness of evaluation procedures, content-validity of tests

- *Instructor enthusiasm:* dynamism, energy, humor, style
- *Workload/difficulty:* perceptions of course difficulty, amount of work required, course pace, number of outside assignments
- *Assignments/readings:* educational value of texts, readings

Marsh and Roche reported that factor analyses of the SEEQ, with data collected in more than 50,000 classes including more than a million students, have confirmed the 9-factor structure of the inventory and their position on the multidimensionality of SETs. They wrote:

> Confusion about the validity and the effectiveness of SETs will continue as long as the various distinct components of students' ratings are treated as a single "puree" rather than as the "apples and oranges" that make up effective teaching. (Marsh & Roche, 1997, p. 1195)

Other investigators, in contrast, feel that the global items on the SETs are the more valid items—particularly when the evaluation will be used to make personnel decisions (e.g., Cashin, 1995; Centra, 1993; McMillan, Wergin, Forsyth, & Brown, 1987). McMillan et al. (1987) suggested that students' general perceptions of instructional effectiveness are more accurate than their perceptions of less "visible" aspects of teaching: for example, their ability to assess their professors' level of preparation, respect for students, or scholarly heft (Funder & Dobroth, 1987). Scriven (1981) argued that many professors are very successful instructors even though they do not score high on scales that measure enthusiasm, warmth, or organization. D'Apollonia and Abrami (1997), after reexamining the results of prior factor analytic studies of SETs, concluded that a single principle component accounts for 63% of the variance in SETs. They speculated that this teaching "g-factor" can be divided into subcomponents, including presentation, facilitation, and evaluation skills, but these subskills are all included in a General Instructional Skill factor (Abrami, d'Apollonia, & Rosenfield, 1997).

Construct Validity of SETs

Researchers and educational experts have yet to agree on a single indicator of the construct "teaching quality," so the definitive study of SETs has yet to be conducted. Researchers have, however, examined the relationship between SETs and a number of variables that should be related to teaching quality. They have found, for example, that SETs are generally highly correlated with the ratings of the instructor provided by other, presumably more objective, observers. For example, researchers have confirmed that SETs are significantly correlated with ratings provided by

- administrators (Feldman, 1989; Kulik & McKeachie, 1975),
- colleagues (Feldman, 1989; cf. Marsh & Roche, 1997),

- alumni (Braskamp & Ory, 1994),
- trained observers (Feldman, 1989),
- trained coders of specific instructional behaviors ("low inference" ratings, H. G. Murray, 1983), and
- faculty rating themselves (Feldman, 1989).

SETs are also related to student performance. Investigators have confirmed that the students in classes taught by professors who are more skilled—as indicated by their higher SETs—get better grades and higher scores on exams. Correlational studies of this grades–ratings relationship cannot rule out the possibility that these higher grades reflect the leniency of the professor rather than the professor's teaching skill. However, quasi-experimental studies have suggested that (a) some instructors teach better than others and (b) SETs are accurate indicators of who these teachers are. Researchers have carried out these multisection validity studies at colleges and universities that offer multiple sections of the same course. These sections, even though taught by different instructors, use the same syllabus, text, and—most important—the same final examination. Meta-analyses of dozens of these multisection studies generally confirm the relationship between students' scores on the final examination and instructors' ratings; students with better teachers—as identified through student evaluations—get higher grades on their finals (Abrami, Cohen, & d'Apollonia, 1988; Cohen, 1981; McCallum, 1984).

Bias in SETs

College courses vary dramatically in size, level, and content. Some require students to pore over original texts, some use elementary textbooks, and others use no book at all. Some meet at 8 a.m., others at 7 p.m. The professors teaching these courses vary in race, gender, age, experience, and so on. These factors do not affect the quality of the instruction, but do they not influence students' perceptions and ratings?

Table 8.1 summarizes some of the many and varied findings pertaining to the impact of extraneous factors—such as amount of work assigned, sex of instructor, and size of class—on SETs. As most faculty realize, factors beyond their control—such as the number of students in the class, their interest in the material prior to registering, the course level, and even the printed instructions on the evaluation form—are systematically related to ratings. But what faculty may not realize is that these factors account for only a small percentage of the variance in ratings. For example, one study indicated that teachers who voluntarily have their courses rated get better evaluations, but this statistically significant relationship accounted for less than 1% of the total variance in evaluations (Cashin & Perrin, 1983). Marsh (1980) suggested that extraneous factors taken together probably

TABLE 8.1
A Sampling of Research Conclusions From Studies of Biasing Factors in Student Evaluations of Teaching

Possible bias	Students' ratings of instruction
Academic discipline	Highest in humanities, lowest in hard sciences and math, and moderate for psychology and other social sciences (Cashin, 1990)
Administration procedures	Lower if anonymous and professor not present (Marsh & Dunkin, 1992); no difference if ratings taken at mid-semester or end of semester (Feldman, 1978)
Class size, time of day it meets	Higher in smaller classes than larger classes (Sixbury & Cashin, 1995); no effect of meeting time (Aleamoni, 1981)
Course level	Higher in graduate courses; some evidence that upper level courses higher than lower level, introductory courses (Aleamoni, 1981)
Description of rating's purpose	Higher if survey states that responses will influence tenure/promotion, salary decisions (Braskamp & Ory, 1994)
Grade	Higher if students get higher grades or expect to receive higher grades (Greenwald & Gillmore, 1997)
Instructor's research productivity	Higher if instructor is active in research (Feldman, 1987)
Instructor's age and rank	Slight tendency for younger faculty to receive higher ratings, but findings are inconsistent and differences are small (Feldman, 1983); graduate student instructors receive lower evaluations (Braskamp & Ory, 1994)
Instructor's sex	Men receive slightly higher ratings in simulated teaching settings, but women receive slightly higher ratings in field studies (Feldman, 1992, 1993)
Race	Insufficient data to draw conclusions (Centra, 1993)
Student motivation	Higher in elective courses; higher in courses that students rated as more interesting prior to enrolling (Marsh & Dunkin, 1992)
Workload and course difficulty	Higher in more difficult, demanding courses (Centra, 1993; Sixbury & Cashin, 1995)

account for only 12–14% of the variance in ratings. As Marsh and Roche (1997) concluded:

> Particularly for the more widely studied characteristics, some studies have found little or no relationship or even results opposite to those reported here. The size, or even the direction, of relations may vary considerably, depending on the particular component of students' ratings that is being considered. Few studies have found any of these characteristics to be correlated more than .30 with class-average students' ratings, and most relations are much smaller. (p. 1194)

Negative Effects of SETs

SETs are designed to assess how well professors are performing their duties in the classroom, but some analysts worry that SETs may have some deleterious effects. Surveys of faculty at various universities, for example, suggest that evaluations may undermine faculty morale, particularly among faculty with weak publication rates or a strong involvement in teaching (Armstrong, 1998). Because these faculty's careers are defined more by their teaching than by their research and service, a failure in this sphere will have more profound emotional and motivational consequences (Niedenthal, Setterlund, & Wherry, 1992). These professors may, for example, lose interest in teaching, particularly if the evaluations do not reflect the amount of time and energy they put into their teaching. As Armstrong (1998) wrote:

> Faculty members with poor ratings might decide that teaching is not rewarding and spend less time teaching. Teachers might get discouraged by ratings if they see no clear relationship between their attempts to provide a useful learning experience and their ratings. Teachers may get discouraged because time spent on teaching activities has little relationship to ratings or because, as they develop knowledge in the field through their research, there is no increase in their teacher ratings. (p. 1223)

McKeachie (1997) also worried that faculty may alter the way they teach to increase their ratings, but because students "prefer teaching that enables them to listen passively" professors may unwittingly adopt less effective, but more student-pleasing methods (p. 1219).

These evaluations may also contribute to grade inflation: the awarding of higher and higher grades for work of lower and lower quality. Of all the factors listed in Table 8.1, only students' expectations about their grades in the class is correlated with higher evaluations and under the control of the instructor. Some educators therefore fear that professors may be tempted to use grades to "buy" better ratings from students. They grade more leniently and lighten the workload for students, who reciprocate by giving them higher evaluations. Given the compressed nature of SET ratings on most campuses, if a lenient grading policy gains the instructor as little as a half-point on his or her average class evaluation, he or she may be catapulted from the lower third of teachers in the department to the upper third (Redding, 1998).

Faculty may not deliberately "dumb down" their courses to get higher evaluations. Instead, once-strict graders may unwittingly relax their standards as a result of pressure from students and administrators. Faced with complaints that their courses are too difficult and grades too low, they alter the way they test, the number of readings they assign, and reduce the workload. The course becomes easier, grades rise, and so do SETs (Green-wald & Gillmore, 1997). On the other hand, they may grade leniently on purpose and cheat the system. Tabachnick et al. (1991), in their survey of teaching psychologists, found that only 40% felt that deliberately inflating grades was unethical, and a substantial proportion admitted they sometimes gave students better grades than they deserved just to "ensure popularity with students" (p. 510; see also Table 6.1 in this volume, chapter 6).

Even though SETs stand accused of fueling grade inflation, they may not deserve the blame. The *grading-leniency explanation* of the findings assumes that students appreciate receiving higher grades than they deserve and so they reciprocate by rating these kindly professors more favorably. But the *validity hypothesis* suggests that SETs and grades are correlated only because they are both caused by a third variable: the professor's superior teaching skills. The students in the class get better grades not because their professor is a lenient grader and the course is not demanding, but because the professor teaches so well that students learn more and so score higher on assessments. The *preexisting differences hypothesis*, on the other hand, suggests that students' prior interest in the course determines both their grade and their rating of the professor. Those students who are excited about learning psychology do well, and their excitement for the course raises the professor's rating, but students who are uninterested in psychology do less well and they do not give their professor high marks. It may be, too, that professors have a natural tendency to teach to the better students in their class, and these students therefore give their instructor higher ratings (McKeachie, 1997). Whereas Greenwald and Gillmore (1997), drawing on their structural equations modeling of the relationships between expected grade and course evaluation, recommended that statistical interventions should be taken to adjust SET ratings for leniency, McKeachie (1997), Marsh and Roche (1997), d'Apollonia and Abrami (1997) and other researchers in this area did not feel the findings are sufficiently strong to warrant this step.

Controversies and Convergences

What is the final word on SETs? Are they valid indicators of teaching effectiveness, or are they so easily manipulated by unprincipled professors that high ratings, like students' high grades, have lost their value? As Table 8.2 indicates, researchers have yet to reach complete consensus on matters of construct, convergent, and discriminant validity. d'Apollonia and Abrami (1997) and Greenwald and Gillmore (1997), for example, felt that ratings reflect students' general appraisal of their instructors, but Marsh and Roche (1997) felt that ratings, and the perceptions they measure, are differentiated and multidimensional. Whereas Greenwald and Gillmore (1997) concluded that ratings are substantially influenced by irrelevant

TABLE 8.2

Four Perspectives in the Debate Over the Validity of Student Evaluations of Teaching

| Authors | Conceptual structure: Are ratings conceptually unidimensional or multidimensional? | Validity concerns and focal questions | | |
		Convergent validity: How well are ratings measures correlated with other indicators of effective teaching?	Discriminant validity: Are ratings influenced by variables unrelated to effective teaching?	Consequential validity: Are ratings results used in a fashion that is beneficial to the educational system?
Marsh & Roche	Like effective teaching, ratings are conceptually and empirically multidimensional. Their validity and particularly their usefulness as feedback are undermined by ignoring this multidimensionality.	Different dimensions of student ratings are consistently related to effective teaching criteria with which they are most logically related, thus supporting their construct validity.	Ratings are relatively unaffected by potential biases. Bias (mis)interpretations typically fail to control valid effects on teaching (e.g., class size, enthusiasm) that ratings accurately reflect.	Multidimensional ratings, augmented by consultation, improve teaching effectiveness (their most important purpose). Their use in personnel decisions, however, should be more informed and systematic.
d'Apollonia & Abrami	Although teaching is multidimensional, ratings contain a large global factor, which consists of several highly correlated lower order factors.	Global student ratings or a weighted average of specific ratings are moderately correlated with teacher-produced student learning.	There is little evidence of bias in ratings; few characteristics have been shown to differentially affect ratings and teacher-produced student learning.	Ratings provide valid information on instructor effectiveness. However, they should not be the only source of information, nor should they be over interpreted.

Greenwald & Gillmore	Because student ratings are dominated by a global evaluative factor, many ratings items detect only this global evaluation rather than their intended distinctive content.	Ratings measures show moderate correlations with achievement in multisection design.	The same instructor gets higher ratings when giving higher grades or teaching smaller classes. Older research indicates also that ratings are increased by enthusiastic style.	The quest for high ratings subtly induces lenient grading, which can both (a) reduce academic content of courses and (b) feed grade inflation.
McKeachie	There is a g factor in ratings, but there are also discriminable lower order factors.	Student ratings provide valid, albeit imperfect, measures of teaching effectiveness.	Influences on ratings by variables other than teaching effectiveness are of concern in the context of the deplorable practice of computing ratings averages that are compared with norms.	Ratings contribute to judgments of teaching effectiveness, but their use could be improved.

Note. From "Validity Concerns and Usefulness of Student Ratings of Instruction," by A. G. Greenwald, 1997, *American Psychologist, 52,* p. 1185. Copyright 1997 by the American Psychological Association. Adapted with permission.

factors, including the grades students expect to receive, d'Apollonia and Abrami (1997), Marsh and Roche (1997) and McKeachie (1997) felt that these biasing factors account for so little of the variance in ratings that they can be ignored with little risk. These latter investigators are more convinced that SETs provide a relatively accurate picture of a professor's classroom skills, but even they noted that SETs can be easily misinterpreted. They suggested that SETs are essential to the formative and summative review process, but as the next section notes, these ratings are only one source of information about teaching.

IMPROVING THE EVAULATION PROCESS

Teaching evaluation systems, like professors' systems for grading their students' performance, serve formative and summative functions. As formative reviews, they can provide specific, useful feedback about what does and does not work in the classroom. When the review is positive, the formative review inspires faculty to continue their good work, but when it is negative, it guides their personal development efforts. As summative reviews, evaluation systems provide evidence of the overall quality of the institution's effectiveness, and they also provide information relevant to administrative decisions on faculty hiring, salary, contract renewal, tenure, and promotion. Formative evaluations may help faculty improve their teaching skills, but summative evaluations provide the extrinsic motivation that translates the feedback into action.

Improving Formative Assessments

Formative assessments are more descriptive than evaluative, for they are designed to give instructors information about their success as lecturers, discussion leaders, testers, graders, and classroom managers. They do not yield grades or scores or rankings, but instead context-specific information about professors' progress toward their teaching goals. Professors who have not yet mastered all the intricacies of teaching should use these assessments to identify the factors that are blocking their progress. And even highly successful teachers should use formative assessments to check for unexpected problems in their teaching.

Student Rating Scales

Students, given their vantage point in the classroom and their familiarity with a variety of professors and their methods, are an excellent source of descriptive information about their professor's practices. Although, as noted previously, their perceptions are not in all cases 100%

veridical, when students' opinions about strengths and weaknesses converge, professors should take heed.

Because the more specific the feedback the better, global items such as "How effective is your instructor?" should be supplemented with items that ask about specific characteristics of the professor and class. The SEEQ, for example, collects students' judgments on a series of relatively specific items, such as, "You found the course intellectually challenging and stimulating," "Instructor's explanations were clear," and "Methods of evaluating student work were fair and appropriate" (Marsh, 1982, pp. 90–91). Other assessment systems, such as the Purdue Research Foundation's Cafeteria Course and Instructor Appraisal System, let faculty select the items they wish to have included on their assessment from a bank of over 140 items. Faculty may also want to develop their own list of items to include on a survey, particularly when they seek feedback about a particular nuance or innovation.

Open-Ended Verbal Descriptions

Many faculty feel that the most useful information they receive about their teaching comes from student responses to such items as, "Do you have any additional comments?" or "Please describe why you rated this course as you did" that are included in many assessment surveys. Even though Braskamp, Ory, and Pieper found that open-ended and fixed-response formats yield similar types of information, with correlations between these two types of measures ranging from .75 to .93 (Braskamp & Ory, 1994; Braskamp, Ory, & Pieper, 1981; Ory, Braskamp, & Pieper, 1980), the open-ended measures are more diagnostic—and painful—in some cases. To reduce the number of incomplete forms and increase the number of useful comments professors should

- explicitly ask students to add written comments,
- assure them that these comments will be read,
- administer the evaluation forms at the beginning of class rather than at the end, and
- code these responses rather than reviewing them haphazardly.

Individual and Group Feedback

Faculty, mindful that the official SETs will be administered at the end of the semester, sometimes overlook opportunities to assess their teaching earlier in the semester. Such assessments, because they can be gathered quickly and analyzed informally, provide useful information about the current class, and so may suggest changes that can be put into practice immediately.

The *midterm course check* procedure, for example, collects students' responses to the following three questions: What do you like the most about this class? What do you like the least about this class? What one thing would you like to see changed? Or, as Angelo and Cross (1993) recommended, ask students to give examples of specific things that help them learn psychology, specific things that make learning more difficult, and practical suggestions for improving their learning. Students should be cautioned to not put their names on their comments, and also be reminded to try to focus on things that can be changed (e.g., amount of discussion, lecture style) rather than things that cannot be changed (when the class meets). Their comments can be categorized and discussed in a feedback session in the following class.

This approach can also be carried out as a collaborative group activity by asking a colleague to administer a Small Group Instructional Diagnosis. The colleague should separate the class into groups of five and give the groups about 20 minutes to answer the three questions in the previous paragraph. The groups must also select a recorder or spokesperson. Then, in a plenary session, the colleague pools all the ideas on the overhead and pushes the group toward consensus. Later, in a private meeting, the colleague relays the feedback to the instructor. This approach promotes collaboration and the development of consensus among class members on issues of classroom management and evaluation (Bennett, 1987).

Classroom Assessment Techniques (CATs)

Some of the most useful information about teaching effectiveness can be gathered by focusing on a particular aspect of the class rather than by seeking general information about overall course quality. A professor may, for example, wonder if students have too much time or too little time to complete the work assigned. Another may be worried that students' notes do not accurately reflect the contents of his lecture. Another may hope that students are learning to apply class material in their everyday lives, but be unable to assess her success in reaching this goal.

Angelo and Cross (1993) recommended using classroom assessment techniques, or CATs, to measure these specific instructional outcomes. They outlined a series of steps that faculty should follow in such assessments:

1. Select a course. Identify a single course that you will review using a CAT. This course should be one that you teach regularly, that you would like to improve in some way, but that has no glaring problems.
2. Identify a relatively specific teaching goal or question for this class. You can begin by reviewing the overall goals of the class, and narrowing down the focus of the review as much as possible. You may also want to think about portions of the class that usually do not go as well as you think they should,

and focus on that problem in your review. Angelo and Cross (1993) recommended that faculty begin by completing their Teaching Goals Inventory discussed in chapter 1. The professor may wish instead to begin with a specific question about some aspect of the class, such as why students are not interested in the material, what nonmajors and majors hope to get out of the course, or why students respond so negatively to classroom discussions.

3. Design an assessment method that will yield information about the question. The assessment should focus on what students have learned. As the instructions to contributors page in the journal *Teaching of Psychology* recommends, "empirical assessment should directly measure the impact of the technique on student learning (e.g., a pretest/posttest analysis of learning) rather than student self-report of learning" (Smith, 2001). The assessment may also include questions that will provide information needed to interpret the results, such as students' perceptions of problems, strengths, and weaknesses. Angelo and Cross (1993) and Table 8.3 describe several of these relatively simple, qualitative approaches to assessment.

4. Conduct the session that you wish to examine as you normally would. The assessment intervention, because it focuses on student learning, should fit naturally into the session's teaching and provide students with feedback about goals.

5. Carry out the assessment procedure, being certain that students understand that the intervention is not a test of their learning, but an indication of the adequacy of the lesson. Angelo and Cross recommended giving students credit for participating, but also keeping responses anonymous.

6. Analyze the data. The professor should review the responses generally, perhaps by reading them over in a single session to get a general sense of their contents. The data can then be reviewed more thoroughly by taking counts on the number of students who missed specific types of material or voiced similar concerns about the class. Specific cases should also be culled to use as illustrative examples of strengths, weaknesses, and areas for improvement.

7. Draw conclusions based on the data. If the results are unexpected or inconsistent, spend some time mulling them over, discussing them with students in the class individually, or sharing them with colleagues. Consider such general questions as, "Do your data indicate how well (or poorly) students achieved the teaching/learning goal or task?" and "Can you

TABLE 8.3
Examples of Classroom Assessment Techniques Discussed by
Angelo and Cross (1993)

Assessment technique	Objective checked	Description
Empty outlines	Accuracy and depth of student's notes	At the end of the day's lecture the professor gives students a sheet of paper with only the major headings of the lecture listed, and asks students to fill in subheadings and key points
Memory matrix	Students' ability to compare and contrast concepts	Students complete a table that lists concepts or theories down the rows and their characteristics across the columns (e.g., classical and operant condition are row entries and terms such as "reinforcement," "extinction," and "shaping" are column headings)
Minute paper	Grasp of key points of presentation	Students are given 1 minute to identify the points that they feel were the most important ones in the day's presentation and ask questions they want answered
Muddiest point	Identification of areas of uncertainty	Students are asked to identify the area of the lesson that was the muddiest, or least clear, to them
One-sentence summary	Students' ability to integrate information	Students must write a grammatically correct single sentence that summarizes a topic; one variation asks students to answer the questions "Who does what to whom, when, where, how, and why" in one sentence
Application cards	Student's ability to apply course material to new examples	The professor hands out large index cards to students, who are asked to write down at least one application of the day's presentation to a real-world situation or problem

interpret why you got the results you did?" (Angelo & Cross, 1993, p. 55).

8. Give the students feedback about the assessment. The results of the assessment can be communicated with students through a didactic session where the professor covers the findings and offers interpretations or by the preparation of a more formal report that is distributed to students. If the re-

sults suggest changes in method, these possible changes should be discussed carefully with students and, depending on the specificity of the syllabus, initiated the next time the course is taught.

9. Evaluate the assessment. Angelo and Cross recommended reviewing the effectiveness of the assessment procedures, noting any ways that the intervention could be improved to yield clearer, more interpretable information.

Consider, as an example, the use of classroom assessment by a professor who teaches a course in learning and cognition. His assessment is triggered by his suspicion that students are not connecting the course content to problems that they face in the own lives. After explaining the reasons for the exercise with the class, he puts this question on the overhead (Angelo & Cross, 1993, p. 68):

> Have you tried to apply anything you learned in this unit on human learning to your own life? Yes or No.
>
> If "yes," please give as many specific, detailed examples of your applications as possible.
>
> If "no," please explain briefly why you have not tried to apply what you learned in this unit.

Students were asked to use a word processor to generate a one-page response, and the paper's due date was set for the next class period. Students were not to put their names on the papers, but the professor noted who turned in a paper and gave each student credit.

One professor who used this method reported that 60% of his students claimed they were using the course's content to improve their studying methods, enhance their memory, reduce their stress, deal with their children's behavior, and so on. At the next class he reviewed the findings with students, and with the class developed a more detailed listing of possible applications. The professor now stresses applications as a specific goal in this course, and conducts the assessment regularly to check his teaching effectiveness.

Collaboration With Colleagues

Colleagues can be an excellent source of formative feedback. Informally, they can act as a sounding board for new ideas, a supportive audience to listen to difficulties, and an advisor who can recommend solutions. More formally, they can review the materials of the course—syllabi, tests, lecture notes, Web materials, and so on—and identify strengths, weaknesses, and revisions. They can also visit the classroom itself, and write up the results of their visit in a report or share them with the instructor over a cup of coffee. Faculty observers, however, tend to be lenient reviewers, and one colleague's high appraisal of a learning strategy might not be shared by another colleague down the hall (Centra, 1975). One may therefore wish to consider providing a checklist for observers to use to structure their comments. Murray (1983) and Mintzes (1979) described observational inventories that are less vulnerable to observer bias because they focus on discrete, specific types of behavior. These low-inference ratings ask observers to indicate only the extent to which the professor displayed behaviors that are related to effective and ineffective teaching, such as speaking clearly and expressively, smiling or laughing, using concrete examples, using headings and subheadings, showing interest in the subject, showing concern for students, and so on (Murray, 1983, pp. 140–141).

Improving Summative Assessment

In teaching, as in all things, many paths lead to excellence. One professor may be a superb lecturer who teaches students so stealthily they do not even realize their neural networks are being rewoven. Another may be the quintessential discussion leader who can draw out and organize students' viewpoints in a rich texture of insights. Others may develop novel methods of instruction, write textbooks that inspire students, or mentor colleagues in the craft of teaching. The steps taken in evaluating teaching must reflect this diversity. Because professors reach excellence through many different paths, no single index or indicator of quality fairly captures this diversity in style and substance. A summative review should take into account not only professors' classroom teaching but also the caliber of the instructional and evaluative materials they develop and use in their classes, the academic quality of the course's contents, the quantity and quality of their nonclassroom teaching activities, and their overall contributions to the discipline's educational mission.

Classroom Teaching

What is the best source of information about professors' competence in the classroom itself: their skill when lecturing, when leading discussions, and when answering questions; their ability to motivate students to learn the material; their work in a teaching laboratory; or their effectiveness as tutors when discussing recent empirical findings with advanced students? As noted earlier in the chapter, studies of the validity of student ratings of their teachers' effectiveness, although not entirely consistent in their conclusions, suggest that summative evaluators should solicit students' opinions rather than rely on their own. Annual reviews of faculty, tenure and promotion decisions, and considerations for wage increase, if they are at least partially based on the quality of professor's teaching, should therefore consider what students say about what goes on when their professor is teaching. Specific suggestions include:

- Although some assessment experts recommend providing reviewers with detailed information about specific facets of teaching, most favor the use of a small number of items that require a general, overall evaluation of teaching. Rather than asking, for example, about skill in lecturing, leading discussions, enthusiasm, building rapport, or providing feedback, summative rating items such as, "How would you rate this instructor's overall teaching effectiveness?" and "Rate this course on a scale from 1 (very poor) to 5 (outstanding)" are preferable. These items are general enough to be asked in any class, no matter what its size, procedures, or level, yet they are highly correlated with other indices of student learning (cf. d'Apollonia & Abrami, 1997; Marsh & Roche, 1997).

- SETs should be used to generate only overall ratings of faculty's teaching—for example, *exceptional, meets standards*, or *unacceptable*—rather fine-grained, multicategory discriminations (d'Apollonia & Abrami, 1997). This conservative approach prevents reviewers from reading too much into the numbers and reaching conclusions that are not warranted given the possibility of measurement error. Moreover, as McKeachie (1997) noted, in most cases

> personnel committees do not need to make finer distinctions. The most critical decision requires only two categories—"promote" or "do not promote." Even decisions about merit increases require no more than a few categories, for example, "deserves a merit increase," "deserves an average pay increase," or "needs help to improve." (p. 1218)

- Because SETs are survey data, they should be discounted if their validity is threatened by unusual administrative procedures and inadequate sample sizes. Cashin (1995) recommended that evaluations should be based on at least five sections, taught in different years. SETs should be interpreted cautiously in classes with fewer than 10 students, and if a substantial portion of the class (30%) did not complete the forms.

- SET information should also include data pertaining to grade expectations, grade distribution, and student motivation; scores can also be statistically adjusted to control for these influences (Greenwald & Gillmore, 1997).

- If merit pay and promotions are based, in part, on teaching effectiveness, then SETs should be administered in all classes, and the same generic questions should be used on all surveys. The use of standardized items promotes the development of norms pertaining to teaching, but only if all faculty are required to have students complete evaluations: professors should not have the option of not evaluating their instruction.

The Quality of Instructional and Evaluative Materials

Outstanding teachers, in addition to stimulating learning through direct instructional activities, also teach by developing effective instructional materials, activities, assignments, and assessment methods. They may not be mesmerizing presenters or skilled discussion leaders, but they can teach effectively with well-designed Web sites, by giving students detailed feedback about their individual work and by setting clear classroom goals and providing students with the resources they need to achieve them. The quality of these procedures will likely be indicated by students' evaluations of the course itself, rather than their rating of the instructor. Colleagues can also review these instructional materials. As Centra (1975) noted, colleagues are too inaccurate for use as classroom observers. They are, however, excellent judges of instructional material and course management. Just as faculty are skilled in reviewing a scholarly article and determining its publishability, faculty are capable of reviewing a colleague's teaching materials to determine if they are excellent, adequate, or need improvement. Instructors can facilitate this process, however, by preparing a dossier, or portfolio, that describes their teaching methods, their educational philosophy, and includes copies of material used in classes (e.g., syllabi, tests, handouts, classroom exercises, sample lecture notes, graded examinations). This important element in summative evaluation in teaching is examined in detail in chapter 9.

The Academic Quality of the Course

There are good courses in psychology, but there are also great courses. One professor may cover all the topics when teaching introductory psychology and measure students' performance adequately, but another may challenge students to think critically about the field's key issues, coordinate a series of student-generated research studies, provide students with opportunities to express their understanding of psychology in their own writing, and have time left over to help students apply psychology in their everyday lives. Summative evaluations should attempt to gauge the relative academic quality of the course itself by looking past *how* the class is taught to focus on *what* is being taught. In most cases, members of the professor's own academic unit can judge whether a course meets the discipline's standards for academic quality by asking such questions as:

- Is the course material current?
- Is the instructor adequately trained in the subject that he or she is teaching?
- Is the course pitched too low, in that it is so easy that students who learn very little nonetheless pass it?
- Does it cover the material that the college catalog says it is supposed to cover, or has it wandered from its purpose to focus on trivia?
- Is the course intellectually challenging?

The Quantity and Quality of Nonclassroom Teaching Activities

When summative evaluators base their ratings of faculty only on classroom teaching, they unwittingly endorse the view of those who criticize faculty for spending too little time teaching. Yet much teaching occurs outside of classroom settings, through the following indicators:

- *Advising and mentoring:* the number of advisees; participation as advisor on undergraduate thesis, graduate thesis, and dissertation committees; any reports (both favorable and unfavorable) from advisees pertaining to advising.
- *Publications dealing with teaching in higher education:* (a) papers and texts published or presented on educational topics, (b) manuals developed for classroom use, (c) papers published or presented with student-coauthors (both graduate and undergraduate), and (d) textbooks.
- *Specialized teaching:* nonclassroom-based teaching, such as (a) public teaching (presentations to the community at large, including speeches, workshops, educational newspaper articles, and interviews); (b) individualized instruction, including mentoring and tutoring; (c) workshops for colleagues and advanced students; (d) distance education; (e) interdisciplinary teaching.
- *Curriculum development activities:* description of courses developed or substantially changed. Innovations in teaching courses or topics should also be noted.
- *Service contributions in teaching:* administrative duties or service that focuses primarily on teaching, such as participation on any departmental, college, or university committees and task forces dealing with teaching.
- *Supervision and mentoring:* guiding students' work on individual research projects, thesis and dissertation research, the development of clinical skills, and other forms of graduate teaching.

Overall Contributions to the Discipline's Educational Mission

Ideal professors do all things well. They teach in the classroom, on the sidewalk, in their offices, through technology, with dramatic effect. Whether they are lecturing, leading discussions, questioning, or mentoring, their students learn. But ideal professors reach beyond fine teaching, per se: They make broader contributions to teaching practices in their disciplines and to higher education in general. Such contributions as research into pedagogical practices, curricular reform, university- and national-level service in teaching, public teaching, and mentorship of other teachers dot the vitae of the finest teachers. They are concerned with their own and others' teaching, to the point that they study the process and hone their own skills. They participate in formal and informal analyses of teaching not because they are experts, but because they are always seeking improvement.

Evaluating Evaluation

Faculty evaluations, whether conducted to help faculty improve their teaching or for input into personnel decisions, should be conducted with care. Formative reviews can provide professors with suggestions on how to improve their teaching, but not if the evaluations themselves are invalid —or thought to be invalid. Summative evaluations, too, must be based on more than a simplistic bean count of faculty's gold stars given them by their students. Summative evaluators who factor teaching skill into their reviews of faculty are to be commended for not basing merit awards only on research productivity, but if they base their review on incomplete data, their good intentions will be for naught. Faculty should be evaluated, but these reviews must be based on procedures that are consistent the current state of knowledge in the field of teaching evaluation rather than the personal predilections of faculty or administrators.

9

DOCUMENTING: DEVELOPING A
TEACHING PORTFOLIO

The outstanding characteristic of man is his individuality. He is a unique creation of the forces of nature. Separated spatially from all other men he behaves throughout his own particular span of life in his own distinctive fashion.

—Gordon W. Allport
Personality: A Psychological Interpretation (1937, p. 3)

*   *   *

Teaching psychologists' professional responsibilities are staggering, yet their work in and out of the classroom can be ignored and forgotten if it is never documented. Many teaching psychologists therefore gather together the artifacts of their teaching in a portfolio or dossier that describes their involvement in, and success at, teaching. Portfolios are unique, individualistic summaries of one's work in the teaching arena, but most will include a teaching vita, a personal statement about teaching, a selective sample of teaching materials, and documents that provide objective evidence of teaching effectiveness. Portfolios describe the teaching professor's work, but they can also be used to guide development, innovation, and assessment.

*   *   *

Gordon W. Allport (1968) summarized his years of research into personality and prejudice with these questions: "How shall a psychological life history be written? What processes and what structures must a full-bodied account of personality include? How can one detect unifying threads in a life, if they exist?" (p. 377). Allport believed answers to these questions elude psychologists because each personality is a unique configuration of patterns and combinations. In his now-classic distinction between the nomothetic and idiographic, he argued that generalities can be applied to personality, but these generalities underestimate the richness of each case. Personalities change over the course of a lifetime as individuals react to

283

new experiences, make choices based on their goals and values, and grapple with issues of self and satisfactions. As Allport said (1955, p. 19): "Personality is less a finished product than a transitive process. While it has some stable features, it is at the same time continually undergoing change." Allport, drawing on the work of humanistic psychologists, called this process of change "becoming" or "individuation."

Allport's conclusions about personality apply to that part of the professor's life that has been spent teaching. His questions, when put to the professor, ask: How shall the life history of the teaching psychologist be written? What processes and what structures must a full-bodied account of college and university teaching include? How can one detect the unifying threads that run throughout a career in the classroom? Here I consider how teaching professors can chart the process of "becoming" a professor by detailing their unique accomplishments in teaching.

THE TEACHING PORTFOLIO

Allport did not favor simple approaches to measuring personality. He sometimes gauged traits and temperament with checklists, surveys, and inventories, but he believed that these methods overlook the unique qualities of the individual. Traits like gregariousness or aggressiveness are more widespread than others, for "the original endowment of most human beings, their stages of growth, and the demands of their particular society, are sufficiently standard and comparable to lead to some basic modes of adjustment that from individual to individual are *approximately* the same" (Allport, 1937, p. 298). But the way in which people's actions are consistent over time and situations is unique to each person: an idiographic tendency, rather than a nomothetic one. "Everyone knows that each human neuropsychic system is unique. With unique genotypes of inheritance and never-repeated personal environments, it could not be otherwise" (Allport, 1968, p. 107).

Allport sought to capture the uniqueness of each person's life by analyzing personal documents: "any self-revealing record that intentionally or unintentionally yields information regarding the structure, dynamics, and functioning of the author's mental life" (Allport, 1942, p. xii). Allport believed that people are relatively accurate when judging their own motives, values, and interests, and so their letters, diaries, journals, and autobiographies yield information that a more standardized assessment would overlook. His famous "Letters from Jenny," for example, offered a detailed analysis of Jenny's unique relationship with her son, with Jenny herself providing all the raw material for the analysis by expressing herself in letters written to friends for many years (Allport, 1946).

A *teaching portfolio* or *teaching dossier* is just such a personal document, for like the personal documents that Allport studied so earnestly, it reveals the personality, accomplishments, and plans of its author. The portfolio strategy comes from fields and professions that make things. Marketing firms' portfolios of their prior advertising successes impress new clients. Architects' portfolios of previous designs and structures convey their style and proficiencies. Actors bring with them to each casting call a history of their prior appearances and accomplishments. And so professors' portfolios should include a detailed account of their *products*; the artifacts of their teaching and scholarship, including capsule summaries of the classes they have taught, the lectures they have crafted, the educational materials they have developed, and the curricula they have built. It is "a comprehensive record of teaching activities and accomplishments drawn up by the professor" himself or herself (O'Neil & Wright, 1992, p. 6).

Portfolios, as personal documents in the Allportian sense, combine both idiographic and nomothetic elements. Each portfolio is unique, for it documents the activities of a single individual's work in teaching. But, as nomothetic records of teaching, they also reflect the common experiences of most professors. Just as the press of environmental circumstances creates dimensions of variation in people's personalities, so the university setting with its demands for teaching, research, and service creates consistencies in the life history of the teaching psychologist. These common themes create similarities in professors' portfolios, so that even though each portfolio is a unique description of a unique professor's life, most nonetheless contain the categories of information summarized in Table 9.1: (a) a vita-like listing of all professional accomplishments related to teaching; (b) a personal statement or narrative that provides the reader with the professor's personal perspective on his or her work in teaching; (c) teaching materials, annotated so that readers can understand their connection to the professor's educational mission; (d) objective and subjective indicators of teaching effectiveness; and (e) ancillaries that the portfolio-builders believe are essential for conveying a sense of their teaching to the reader.

Why Develop a Teaching Portfolio?

It takes time to develop a teaching portfolio, and most teaching professors are short on that commodity. So, why take the trouble to document one's teaching in a portfolio? The motivations that prompt professors to create portfolios are as diverse as the motivations that Allport (1942, pp. 69–75) identified in his analysis of why people write diaries, letters, and journals. Some write to explain their actions, others are driven by "a single-minded desire to display one's virtues and vices," and others desire to put their accomplishments in order. But across the gamut of motives, portfolio experts most frequently cite these five purposes: documentation, develop-

TABLE 9.1
Possible Components of a Teaching Portfolio or Dossier

Component	Characteristics
Vita	A comprehensive listing of all professional activities related to teaching, including courses taught, service on teaching-related committees, and scholarly activities related to teaching
Personal statement	A narrative describing one's teaching, often containing sections pertaining to personal principles and assumptions about learning, general and specific goals, and autobiographical materials
Teaching materials	An annotated and selective sample of materials used in teaching, including syllabi, lecture notes, reading lists, session plans, self-constructed learning activities and assignments, hypertext documents, tests and examinations, and unique instructional tools
Assessments	Text, numerical, and graphic summaries of evidence of teaching effectiveness gathered from such sources as student evaluations, peer observations, self-assessments, and exit interviews with students
Supplemental materials	Individualized indicators of teaching style and quality, such as videotaped lectures, transcribed supervision sessions and discussions, copies of students' graded assignments, scholarly publications pertaining to teaching and learning

ment, enrichment, innovation, and assessment (Cerbin, 2001; Murray, 1995; Seldin, 1998).

Documentation

Teaching portfolios provide a glimpse (ideally, a reassuring glimpse) into the inner world of the teaching professor. For even though teaching is a very public activity, it often occurs in an exclusive, almost secret, setting. The professor typically meets with many students, but in isolation from fellow professors or administrators. Although everyone remembers what is involved in teaching, for they were students themselves at one time, professors' actual activities in and out of the classroom require specification. The portfolio provides that by cataloging the various obligations of a teacher—such activities as meeting class, lecturing, leading discussions, developing and administering tests, advising, developing curricula, and so on. But the portfolio goes beyond these general, categorical listings by identifying concrete actions and activities that comprise them, while also describing any uncommon, unusual, and innovative activities undertaken by the instructor. They also provide a more complete picture of the professor's accomplishments by offering a long-range look at the teacher rather than a time-limited sample of a year or two's work. A portfolio generates longitudinal data that describe the professor's accomplishments across a longer period of time, and so provides evidence of changes in patterns and qualities.

Development

The teaching portfolio is a useful tool for stimulating adaptive change across the life history of the teaching professor. Studies of experts in such spheres as sports, chess, problem solving, and science all converge on one conclusion: Experts are particularly good at seeking out feedback about their performances, and then using that feedback to improve their overall performance (Ericsson & Lehmann, 1996). The portfolio is an excellent means of gathering such feedback, particularly because the portfolio forces the professor to create a context for this information. During the day-to-day demands of teaching, one can easily lose sight of the overall reasons behind one's practices. Teaching becomes a series of discrete actions, such as giving lectures, making up exams, giving out grades, and holding office hours. Preparing a portfolio forces the professor to put these specific actions into a broader context and so see the forest rather than just the individual trees. The very act of developing a portfolio helps professors gain an over-arching perspective on their varied accomplishments and activities.

The portfolio-building process also provides the opportunity to discover inconsistencies in one's practices, identify weaknesses, and devise ways to improve. In many cases portfolios include sections that ask the professors to describe ways in which they expect their teaching will change in the future, so that they can identify new goals and plan for their implementation.

Enrichment

Administrators in higher education often confuse job enrichment strategies with job enlargement strategies. Job enlargement is most useful when individuals, bored with the routine of their work and its minimal demands, are given the opportunity to take on new duties. Job enhancement, in contrast, increases the value of the individual's work, particularly by stressing the intrinsic rewards the work generates.

Teaching portfolios should not be just one more burden placed on an already overburdened teaching professor. Rather, building a teaching portfolio gives professors an opportunity to revisit their motivations for teaching and redefine the intrinsic satisfactions that teaching provides. When professors catalog all the many and varied activities that are associated with teaching, they can better recognize the magnitude of their contribution to others' learning. Portfolios, by providing an opportunity to plan future directions, also increase a sense of efficacy as individual faculty chart out their own goals. Portfolios are also protective and empowering. They protect faculty, to a degree, from the disappointment, disillusionment, and distress that can occur when they receive negative evaluations about their teaching from their students. If these evaluations are their sole source of data pertaining to their teaching, then the professor must accept their students' pronouncements. But professors who have assembled a cumulative teaching portfolio can consider student opinions in the overall context of their work as teachers. Portfolios also provide professors with the means to influence how their teaching is evaluated by colleagues and administrators, for they give professors the opportunity to create and select the materials that will determine how they are evaluated.

Innovation

Portfolios benefit not only individual instructors, but also their departments, institutions, and disciplines. Portfolios are often recommended as a tool for refocusing the faculty's attention on teaching, particularly when teaching is afforded little time or energy relative to research. The process of portfolio-building can also increase the amount of time faculty spend discussing teaching, as they share ideas for what elements to include in portfolios, gather information from peers to include in their reports, and identify examples of good portfolios to emulate.

Assessment

As noted in chapter 8, many colleges and universities use portfolios in their annual review of faculty, when identifying faculty for special awards and honors, and when making tenure and promotion decisions. Portfolios, because they meld many sources of information about teaching, provide a more complete assessment of the quality of the instruction. Portfolios also take some of the sting out of the review process. Faculty reviews can, in some cases, create feelings of competition among the faculty, for when evaluations follow identical formats and use comparative scales, then relative rankings of individuals are unavoidable (e.g., "Relative to the other teachers at this university, how would you rate *this* professor?"). Portfolios, because they are individualized, reduce the tendency to rank order faculty. Many faculty also feel less threatened by the prospect of portfolio-based reviews. The judgments of students and peers are often summarized in portfolios, but the professor has the opportunity to put this information into perspective for the reader.

Types of Teaching Portfolios

Just as the vita or resume is deliberately shaped and recast for differing purposes—the vita one sends when applying for a position as a scientist at a research institute should look very different from the vita sent with one's application for a tenure-track position at a small, liberal arts college—the teaching portfolio's structure and content change depending on its overall purpose. For example, a *showcase portfolio* that is created when a faculty member is nominated for a teaching award will differ substantially from the *evaluation portfolio* that is requested by the professor's tenure and promotion review committee. A showcase portfolio is deliberately designed to highlight the professor's strengths rather than weaknesses. Just as researchers don't list on their vita their many failed studies or the papers that never were accepted for publication, the portfolio need not catalog every teaching catastrophe. It should be "a factual description of a professor's major strengths and teaching achievements" (Seldin, 1991, p. 3), a "collection of documents that represent the best of one's teaching" (Murray, 1994, p. 34). An evaluation portfolio, on the other hand, should be a more evenhanded review of the prior work in teaching. Such portfolios, too, should adhere more closely to the standards for such documents as established by the department, college, or school. The evaluation portfolio's goal: to "describe, through documentation over an extended period of time, the full range of your abilities as a college teacher" (Urbach, 1992, p. 71). Other portfolio forms include the archival portfolio, the course-limited portfolio, the time-limited portfolio, and the developmental portfolio.

The portfolio will also differ depending on the instructor's stage of development as a teaching professor. A graduate student may begin building a portfolio to qualify for an academic post, a new professor's motivation may be tenure review, and the full professor's motives may reflect exhibitionism or a quest to find order in the accumulated events of a long and distinguished career. As Table 9.2 suggests, graduate students and senior professors might develop portfolios, but the final document reflects their varying purposes (Brems, Lampman, & Johnson, 1995; Stewart, 1997).

BUILDING THE PORTFOLIO

Languishing in those filing cabinets, scattered across the desk top, and interweaved randomly into stacks of last semester's correspondence is the raw material needed to build a teaching portfolio. Teaching evaluations, thank you notes for guest lectures given, old tests and syllabi, handouts and homework assignments, and the lecture notes used on the first day of class that outline the course's larger purposes provide the foundation for what will grow into a more comprehensive life history of the teaching psychologist. Once organized into the basic categories listed in Table 9.1 and discussed in more detail in this chapter, the scattered bits of information will grow into a full fledged portfolio that charts the changes and achievements of its author.

TABLE 9.2
The Purposes of Portfolios for Particular Professors

Position	Purposes
Graduate student instructors	Gaining a perspective on teaching and its relationship to one's professional identity
	Developing the credentials and experiences needed for faculty positions
	Increasing sense of efficacy in teaching
New faculty	Defining and implementing a balance across demands for research, teaching, and service
	Increasing the quality of instruction
	Documenting teaching quality for tenure review
Tenured faculty	Developing and diversifying teaching activities
	Renewing teaching methods
	Maintaining and enhancing motivation for teaching
	Documenting teaching quality for honors, awards, promotion, pay
Adjunct faculty	Developing credentials and experiences required by employers
	Increasing preparedness for teaching
	Developing and sustaining an identity as a teaching professor

The Eruditio Vitae

The curriculum vitae, or C.V., is both the birth certificate and the headstone of the academic. It is literally the "course of the scholar's life," the autobiographical record of all scholarly accomplishments. It should therefore be extraordinarily detailed, with no accomplishment excluded. At the same time, though, the C.V. is usually a terse document that lists achievements, organizing them into appealing clusters with meaningful headings and subheadings. The traditional C.V. usually stresses the scholar's own study, training, and research rather than his or her impact on others' learning.

Unlike the traditional C.V., the vita in a teaching portfolio should stress *eruditio*: instruction, or one's accomplishments as an educator, teacher, and disseminator of knowledge. As Table 9.3 suggests, the Eruditio Vitae (or E.V.) should go beyond information pertaining to degrees received, academic appointments held, membership in professional associations, courses taught, and research published to include sections rarely seen on a C.V.—sections that provide more detailed information about the course of the scholar's teaching life. Because it is a personal document, designed to convey information about the professor's instructional practices, values, and achievements, its author must consider what impression the E.V. leaves with the reader. As you build a E.V. you must ask yourself: "What do I want to tell people about myself and my teaching?"

TABLE 9.3
Information Often Included in a Curriculum Vitae and in an Expanded Teaching Vitae (Eruditio Vitae)

Category	Example
The curriculum vitae	
Academic appointments	Professorships, lecturerships, significant work experiences
Awards and honors	Fellowships, memberships in scholarly societies
Education	Universities attended, degrees
Grants and contracts	Support garnered from government agencies, private foundations, private industry
Memberships	Disciplinary and professional memberships, such as APA member, state-association membership, etc.
Professional and disciplinary service	Editorships, reviewing for scholarly journals, service to community organizations, etc.
Research and scholarship	Books (monographs, texts, edited volumes, etc.); articles (both refereed or non-refereed), review articles, semi-popular or popular magazine articles; professional reports, journal editorships, proceedings or symposium editorships; conference paper presentations, participation as a panel chair or discussant, invited colloquia, etc.
Service	Involvement with and role taken in departmental, school, and university committees and organizations
Teaching experience	Teaching interests, courses taught, graduate student supervision experience, advising
The eruditio vitae	
Advising	Assisting students in curriculum planning and career exploration
Courses taught	Undergraduate and graduate courses taught, including descriptions of topics covered
Curriculum development	Creating new courses, extensively revising existing courses, developing new methods of instruction, developing entirely new educational programs
Faculty development	Activities that enhance other faculty members' skills in teaching (developing and conducting teaching workshops, consulting with faculty regarding their teaching, conducting informal and formal assessments of teaching)
Graduate student mentoring and supervision	Mentoring graduate students in research and practice (e.g., laboratory supervision, thesis and dissertation research)
Grants and contracts	Grants dealing specifically with educational issues, such as projects supported by the Funds for the Improvement of Post-Secondary Education

Table continues

TABLE 9.3 (*Continued*)

Category	Example
The eruditio vitae (continued)	
Memberships	Membership in associations focused on teaching, such as Division 2 of APA, local faculty consortiums
Self-development	Participation in workshops dealing with teaching skills, attendance at conferences on teaching, continuing education enrollments
Service in teaching	Participation in and leadership of committees and task forces dealing with teaching (departmental curriculum committee, university task force on instruction, etc.)
Specialized forms of teaching	Nonroutine types of teaching, including guest lectures, public teaching (speeches to lay audiences, educational newspaper articles, and interviews), interdisciplinary teaching, colloquia at one's own university and other universities
Teaching scholarship	Publications, presentations, and talks dealing with teaching and learning (research into teaching effectiveness, publications in *Teaching of Psychology*, etc.)
Technology and teaching	Using technology for instructional purposes, including development of multimedia, films, distance education, Internet-based instruction
Texts and teaching materials	Authored materials used in teaching, including textbooks, instruction manuals, test item banks, and websites
Undergraduate student mentoring and supervision	Individualized forms of instruction (student internships, field work, honors theses, membership on thesis committees)

I Am Involved in Teaching

Each publication usually gets some mention on the vita: every conference paper, chapter, book, and article gets a line or more. Yet, professors who have taught two sections of personality each semester for 15 years humbly list only "Psychology of Personality" on their vita, hoping the reader will imagine the scope of the work summarized by that one line. The E.V. distrusts imagination, and so provides a detailed listing of each semester's classes taught, and it may even include essential details such as size, text, and time. The seasoned scholar, looking back at many years of classes, often stops counting each contribution. But if a class is not noted, then a casual reader of the vita may mistakenly think very little teaching has been done.

My Teaching Takes Many Forms

Professors teach in many places and in many ways. They teach in the classroom, on the sidewalk, in their offices, through technology, by lecturing, leading discussions, questioning, and mentoring. The E.V. should reflect this diversity, and so disconfirm the lay belief that teaching involves classroom instruction only. If professors describe their teaching solely in terms of specific classes offered and they omit other forms of instruction from the E.V., then their message is obvious: these other activities must not qualify as teaching.

The portfolio must document these forms by painstakingly listing supervision of internships, field work, thesis and dissertation research; membership on honors, thesis, and dissertation committees; colloquia; guest lectures; workshops; and so on. Moreover, the concept of teaching itself should be enlarged so that it includes nontraditional forms of instruction, including

- public teaching (presentations to the community at large, including speeches, workshops, educational newspaper articles, and interviews);
- workshops for colleagues and advanced students;
- distance education;
- interdisciplinary teaching;
- colloquia at one's own university and other universities; and
- Internet-based instruction.

The idea here is that outstanding teachers teach—they are literally involved in the act of teaching—in the classroom and in other teaching settings.

I Am a Practicing Teacher

Many professions, including medicine and the law, put great emphasis on improving their work over time. Physicians or lawyers, for example, are called practitioners, and their work is called a practice. Similarly, the E.V. should stress 'teaching professors' development as they "practice" and hone their technique. The outstanding educator who has never attended a workshop dealing with teaching skills or a conference on teaching or earned continuing education credit while studying his or her teaching is a rarity. If you attend the annual convention of American Psychological Association, be sure to go to the poster session dealing with teaching and note your attendance on your E.V. If your university offers workshops in teaching skills, take part and record your participation on your E.V. Join online e-mail groups devoted to teaching. Even informal meetings where you and your colleagues discuss teaching can be upgraded into self-development forums by titling the group and formally defining its focus on teaching.

I Contribute to the Teaching Side of Psychology

Many of the activities of a professor focus on the way knowledge generated in his or her field can be best conveyed to learners. The E.V. should, when possible, mention contributions to teaching in psychology and to higher education in general. Such contributions as research into pedagogical practices, curricular reform, university- and national-level service in teaching, public teaching, and mentorship of other teachers dot the vitas of the finest teachers. They also provide considerable service to their unit and to their discipline by developing courses, organizing offerings, and providing guidance on curriculum, including

- membership in or leadership of state or national committees or organizations that examine questions of teaching methods and curriculum,
- mentorship of other teachers,
- grant activities related to higher education,
- consultations at other universities regarding teaching,
- leadership in faculty development,
- development of educational models adopted elsewhere, and
- conducting workshops for colleagues at professional meetings.

Advanced teaching professors are concerned with their own and others' teaching, to the point that they study the process of teaching their discipline itself. Indeed, the professor's dictum, "publish or perish," applies to some degree to the teaching professor—for well-rounded professors communicate their ideas and experiences about teaching to others through papers and texts published or presented on educational topics, manuals developed for classroom use, and textbooks.

I Value Teaching

A traditional C.V., with 90% of its content devoted to research, screams the message TEACHING DOES NOT MATTER. And although this message is attributed to the individual professor who has crafted the C.V., it implies that the professor's college or university agrees with this assessment. When students, parents, or legislators read over a traditional C.V., all they see is evidence of the scholarly credentials and accomplishments. It is little wonder that they often complain that teaching is given too low a priority, for they are misled by the C.V.'s myopia. An E.V., by giving a voice to accomplishments in teaching, underscores the value of this activity.

Personal Statement of Teaching

A teaching portfolio is a personal document that should reflect the unique qualities of the particular teacher and so no uniform table of contents can be either offered or enforced. But most analyses of portfolios in higher education agree that it should contain a statement by the professor that describes his or her beliefs about learning and education, and how these beliefs influence teaching practice. Murray writes: "The only essential component of the teaching portfolio is a statement of what the author believes about teaching and learning" (Murray, 1995, pp. 24–25).

The actual contents of these narratives vary, but the best teaching philosophies are lucid analyses of the professors' views of their mission as a scholar, a teacher, and a psychologist. They are sometimes written in a personal, revealing style, but they nonetheless contain substantive information about teaching professors' theoretical and conceptual orientation, the goals they seek when teaching their students about psychology, and their general assumptions about higher education and learning.

Paradigmatic Assumptions and Outlook

Because college professors integrate the values of the traditional teacher—one who educates and imparts knowledge—and the scholar—a learned person who has a profound knowledge of a particular subject matter —they do not simply serve as relay points for the transmission of information from authorities in the field to the student. Rather, they actively participate in the analysis, construction, and elaboration of psychology's basic findings, theories, and applications, and so have developed a unique understanding of their field. That unique understanding will permeate their teaching just as it permeates their research.

The portfolio provides an opportunity to describe, albeit briefly, one's fundamental assumptions about psychology, in general, and one's subfield, in particular. A behaviorist teaching introductory psychology, for example, may explain that her training prompts her to stress measurement over theory and the experimental analysis of behavior rather than difficult-to-observe psychological events such as cognitions and unconscious tensions. A personality theorist may state that his training and orientation are reflected in his continuing interest in human potentialities, prejudice, religion, and the value of self-reflection. An expert on multicultural issues may introduce a particular model of emic–etic distinctions and note the implications of this view for understanding socialization and development. A social psychologist may describe the basic tenets that she feels sustain that subfield's paradigm, including the concepts of interactionism, constructivism, dynamism, and empiricism. A psychologist teaching perception may explain that, even though he was trained in the psychophysical research tradition, his current work focuses more on the neural systems that sustain perception and attention. These brief descriptions of the professor's background and paradigmatic assumptions remind the reader that the author of the portfolio is not simply someone who teaches psychology, but rather a psychologist who has chosen to advance the discipline by teaching it to others.

Principles

Skilled professors' base their teaching interventions on a set of assumptions, or principles, about learning and higher education in general. These principles can be one's that the teaching professor personally finds to be important, but they can also be drawn from extant analyses of college-level instruction like those discussed briefly in chapter 1. A professor may, for example, briefly summarize the American Psychological Association's Committee on Undergraduate Education's 1991 report (McGovern et al., 1991) on teaching or Chickering and Gamson's (1987) *Seven Principles for Good Practice in Undergraduate Education* before giving examples of their application in the professor's class on history and systems, experimental methods, or child psychology. Another effective approach is to tie the principles directly to the particular field's paradigmatic assumptions. For example, developmentalists could note what theories of cognitive development say about how a college class should be structured, behaviorists could stress the importance of behavioral objectives and rewards, and personality theorists could explain their student-centered approach by examining individual differences in learning styles.

Recognized expert teachers in the field of psychology are also excellent sources of points to include and discuss in this segment of the narrative. The chapters in Sternberg's (1997b) *Teaching Introductory Psychology: Survival Tips from the Experts* and Perlman, McCann, and McFadden's (1999) *Lessons Learned: Practice Advice for the Teaching of Psychology* are founts of principled insights into how psychology is best taught. Lefton (1997, pp. 65–66), for example, explained his approach as follows:

> I design my class and my textbook according to certain guiding principles. I try to (a) be selective in what I teach; (b) adapt to my students' learning styles; (c) teach critical thinking and learning strategies; (d) work from application to theory; (e) help students recognize and be sensitive to issues of diversity, including age, gender, and ethnicity; (f) keep the course current and exciting; (g) engage students; and (h) teach psychology as a unified, coherent discipline.

He then expands on each of these principles, explaining how they determine the strategies he uses in the classroom. In doing so he deals with questions of breadth vs. depth of coverage, the emphasis on facts vs. ideas, the need to organize material vs. the need to let students structure the material themselves, the use of questions to stimulate critical thinking, and the balance between theory and its application to issues.

Gray (1997), whose teaching duties include physiological and introductory psychology, introduced his own approach to teaching by first describing a comic strip that features a college professor struggling to prompt a reaction from his students. The professor, to goad the students into challenging the ideas he is presenting, makes statements that grow ever more extreme, until eventually he proclaims "Democracy is the source of all evil! Up is down! Right is wrong!" In the comic strips' final panel two students comment to each other "Boy, this course is really getting interesting," and "Yeah, I didn't know half this stuff" (Gray, 1997, p. 49). To Gray, this comic illustrated the tendency for students, and professors, to focus too much on facts and information—to the point that students stop thinking critically about the information presented. Gray then explained how he shifts students' attention to ideas and arguments (1997):

> The essence of the approach is to focus explicitly on ideas as the subject matter of the course, rather than on facts, terms, topics, textbook pages, the unsupported opinions of famous psychologists, or any of the other substitutes for ideas that may attempt to force their way to center stage. An idea, by definition, is something to think about; it is something to defend or refute with evidence and logic. (p. 50)

Bernstein (1997) began by explaining that he "makes no claim to special insight about the best way to teach this, or any other, course. My approach to teaching makes sense to me, but I don't expect everyone to agree with it" (p. 35). He also prefaced this overview of his principles with engaging autobiographical material that describes the first course he ever taught and his decision to cope with feelings of incompetence by basing his teaching on the Hippocratic oath: "First of all, do no harm." The narrative set forth a number of key assumptions (pp. 40–44):

- Portray psychology as an empirical science based on critical thinking.
- Portray psychology knowledge as dynamic, not static.
- Portray the breadth and diversity of psychology.
- Promote active learning.
- Emphasize the importance of psychology in everyday life.
- Portray psychology as an integrated discipline.

Techniques and Strategies

The generality of the section dealing with assumptions and philosophies of learning should be tempered by a section that provides concrete examples of how these principles are applied in specific courses, to specific topics, and to specific types of students. If your teaching responsibilities include the introductory course, advanced senior courses, large proseminar courses, and graduate seminars, you need to describe each of these courses, and at least briefly explain your specific goals, strategies, and procedures.

You may, too, wish to provide far more details about your methods for one or two of your classes. If, for example, you teach a large section of introductory psychology, you may wish to use this class to illustrate how you put your principles about learning into practice by stressing critical thinking in your lecturing, breaking the class down into small groups for collaborative learning, by using computer-based technologies, and so on.

Unique Strengths and Concerns

The teaching narrative provides professors with the opportunity to explain, and even highlight, those features of their teaching that are unique, controversial, or even eccentric. Some professors spend a good deal of time describing some specific, if idiosyncratic, concern that they consider to be of paramount importance; Professor X might discuss the rigor of her course in some detail, noting the close connection between exams, final grades, and the primary objectives of the course. Professor Y might stress the importance of remaining sensitive to how men and women are treated in the classroom, because evidence has suggested that in many educational settings women receive less attention relative to men. Professor Z may discuss how students earn points in the class through service learning at local mental health agencies.

Pitfalls of the Personal Narrative

The narrative section of the portfolio is not easily crafted, for professors who do not exercise caution often convey the wrong impression to the reader. The reader of the narrative needs answers to many questions about teaching: What are the writer's teaching values? What is her teaching style? Is this instructor liked or disliked by his students? Does the teacher seem experienced and "wise" in her approach to instruction, or naive and uncertain? Does the teacher seem interested in his discipline and in teaching it to others? Does she seem well-informed or dogmatic? Does he let his personal values surface unnecessarily, or does he set the correct level of personalization?

These narratives should also be carefully written so they are coherent, articulate, and free of grammatical error. This element of the portfolio gives professors the opportunity to explain the reasons behind their teaching methods, but they can also reveal other, less positive, messages. A narrative that is garbled or unstructured raises, sometimes unfairly, warning signs for the reader. If authors cannot communicate their ideas about the teaching clearly, then how well do they communicate information about psychology to their students? A lack of care in developing the narrative can also generate one that sounds pretentious or trite. The professor may explain "I am deeply committed to teaching, for my first obligation is to my students." Another writes, "I love to teach. I've always felt at home in the classroom, surrounded by young minds." A third claims "I strive to instill a love of learning in my students, for I believe that education and the ability to acquire knowledge hold the keys to our world's survival." These statements are the professorial versions of the painful "What my education means to me" essays that students must write on admission applications. These statements should not be written at the last moment, but well in advance of the deadline so revisions recommended by colleagues and mentors can be made.

Teaching Materials

Portfolios should contain actual samples of the professor's work. These samples should be carefully organized so the reader can grasp the connections among the various documents. This section can be prefaced with a brief overview of the scheme that organized the various elements, and annotations should be added as needed to help the reader grasp the importance of each exhibit. Again, these materials should be consistent with, and even elaborate upon, the principles and strategies of instruction noted in the personal narrative.

Syllabi

The syllabus, or course outline, is often the very first piece of paper that professors drop into that file folder labeled "Teaching Portfolio Project." Syllabi, as noted in chapter 1, are designed to give students a clear idea of the professor's goals, methods, standards, and policies, which is precisely the type of information that should be conveyed in a teaching portfolio. Professors should, however, be mindful of the fit between the principles that they espouse in their narrative and the objective data of the syllabus. Professors who claim to use teacher-centered methods and engaging activities that demand critical thinking, but whose syllabi list only the chapter topics and the dates for the multiple choice exams, signal their hypocrisy rather than competency. A syllabus that omits critical information, such as the course goals, contact information, and course prerequisites, makes a poor impression, as does a syllabus that goes on and on about attendance, make-ups, and classroom etiquette but says little about the course's overall purpose and procedures.

Handouts, Assignments, Activities

A college course can be the wellspring of a river of paper. During the course of a semester or quarter, professors inundate their students with lecture outlines, learning objectives, exam prep sheets, reading lists, research summaries, homework assignments, exercises, observation guides, study hints, thought questions, and so on, and these documents are telling indicators of teaching practices. Even electronic communications and handouts should be included, such as e-mails to students, screen shots of Web pages, online discussion questions, and forum topics. Your classroom might be paperless, but your portfolio should not be (unless you mount it on a Web page).

Notes and Planning Materials

College professors rarely develop the elaborate curriculum guides favored by elementary and secondary education teachers, but some use detailed worksheets to describe topics and objectives, lists of the media to use and readings to cover, key examples to share with students, clippings from magazines and newspapers about course topics, and notes about potential projects. These types of material provide background information about the professor's level of preparation, as do the notes they use when giving a lecture or leading a discussion. Lecture and discussion notes, for example, provide the reader with an idea of how each presentation is structured, and its relationship to the professor's overall assumptions about teaching. The reading list serves a similar function, even if the list was used only by the professor during his or her preparation for the class and was not shared with the students. Such lists of scholarly books, references, and readings impress laypersons, but they also give colleagues a good indication of the instructor's basic approach and emphases.

Tests, Quizzes, and Examinations

The portfolio should include, at a minimum, a description of the procedures used to give students feedback about their progress toward the course's objectives. In many cases, this section will include samples of quizzes, tests, exams, and term paper assignments made in a recently taught class, but professors who use alternative strategies such as graded participation, term projects, observation of students, and oral exams should provide some details about how they carry out these evaluations. This section may also contain examples of the types of feedback given to students about their performance, including graded papers (with student names removed).

Given the importance of assessment in teaching, professors should also include additional information about the reliability and validity of the procedures they use. Examples of tables of specification that indicate the relationship between each item and the course's learning objectives, indexes of difficulty and discrimination, item-to-total correlations, and other psychometric data can give readers of the portfolio reassuring information about the quality of assessment procedures. The professor may also wish to give some indication of the typical distribution of grades—particularly when the portfolio will be reviewed by external audiences that have no way of estimating the difficulty of the exam and the overall course content.

Evaluations of Teaching Effectiveness

The portfolio should include digests of the results of past and current evaluations of teaching effectiveness based on student evaluations, peer evaluations, and other types of summative evaluation systems. Some of this information may be available on the E.V. but this section should provide much more orientation and interpretation so that the reader interprets the data appropriately. A professor might, for example, list all his PhD students and where they are currently employed on his E.V., but draw attention to these data in this section of the portfolio in a heading named "Mentoring Advance Students" or "Graduate Student Instruction."

Student-Based Evaluations

As noted in chapter 8, the validity of students' perceptions of teaching quality is a matter of debate. This information should nonetheless be included in the complete portfolio, for the portfolio's flexibility provides the author with an opportunity to suggest his or her own interpretation of the data.

Most colleges and universities use a specific system for soliciting data from students pertaining to teaching effectiveness, and they provide professors with feedback from this evaluation on a regular basis. This material provides the basis for clarifying one's success in teaching, particularly if the data are carefully mined and artfully summarized. These inventories often include items with dubious psychometric quality, so the portfolio should focus on those items with the best validity and reliability (e.g., global items that assess satisfaction with the course, the professor, and learning rate; compare d'Apollonia & Abrami, 1997 and Marsh & Roche, 1997). The portfolio should not assume that the reader understands concepts such as range, standard deviation, mean, median, mode, or even the item's metric, so this section requires annotations that provide a verbal interpretation of the numeric data and descriptions of any special conditions that should be taken into account when interpreting the results.

Charts, plots, figures, and other graphics also increase the ease of interpretation of the items, particularly when the data are extensive, inconsistent, or confusing. Figure 9.1, for example, provides a graphic illustration of the charted data from a professor teaching an introductory course over a 5-year period (perhaps the 5 years prior to tenure). A overall mean for this instructor's teaching would not be particularly positive: only a 3.5 on a 5-point scale, where 5 indicates "excellent." The charted data, however, tell a different story; one of remarkable improvement over time, and the promise that future classes will be evaluated very positively. The figure should be annotated, however, to provide an explanation for the trend: Perhaps this professor was developing excellence in teaching over this pe-

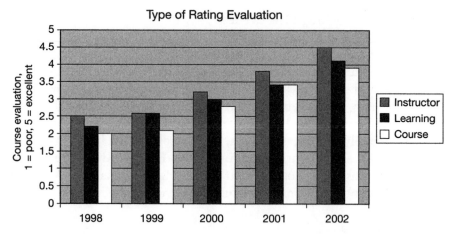

Figure 9.1. Example of figure depicting teaching evaluations over a 5-year period.

riod rather than merely devoting more time to teaching as the deadline for tenure and promotion approached.

Peer-Based Evaluations

Fellow instructors can often provide considerable information about teaching performance; information that goes well beyond that provided by students. In many cases colleagues have seen each other give colloquia, guest lectures, and presentations at meetings, and these experiences can form the basis for a brief commentary about one's communication and presentation skills. Peers also have considerable information about effectiveness gained by participation in joint teaching situations, such as membership on student committees and team teaching situations. Some universities even have objective "teacher evaluators" visit classrooms and provide analyses of the quality of instruction.

Outcome-Based Evaluations

Most indices of teaching excellence focus on the instructor, asking the question "How effective is this instructor?" Yet some universities suggest that the portfolio should also include evidence of the impact of instruction. It is difficult to determine instructors' contribution to their students' achievement, but the following types of information provide some evidence of learning outcomes:

- High scores on standardized or locally developed tests of knowledge
- High-quality essays, projects, and reports written by students

- Publications or presentations with students as coauthors
- Evidence of success following graduation in careers closely connected to specific course
- The performance of students in related or subsequent courses
- Employers' reports after hiring students

Additional Indicators

Teaching effectiveness can be assessed in a variety of ways in addition to the usual student ratings (see chapter 8). In addition to data pertaining to the most critical dependent measure in higher education—Did students learn anything?—one may also wish to include other types of evidence of impact: success in placing students in jobs or graduate schools, comments from parents, testimonials written by students (both those written in response to a direct request and spontaneous submissions), interviews with students or alumni, and special surveys of opinion (often conducted prior to tenure and promotion).

Supplemental Materials

The teaching professor's creativity, and not the standards set by others' portfolios, determines what goes in to and is left out of the portfolio. Depending on the individual teacher, the portfolio may include such novelties as the following items:

- A videotape of a lecture from a class or a presentation at a national conference.
- A computer disk containing the interactive programs that teach a range of psychological topics.
- A map of the United States, with a star marking the location of each PhD student mentored.
- The verbatim, unedited comments made by students on the open-ended portion of the student evaluations.
- Copies of the forms, descriptions, and memoranda created when a new course was guided through the various school curricula committees and into the course catalog.
- Dozens of eloquent recommendation letters written for undergraduate and graduate students.
- A letter from the department chairperson describing the professor's teaching skills.
- Photographs of chalk-filled blackboards after a particularly passionate lecture.

All these varied forms of evidence that testify to the professor's skills as an educator are possibilities for inclusion in the portfolio. For just as evaluators of teaching quality must cast their net widely if they are to catch all the indicators of teaching discussed in chapter 8, so professors must do all they can to provide readers with the information they need to understand what it means to be a teaching psychologist.

Indicators of sometimes overlooked aspects of teaching are particularly important to include. *Teaching-related service*, for example, can absorb an enormous amount of time, but this contribution to teaching is often overlooked by review committees whose attention is riveted on classroom instruction. Yet, each new course developed or modified, service on committees devoted to issues related to teaching and curriculum, and administrative duties that are primarily focused on teaching all underscore the professor's commitment to teaching. Evidence of effective *mentoring and advising* should also be highlighted, for all teaching does not happen in a classroom lecture or discussion; the portfolio should not overlook indicators of the professor's accomplishments in one-on-one and small group teaching settings. Evidence of teaching scholarship—such as papers on teaching, manuals developed for classroom use, research into the learning and teaching process, textbooks, and books—that examines critical processes and issues in teaching psychology (like this one!), too, are appropriate additions to the teaching portfolio.

BECOMING THE TEACHING PSYCHOLOGIST

Allport, like many psychologists whose views of people were shaped by humanistic assumptions, believed that each human's life is a process of becoming. His studies of religion, personality, and mental health all converged on one conclusion: People are not complacently satisfied with their accomplishments but rather goal-oriented creatures who pursue mastery with great fervor. Psychologically healthy people constantly reflect on their potentialities, set new aspirations, deepen their self-understanding, and strive toward perfection. And so it is for the teaching psychologist. Each day brings new demands and new experiences: new courses to teach when the developments of our field make the ideas and information offered in older formulations obsolete; new studies to conduct as new questions arise that can only be answered empirically; new students to help understand the nature of psychology through teaching and training; and new lectures to give, discussions to lead, activities to design and implement, tests to write, grades to assign, classes to manage, technologies to learn, and courses to evaluate. But each activity, each course, each term, and each year contributes to the process of becoming, and in time the neophyte instructor is transformed into the teaching psychologist.

REFERENCES

Abrami, P. C., Cohen, P. A., & d'Apollonia, S. (1988). Implementation problems in meta-analysis. *Review of Educational Research, 58,* 151–179.

Abrami, P. C., d'Apollonia, S., & Rosenfield, S. (1997). The dimensionality of student ratings of instruction: What we know and what we do not. In R. P. Perry & J. C. Smart (Eds.), *Effective teaching in higher education: Research and practice* (pp. 321–367). New York: Agathon Press.

Aiken, E. G., Thomas, G. S., & Shennum, W. A. (1975). Memory for a lecture: Effects of notes, lecture rate, and informational density. *Journal of Educational Psychology, 67,* 439–444.

Albanese, M. A., & Mitchell, S. (1993). Problem-based learning: A review of literature on its outcomes and implementation issues. *Academic Medicine, 68,* 52–81.

Albom, M. (1997). *Tuesdays with Morrie.* New York: Doubleday.

Aleamoni, L. M. (1981). Student ratings of instruction. In J. Millman (Ed.), *Handbook of teacher evaluation* (pp. 110–145). Thousand Oaks, CA: Sage.

Allen, M. J. (2000). Teaching non-traditional students. *Observer, 13*(7), 16–17, 21, 23.

Allport, G. W. (1937). *Personality: A psychological interpretation.* New York: Holt, Rinehart, & Winston.

Allport, G. W. (1942). *The use of personal documents in psychological science.* New York: Social Science Research Council.

Allport, G. W. (1946). Letters from Jenny. *Journal of Abnormal and Social Psychology, 41,* 315–350.

Allport, G. W. (1955). *Becoming: Basic considerations for a psychology of personality.* New Haven, CT: Yale University Press.

Allport, G. W. (1968). *The person in psychology: Selected essays by Gordon W. Allport.* Boston: Beacon Press.

Alwin, D. F., Cohen, R. L., & Newcomb, T. M. (1991). *Personality and social change: Attitude persistence and changes over the lifespan.* Madison: University of Wisconsin Press.

Amabile, T. M. (2001). Beyond talent: John Irving and the passionate craft of creativity. *American Psychologist, 56,* 333–336.

American Psychological Association (n.d.). *Undergraduate psychology courses important in obtaining current primary position, 1992: Baccalaureate recipients in psychology.* Retrieved August 2, 2001, from http://research.apa.org/bac5.html

American Psychological Association. (2001). *Publication manual of the American Psychological Association* (5th ed.). Washington, DC: Author.

American Psychological Association. (2002). Ethical principles of psychologists and code of conduct. *American Psychologist, 57*(12).

Ames, C. (1987). The enhancement of student motivation. In M. L. Maehr &

D. A. Kleiber (Eds.), *Advances in motivation and achievement* (Vol. 5, pp. 123–148). Greenwich, CT: JAI Press.

Anastasi, A. (1988). *Psychological testing* (6th ed.). New York: MacMillan.

Anderson, J. A. (1988). Cognitive styles and multicultural populations. *Journal of Teacher Education, 39*(1), 2–9.

Anderson, L. W., & Sosniak, L. A. (Eds.). (1994). *Bloom's taxonomy: A forty-year retrospective*. Chicago: University of Chicago Press.

Angelo, T. A., & Cross, K. P. (1993). *Classroom assessment techniques: A handbook for college teachers* (2nd ed.). San Francisco: Jossey-Bass.

Appleby, D. C. (1999). How to improve your teaching with the course syllabus. In B. Perlman, L. I. McCann, & S. H. McFadden (Eds.), *Lessons learned: Practical advice for the teaching of psychology* (pp. 19–24). Washington, DC: American Psychological Society.

Armstrong, J. S. (1998). Are student ratings of instruction useful? *American Psychologist, 53,* 1223–1224.

Aronson, E., Stephan, C., Sikes, J., Blaney, N., & Snapp, M. (1978). *The jigsaw classroom*. Thousand Oaks, CA: Sage.

Asch, S. E. (1946). Forming impressions of personality. *Journal of Abnormal and Social Psychology, 41,* 258–290.

Astin, A. W. (1977). *Four critical years: Effects of college on beliefs, attitudes, and knowledge*. San Francisco: Jossey-Bass.

Astin, A. W. (1993). *What matters in college? Four critical years revisited*. San Francisco: Jossey-Bass.

Austin, J. T., & Vancouver, J. B. (1996). Goal constructs in psychology: Structure, process, and content. *Psychological Bulletin, 120,* 338–375.

Avery, P. B., & Gray, P. L. (1995). Mentoring graduate teaching assistants: Creating an effective mentor/mentee relationship. *Journal of Graduate Teaching Assistant Development, 3*(1), 9–19.

Axtell, J. (1998). *The pleasures of academe: A celebration and defense of higher education*. Lincoln: University of Nebraska Press.

Babad, E., Darley, J. M., & Kaplowitz, H. (1999). Developmental aspects in students' course selection. *Journal of Educational Psychology, 91,* 157–168.

Babad, E., Kaplowitz, H., & Darley, J. M. (1999). A "classic" revisited: Students' immediate and delayed evaluations of a warm/cold instructor. *Social Psychology of Education, 3,* 81–102.

Balch, W. R. (1986). The use of student-performed developmental exercises in the classroom. *Teaching of Psychology, 13,* 140–142.

Bandura, A. (1969). *Principles of behavior modification*. Stanford, CA: Stanford University Press.

Bandura, A. (1977). *Social-learning theory*. Englewood Cliffs, NJ: Prentice-Hall.

Banyard, P., & Grayson, A. (1999). Teaching with original sources. In B. Perlman, L. I. McCann, & S. H. McFadden (Eds.), *Lessons learned: Practical advice for the teaching of psychology* (pp. 29–35). Washington, DC: American Psychological Society.

Bar-Tal, D. (2000). *Shared beliefs in a society: Social psychological analysis.* Thousand Oaks: Sage.

Bates, J. A. (1991). Teaching hypothesis testing by debunking a demonstration of telepathy. *Teaching of Psychology, 18,* 94–97.

Bayer, A. E. (1975). Faculty composition, institutional structure, and students' college environment. *Journal of Higher Education, 46,* 549–555.

Becker, A. H., & Calhoon, S. K. (1999). What introductory psychology students attend to on a course syllabus. *Teaching of Psychology, 26,* 6–11.

Bednar, R. L., & Kaul, T. (1978). Experiential group research: Current perspectives. In S. L. Garfield & A. E. Bergin (Eds.), *Handbook of psychotherapy and behavior change* (2nd ed., pp. 769–815). New York: Wiley.

Beers, S. E. (1986). Questioning and peer collaboration as techniques for thinking and writing about personality. *Teaching of Psychology, 13,* 75–77.

Beins, B. C. (1993). Using the Barnum effect to teach about ethics and deception in research. *Teaching of Psychology, 20,* 33–35.

Beins, B. C. (1999). The interaction of taste and smell to create flavor. In L. T. Benjamin, B. F. Nodine, R. M. Ernst, & C. B. Broeker (Eds.), *Activities handbook for the teaching of psychology* (pp. 154–156). Washington, DC: American Psychological Association.

Belar, C. D., & Perry, N. W. (1992). The National Conference on Scientist-Practitioner Education and Training for the Professional Practice of Psychology. *American Psychologist, 47,* 71–75.

Bellezza, F. S., & Bellezza, S. F. (1995). Detection of copying on multiple-choice tests: An update. *Teaching of Psychology, 22,* 180–182.

Beloit College. (2001). *Class of 2004 mindset list.* Retrieved August 3, 2001, from Beloit College Web site http://www.beloit.edu/~pubaff/releases/Mindset-List-2004.html

Benassi, V. A., & Fernald, P. S. (1993). Preparing tomorrow's psychologists for careers in academe. *Teaching of Psychology, 20,* 149–155.

Benjamin, L. T., Jr. (1988). A history of teaching machines. *American Psychologist, 43,* 703–712.

Benjamin, L. T. (1991). Personalization and active learning in the large introductory psychology class. *Teaching of Psychology, 18,* 68–74.

Benjamin, L. T., Nodine, B. F., Ernst, R. M., & Broeker, C. B. (Eds.). (1999). *Activities handbook for the teaching of psychology.* Washington, DC: American Psychological Association.

Bennett, R., Rock, D., Braun, H., Frye, D., Spohrer, J., & Soloway, E. (1990). The relationship of constrained free-response to multiple-choice and open-ended items. *Applied Psychological Measurement, 14,* 151–162.

Bennett, R., Rock, D., & Wang, M. (1991). Equivalence of free-response and multiple-choice items. *Journal of Educational Measurement, 28,* 77–92.

Bennett, W. E. (1987). Small group instructional diagnosis: A dialogic approach to instructional improvement for tenured faculty. *Journal of Staff, Program, and Organizational Development, 5,* 100–104.

Bent, D. (1997). A neophyte constructs a Web site: Lessons learned. *The Internet and Higher Education, 1*(1), 21–30.

Benz, J. J., & Miller, R. L. (1996). Panel discussions as a means of enhancing student directed learning. *Journal of Instructional Psychology, 23,* 131–136.

Bernstein, D. A. (1997). Reflections on teaching introductory psychology. In R. J. Sternberg (Ed.), *Teaching introductory psychology: Survival tips from the experts* (pp. 35–47). Washington, DC: American Psychological Association.

Bernstein, D. A. (1999). Tell and show: The merits of classroom demonstrations. In B. Perlman, L. I. McCann, & S. H. McFadden (Eds.), *Lessons learned: Practical advice for the teaching of psychology* (pp. 105–108). Washington, DC: American Psychological Society.

Bernt, F. M. (1999). The ends and means of raising children: A parent interview activity. In L. T. Benjamin, B. F. Nodine, R. M. Ernst, & C. B. Broeker (Eds.), *Activities handbook for the teaching of psychology* (pp. 244–252). Washington, DC: American Psychological Association.

Biggs, J. B. (1987). *Student approaches to learning and studying.* Hawthorn, Victoria: Australian Council for Educational Research.

Binet, A., & Simon, T. (1905). New methods for the diagnosis of the intellectual level of subnormals. *L'Année Psychologique, 11,* 191–244.

Bjork, R. A. (2001). How to succeed in college: Learn how to learn. *Observer, 14*(3), 9–10.

Blair-Broeker, C. T., & Bernstein, D. A. (1999). Distribution of rods, cones, and color vision in the retina. In L. T. Benjamin, B. F. Nodine, R. M. Ernst, & C. B. Broeker (Eds.), *Activities handbook for the teaching of psychology* (pp. 125–126). Washington, DC: American Psychological Association.

Blanchard, F. A., Tilly, T., & Vaughn, L. A. (1991). Reducing the expression of racial prejudice. *Psychological Science, 2,* 101–105.

Bligh, D. (1998). *What's the use of lectures?* (5th ed.). [Electronic version]. Exeter, England: Intellect. Retrieved from netLibrary ebooks.

Bligh, D. (2000). *What's the point in discussion?* [Electronic version]. Exeter, England: Intellect Books. Retrieved from netLibrary ebooks.

Block, J. H. (1974). *Schools, society, and mastery learning.* New York: Holt, Rinehart, & Winston.

Bloom, B. S. (1976). *Human characteristics and school learning.* New York: McGraw-Hill.

Bloom, B. S., Englehart, M. D., Furst, E. J., Hill, W. H., & Krathwohl, D. R. (1956). *Taxonomy of educational objectives: The classification of educational goals. Handbook I: Cognitive domain.* White Plains, NY: Longman.

Boice, R. (1982). Teaching of writing in psychology. *Teaching of Psychology, 9,* 143–147.

Boice, R. (1994). *How writers journey to comfort and fluency*. Westport, CN: Praeger.

Boice, R. (2000). *Advice for new faculty members: Nihil nimus*. Boston: Allyn and Bacon.

Boniface, D. (1985). Candidates' use of notes and textbooks during an open-book examination. *Educational Research, 27*, 201–209.

Border, B., & Chism, N. V. N. (Eds.). (1992). *New Directions for Teaching and Learning: Teaching for Diversity, 49*. San Francisco: Jossey-Bass.

Bornstein, R. F. (1996). Face validity in psychological assessment: Implications for a unified model of validity. *American Psychologist, 51*, 983–984.

Bowen, H. R. (1977). *Investment in learning*. San Francisco: Jossey-Bass.

Braskamp, L. A., & Ory, J. C. (1994). *Assessing faculty work: Enhancing individual and institutional performance*. San Francisco: Jossey-Bass.

Braskamp, L. A., Ory, J. C., & Pieper, D. M. (1981). Student written comments: Dimensions of instructional quality. *Journal of Educational Psychology, 73*, 65–70.

Brems, C., Lampman, C., & Johnson, M. E. (1995). Preparation of applications for academic positions in psychology. *American Psychologist, 50*, 533–537.

Bridgeman, B. (1992). A comparison of quantitative questions in open-ended and multiple-choice formats. *Journal of Educational Measurement, 29*, 253–271.

Bringle, R. G., & Duffy, D. K. (Eds.). (1998). *With service in mind: Concepts and models for service learning in psychology*. Washington, DC: American Association for Higher Education.

Britton, B. K., Guelgoez, S., Van Dusen, L., Glynn, S. M., & Sharp, L. (1991). Accuracy of learnability judgments for instructional texts. *Journal of Educational Psychology, 83*, 43–47.

Bromage, B. K., & Mayer, R. E. (1986). Quantitative and qualitative effects of repetition on learning from technical text. *Journal of Educational Psychology, 78*, 271–278.

Brookhart, S. M. (1999). *The art and science of classroom assessment: The missing part of pedagogy*. Washington, DC: The George Washington University.

Brooks, C. I. (1985). A role-playing exercise for the history of psychology course. *Teaching of Psychology, 12*, 84–85.

Brown, G. A., Bakhtar, M., & Youngman, M. B. (1984). Toward a typology of lecturing styles. *British Journal of Educational Psychology, 54*, 93–100.

Brown, L. T. (1980). What the consumer thinks is important in the introductory psychology course. *Teaching of Psychology, 7*, 215–218.

Bruner, J. (1996). Frames for thinking: Ways of making meaning. In D. R. Olson & N. Torrance (Eds.), *Modes of thought: Explorations in culture and cognition* (pp. 93–105). New York: Cambridge University Press.

Bruning, R., & Horn, C. (2000). Developing motivation to write. *Educational Psychologist, 35*, 25–37.

Burchfield, C. M., & Sappington, J. (2000). Compliance with required reading assignments. *Teaching of Psychology, 27*, 58–60.

Buskist, W., & Saville, B. K. (2001). Rapport-building: Creating positive emotional contexts for enhancing teaching and learning. *Observer, 14*(3), 12–13, 19.

Cacioppo, J. T., & Petty, R. E. (1979). Effects of message repetition and position on cognitive response, recall, and persuasion. *Journal of Personality and Social Psychology, 37,* 97–109.

Carbone, E. (1998). *Teaching large classes.* Thousand Oaks, CA: Sage.

Carlson, J. F. (2000). Psychosexual pursuit: Enhancing learning of theoretical psychoanalytic constructs. In M. E. Ware & D. E. Johnson (Eds.), *Handbook of demonstrations and activities in the teaching of psychology: III. Personality, abnormal, clinical-counseling, and social* (2nd ed., pp. 25–27). Mahwah, NJ: Erlbaum.

Carnegie, D. (1937). *How to win friends and influence people.* New York: Simon and Schuster.

Caron, M. D., Whitbourne, S. K., & Halgin, R. P. (1992). Fraudulent excuse making among college students. *Teaching of Psychology, 19,* 90–93.

Carroll, D. W. (2001). Using ignorance questions to promote thinking skills. *Teaching of Psychology, 28,* 98–100.

Cashin, W. E. (1988). *Student ratings of teaching: A summary of research (IDEA Paper No. 20).* Manhattan, KS: Kansas State University, Division of Continuing Education.

Cashin, W. E. (1990). *Student ratings of teaching: Recommendations for use (IDEA Paper No. 22).* Manhattan, KS: Kansas State University, Center for Faculty Evaluation and Development. (ERIC Document Reproduction Service No. ED 339 732)

Cashin, W. E. (1995). *Student ratings of teaching: The research revisited (IDEA Paper No. 32).* Manhattan, KS: Kansas State University, Center for Faculty Evaluation and Development.

Cashin, W. E., & Perrin, B. M. (1983). Do college teachers who voluntarily have courses evaluated receive higher student ratings? *Journal of Educational Psychology, 75,* 595–602.

Cattell, R. B. (1986). Structured tests and functional diagnoses. In R. B. Cattell & R. C. Johnson (Eds.), *Functional psychological testing: Principles and instruments* (pp. 3–14). New York: Brunner/Mazel.

Centra, J. A. (1975). Colleagues as raters of classroom instruction. *Journal of Higher Education, 46,* 327–337.

Centra, J. A. (1993). *Reflective faculty evaluation: Enhancing teaching and determining faculty effectiveness.* San Francisco: Jossey-Bass.

Cerbin, W. (2001). The course portfolio. *Observer, 14*(4), 16–17, 30–31.

Chamberlin, J. (2001). Digital dissemination. *Monitor on Psychology, 32*(1), 64–67.

Chaparro, B. S., & Halcomb, C. G. (1990). The effects of computerized tutorial usage on course performance in general psychology. *Journal of Computer-Based Instruction, 17,* 141–146.

Chickering, A. W. (1969). *Education and identity.* San Francisco: Jossey-Bass.

Chickering, A. W. (1981). *The modern American college: Responding to the new realities of diverse students and a changing society.* San Francisco: Jossey-Bass.

Chickering, A. W., & Ehrmann, S. C. (1996). Implementing the seven principles: Technology as a lever. *AAHE Bulletin, 49*(2), 3–6.

Chickering, A. W., & Gamson, Z. F. (1987). Seven principles for good practice in undergraduate education. *AAHE Bulletin, 39*(7), 3–7.

Chism, N. V. N. (1999). Taking student social diversity into account. In W. J. McKeachie, *McKeachie's teaching tips: Strategies, research, and theory for college and university teachers* (pp. 218–234). New York: Houghton Mifflin.

Chute, D. L. (1986). MacLaboratory for psychology: General experimental psychology with Apple's Macintosh. *Behavior Research Methods, Instruments, and Computers, 18,* 205–209.

Clarke, J. H. (1988). Designing discussions as group inquiry. *College Teaching, 36*(4), 140–143.

Claxton, C. S., & Murrell, P. H. (1987). Learning styles: Implications for improving educational practices. *ASHE-ERIC Higher Education Report No. 4.* Washington, DC: Association for the Study of Higher Education.

Cohen, P. A. (1981). Student ratings of instruction and student achievement: A meta-analysis of multisection validity studies. *Review of Educational Research, 51,* 281–309.

Confucius. (1994). *The analects.* Retrieved May 21, 2001, from Massachusetts Institute of Technology, The Internet Classics Archive Web site: http://classics.mit.edu/Confucius/analects.html (Original work produced in 500 BC)

Conyne, R. K. (1999). *Failures in group work: How we can learn from our mistakes.* Thousand Oaks, CA: Sage.

Cook, S. W. (1985). Experimenting on social issues: the case of school desegregation. *American Psychologist, 40,* 452–460.

Corrigan, J. D., Dell, D. M., Lewis, K. N., & Schmidt, L. D. (1980). Counseling as a social influence process: A review. *Journal of Counseling Psychology, 27,* 395–441.

Cortina, J. M. (1993). What is coefficient alpha? An examination of theory and applications [Electronic version]. *Journal of Applied Psychology, 78,* 98–104.

Cotton, K., & Wikelund, K. R. (1989). *School Improvement Research Series (SIRS): Educational time factors.* Retrieved February 5, 2001, from Northwest Regional Educational Laboratory Web site: http://www.nwrel.org/scpd/sirs/4/cu8.html

Covington, M. V., & Beery, R. (1976). *Self-worth and school learning.* New York: Holt, Rinehart & Winston.

Covington, M. V., & Wiedenhaupt, S. (1997). Turning work into play: The nature and nurturing of intrinsic task engagement. In R. Perry & J. C. Smart (Eds.), *Effective teaching in higher education: Research and practices* (pp. 101–114). New York: Agathon Press.

Craik, F. I., & Tulving, E. (1975). Depth of processing and the retention of words in episodic memory. *Journal of Experimental Psychology: General, 104,* 268–294.

Cronbach, L. J. (1977). *Educational psychology* (3rd. ed.). New York: Harcourt Brace Jovanovich.

Cronbach, L. J., & Meehl, P. E. (1955). Construct validity in psychological tests. *Psychological Bulletin, 52,* 281–302.

d'Apollonia, S., & Abrami, P. C. (1997). Navigating student ratings of instruction. *American Psychologist, 52,* 1198–1208.

Davis, B. G. (1993). *Tools for teaching.* San Francisco: Jossey-Bass.

Davis, S. F. (1999). The value of collaborative scholarship with undergraduates. In B. Perlman, L. I. McCann, & S. H. McFadden (Eds.), *Lessons learned: Practical advice for the teaching of psychology* (pp. 201–205). Washington, DC: American Psychological Society.

Davis, S. F., Grover, C. A., Becker, A. H., & McGregor, L. N. (1992). Academic dishonesty: Prevalence, determinants, techniques, and punishments. *Teaching of Psychology, 19,* 16–20.

Day, R. S. (1980). Teaching from notes: Some cognitive consequences. *New Directions for Teaching and Learning: Learning, Cognition, and College Teaching, 2,* 95–112.

Deci, E. L., & Ryan, R. M. (1985). *Intrinsic motivation and self determination in human behavior.* New York: Plenum.

Deloughry, T. J. (1995, November 24). High-tech efficiency? Colleges ask whether technology can cut their costs and improve productivity. *Chronicle of Higher Education,* A17, A19.

Dempster, F. N., & Perkins, P. G. (1993). Revitalizing classroom assessment: Using tests to promote learning. *Journal of Instructional Psychology, 20,* 197–203.

Deutsch, M. (1994). Constructive conflict resolution: Principles, training, and research. *Journal of Social Issues, 50*(1), 13–32.

Devine, P. G. (1989). Stereotypes and prejudice: Their automatic and controlled components. *Journal of Personality and Social Psychology, 56,* 5–18.

DeVries, D. L., Edwards, K. J., & Fennessey, G. M. (1973). *Using Teams-Games-Tournaments (TGT) in the classroom.* Baltimore: Center for Social Organization in Schools, Johns Hopkins University.

Dewey, R. A. (1999). Finding the right introductory psychology textbook. In B. Perlman, L. I. McCann, & S. H. McFadden (Eds.), *Lessons learned: Practical advice for the teaching of psychology* (pp. 25–28). Washington, DC: American Psychological Society.

Dodd, D. K. (1985). Robbers in the classroom: A deindividuation exercise. *Teaching of Psychology, 12,* 89–91.

Dreeben, R. (1972). *The nature of teaching.* Glenview, IL: Scott, Foresman.

Duffy, D. K., & Jones, J. W. (1995). *Teaching within the rhythms of the semester.* San Francisco: Jossey-Bass.

Duncan, N. C. (1991). CAI-enhanced exam performance in a research design course. *Behavior Research Methods, Instruments, and Computers, 23,* 324–327.

Duncan, N. C. (1993). Evaluation of instructional software: Design considerations and recommendations. *Behavior Research Methods, Instruments, and Computers, 25*, 223–227.

Dunn, D. S. (2000). Letter exchanges on statistics and research methods: Writing, responding, and learning. *Teaching of Psychology, 27*, 128–130.

Dweck, C. S. (1999). *Self-theories: Their role in motivation, personality, and development.* Philadelphia: Psychology Press/Taylor & Francis.

Dweck, C. S., & Leggett, E. L (1988). A social-cognitive approach to motivation and personality. *Psychological Review, 95*, 256–273.

Dyck, J. L., & Gee, N. R. (1998). A sweet way to teach students about the sampling distribution of the mean. *Teaching of Psychology, 25*, 192–195.

Ebel, K. E. (1988). *The craft of teaching* (2nd ed.). San Francisco: Jossey-Bass.

Ebel, R. L. (1974). Shall we get rid of grades? *Measurement in Education, 5*(4), 1–5.

Egeth, H. E., & Yantis, S. (1997). Visual attention: Control, representation, and time course. *Annual Review of Psychology, 48*, 269–297.

Elliot, A. J. (1999). Approach and avoidance motivation and achievement goals. *Educational Psychologist, 34*, 169–189.

Emmer, E. T., & Stough, L. M. (2001). Classroom management: A critical part of educational psychology, with implications for teacher education. *Educational Psychologist, 36*, 103–112.

English, S. L. (1985). Kinetics in academic lectures. *ESP Journal, 4*, 161–170.

Ericsson, K. A., & Lehmann, A. C. (1996). Expert and exceptional performance: Evidence of maximal adaptation to task constraints. *Annual Review of Psychology, 47*, 273–305.

Ewens, W. (1985). Teaching using discussion. *Footnotes, 13*(10), 8.

Exline, R., & Messick, D. (1967). The effects of dependency and social reinforcement upon visual behavior during an interview. *British Journal of Social and Clinical Psychology, 6*, 256–266.

Fay, N., Garrod, S., & Carletta, J. (2000). Group discussion as interactive dialogue or as serial monologue: The influence of group size. *Psychological Science, 11*, 481–486.

Feldman, K. A. (1978). Course characteristics and college students' ratings of their teachers and courses: What we know and what we don't. *Research in Higher Education, 9*, 199–242.

Feldman, K. A. (1983). Seniority and experience of college teachers as related to evaluations they receive from students. *Research in Higher Education, 18*, 3–124.

Feldman, K. A. (1987). Research productivity and scholarly accomplishment of college teachers as related to their instructional effectiveness: A review and exploration. *Research in Higher Education, 26*, 227–298.

Feldman, K. A. (1989). Instructional effectiveness of college teachers as judged by teachers themselves, current and former students, colleagues, administrators and external (neutral) observers. *Research in Higher Education, 30*, 137–194.

Feldman, K. A. (1992). College students' views of male and female college teachers: Part IB, Evidence from the social laboratory and experiments. *Research in Higher Education, 33,* 317–375.

Feldman, K. A. (1993). College students' views of male and female college teachers: Part IIB, Evidence from students' evaluations of their classroom teachers. *Research in Higher Education, 34,* 151–211.

Feldman, K. A., & Newcomb, T. M. (1969). *The impact of college on students.* San Francisco: Jossey-Bass.

Festinger, L. (1954). A theory of social comparison processes. *Human Relations, 7,* 117–140.

Fish, T. A., & Fraser, I. H. (1993). The science fair: A supplement to the lecture technique. *Teaching of Psychology, 20,* 231–233.

Fisher, R., & Ury, W. (with B. Patton, Ed.). (1981). *Getting to YES: Negotiating agreement without giving in.* Boston: Houghton-Mifflin.

Fisher, R., Ury, W., & Patton, B. (1991). *Getting to YES: Negotiating agreement without giving in* (2nd ed.). New York: Penguin Books.

Fitzgerald, H. G. (1947). *Projector for handling transparent plates.* United States Patent and Trademark Office, Serial No. 769,741. Retrieved August 4, 2001, from United States Patent and Trademark Office Web site http://www.uspto.gov/patft/index.html

Fitzgerald, J., & Shanahan, T. (2000). Reading and writing relations and their development. *Educational Psychologist, 35,* 39–50.

Fleming, N. D., & Bonwell, C. C. (1998). *The active learning site: VARK Inventory.* Retrieved August 2, 2001, from http://www.active-learning-site.com/inventory.html

Forer, B. R. (1949). The fallacy of personal validation: A classroom demonstration of gullibility. *Journal of Abnormal and Social Psychology, 44,* 118–123.

Forsyth, D. R. (1982). *An introduction to group dynamics.* Monterey, CA: Brooks Cole.

Forsyth, D. R. (1986). An attributional analysis of students' reactions to success and failure. In R. Feldman (Ed.), *The social psychology of education* (pp. 17–38). New York: Cambridge University Press.

Forsyth, D. R. (1991). Change in therapeutic groups. In C. R. Snyder & D. R. Forsyth (Eds.), *Handbook of social and clinical psychology: The health perspective* (pp. 664–680). New York: Pergamon.

Forsyth, D. R. (1999). *Group dynamics* (3rd ed.). Belmont, CA: Wadsworth.

Forsyth, D. R., & Archer, C. R. (1997). Technologically assisted instruction and student mastery, motivation, and matriculation. *Teaching of Psychology, 24,* 207–212.

Forsyth, D. R., & Berger, R. E. (1982). The effects of ethical ideology on moral behavior. *Journal of Social Psychology, 117,* 53–56.

Forsyth, D. R., & McMillan, J. (1981a). Attributions, affect, and expectations: A test of Weiner's three-dimensional model. *Journal of Educational Psychology*, *73*, 393–401.

Forsyth, D. R., & McMillan, J. (1981b). The attribution cube and reactions to educational outcomes. *Journal of Educational Psychology*, *73*, 632–641.

Forsyth, D. R., & McMillan, J. H. (1991). Some practical proposals for motivating students. *New Directions for Teaching and Learning: Approaching Instructional Problems Through Theoretical Perspectives*, *44*, 53–66.

Forsyth, D. R., & Wibberly, K. H. (1993). The self-reference effect: Demonstrating schematic processing in the classroom. *Teaching of Psychology*, *20*, 237–238.

Freud, S. (1953). *The standard edition of the complete psychology works: Vol 7* (J. Strachey, Ed.). London: Hogarth Press. (Original work published 1905)

Friedman, M., & Rosenman, R. (1974). *Type A behavior and your heart*. New York: Knopf.

Friedrich, J. (1996). Assessing students' perceptions of psychology as a science: Validation of a self-report measure. *Teaching of Psychology*, *23*, 6–13.

Friedrich, J. (1998). Teaching evaluations: Concerns for psychologists? *American Psychologist*, *53*, 1226–1227.

Frisbie, D. A. (1992). The multiple true/false item format: A status review. *Educational Measurement: Issues and Practice*, *11*, 21–26.

Froese, A. D., Gantz, B. S., & Henry, A. L. (1998). Teaching students to write literature reviews: A meta-analytic model. *Teaching of Psychology*, *25*, 102–105.

Fuhrmann, B. S., & Grasha, A. F. (1983). *A practical handbook for college teachers*. Boston: Little, Brown.

Fujishin, R. (2001). *Creating effect groups: The art of small group communication*. San Francisco: Acada.

Funder, D. C., & Dobroth, K. M. (1987). Differences between traits: Properties associated with interjudge agreement. *Journal of Personality and Social Psychology*, *52*, 409–418.

Gaertner, S. L., & Dovidio, J. F. (2000). *Reducing intergroup bias: The common ingroup identity model*. Philadelphia: Psychology Press/Taylor & Francis.

Galanter, E. (1962). Contemporary psychophysics. In R. Brown, E. Galanter, E. Hess, & G. Mandler (Eds.), *New directions in psychology* (pp. 87–156). New York: Holt, Rinehart & Winston.

Galliano, G. (1999). Enhancing student learning through exemplary examples. In B. Perlman, L. I. McCann, & S. H. McFadden (Eds.), *Lessons learned: Practical advice for the teaching of psychology* (pp. 93–97). Washington, DC: American Psychological Society.

Gamson, Z. F. (1991). A brief history of the seven principles for good practice in undergraduate education. *New Directions for Teaching and Learning: Applying the Seven Principles for Good Practice in Undergraduate Education*, *47*, 5–12.

Gardiner, L. F. (1998). Why we must change: The research evidence. *Thought and*

Action, 16, 71–88. Retrieved April 26, 2001, from National Education Association; http://www.nea.org/he/heta98/spring98.html

Gates, B. (with Hemingway, C.). (1999). *Business @ the speed of thought: Using a digital nervous system.* New York: Warner Books.

Gee, N. R., & Dyck, J. L. (1998). Using a videotape clip to demonstrate the fallibility of eyewitness testimony. *Teaching of Psychology, 25,* 138–140.

Gibb, J. R. (1973). Defensive communication. In W. G. Bennis, D. E. Berlew, E. H. Schein, & F. I. Steele (Eds.), *Interpersonal dynamics: Essays and readings on human interaction* (3rd ed., pp. 488–493). Homewood, IL: Dorsey.

Ginsberg, A., & Morecroft, J. (1997). Weaving feedback systems thinking into the case method: An application to corporate strategy. *Management Learning, 28,* 455–473.

Glaser, R. (1963). Instructional technology and the measurement of leading outcomes: Some questions. *American Psychologist, 18,* 519–521.

Gleason, M. (1986). Better communication in large courses. *College Teaching, 34*(1), 20–24.

Goetsch, G. G., & McFarland, D. D. (1980). Models of the distribution of acts in small discussion groups. *Social Psychology Quarterly, 43,* 173–183.

Goffman, E. (1967). Normal deviants. In T. J. Scheff (Ed.), *Mental illness and social processes* (pp. 267–271). New York: Harper & Row.

Goldman, L. (1985). The betrayal of the gatekeepers: Grade inflation. *The Journal of General Education, 37,* 97–121.

Goolkasian, P. (1989). Computerized laboratories for psychology instruction: How successful are they? *Behavior Research Methods, Instruments, and Computers, 21,* 148–150.

Goolkasian, P., & Lee, J. (1988). A computerized laboratory for general psychology. *Teaching of Psychology, 15,* 98–100.

Goss, S. S., & Bernstein, D. A. (1999). Research methods and critical thinking: Explaining "psychic" phenomena. In L. T. Benjamin, B. F. Nodine, R. M. Ernst, & C. B. Broeker (Eds.), *Activities handbook for the teaching of psychology* (pp. 25–27). Washington, DC: American Psychological Association.

Grabe, M. (1994). Motivational deficiencies when multiple examinations are allowed. *Contemporary Educational Psychology, 19,* 45–52.

Grabe, M., Petros, T., & Sawler, B. (1989). An evaluation of computer assisted study in controlled and free access settings. *Journal of Computer-Based Instruction, 16,* 110–116.

Graham, S., & Donaldson, J. F. (1999). Adult students' academic and intellectual development in college. *Adult Education Quarterly, 49,* 147–161.

Grasha, A. F. (1972). Observations on relating teaching goals to student response styles and classroom methods. *American Psychologist, 27,* 144–147.

Grasha, A. F. (1998). "Giving psychology away": Some experiences teaching undergraduates practical psychology. *Teaching of Psychology, 25,* 85–88.

Gray, P. (1997). Teaching is a scholarly activity: The idea-centered approach to introducing psychology. In R. J. Sternberg (Ed.), *Teaching introductory psychology: Survival tips from the experts* (pp. 49–64). Washington, DC: American Psychological Association.

Greenwald, A. G. (1997). Validity concerns and usefulness of student ratings of instruction. *American Psychologist, 52,* 1182–1186.

Greenwald, A. G., & Gillmore, G. M. (1997). Grading leniency is a removable contaminant of student ratings. *American Psychologist, 52,* 1209–1217.

Gregorc, A. F. (1982). *Gregorc style delineator—Research edition.* Columbia, CT: Gregorc Associates.

Griffith, C. R. (1921). A comment upon the psychology of the audience. *Psychological Monographs, 30,* 36–47.

Gronlund, N. E. (1998). *Assessment of student achievement* (6th ed.). Boston: Allyn & Bacon.

Gronlund, S. D., & Lewandowsky, S. (1992). Making TV commercials as a teaching aid for cognitive psychology. *Teaching of Psychology, 19,* 158–160.

Gruber, H. E., & Wallace, D. B. (2001). Creative work: The case of Charles Darwin. *American Psychologist, 56,* 346–349.

Gustafson, D. H., Shukla, R. M., Delbecq, A. L., & Walster, G. W. (1973). A comparative study of differences in subjective likelihood estimates made by individuals, interacting groups, Delphi groups, and nominal groups. *Organizational Behavior and Human Performance, 9,* 280–291.

Guthrie, R. V. (1997). *Even the rat was white: A historical view of psychology.* Boston: Allyn & Bacon.

Haber, G. M. (1980). Territorial invasion in the classroom: Invadee response. *Environment and Behavior, 12,* 17–31.

Hairston, M., Ruszkiewicz, J., & Friend, C. (1999). *The Scott, Foresman handbook for writers* (5th ed.). New York: Longman.

Haladyna, T. M. (1994). *Developing and validating multiple-choice test items.* Mahwah, NJ: Erlbaum.

Haladyna, T. M. (1997). *Writing test items to evaluate higher order thinking.* Boston: Allyn & Bacon.

Haladyna, T. M., & Downing, S. M. (1989a). A taxonomy of multiple-choice item-writing rules. *Applied Measurement in Education, 2,* 37–50.

Haladyna, T. M., & Downing, S. M. (1989b). Validity of a taxonomy of multiple-choice item-writing rules. *Applied Measurement in Education, 2,* 51–78.

Halamandaris, K. F., & Power, K. G. (1999). Individual differences, social support and coping with the examination stress: A study of the psychosocial and academic adjustment of first year home students. *Personality and Individual Differences, 26,* 665–685.

Hall, R. M., & Sandler, B. R. (1986). *The classroom climate: A chilly one for women? Project on the status and education of women.* Washington, DC: Association of American Colleges.

Halliday, G. (1991). Psychological self-help books: How dangerous are they? *Psychotherapy, 28,* 678–680.

Halpern, D. F., Appleby, D. C., Beers, S. E., Cowan, C. L., Furedy, J. J., Halonen, J. S., et al. (1993). Targeting outcomes: Covering your assessment concerns and needs. In T. V. McGovern (Ed.), *Handbook for enhancing undergraduate education in psychology* (pp. 23–46). Washington, DC: American Psychological Association.

Hamilton, S. B., & Knox, T. A. (1985). The colossal neuron: Acting out physiological psychology. *Teaching of Psychology, 12,* 153–156.

Handelsman, M. M., & Krest, M. (1996). Improving your students' writing: Arts and drafts. *Observer, 9*(3), 22, 23, 31.

Harackiewicz, J. M., Barron, K. E., & Elliot, A. J. (1998). Rethinking achievement goals: When are they adaptive for college students and why? *Educational Psychologist, 33,* 1–21.

Harlow, R. E., & Cantor, N. (1995). To whom do people turn when things go poorly? Task orientation and functional social contacts. *Journal of Personality and Social Psychology, 69,* 329–340.

Harris, M. J., & Rosenthal, R. (1986). Four factors in the mediation of teacher expectancy. In R. S. Feldman (Ed.), *The social psychology of education: Current research and theory* (pp. 91–114). New York: Cambridge.

Harris, P. C., Harris, M. H., & Hannah, S. A. (1998). Confronting hypertext: Exploring divergent responses to digital coursework. *The Internet and Higher Education, 1*(1), 45–57.

Hendrix, K. G. (1998). Student perceptions of the influence of race on professor credibility. *Journal of Black Studies, 28,* 738–763.

Herman, W. E. (2000). An interview with Wilbert (Bill) J. McKeachie. *Newsletter for Educational Psychologists (NEP/15), 24*(1), 7–10.

Hettich, P. (1990). Journal writing: Old fare or nouvelle cuisine? *Teaching of Psychology, 17,* 36–39.

Higgenbotham, H. N., West, S. G., & Forsyth, D. R. (1988). *Psychotherapy and behavior change: Social, cultural, and methodological perspectives.* New York: Pergamon.

Hill, G. W., Palladino, J. J., & Eison, J. A. (1993). Blood, sweat, and trivia: Faculty ratings of extra-credit opportunities. *Teaching of Psychology, 20,* 209–213.

Hilton, J. L. (1999). Teaching large classes. In B. Perlman, L. I. McCann, & S. H. McFadden (Eds.), *Lessons learned: Practical advice for the teaching of psychology* (pp. 115–120). Washington, DC: American Psychological Society.

Hinds, K., Schneider, W., & St. James, J. D. (1990). *MEL LAB: Instructor's Guide, Experiments in perception, cognition, social psychology and human factors.* Pittsburgh, PA: Psychology Software Tools.

Hinkle, S., & Hinkle, A. (1990). An experimental comparison of the effects of focused freewriting and other study strategies on lecture comprehension. *Teaching of Psychology, 17,* 31–35.

Hock, R. R. (Ed.). (1999). *Forty studies that changed psychology: Explorations into the history of psychological research* (3rd ed.). Upper Saddle River, NJ: Prentice-Hall.

Hokanson, J. E., & Burgess, M. (1962). The effects of three types of aggression on vascular processes. *Journal of Abnormal and Social Psychology, 64,* 446–449.

Homer, P. M., & Kahle, L. R. (1988). A structural equation test of the value-attitude-behavior hierarchy. *Journal of Personality and Social Psychology, 54,* 638–646.

Horner, D. T., Stetter, K. R., & McCann, L. I. (1998). Adding structure to unstructured research courses. *Teaching of Psychology, 25,* 126–128.

Hovland, C. I., Janis, I. L., & Kelley, H. H. (1953). *Communication and persuasion.* New Haven, CT: Yale University Press.

Howard, D. J. (1990). Rhetorical question effects on message processing and persuasion: The role of information availability and the elicitation of judgment. *Journal of Experimental Social Psychology, 26,* 217–239.

Husman, J., & Lens, W. (1999). The role of the future in student motivation. *Educational Psychologist, 34,* 113–125.

Jackson, S. E. (1992). Team composition in organizational settings: Issues in managing an increasingly diverse workforce. In S. Worchel, S. Wood, & J. A. Simpson (Eds.), *Group process and productivity* (pp. 138–172). Thousand Oaks, CA: Sage.

Jackson, S. E., May, K. E., & Whitney, K. (1995). Understanding the dynamics of diversity in decision-making teams. In R. A. Guzzo, E. Salas, & Associates (Eds.), *Team effectiveness and decision making in organizations* (pp. 204–261). San Francisco: Jossey-Bass.

Jacobs, L. C., & Chase, C. I. (1992). *Developing and using tests effectively: A guide for faculty.* San Francisco: Jossey-Bass.

James, W. (1892). *Psychology.* New York: Henry Holt.

Jarboe, S. C., & Witteman, H. R. (1996). Intragroup conflict management in task-oriented groups: The influence of problem sources and problem analyses. *Small Group Research, 27,* 316–338.

Jemmott, J. B., & Magloire, K. (1988). Academic stress, social support, and secretory immunoglobulin A. *Journal of Personality and Social Psychology, 55,* 803–810.

Johnson, J. T., Cain, L. M., Falke, T. L., Hayman, J., & Perillo, E. (1985). The "Barnum effect" revisited: Cognitive and motivational factors in the acceptance of personality descriptions. *Journal of Personality and Social Psychology, 49,* 1378–1391.

Johnston, J. (1989). *Accent on improving college teaching and learning: The computer revolution in teaching.* Ann Arbor, MI: National Center for Research to Improve Postsecondary Teaching and Learning.

Jones, E. E., & Berglas, S. (1978). Control of attributions about the self through self-handicapping strategies: The appeal of alcohol and the role of underachievement. *Personality and Social Psychology Bulletin, 4,* 200–206.

Jordan, A. E. (2001). College student cheating: The role of motivation, perceived norms, attitudes, and honors codes. *Ethics and Behavior, 11*, 233–248.

Kalat, J. W. (1999). Parsimonious explanations of apparent mind reading. In L. T. Benjamin, B. F. Nodine, R. M. Ernst, & C. B. Broeker (Eds.), *Activities handbook for the teaching of psychology* (pp. 18–21). Washington, DC: American Psychological Association.

Karoly, P. (1993). Mechanisms of self-regulation: A system view. *Annual Review of Psychology, 44*, 23–52.

Karoly, P., & Ruehlman, L. S. (1995). Goal cognition and its clinical implications: Development and preliminary validation of four motivational assessment instruments. *Assessment, 2*, 113–129.

Kaufman, B. (1964). *Up the down staircase.* Englewood Cliffs, NJ: Prentice-Hall.

Kaufman, J. C., & Bristol, A. S. (2001). When Allport met Freud: Using anecdotes in the teaching of psychology. *Teaching of Psychology, 28*, 44–46.

Keith-Spiegel, P. C., Tabachnick, B. G., & Allen, M. (1993). Ethics in academia: Students' views of professors' actions. *Ethics and Behavior, 3*, 149–162.

Keith-Spiegel, P. C., Tabachnick, B. G., Whitley, B. E., Jr., & Washburn, J. (1998). Why professors ignore cheating: Opinions of a national sample of psychology instructors. *Ethics and Behavior, 8*, 215–227.

Keller, F. S. (1968). "Good-bye, teacher. . ." *Journal of Applied Behavior Analysis, 1*, 79–89.

Kelley, H. H. (1967). Attribution theory in social psychology. *Nebraska Symposium on Motivation, 15*, 192–241.

Kelvin, Lord (W. Thompson). (1891). *Popular lectures and addresses* (Vol. 1). London: Macmillan.

Kleinbeck, U., Quast, H., & Schwarz, R. (1989). Volitional effects on performance: Conceptual considerations and results from dual-task studies. In R. Kanfer, P. L. Ackerman, & R. Cudeck (Eds.), *Abilities, motivation, and methodology: The Minnesota Symposium on Learning and Individual Differences* (pp. 23–42). Mahwah, NJ: Erlbaum.

Kimble, G. A. (1984). Psychology's two cultures. *American Psychologist, 39*, 833–839.

King, P. M. (1978). William Perry's theory of intellectual and ethical development. In L. Knefelkamp, C. Widick, & C. A. Parker (Eds.), *Applying new developmental findings: New directions for student services* (No. 4, pp. 35–52). San Francisco: Jossey-Bass.

Kintsch, W., & Bates, E. (1977). Recognition memory for statements from a classroom lecture. *Journal of Experimental Psychology: Human Learning and Memory, 3*, 150–159.

Kitchener, K. S. (2000). *Foundations of ethical practice, research, and teaching in psychology.* Mahwah, NJ: Erlbaum.

Kleinpenning, G., & Hagendoorn, L. (1993). Forms of racism and the cumulative dimension of ethnic attitudes. *Social Psychology Quarterly, 56*, 21–36.

Knight, L. J., & McKelvie, S. J. (1986). Effects of attendance, note-taking, and review on memory for a lecture: Encoding vs. external storage functions of notes. *Canadian Journal of Behavioural Science, 18,* 52–61.

Knowles, E. S. (1982). A comment on the study of classroom ecology: A lament for the good old days. *Personality and Social Psychology Bulletin, 8,* 357–361.

Kochenour, E. O., Jolley, D. S., Kaup, J. G., Patrick, D. L., Roach, K. D., & Wenzler, L. A. (1997). Supplemental instruction: An effective component of student affairs programming. *Journal of College Student Development, 38,* 577–586.

Kohut, H. (1984). *How does analysis cure? Contributions to the psychology of the self* (A. Goldberg, Ed., with the collaboration of P. Stepansky). Chicago: University of Chicago Press.

Kolb, D. A. (1976). *The learning style inventory.* Boston: McBer.

Kramer, T. J., & Korn, J. H. (1999). Class discussions: Promoting participation and preventing problems. In B. Perlman, L. I. McCann, & S. H. McFadden (Eds.), *Lessons learned: Practical advice for the teaching of psychology* (pp. 99–104). Washington, DC: American Psychological Society.

Krauss, R. M., Morrel-Samuels, P., & Colasante, C. (1991). Do conversational hand gestures communicate? *Journal of Personality and Social Psychology, 61,* 743–754.

Kulik, C. L. C., & Kulik, J. A. (1991). Effectiveness of computer-based instruction: An updated analysis. *Computers in Human Behavior, 7,* 75–94.

Kulik, J. A., Bangert, R. C., & Williams, G. W. (1983). Effects of computer-based teaching on secondary school students. *Journal of Educational Psychology, 75,* 119–126.

Kulik, J. A., & Kulik, C. L. C. (1987). Review of recent research literature on computer-based instruction. *Contemporary Educational Psychology, 12,* 222–230.

Kulik, J. A., & McKeachie, W. J. (1975). The evaluation of teachers in higher education. *Review of Research in Education, 3,* 210–240.

Laghans, W. (1996). Metabolic and glucostatic control of feeding. *Proceedings of the Nutrition Society, 55,* 497–515.

Langer, E. J. (1989). *Mindfulness.* Reading, MA: Addison-Wesley.

Larson, C. E., & LaFasto, F. M. (1989). *Teamwork: What must go right/What can go wrong.* Thousand Oaks, CA: Sage.

Leary, M. R., & Kowalski, R. M. (1995). *Social anxiety.* New York: Guilford Press.

Leary, M. R., Rogers, P. A., Canfield, R. W., & Coe, C. (1986). Boredom in interpersonal encounters: Antecedents and social implications. *Journal of Personality and Social Psychology, 51,* 968–975.

Lefton, L. A. (1997). Why I teach the way I do: Repackaging psychology. In R. J. Sternberg (Ed.), *Teaching introductory psychology: Survival tips from the experts* (pp. 65–71). Washington, DC: American Psychological Association.

Levine, D. W., McDonald, P. J., O'Neal, E. C., & Garwood, S. G. (1982). Classroom seating effects: Environment or self-selection—neither, either, or both. *Personality and Social Psychology Bulletin, 8,* 365–369.

Levinson, E., & Grohe, B. (2001). How do you act intelligently when you don't know what you are doing? *Converge, 4*(3), 58, 60.

Levy, J., Burton, G., Mickler, S., & Vigorito, M. (1999). A curriculum matrix for psychology program review. *Teaching of Psychology, 26,* 291–294.

Lindgren, H. C. (1969). *The psychology of college success: A dynamic approach.* New York: Wiley.

Lloyd, M. A. (1999). Aggression on television. In L. T. Benjamin, B. F. Nodine, R. M. Ernst, & C. B. Broeker (Eds.), *Activities handbook for the teaching of psychology* (pp. 346–349). Washington, DC: American Psychological Association.

Loevinger, J. (1998). *Technical foundations for measuring ego development.* Mahwah, NJ: Erlbaum.

Lowman, J. (1984). *Mastering the techniques of teaching.* San Francisco: Jossey-Bass.

Lowman, J. (1995). *Mastering the techniques of teaching* (2nd ed.). San Francisco: Jossey-Bass.

Ludewig, L. M. (1994). 10 worst student behaviors. *The Teaching Professor, 8*(5), 3.

Ludwig, T. (1996). *PsychSim: Interactive graphic simulations for psychology* (Version 4). New York: Worth.

Lukhele, R., Thissen, D., & Wainer, H. (1994). On the relative value of multiple-choice, constructed-response, and examinee-selected items on two achievement test. *Journal of Educational Measurement, 31,* 234–250.

Luthans, F. (1998). *Organization behavior* (8th ed.). New York: McGraw-Hill.

Luthans, F., Hodgetts, R. M., & Rosenkrantz, S. A. (1988). *Real managers.* Cambridge, MA: Balinger.

Lutsky, N. (1986). Undergraduate research experience through the analysis of data sets in psychology courses. *Teaching of Psychology, 13,* 119–122.

Lutsky, N. (1999). Teaching with overheads: low tech, high impact. In B. Perlman, L. I. McCann, & S. H. McFadden (Eds.), *Lessons learned: Practical advice for the teaching of psychology* (pp. 67–72). Washington, DC: American Psychological Society.

Mager, R. F. (1962). *Preparing instructional objectives.* Belmont, CA: Fearon.

Malin, J. T., & Timmreck, C. (1979). Student goals and the undergraduate curriculum. *Teaching of Psychology, 6,* 136–139.

Mann, R. D., Arnold, S. M., Binder, J. L., Cytrynbaum, S., Newman, B. M., Ringwald, B. E., et al. (1970). *The college classroom: Conflict, change, and learning.* New York: Wiley.

Marcoulides, G. A. (1990). Improving learner performance with computer based programs. *Journal of Educational Computing Research, 6,* 147–155.

Marques, J. F. (1999). Raiders of the lost reference: Helping your students do a literature search. In B. Perlman, L. I. McCann, & S. H. McFadden (Eds.), *Lessons learned: Practical advice for the teaching of psychology* (pp. 173–178). Washington, DC: American Psychological Society.

Marsh, H. W. (1980). The influence of student, course, and instructor characteristics on evaluations of university teaching. *American Educational Research Journal, 17,* 219–237.

Marsh, H. W. (1982). SEEQ: A reliable, valid, and useful instrument for collecting students' evaluations of university teaching. *British Journal of Educational Psychology, 52,* 77–95.

Marsh, H. W. (1983). Multidimensional ratings of teaching effectiveness by students from different academic settings and their relation to student/course/instructor characteristics. *Journal of Educational Psychology, 75,* 150–166.

Marsh, H. W. (1984). Students' evaluations of university teaching: Dimensionality, reliability, validity, potential biases, and utility. *Journal of Educational Psychology, 76,* 707–754.

Marsh, H. W., & Dunkin, M. (1992). Students' evaluations of university teaching: A multidimensional perspective. In J. C. Smart (Ed.), *Higher education: Handbook of theory and research* (Vol. 8, pp. 143–233). New York: Agathon.

Marsh, H. W., & Hocevar, D. (1991). Students' evaluations of teaching effectiveness: The stability of mean ratings of the same teachers over a 13-year period. *Teaching and Teacher Education, 7,* 303–314.

Marsh, H. W., & Roche, L. A. (1993). The use of students' evaluations and an individually structured intervention to enhance university teaching effectiveness. *American Educational Research Journal, 30,* 217–251.

Marsh, H. W., & Roche, L. A. (1997). Making students' evaluations of teaching effectiveness effective: The critical issues of validity, bias, and utility. *American Psychologist, 52,* 1187–1197.

Marsh, H. W., & Ware, J. E. (1982). Effects of expressiveness, content coverage, and incentive on multidimensional student rating scales: New interpretations of the Dr. Fox effect. *Journal of Educational Psychology, 74,* 126–134.

Marsh, R. (1984). A comparison of take-home versus in-class exams. *Journal of Educational Research, 78,* 111–113.

Martin, E. (1984). Power and authority in the classroom: Sexist stereotypes in teaching evaluations. *Signs, 9,* 482–492.

Martinez, M. E. (1999). Cognition and the question of test item format. *Educational Psychologist, 34,* 207–218.

Mathie, V. A., Beins, B., Benjamin, L. T., Jr., Ewing, M. M., Iljima Hall, C. C., Henderson, B., et al. (1993). Promoting active learning in psychology courses In T. V. McGovern (Ed.), *Handbook for enhancing undergraduate education in psychology* (pp. 183–214). Washington, DC: American Psychological Association.

Mayer, R. E. (1997). Multimedia learning: Are we asking the right questions? *Educational Psychologist, 32,* 1–19.

Mayer, R. E., & Anderson, R. B. (1991). Animations need narrations: An experimental test of a dual-coding hypothesis. *Journal of Educational Psychology, 83,* 484–490.

Mayer, R. E., & Gallini, J. K. (1990). When is an illustration worth ten thousand words? *Journal of Educational Psychology, 82,* 715–726.

McBurney, D. H. (1999). Cheating: Preventing and dealing with academic dishonesty. In B. Perlman, L. I. McCann, & S. H. McFadden (Eds.), *Lessons learned: Practical advice for the teaching of psychology* (pp. 213–217). Washington, DC: American Psychological Society.

McBurney, D. H. (2000). The problem method of teaching research methods. In M. E. Ware & D. E. Johnson (Eds.), *Handbook of demonstrations and activities in the teaching of psychology: Vol. I. Introductory, statistics, research methods, and history* (2nd ed., pp. 134–136). Mahwah, NJ: Erlbaum.

McCabe, D. L., & Bowers, W. J. (1996). The relationship between student cheating and college fraternity or sorority membership, *NASPA Journal, 33*(4), 280–291.

McCabe, D. L., & Treviño, L. K. (1997). Individual and contextual influences on academic dishonesty: A multicampus investigation. *Research in Higher Education, 38*(3), 379–396.

McCabe, D. L., Treviño, L. K., & Butterfield, K. D. (2001). Cheating in academic institutions: A decade of research. *Ethics and Behavior, 11,* 219–232.

McCallum, L. W. (1984). A meta-analysis of course evaluation data and its use in the tenure decision. *Research in Higher Education, 21,* 150–158.

McDade, S. A. (1995). Case study pedagogy to advance critical thinking. *Teaching of Psychology, 22,* 9–10.

McGovern, T. V. (1987). *Large class instruction: Models and processes.* Richmond, VA: Virginia Commonwealth University.

McGovern, T. V. (Ed.). (1993). *Handbook for enhancing undergraduate education in psychology.* Washington, DC: American Psychological Association.

McGovern, T. V., Furumoto, L., Halpern, D. F., Kimble, G. A., & McKeachie, W. (1991). Liberal education, study in depth, and the arts and sciences major: Psychology. *American Psychologist, 46,* 598–605.

McGovern, T. V., & Hawks, B. K. (1986). The varieties of undergraduate experience. *Teaching of Psychology, 13,* 174–181.

McGovern, T. V., & Hogshead, D. L. (1990). Learning about writing, thinking about teaching. *Teaching of Psychology, 17,* 5–10.

McGovern, T. V., & Reich, J. (1996). A comment on the quality principles. *American Psychologist, 51,* 252–255.

McGrath, J. E. (1984). *Groups: Interaction and performance.* Englewood Cliffs, NJ: Prentice Hall.

McKeachie, W. J. (1978). *Teaching tips: A guidebook for the beginning college teacher* (7th ed.). Lexington, MA: D. C. Heath.

McKeachie, W. J. (1980). Implications of cognitive psychology for college teaching. *New Directions for Teaching and Learning: Learning, Cognition, and College Teaching, 2,* 85–93.

McKeachie, W. J. (1997). Student ratings: The validity of use. *American Psychologist, 52,* 1218–1225.

McKeachie, W. J. (1999). *McKeachie's teaching tips: Strategies, research, and theory for college and university teachers.* New York: Houghton Mifflin.

McKeachie, W. J., Pintrich, P. R., Lin, Y.-G., & Smith, D. A. F. (1986). *Teaching and learning in the college classroom: A review of the research literature.* Ann Arbor, MI: National Center for Research to Improve Postsecondary Teaching and Learning, University of Michigan.

McManus, J. L. (1986). "Live" case study/journal record in adolescent psychology. *Teaching of Psychology, 13,* 70–74.

McMillan, J. H. (1997). *Classroom assessment: Principles and practice for effective instruction.* Boston: Allyn & Bacon.

McMillan, J. H., & Forsyth, D. R. (1991). Why do learners learn? Answers offered by current theories of motivation. *New Directions for Teaching and Learning: Approaching Instructional Problems Through Theoretical Perspectives, 44,* 39–52.

McMillan, J. H., Wergin, J. F., Forsyth, D. R., & Brown, J. C. (1987). Student ratings of instruction: A summary of the literature. *Instructional Evaluation, 8,* 2–13.

Mehrabian, A. (1972). *Nonverbal communication.* Chicago: Aldine.

Messick, S. (1995). Validity of psychological assessment: Validation of inferences from persons' responses and performances as scientific inquiry into score meaning. *American Psychologist, 50,* 741–749.

Meyer, G. J., Finn, S. E., Eyde, L. D., Kay, G. G., Moreland, K. L., Dies, R. R., et al. (2001). Psychological testing and psychological assessment: A review of evidence and issues. *American Psychologist, 56,* 128–165.

Meyers, S. A. (1997). Increasing student participation and productivity in small-group activities for psychology classes. *Teaching of Psychology, 24,* 105–115.

Meyers, S. A., & Prieto, L. R. (2000). Training in the teaching of psychology: What is done and examining the differences. *Teaching of Psychology, 27,* 258–261.

Milgram, S. (1963). Behavioral study of obedience. *Journal of Abnormal and Social Psychology, 67,* 371–378.

Milgram, S. (1974). *Obedience to authority.* New York: Harper & Row.

Miller, B., & Gentile, B. F. (1998). Introductory course content and goals. *Teaching of Psychology, 25,* 89–96.

Miller, G. A. (1956). The magical number seven, plus or minus two: Some limits on our capacity for processing information. *Psychological Review, 63,* 81–97.

Miller, G. A., Galanter, E., & Pribram, K. H. (1960). *Plans and the structure of behavior.* New York: Holt.

Miller, R. L., Brickman, P., & Bolen, D. (1975). Attribution versus persuasion as a means for modifying behavior. *Journal of Personality and Social Psychology, 31*, 430–441.

Millman, J., Bishop, C. H., & Ebel, R. (1965). An analysis of test-wiseness. *Educational and Psychological Measurement, 25*, 707–726.

Mintzes, J. J. (1979). Overt teaching behaviors and student ratings of instructors. *Journal of Experimental Education, 48*, 145–153.

Miserandino, M. (1991). Memory and the seven dwarfs. *Teaching of Psychology, 18*, 169–171.

Miserandino, M. (1999). Those who can do: Implementing active learning. In B. Perlman, L. I. McCann, & S. H. McFadden (Eds.), *Lessons learned: Practical advice for the teaching of psychology* (pp. 109–114). Washington, DC: American Psychological Society.

Miserandino, M. (2000). Freudian principles in everyday life. In M. E. Ware & D. E. Johnson (Eds.), *Handbook of demonstrations and activities in the teaching of psychology: III. Personality, abnormal, clinical-counseling, and social* (2nd ed., pp. 21–24). Mahwah, NJ: Erlbaum.

Monahan, J. S. (1993). A computer lab for undergraduate psychological research. *Behavior Research Methods, Instruments, and Computers, 25*, 295–297.

Montepare, J. M., & Zebrowitz-McArthur, L. (1988). Impressions of people created by age-related qualities in their gaits. *Journal of Personality and Social Psychology, 55*, 547–556.

Montessori, M. (1995). *The absorbent mind* (C. A. Claremont, Trans.). New York: Henry Holt. (Original work published 1949)

Moreland, R. L., Levine, J. M., & Wingert, M. L. (1996). Creating the ideal group: Composition effects at work. In E. Witte & J. Davis (Eds.), *Understanding group behavior: Small group processes and interpersonal relations* (Vol. 2, pp. 11–35). Mahwah, NJ: Erlbaum.

Morris, E. J. (1991). Classroom demonstration of behavioral effects of the split-brain operation. *Teaching of Psychology, 18*, 226–228.

Murray, B., Gillese, E., Lennon, M., Mercer, P., & Robinson, M. (1996). *Ethical principles for college and university teaching.* Retrieved July 18, 2001, from University of Guelph, Society for Teaching and Learning in Higher Education Web site: http://www.tss.uoguelph.ca/stlhe/ethical.html

Murray, D. M. (1985). *A writer teaching writing* (2nd ed). Boston: Houghton Mifflin.

Murray, H. G. (1983). Low-inference classroom teaching behaviors and student ratings of college teaching effectiveness. *Journal of Educational Psychology, 75*, 138–149.

Murray, H. G., & Lawrence, C. (1980). Speech and drama training for lecturers as a means of improving university teaching. *Research in Higher Education, 13*, 73–90.

Murray, J. P. (1994). Why teaching portfolios? *Community College Review, 22*, 33–43.

Murray, J. P. (1995). *Successful faculty development and evaluation: The complete* teaching portfolio. *ASHE-ERIC Higher Education Report No. 8.* Washington, DC: The George Washington University, Graduate School of Education and Human Development.

Nakamura, J., & Csikszentmihalyi, M. (2001). Catalytic creativity: The case of Linus Pauling. *American Psychologist, 56,* 337–341.

National Center for Education Statistics (1999). *Digest of educational statistics: Chapter 3. Postsecondary education.* Retrieved July 18, 2001, from http://nces. ed.gov/pubs2000/Digest99/chapter3.html

National Institute of Education. (1984). *Involvement in learning: Realizing the potential of American higher education.* Washington, DC: National Institute of Education.

National Survey of Student Engagement. (2000). *National benchmarks of effective educational practice.* Bloomington, IN: Indiana University Center for Postsecondary Research and Planning.

Naveh-Benjamin, M., McKeachie, W. J., Lin, Y., & Holinger, D. P. (1981). Test anxiety: Deficits in information processing. *Journal of Educational Psychology, 73,* 816–824.

Newcomb, T. M., Koenig, K. E., Flacks, R., & Warwick, D. P. (1967). *Persistence and change: Bennington College and its students after twenty-five years.* New York: Wiley.

Newman, J. H. (1973). *The idea of a university.* New York: Doubleday. (Original work published 1852)

Niedenthal, P. M., Setterlund, M. B., & Wherry, M. B. (1992). Possible self-complexity and affective reactions to goal-relevant evaluation. *Journal of Personality and Social Psychology, 63,* 5–16.

Niemiec, R., & Walberg, H. J. (1987). Comparative effects of computer-assisted instruction: A synthesis of reviews. *Journal of Educational Computing Research, 3,* 19–37.

Nitko, A. J. (2001). *Educational assessment of students.* Upper Saddle River, NJ: Prentice-Hall.

Nodine, B. F. (1999). Why not make writing assignments? In B. Perlman, L. I. McCann, & S. H. McFadden (Eds.), *Lessons learned: Practical advice for the teaching of psychology* (pp. 167–172). Washington, DC: American Psychological Society.

Noel, J., Forsyth, D. R., & Kelley, K. (1987). Improving the performance of failing students by overcoming their self-serving attributional biases. *Basic and Applied Social Psychology, 8,* 151–162.

O'Neil, C., & Wright, A. (1992). *Recording teaching accomplishment: A Dalhousie guide to the teaching dossier* (3rd ed.). Halifax, Nova Scotia: Dalhousie University Press.

O'Neil, J. (1990). Making sense of style. *Educational Leadership, 48*(2), 4–9.

Olds, J. (1958). Self-stimulation of the brain: Its use to study local effects of hunger, sex, and drugs. *Science, 127,* 315–324.

Onifade, E. O., Nabangi, F. K., Reynolds, R., & Allen, C. (2000). The relationship between grade point average and cheating behavior, and the effect of both on the usefulness of take-home tests. *Proceedings of the Annual Meeting of the Academy of Business Education*. Retrieved June 7, 2000, from Journal of Business Education Proceedings at www.abe.villanova.edu/proceeding.html

Onifade, E., Nabangi, F. K., & Trigg, R. R. (1998). Comparative effects of take-home tests, quizzes, and home-works on accounting students' performance. *Journal of Accounting and Finance Research, 5*(2), 6–14.

Ory, J. C., Braskamp, L. A., & Pieper, D. M. (1980). Congruency of student evaluative information collected by three methods. *Journal of Educational Psychology, 72,* 181–185.

Ory, J. C., & Ryan, K. E. (1993). *Tips for improving testing and grading.* Thousand Oaks, CA: Sage.

Osborn, A. F. (1957). *Applied imagination.* New York: Scribner.

Overall, J. U., & Marsh, H. W. (1980). Students' evaluations of instruction: A longitudinal study of their stability. *Journal of Educational Psychology, 72,* 321–325.

Palladino, J. J., Hill, G. W., IV, & Norcross, J. C. (1999). Using extra credit. In B. Perlman, L. I. McCann, & S. H. McFadden (Eds.), *Lessons learned: Practical advice for the teaching of psychology* (pp. 57–60). Washington, DC: American Psychological Society.

Palmer, P. J. (1998). *The courage to teach: Exploring the inner landscape of a teacher's life.* San Francisco: Jossey-Bass.

Parsons, T. S. (1957). A comparison of instruction by kinescope, correspondence study, and customary classroom procedures. *Journal of Educational Psychology, 48,* 27–40.

Pascarella, E. T. (1980). Student-faculty informal contact and college outcomes. *Review of Educational Research, 50,* 545–595.

Pastorino, E. E. (1999). Students with academic difficulty: Prevention and assistance. In B. Perlman, L. I. McCann, & S. H. McFadden (Eds.), *Lessons learned: Practical advice for the teaching of psychology* (pp. 193–199). Washington, DC: American Psychological Society.

Pauk, W. (1993). *How to study in college* (5th ed.). Boston: Houghton Mifflin.

Penner, J. G. (1984). *Why many college teachers cannot lecture: How to avoid communication breakdown in the classroom.* Springfield, IL: C C Thomas.

Percy, B., & Leight, M. (2001). Side by side. *Converge, 4*(3), 13.

Perkins, D. V., & Saris, R. N. (2001). A "jigsaw classroom" technique for undergraduate statistics courses. *Teaching of Psychology, 28,* 111–113.

Perlman, B., & McCann, L. I. (1999a). Student perspectives on the first day of class. *Teaching of Psychology, 26,* 277–279.

Perlman, B., & McCann, L. I. (1999b). The most frequently listed courses in the undergraduate psychology curriculum. *Teaching of Psychology, 26,* 177–182.

Perlman, B., McCann, L. I., & McFadden, S. H. (Eds.). (1999). *Lessons learned:*

Practical advice for the teaching of psychology. Washington, DC: American Psychological Society.

Perone, M. (1991). Computer-based methodology laboratories: An undergraduate course in experimental psychology. *Behavior Research Methods, Instruments, and Computers, 23,* 121–126.

Perry, W. G., Jr. (1970). *Forms of intellectual and ethical development in the college years: A scheme.* New York: Holt, Rinehart & Winston.

Petty, R. E., Cacioppo, J. T., & Heesacker, M. (1981). The use of rhetorical questions in persuasion: A cognitive response analysis. *Journal of Personality and Social Psychology, 40,* 432–440.

Petty, L. C., & Rosen, E. F. (1990). Increase in mastery level using a computer-based tutorial/simulation in experimental psychology. *Behavior Research Methods, Instruments, and Computers, 22,* 216–218.

Pintrich, P. R. (1988). Student learning and college teaching. *New Directions for Teaching and Learning: Preparing for New Commitments, 33,* 47–58.

Pirsig, R. M. (1974). *Zen and the art of motorcycle maintenance.* New York: Bantam.

Plante, T. G. (1998). A laboratory group model for engaging undergraduates in faculty research. *Teaching of Psychology, 25,* 128–130.

Poe, R. E. (1990). A strategy for improving literature reviews in psychology courses. *Teaching of Psychology, 17,* 54–55.

Poe, R. E. (2000). Hitting a nerve: When touchy subjects come up in class. *Observer, 13*(9), 18–19, 31.

Polczynski, J. J., & Shirland, L. E. (1977). Expectancy theory and contract grading combined as an effective motivational force for college students. *Journal of Educational Research, 70,* 238–241.

Polzer, J. T., Kramer, R. M., & Neale, M. A. (1997). Positive illusions about oneself and one's group. *Small Group Research, 28,* 243–266.

Posthuma, B. W. (1999). *Small groups in counseling and therapy* (3rd ed.). Boston: Allyn & Bacon.

Pratt, D. D. (1992). Conceptions of teaching. *Adult Education Quarterly, 42,* 203–220.

Pressley, N., Van Etten, S., Yokoi, L., Freebern, G., & Van Meter, P. (1998). The metacognition of college studentship: A grounded theory approach. In J. D. Hacker, J. Dunlosky, & A. Graesser (Eds.), *Metacognition in educational theory and practice* (pp. 347–363). Mahwah, NJ: Erlbaum.

Procidano, M. E. (1991). Students' evaluation of writing assignments in an abnormal psychology course. *Teaching of Psychology, 18,* 164–167.

Puente, A. E., Blanch, E., Candland, D. K., Denmark, F. L., Laman, C., Lutsky, N., et al. (1993). Toward a psychology of variance: Increasing the presence and understanding of ethnic minorities in psychology. In T. V. McGovern (Ed.), *Handbook for enhancing undergraduate education in psychology* (pp. 71–92). Washington, DC: American Psychological Association.

Quereshi, M. Y. (1988). Evaluation of an undergraduate psychology program: Occupational and personal benefits. *Teaching of Psychology, 15,* 119–123.

Radmacher, S. A., & Latosi-Sawin, E. (1995). Summary writing: A tool to improve student comprehension and writing in psychology. *Teaching of Psychology, 22,* 113–115.

Ralston, J. V., & Beins, B. (1999). Thirteen ideas to help computerize your course. In B. Perlman, L. I. McCann, & S. H. McFadden (Eds.), *Lessons learned: Practical advice for the teaching of psychology* (pp. 73–77). Washington, DC: American Psychological Society.

Redding, R. E. (1998). Students' evaluations of teaching fuel grade inflation. *American Psychologist, 53,* 1227–1228.

Reimann, P., & Schult, T. J. (1996). Turning examples into cases: Acquiring knowledge structures for analogical problem solving. *Educational Psychologist, 31,* 123–132.

Renner, C. H., & Renner, M. J. (1999). How to create a good exam. In B. Perlman, L. I. McCann, & S. H. McFadden (Eds.), *Lessons learned: Practical advice for the teaching of psychology* (pp. 43–47). Washington, DC: American Psychological Society.

Rheingold, H. L. (1994). *The psychologist's guide to an academic career.* Washington, DC: American Psychological Association.

Riechmann, S., & Grasha, A. F. (1974). A rational approach to developing and assessing the construct validity of a student learning style scale instrument. *Journal of Psychology, 87,* 213–223.

Rietz, H. L., & Manning, M. (1994). *The one-stop guide to workshops.* New York: Irwin.

Roberts, D. M. (1993). An empirical study on the nature of trick test questions. *Journal of Educational Measurement, 30,* 331–344.

Rocklin, T. (2001). Do I dare? Is it prudent? *The National Teaching & Learning Forum, 10*(3), 1–3. Retrieved August 3, 2001, from National Education Association Web site: http://www.ntlf.com/html/pi/0103/v10n3smpl.pdf

Rodabaugh, R. C. (1996). Institutional commitment to fairness in college teaching. In L. Fisch (Ed.), *Ethical dimensions of college and university teaching* (pp. 37–45). San Francisco: Jossey-Bass.

Rogers, C. (1961). *On becoming a person.* Boston: Houghton Mifflin.

Rogers, C. (1969). *Freedom to learn.* Columbus, OH: Charles E. Merrill.

Rohm, R. A., Sparzo, F. J., & Bennett, C. M. (1986). College student performance under repeated testing and cumulative testing conditions: Report on five studies. *Journal of Educational Research, 80,* 99–104.

Roig, M. (2001). Plagiarism and paraphrasing criteria of college and university professors. *Ethics and Behavior, 11,* 307–324.

Rosch, E. H. (1973). Natural categories. *Cognitive Psychology, 4,* 328–350.

Rosch, E. (1975). Cognitive representations of semantic categories. *Journal of Experimental Psychology: General, 104,* 192–233.

Rosen, G. M. (1987). Self-help treatment books and the commercialization of psychotherapy. *American Psychologist, 42,* 46–51.

Rosenfeld, P., & Anderson, D. D. (1985). The effects of humorous multiple-choice alternatives on test performance. *Journal of Instructional Psychology, 12,* 3–5.

Rosenthal, R., & Jacobson, L. (1968). *Pygmalion in the classroom: Teacher expectation and pupils' intellectual development.* New York: Holt, Rinehart & Winston.

Rosenwein, R. (1983). Classroom exercises in social psychology: Muddles, confusions and concerns. *Society for the Advancement of Social Psychology Newsletter, 9, 1,* 6–7.

Rosnow, R. L., & Rosnow, M. (1995). *Writing papers in psychology.* Pacific Grove: Brooks/Cole.

Ross, L., Amabile, T. M., & Steinmetz, J. L. (1977). Social roles, social control, and biases in social perception processes. *Journal of Personality and Social Psychology, 35,* 485–494.

Rudisill, J. R. (1999). Diagnosis of psychological disorders: A group therapy simulation. In L. T. Benjamin, B. F. Nodine, R. M. Ernst, & C. B. Broeker (Eds.), *Activities handbook for the teaching of psychology* (pp. 384–392). Washington, DC: American Psychological Association.

Ruhl, K. L., Hughes, C. A., & Schloss, P. J. (1987). Using the pause procedure to enhance lecture recall. *Teacher Education and Special Education, 10,* 14–18.

Ruscio, J. (2001). Administering quizzes at random to increase students' reading. *Teaching of Psychology, 28,* 204–206.

Ryan, R. M., Mims, V., & Koestner, R. (1983). Relation of reward contingency and interpersonal context to intrinsic motivation: A review and test using cognitive evaluation theory. *Journal of Personality and Social Psychology, 45,* 736–750.

Sabini, J. P., & Silver, M. (1978). Moral reproach and moral action. *Journal for the Theory of Social Behavior, 8,* 103–123.

Sadoski, M., Goetz, E. T., & Avila, E. (1995). Concreteness effects in text recall: Dual coding or context availability. *Reading Research Quarterly, 30,* 278–288.

Sadoski, M., Goetz, E. T., & Rodriguez, M. (2000). Engaging texts: Effects of concreteness on comprehensibility, interest, and recall in four text types. *Journal of Educational Psychology, 92,* 85–95.

Sandler, B. R. (1988). The classroom climate: Chilly for women? In A. L. Deneef, C. D. Goodwin, & E. S. McCrate (Eds.), *The academic handbook* (pp. 146–152). Durham, NC: Duke University Press.

Sarason, I. G. (1984). Stress, anxiety, and cognitive interference: Reactions to tests. *Journal of Personality and Social Psychology, 46,* 929–938.

Sawyer, T. A. (1988). The effects of computerized and conventional study guides on achievement in college students. *Journal of Computer-Based Instruction, 15,* 80–82.

Schommer, M. (1998). The influence of age and education on epistemological beliefs. *British Journal of Educational Psychology, 68,* 551–562.

Schwarz, N., & Hippler, H. (1995). Subsequent questions may influence answers to preceding questions in mail surveys. *Public Opinion Quarterly, 59*, 93–97.

Schweighart Goss, S. (1999). Dealing with problem students in the classroom. In B. Perlman, L. I. McCann, & S. H. McFadden (Eds.), *Lessons learned: Practical advice for the teaching of psychology* (pp. 209–212). Washington, DC: American Psychological Society.

Scialfa, C., Legare, C., Wenger, L., & Dingley, L. (2001). Difficulty and discriminability of introductory psychology test items. *Teaching of Psychology, 28*, 11–15.

Scogin, F., & Rickard, H. C. (1987). A volunteer program for abnormal psychology students: Eighteen years and still going strong. *Teaching of Psychology, 14*, 95–97.

Scott, J. M., Koch, R. E., Scott, G. M., & Garrison, S. M. (1999). *The psychology student writer's manual.* Upper Saddle River, NJ: Prentice Hall.

Scriven, M. (1981). Summative teacher evaluation. In J. Millman (Ed.), *Handbook of teacher evaluation* (pp. 244–271). Thousand Oaks, CA: Sage.

Sechrest, L., Kihlstrom, J. F., & Bootzin, R. R. (1999). How to develop multiple-choice tests. In B. Perlman, L. I. McCann, & S. H. McFadden (Eds.), *Lessons learned: Practical advice for the teaching of psychology* (pp. 49–56). Washington, DC: American Psychological Society.

Seldin, P. (1991). *The teaching portfolio: A practical guide to improved performance and promotion/tenure decisions.* Bolton, MA: Anker.

Seldin, P. (1998). *The teaching portfolio: A practical guide to improved performance and promotion/tenure decisions* (2nd ed.). Bolton, MA: Anker.

Shepard, L. A. (1993). Evaluating test validity. *Review of Research in Education, 19*, 405–450.

Simmel, G. (1902). The number of members as determining the sociological form of the group. *American Journal of Sociology, 8*, 1–46, 158–196.

Sixbury, G. R., & Cashin, W. E. (1995). *Description of database for the IDEA Disgnostic Form. IDEA Paper No. 10.* Manhattan, KS: Kansas State University, Center for Faculty Evaluation and Development.

Sleigh, M. J., & Ritzer, D. R. (2001). Encouraging student attendance. *Observer, 11.* Retrieved December 27, 2001, from http://www.psychologicalscience.org/observer/1101/tips.html

Slife, D. (2001). *Taking sides: Clashing views on controversial psychological issues* (11th ed.). New York: McGraw-Hill.

Smith, R. A. (2001). Instructions for contributors. *Teaching of Psychology, 28*, 3.

Snodgrass, S. E. (1985). Writing as a tool for teaching social psychology. *Teaching of Psychology, 12*, 91–94.

Snyder, C. R., Cheavens, J., & Sympson, S. C. (1997). Hope: An individual motive for social commerce. *Group Dynamics, 1*, 107–118.

Snyder, C. R., Shenkel, R. J., & Lowery, C. R. (1977). Acceptance of personality interpretations: The "Barnum effect" and beyond. *Journal of Consulting and Clinical Psychology, 45,* 104–114.

Sommer, R. (1969). *Personal space: The behavioral basis of design.* Englewood Cliffs, NJ: Prentice-Hall.

Sorcinelli, M. D. (1991). Research findings on the seven principles. *New Directions for Teaching and Learning: Applying the Seven Principles for Good Practice in Undergraduate Education, 47,* 13–25.

Sperling, G. (1960). The information available in brief visual presentations. *Psychological Monographs, 74* (Whole No. 498).

Stanovich, K. E. (1993). Does reading make you smarter? Literacy and the development of verbal intelligence. In H. Reese (Ed.), *Advances in child development and behavior* (Vol. 24, pp. 133–180). San Diego: Academic Press.

Stanovich, K. E., & Cunningham, A. E. (1993). Where does knowledge come from? Specific associations between print exposure and information acquisition. *Journal of Educational Psychology, 85,* 211–229.

Stark, J. S., Lowther, M. A., Ryan, M. P., & Genthon, M. (1988). Faculty reflect on course planning. *Research in Higher Education, 29,* 219–240.

Starker, S. (1987). Psychologists and self-help books: Attitudes and prescriptive practices of clinicians. *American Journal of Psychotherapy, 42,* 448–455.

Statman, S. (1988). Ask a clear question and get a clear answer: An enquiry into the question/answer and the sentence completion formats of multiple-choice items. *Systems, 16,* 357–376.

Stearns, S. A. (2001). The student-instructor relationship's effect upon academic integrity. *Ethics and Behavior, 11,* 275–286.

Sternberg, R. J. (1985). *Beyond IQ: A triarchic theory of human intelligence.* New York: Cambridge University Press.

Sternberg, R. J. (1997a). *Successful intelligence.* New York: Plume.

Sternberg, R. J. (Ed.). (1997b). *Teaching introductory psychology: Survival tips from the experts.* Washington, DC: American Psychological Association.

Sternberg, R. J. (1997c). Teaching students to think as psychologists. In R. J. Sternberg (Ed.), *Teaching introductory psychology: Survival tips from the experts* (pp. 137–149). Washington, DC: American Psychological Association.

Sternberg, R. J. (1999a). A propulsion model of types of creative contributions. *Review of General Psychology, 3,* 83–100.

Sternberg, R. J. (1999b). The theory of successful intelligence. *Review of General Psychology, 3,* 292–316.

Sternberg, R. J. (1999c). Twenty tips for teaching introductory psychology. In B. Perlman, L. I. McCann, & S. H. McFadden (Eds.), *Lessons learned: Practical advice for the teaching of psychology* (pp. 37–41). Washington, DC: American Psychological Society.

Sternberg, R. J. (2001). What is the common thread of creativity? Its dialectical relation to intelligence and wisdom. *American Psychologist, 56,* 360–362.

Sternberg, R. J., & Lubart, T. I. (1996). Investing in creativity. *American Psychologist, 51,* 677–688.

Stevens, S. S. (1951). Mathematics, measurement, and psychophysics. In S. S. Stevens (Ed.), *Handbook of Experimental Psychology* (pp. 1–49). New York: Wiley.

Stewart, K. E. (1997). Applying for academic positions: Guidelines from a survivor. *Newsletter of the American Psychological Association of Graduate Students, 9*(2), 1, 3–6.

Stires, L. K. (1982). Classroom seating location, order effects, and reactivity. *Personality and Social Psychology Bulletin, 8,* 362–364.

Stokes, P. D. (2001). Variability, constraints, and creativity: Shedding light on Claude Monet. *American Psychologist, 56,* 355–359.

Sunwolf, & Siebold, D. R. (1999). The impact of formal procedures on group processes, members, and task outcomes. In L. R. Frey (Ed.), *The handbook of group communication theory and research* (pp. 395–431). Thousand Oaks, CA: Sage.

Swenson, L. C. (1997). *Psychology and law for the helping profession.* Pacific Grove, CA: Brooks/Cole.

Sykes, C. J. (1988). *ProfScam: Professors and the demise of higher education.* Washington, DC: Regnery Gateway.

Tabachnick, B. G., Keith-Spiegel, P., & Pope, K. S. (1991). Ethics of teaching: Beliefs and behaviors of psychologists as educators. *American Psychologist, 46,* 506–515.

Tenenbaum, S. (1961). Carl R. Rogers and non-directive teaching. In C. R. Rogers, *On becoming a person* (pp. 299–310). Boston: Houghton Mifflin.

Thomas, K. W. (1992). Conflict and negotiation processes in organizations. In M. D. Dunnette & L. M. Hough (Eds.), *Handbook of industrial and organizational psychology* (2nd ed., Vol. 3, pp. 651–717). Palo Alto, CA: Consulting Psychologists Press.

Thorndike, E. L. (1918). The nature, purposes, and general methods of measurement of educational products. In G. M. Whipple (Ed.), *Seventeenth yearbook of the National Society for the Study of Education* (Vol. 2, pp. 16–24). Bloomington, IL: Public School Publishing.

Thorne, B. M. (2000). Extra credit exercise: A painless pop quiz. *Teaching of psychology, 27,* 204–205.

Thurstone, L. L. (1928). Attitudes can be measured. *American Journal of Sociology, 33,* 529–554.

Towbes, L. C., & Cohen, L. H. (1996). Chronic stress in the lives of college students: Scale development and prospective prediction of distress. *Journal of Youth and Adolescence, 25,* 199–217.

Traub, R. (1993). On the equivalence of the traits assessed by multiple-choice and constructed-response tests. In R. Bennett & W. Ward (Eds.), *Construction versus choice in cognitive measurement* (pp. 29–44). Mahwah, NJ: Erlbaum.

Triandis, H. C. (1995). A theoretical framework for the study of diversity. In M. M.

Chemers, S. Oskamp, & M. A. Costanzo (Eds.), *Diversity in organizations: New perspectives for a changing workplace* (pp. 11–36). Thousand Oaks, CA: Sage.

Tuckman, B. W. (1965). Developmental sequences in small groups. *Psychological Bulletin, 63,* 384–399.

Urbach, F. (1992). Developing a teaching portfolio. *College Teaching, 40,* 71–74.

Vallacher, R. R., & Wegner, D. M. (1987). What do people think they're doing? Action identification and human behavior. *Psychological Review, 94,* 3–15.

van de Vliert, E., & Euwema, M. C. (1994). Agreeableness and activeness as components of conflict behaviors. *Journal of Personality and Social Psychology, 66,* 674–687.

Vernoy, M. W. (1987). Demonstrating classical conditioning in introductory psychology: Needles do not always make balloons pop! *Teaching of Psychology, 14,* 176–177.

Wade, C. (1995). Using writing to develop and assess critical thinking. *Teaching of Psychology, 22,* 24–28.

Wagor, W. F. (1990). Using student projects to acquire demonstrations for the classroom and laboratory. *Teaching of Psychology, 17,* 253–255.

Wajda-Johnston, V. A., Handal, P. J., Brawer, P. A., & Fabricatore, A. N. (2001). Academic dishonesty at the graduate level. *Ethics and Behavior, 11,* 287–306.

Wales, C. E., & Stager, R. A. (1978). *The guided design approach.* Englewood Cliffs, NJ: Educational Technology Publications.

Wall, V. D., Jr., & Nolan, L. L. (1987). Small group conflict: A look at equity, satisfaction, and styles of conflict management. *Small Group Behavior, 18,* 188–211.

Walvoord, B. E. F. (1982). *Helping students write well.* New York: The Modern Language Association of America.

Walvoord, B. E., & Anderson, V. J. (1998). *Effective grading: A tool for learning and assessment.* San Francisco: Jossey-Bass.

Wang, X., Wainer, H., & Thissen, D. (1995). On the viability of some untestable assumptions in equating exams that allow examinee choice. *Applied Measurement in Education, 8,* 211–225.

Ward, D. A., & Beck, W. L. (1990). Gender and dishonesty. *Journal of Social Psychology, 130,* 333–339.

Ware, J. E., & Williams, R. G. (1977). Discriminant analysis of student ratings as a means for identifying lecturers who differ in enthusiasm or information-giving. *Educational and Psychological Measurement, 37,* 627–639.

Ware, M. E., & Johnson, D. E. (Eds.). (2000a). *Handbook of demonstrations and activities in the teaching of psychology: Vol. I. Introductory, statistics, research methods, and history* (2nd ed.). Mahwah, NJ: Erlbaum.

Ware, M. E., & Johnson, D. E. (Eds.). (2000b). *Handbook of demonstrations and activities in the teaching of psychology: Vol II. Physiological-comparative, perception, learning, cognitive, and developmental* (2nd ed.). Mahwah, NJ: Erlbaum.

Ware, M. E., & Johnson, D. E. (Eds.). (2000c). *Handbook of demonstrations and activities in the teaching of psychology: Vol. III. Personality, abnormal, clinical-counseling, and social* (2nd ed.). Mahwah, NJ: Erlbaum.

Watson, D., & Clark, L. A. (1992). Affects separable and inseparable: On the hierarchical arrangement of the negative affects. *Journal of Personality and Social Psychology, 62*, 489–505.

Watson, J. B. (1924). *Behaviorism*. New York: Norton.

Webb, E. J., Campbell, D. T., Schwartz, R. D., & Sechrest, L. (1966). *Unobtrusive measures: Nonreactive measures in the social sciences*. Chicago: Rand McNally.

Weber, A. L. (1983). The dark side of classroom exercises in social psychology: A response to Rosenwein. *Society for the Advancement of Social Psychology Newsletter, 9*, 23–25.

Weber, L. J., McBee, J. K., & Krebs, J. E. (1983). Take home tests: An experimental study. *Research in Higher Education, 18*, 473–483.

Weldon, E., & Weingart, L. R. (1993). Group goals and group performance. *British Journal of Social Psychology, 32*, 307–334.

Welsh, J. A., & Null, C. H. (1991). The effects of computer-based instruction on college students' comprehension of classic research. *Behavior Research Methods, Instruments, and Computers, 23*, 301–305.

White, K. W., & Weight, B. H. (Eds.). (1999). *The online teaching guide: A handbook of attitudes, strategies, and techniques for the virtual classroom*. Boston: Allyn & Bacon.

Whitford, F. W. (1992). *Teaching psychology*. Englewood Cliffs, NJ: Prentice Hall.

Whitley, B. E. (1998). Factors associated with cheating among college students: A review. *Research in Higher Education, 39*(3), 235–274.

Whitley, B. E., Jr., & Keith-Spiegel, P. (2001). Academic integrity as an institutional issue. *Ethics and Behavior, 11*, 325–242.

Whitley, B. E., Jr., Perkins, D. V., Balogh, D. W., Keith-Spiegel, P., & Wittig, A. F. (2000). Fairness in the classroom. *Observer, 13*. Retrieved May 20, 2001, from http://www.psychologicalscience.org/newsresearch/tips/0700tips.html

Wicker, A. W., & August, R. A. (1995). How far should we generalize? The case of a workload model. *Psychological Science, 6*, 39–44.

Widick, P., Parker, C. A., & Knefelkamp, L. (1978). Arthur Chickering's vectors of development. *Applying New Developmental Findings, 4*, 19–34.

Widmeyer, W. N., & Loy, J. W. (1988). When you're hot, you're hot: Warm-cold effects in first impressions of persons and teaching effectiveness. *Journal of Educational Psychology, 80*, 118–121.

Williams, R. G., & Ware, J. E. (1976). Validity of student ratings of instruction under different incentive conditions: A further study of the Dr. Fox effect. *Journal of Educational Psychology, 68*, 48–56.

Williams, R. G., & Ware, J. E. (1977). An extended visit with Dr. Fox: Validity of student satisfaction with instruction ratings after repeated exposures to a lecturer. *American Educational Research Journal, 14*, 449–457.

Willingham, D. B. (1990). Effective feedback on written assignments. *Teaching of Psychology, 17,* 10–13.

Wills, T. A. (1987). Help-seeking as a coping mechanism. In C. R. Snyder & C. E. Ford (Eds.), *Coping with negative life events* (pp. 19–50). New York: Plenum.

Wilson, J. H., & Taylor, K. W. (2001). Professor immediacy as behaviors associated with liking students. *Teaching of Psychology, 28,* 136–138.

Wilson, T. D., & Linville, P. W. (1982). Improving the academic performance of college freshmen: Attribution therapy revisited. *Journal of Personality and Social Psychology, 42,* 367–376.

Wilson, T. D., & Linville, P. W. (1985). Improving the academic performance of college freshmen with attributional techniques. *Journal of Personality and Social Psychology, 49,* 287–293.

Wilson, C., & Marcus, D. K. (1992). Teaching anatomy of the sheep brain: A laboratory exercise with PlayDoh. *Teaching of Psychology, 19,* 223–225.

Witkins, H. A. (1977). Cognitive styles in the educational setting. *New York University Educational Quarterly, 8,* 14–20.

Wolfe, M. B., Schreiner, M. E., Rehder, B., Laham, D., Foltz, P. W., Kintsch, W., et al. (1998). Learning from text: Matching readers and texts by latent semantic analysis. *Discourse Processes, 25,* 309–336.

Woods, S. C., Schwartz, M. W., Baskin, D. G., & Seeley, R. J. (2000). Food intake and the regulation of body weight. *Annual Review of Psychology, 51,* 255–277.

Woodworth, R. S. (1958). *Dynamics of behavior.* New York: Holt.

Worthington, E. L., Jr., Welsh, J. A., Archer, C. R., Mindes, E. J., & Forsyth, D. R. (1996). Computer-assisted instruction as a supplement to lectures in an introductory psychology class. *Teaching of Psychology, 23,* 175–180.

Wright, J. J. (1967). Reported personal stress sources and adjustment of entering freshman. *Journal of Counseling Psychology, 14,* 371–373.

Wright, S. C., Aron, A., McLaughlin-Volpe, T., & Ropp, S. A. (1997). The extended contact effect: Knowledge of cross-group friendships and prejudice. *Journal of Personality and Social Psychology, 73,* 73–90.

Wright, S. S. (2000). Looking at the self in a rose-colored mirror: Unrealistically positive self-views and academic performance. *Journal of Social and Clinical Psychology, 19,* 451–462.

Zakrajsek, T. (1999). Developing effective lectures. In B. Perlman, L. I. McCann, & S. H. McFadden (Eds.), *Lessons learned: Practical advice for the teaching of psychology* (pp. 81–86). Washington, DC: American Psychological Society.

Zanna, M. P., & Darley, J. M. (1987). On managing the faculty-graduate student research relationship. In M. P. Zanna & J. M. Darley (Eds.), *The compleat academic: A practical guide for the beginning social scientist* (pp. 139–149). New York: Random House.

Zeidner, M. (1998). *Test anxiety: The state of the art.* New York: Plenum.

Zeren, A. S., & Makosky, V. P. (1986). Teaching observational methods: Time sampling, event sampling, and trait rating techniques. *Teaching of Psychology,* *13,* 80–82.

Zimbardo, P. G. (1997). A passion for psychology: Teaching it charismatically, integrating teaching and research synergistically, and writing about it engaging. In R. J. Sternberg (Ed.), *Teaching introductory psychology: Survival tips from the experts* (pp. 7–34). Washington, DC: American Psychological Association.

Zimiles, H. (1996). Rethinking the validity of psychological assessment. *American Psychologist, 51,* 980–981.

Zimmerman, B. J. (1998). Academic studying and the development of personal skill: A self-regulatory perspective. *Educational Psychologist, 33,* 73–86.

Zimmerman, B. J., & Martinez-Pons, M. (1986). Development of a structured interview for assessing student use of self-regulated learning strategies. *American Educational Research Journal, 23,* 614–628.

Zlokovich, M. S. (2001). Grading for optimal student learning. *Observer, 14*(1). Retrieved May 20, 2001, from http://www.psychologicalscience.org/newsresearch/tips/0101tips.html

Zlotkowski, E. (Ed.). (1998). *Successful service-learning programs: New models of excellence in higher education.* Bolton, MA: Anker.

INDEX

Academic integrity
 cheating and, 203–205
 ethics of professor and, 213–230
 honor code for, 207–208
 internalization of codes for, 208
 maintenance of
  clarification and review of
   acceptable/unacceptable behavior,
   206–207
 moral standards and, 202–203
 norms and, 202–203
 plagiarism and, 205
 plagiarism-detection software for, 250
 policy for, 39
 variations and violations of, 203–205
Academic skill(s)
 development of, 191–196
 note-taking, 193–195
 preparation for tests, 195
 reading, 192–193
 resources for, 196
 studying, 191–192
 as teaching goal, 15
Achievement
 impact of computerized learning laboratories on, 252–253
Active learning, in course planning, 45,
 46, 110
Activities
 in active learning
  design issues for, 113–114
  phases in, 113
  types of, 110–113
 for capturing attention, 77
 on teaching portfolio, 299–300
Advising, in summative evaluation, 281
Allport, G. W.
 on personality, 283, 284
American Psychological Association
 (APA)
 on diversity in classroom, 47
 *Ethical Principles of Psychologists and
  Code of Conduct*
  agreement with and conformity to,
   216
  examples from, 213–216

judgments and self-reports of various
 behaviors, 216–219
laxity in observance of, 216
on plagiarism, 206–207
on ethics in testing, 129
Ames, C.
 on learning vs. performing, 34
Analysis
 as course goal, 13–14
 multiple-choice test items for, 141
Anecdotes
 for capturing attention, 70, 72
Angelo, T. A., 16
 on classroom assessment, 277
 model of teaching goals, 14–16
 on test feedback for professors, 128
Appleby, D. C.
 on syllabus as contract, 39
Application
 as course goal, 13
 multiple-choice test items for, 140–141
Asides
 for capturing attention, 76
Assessment
 in APA code of ethics and conduct,
  215
Assignments
 on teaching portfolio, 299–300
Attendance
 on exam days, 211
 norms for, 223–224
 performance and, 84–85
 policy for, 38
Attention
 asides and personal views for, 76
 humor for, 75
 multimedia material for, 76
 questioning for, 72–74
 quoting original sources for, 74–75
 story telling and anecdotes for, 70, 72
Axell, J.
 on inspirational lecturers, 60

Backlash
 in discussions, 102

339

Bakhtar, M.
  on lecturers, 52–53
Bednar, R. L.
  on class preparation for discussion, 98–
    99
Benjamin, L. T.
  on opportunities in group discussions,
    105
Berstein, D. A.
  on assumptions in teaching, 297
Bias
  in diverse classroom
    intergroup, 228–229
    of professor, 229
  in grading, 173
  in scoring essay tests, 158
  in student evaluations of teaching,
    266–267
Bligh, D.
  on buzz groups, *106–107*
  on pace of lecture, *79*
  on seminars, *122*
Bloom, B. S.
  cognitive domains of, 130
  taxonomy of educational objectives,
    11–14
Boice, R.
  on incivility, 224
Bomb scare, 204
Boredom
  components of, 61, 62
  occurrence of, 61
Brown, G. A.
  on lecturers, 52–53
Browsers
  features in, 257–258
Brunning, R.
  on motivation to write, *120*
Buddha, teaching method of, 8
Buzz groups, 106–107

Carbone, E.
  on classroom management, *221*
Catell, R. B.
  on tests, *129*
Chalkboard
  advantages and disadvantages of, 237–
    238
  as innovation, 234
  in knowledge transmission, 237–238

Change
  motivate for, 199
Cheating
  awareness and investigation of possible
    instances of, 210–211
  clarification of meaning, 206
  definition of, 203
  elimination of temptations to, 208–209
  methods for, 203–205
  modeling integrity and fairness and,
    212–213
  as moral issue, 207
  reduce pressures to, 211–212
  test format and, 133–134
  on tests, 208–209, 211–212
  Web site detection services for, 250
  on written essays, 210
Chickering, A. W.
  on lectures, 44
  on online collaborative learning, 246
  *Seven Principles for Good Practice in
    Undergraduate Education*, 44
Choice-type tests. See also Multiple-
    choice tests
  analysis of, 160–165
    descriptive statistics in, 160
    by item, 160–164
    for reliability, 160
  comparison with supply-type, 132–134
  student preparation for, 195
Civility
  attendance and, 223–224
  creating norms for, 221–222
  social influence and, 222–223
  standards for, 221
Clarity
  note readers and, 58
  practice and, 57–58
  requirements for, 57
Class
  large *vs.* small, 24–25
  size of and techniques, 23–24
Class preparation. *See also* Goals, in
    course planning
  active learning in, 45, 46
  assessments in, 33–37
  class size and, 23–25
  cooperation among students and, 44,
    45, 46
  course content in, 21–22
  course level in, 22–23
  expectations in, 45, 47

time for grading of, 155
written feedback on, 189
Ethical Principles of Psychologists and Code of Conduct (American Psychological Association), 213–216
Ethics
institutional policy for, 207–208
violations of, handling of, 214
Ethics committees
APA code of ethics and conduct and, 214
Evaluation
of computer-based learning, 251–253
as course goal, 14
of faculty, 261–272. *See* Faculty evaluation
on teaching portfolio, 301–303
multiple-choice test items for, 141
of teaching effectiveness
outcome-based, 302–303
peer-based, 302
student-based, 301–302
of technologies, 251–252
types of, 262
Ewens, W.
on discussions, 89
Examinations. *See* Test(s)
Examples
in lectures, 79–80
Expectations
of professor, 45, 47
students', correction of, 42
Expertise
in APA code of ethics and conduct, 213
credibility issues and, 58
student perceptions of, 58–59
Eye contact
in rapport building, 63–64

Face validity
of tests, 136–137
Faculty evaluation, 282
formative assessments in, 262, 272–278
improvement of, 272–282
student evaluations of teaching in, 263–272
summative assessments in, 262, 278–282

Fairness
modeling of, 212–213
students' perceptions of, 190
Falsification
definition of, 203
Feedback, 45, 46–47. *See also* Formative assessment; Summative assessment
on essay tests, 189
formative, 188–189
in formative assessment, of faculty, 273–274
on grades, 185–190
in motivational support, 199
summative, 186–188
technologies in, 249–250
test review in class, 187, 188–189
from tests, 133
for students and professors, 128
Field placement, 124
Final grades
aligning metrics for, 184
assigning weights for, 184
checking records for, 183–184
creating composite score, 184–185
feedback on, 185–190
First class
correction of misunderstandings, 42–43
course goals and, 41–42
motivating, 42
setting tone, 42
Formative assessment of faculty
classroom assessment techniques, 274–277
collaboration with colleagues, 277–278
group feedback in, 274
improvement of, 272–278
individual feedback in, 273–274
open-ended verbal descriptions in, 273
student rating scales in, 272–273
Freud, S.
psychotherapy and, 74

Galanter, G.
on planning, 9, *10*
Gamson, Z. F.
on lecturing, *44*
Seven Principles for Good Practice in Undergraduate Education, *44*
Gap grading, 180
Ghosting, 204
Goals
of course, first class and, 41–42

Internship, in graduate-level training, 124–125
Interpersonal rapport
in effective teaching, 55, 56

James, W.
emotion and, *74*
Janis, I. L.
on lecture listeners, *81*
on lecturing, *49*
on sequencing in lectures, *77*
Jigsaw method of peer instruction, 108–109
Johnston, J.
on computer in statistical analysis, *244*

Kaufman, B.
on proctoring and cheating on exams, *201*
Kaul, T.
class preparation for discussion and, 98–99
Kelley, H. H.
on lecture listeners, *81*
on lecturing, *49*
on sequencing in lectures, *77*
Kitchener, K. S.
on faculty–student sexual relationships, *219*
Knowledge
as course goal, 12–13
discipline-specific
as teaching goal, 15
multiple-choice test items for, 140
Knowledge base
as course goal, 17, 18
Knowledge transmission
computerized instructional packages for, 241–242
E-mail, 240–241
in-class presentation tools for, 237–239
Web sites for, 236, 239–240

Language skills development, 249
e-mail and conferencing in, 245
word-processing programs for, 245

Leadership skills
for discussion
distributed, 98
relationship, 96, 97–98
task, 95–97
Leakage
of test bank items, 149–150
Learning
academic skills for, 191–196
computer-based methods
evaluation of, 251–253
computerized laboratories for, 252–253
helping students with, 190–191
motivational support for, 198–200
professorial social support for, 197–198
self-regulation skills for, 196–197
technological facilitation of, 247–248, 249
Learning readiness, of listener, 83
Learning styles
categories of, 81–83
models of individual differences in, 82
Lecture hall ecology, 85–86
Lecturers
exemplary, 53
types of, 52–53
Lectures
attention in, 70, 71–78
capturing attention in, 70, 72
connection with textbook, 67–68
cues to organizational elements of, 70, 71–72
familiarity with topic in, 66–67
idea-based, 77–78
integration with course textbook, 67–68
learning styles and, 81–83
memorability enhancement and, 78–80
organization of topic for, 68–69
provision to listeners, 69–70, 71
outline of, 70
structure of, 68–70, 71
hierarchical, 68–69
linear, 69
studentship and, 83–86
Lecturing
effective
clarity in, 57–58
enthusiasm in, 59–61
expertise in, 58–59
negativity in, 64–65
rapport in, 61–64
lecture and, 66–80

practical
as course objective, 19
Sleigh, M. J.
on attendance and class structure, 84
Slide projector
in knowledge transmission, 238
Small group discussions (SGDs)
closing summaries in, 106
development of, 104
duration of, 104–106
forms and variations of, 106–110
goal selection for, 104
tasks in, 105
utility of, 103
Smile
in rapport building, 63
Social–interactional learning style, 81, 82
Socratic method of teaching, 87
Stealing and switching assignments, 204
Stevens, S. S.
on measurement, *170*
Stories
for capturing attention, 70, 72
Stress, student, handling of, 231
Student-centered learning
achievement of educational goals in,
126
comparison with lectures, 126
professors' distrust of, 125–126
Student-centered teaching
activities in, 110–114
discussions in
leading, 89–102
small group, 103–110
great exemplars of, 87–88
Rogers on, 87, 88
through composition, 114–122. *See
also* Writing; Written assignments
through field placements, internships,
practica, service learning, 124–
125
through presentations, panels, seminars, 122, 123
types of, 89
Student engagement
class size and, 24
Student evaluations of teaching (SETs)
bias in, 266–267
construct validity of, 265–266
controversies and convergences in,
269–272
influences on, 279
issues concerning, 263

negative effects of, 268–269
on faculty morale, 268
grade inflation, 269
relaxation of standards, 268–269
reliability of, 263–264
structure of
comparison of global summary and
specific items in, 264–265
student performance and, 266
in summative assessments, 279–280
on teaching portfolio, 301–302
graphic display of, 301–302
uses of, 263
Student names
in rapport building, 62–63
Students
backgrounds of, 25
diverse or homogeneous, 26–27
interest in
in rapport building, 64
matching with classes, 26
traditional *vs.* nontraditional, 27
Students' Evaluations of Educational
Quality (SEEQ) inventory
components of effective teaching in,
264–265
factor analyses of, 265
Studentship and lectures, 83–86
Students with disabilities
accommodations for, 230
federal law and institutional policy,
230
types of, 229
Students with special needs, policy and,
39
Study skills
technologies and, 247–248, 249
Study skills, development of, 191–192
Style
class size and, 23
Summative assessment
of academic quality of course, 280–281
classroom teaching in, 278–280
contribution to educational mission of
discipline in, 282
nonclassroom teaching activities in,
281
of quality of instructional and evaluative materials, 280
scope of, 278
Supervision
in summative evaluation, 281

Trivia
    on multiple-choice tests, 138–139
    on test bank tests, 148
True–false test formats
    bundled, 147
    double, 146
    multiple, 146

Urbach, F.
    on teaching portfolios, 289

Validity
    description of, 135
    of student evaluations of teaching
        perspectives in, 270–271
    subcomponents of, 135–137
    of tests, 134–135
Values
    diversity and conflicts in, 227
    liberal arts and academic, as teaching
        goal, 15
    in psychology teaching, 19

Walvoord, B. E. F.
    on writing assignments, *118*
Watson, J. B.
    behaviorism and, *74*
Web-authoring programs
    features in, 258
Web page, for course
    information on, 239–240

Web sites
    in knowledge transmission, 236, 239–
        240
    paper reduction with, 248
    for thinking skill development, 244
Weighting
    in final grade, 184
Whitford, F. W.
    on challenges of score, *189*
Word-processing programs
    features in, 257
    for language skill development, 245
Writing
    guidance on process of, 118
    as learning process, 114–115
    motivation for, 120, 121
Written assignments
    clarification of, 118
    coaching for, 117–118
    feedback on, 118–120
    grading of
        time for, 120, 122
    prevention of cheating on, 210
    types of, 115–117

Youngman, M. B.
    on lecturers, 52–53

Zimbardo, P. G.
    on informal lecture style, 63
Zimmerman, B. J.
    on self-regulation in learning, *196*

ABOUT THE AUTHOR

Donelson R. Forsyth, PhD, is professor of psychology at Virginia Commonwealth University in Richmond. He completed his undergraduate studies at Florida State University, where he changed majors from classical civilizations to psychology after taking a lecture-only social psychology course. He received a PhD in social psychology in 1978 from the University of Florida and joined the faculty of Virginia Commonwealth University in that year.

At the undergraduate level he teaches introductory psychology, social psychology, group dynamics, and honors seminars. His graduate-level courses include research methods in social psychology and specialty seminars on attitude theory and measurement, attribution and social cognition, and group dynamics. He also developed and currently teaches a graduate course on teaching psychology. He received the Virginia Commonwealth University College of Humanities and Sciences Lecturer Award in 1985, as well as the university's Distinguished Teaching Award in 1992 and its Award for Innovative Excellence in Teaching, Learning, and Technology in 2000. In 2002, he received the Outstanding Faculty Award for the State of Virginia.

Dr. Forsyth studies reactions to success and failure, individual differences in moral thought, applications of social psychology in educational and clinical settings, and group dynamics. His research has been published in the *Journal of Personality and Social Psychology*, the *American Psychologist*, the *Journal of Educational Psychology*, and the *Teaching of Psychology*. He has written and edited several books, including *Our Social World* (1995) and *Group Dynamics* (1999). He currently serves on several editorial boards and was the founding editor of the journal *Group Dynamics*.